MW00777668

Cultures of Power

University of Pennsylvania Press
MIDDLE AGES SERIES
Edited by
Edward Peters
Henry Charles Lea Professor
of Medieval History
University of Pennsylvania

A listing of the available books in the series
appears at the back of this volume

Cultures of Power

Lordship, Status, and Process in Twelfth-Century Europe

edited by
Thomas N. Bisson

University of Pennsylvania Press
Philadelphia

Copyright © 1995 by the University of Pennsylvania Press
All rights reserved
Printed in the United States of America

Library of Congress Cataloging-in-Publication Data

Cultures of power : lordship, status, and process in twelfth-century Europe / edited by Thomas N. Bisson.
p. cm. — (Middle Ages series)
Includes bibliographical references and index.
ISBN 0-8122-1555-9 (alk. paper)
1. Papers presented at an interdisciplinary conference, held May 1–4, 1991, and sponsored by the Committee on Medieval Studies at Harvard University. 2. Nobility—Europe—History—Congresses. 3. Aristocracy (Social class)—Europe—History—Congresses. 4. Upper class—Europe—History—Congresses. 5. Elite (Social sciences)—Europe—History—Congresses. I. Bisson, Thomas N. II. Harvard University. Committee on Medieval Studies. III. Series.
HT653.E9C85 1995
305.5'223'094—dc20 95-12349
CIP

Contents

Preface

In this volume are gathered papers originally prepared for an interdisciplinary conference on Power and Society in the Twelfth Century (1050–1225) sponsored by the committee on medieval studies at Harvard University. The occasion and purpose of the conference are explained in the Introduction, which is devoted to the contents of this volume. But no conference is a book to begin with, and in this case some details of the assemblage in Cambridge, Massachusetts on May 1–4 1991 may point usefully to the kind of collaborative strength that we believe justifies publication. Eighteen scholars took part, mostly medievalist historians but including one art historian and two specialists in medieval literature. Lady Sally J. Fielding (Sally Harvey) was unable finally to attend, but kindly submitted a discussion paper on "Fiscal Management in England (1070–1170)," which found its place in a session on means and techniques of power. The sessions were attended by forty or more persons, including graduate students from Harvard and elsewhere, plus interested scholars from other institutions. Georges Duby's lecture (in French) on "Les femmes et le pouvoir" drew nearly one hundred persons. Discussions in each session were opened by chairperson-commentators, whose prepared comments together with the interventions by auditors imparted to the occasion the vitality of a creative workshop.

Four of these chairpersons merit special thanks: Patrick Geary, Fredric L. Cheyette, and my Harvard colleagues Charles Donahue, Jr. and Eckehard Simon. Their suggestions and criticisms not only enlivened the conference but helped contributors to improve their results for publication. Kenneth Pennington kindly contributed a paper on "The Medieval Origins of Due Process and the Power of the Prince" which unfortunately fell outside the chronological boundaries set for the present volume. In his place Charles Duggan was good enough to provide a study, written expressly for this book, of "Papal Judges Delegate and the Making of 'New Law' in the Twelfth Century".

Other persons have helped this enterprise along. I wish to thank Harvard's committee on medieval studies for recommending this conference and the Dean of the Faculty of Arts and Sciences for supporting it financially. Robert Berkhofer not only managed logistics but later undertook to reconstitute the spontaneous comments from tapes. Jennifer Paxton and Nathaniel Taylor helped him record the discussions. Margo Granfors, *domina* of the Committee at 61 Kirkland Street, organized the conference administratively and long continued to assist in the diverse tasks required to bring it to publication. In the later stages of publication I have (again) had reason to be grateful to Professor Eckehard Simon, who lately chaired the Committee on Medieval Studies, for his understanding support. Jerome Singerman, Ridley Hammer, and Alison A. Anderson of the University of Pennsylvania Press have earned the thanks of us all for their expertise and forbearance in handling a difficult manuscript. To these persons as well as to all those who contributed, intervened, and attended I feel myself personally obligated, for the conference addressed problems of high interest to my own research and teaching. I thank the contributors for their good will and patience in the work of rendering this collaboration accessible to a wider readership.

TNB
Cambridge, Massachusetts
February 1995

Abbreviations

AASS	*Acta sanctorum*, ed. J. Bollandus et al. (Antwerp, Brussels, 1643–)
AD	Archives Départementales (France)
AHR	*American Historical Review*
AN	Archives Nationales (Paris)
Annales E.S.C.	*Annales: Economies, Sociétés, Civilisations*
BEC	*Bibliothèque de l'Ecole des Chartes*, Paris
BM	Bibliothèque Municipale
BN	Bibliothèque Nationale (Paris)
CC	*Corpus christianorum (Series latina)*
CCCM	*Corpus christianorum, Continuatio mediaevalis*
CSEL	*Corpus scriptorum ecclesiasticorum latinorum*
EHR	*English Historical Review*
ES	*España sagrada*, ed. Henrique Florez, 58 vols. (Madrid, 1747–1918)
HF	*Recueil des historiens des Gaules et de la France*, ed. Martin Bouquet et al., 24 vols. (Paris, 1738–1904)
Mansi	*Sacrorum conciliorum nova et amplissima collectio*, ed. J. D. Mansi, 31 vols. (Florence-Venice, 1759–98)
JCP	Justice of the Common Pleas
MGH	*Monumenta Germaniae historica*
Diplomata	*Diplomata regum et imperatorum Germaniae*
SRG	*Scriptores rerum Germanicarum in usum scholarum*
SS	*Scriptores* (in folio)
MV	*Cartulaire vendômois de Marmoutier*, ed. A. de Trémault (Vendôme, 1893).
OV	*The Ecclesiastical History of Orderic Vitalis*, ed. Marjorie Chibnall, 6 vols. (Oxford, 1969–80). Citations are by book, chapter, and (in parentheses) Chibnall's edition.
PL	*Patrologiae cursus completus . . . Series latina*, ed. J.-P. Migne, 221 vols. (Paris, 1844–64)

RH	*Revue Historique*
TV	*Cartulaire de l'abbaye cardinale de la Trinité de Vendôme* . . . , ed. Ch. Métais, 5 vols. (Paris, 1893–1904)
ZRG Kan. Abt	*Zeitschrift der Savigny-Stiftung für Rechtsgeschichte, Kanonistische Abteilung*

Thomas N. Bisson

Introduction

In 1988 the Committee on Medieval Studies at Harvard University authorized me to organize an interdisciplinary conference. I welcomed the invitation not only as an opportunity to carry on in a worthy tradition of the Committee but also as an occasion for trying out an idea well suited to collaborative exploration. I wanted to see what would happen if specialists in political, social, ecclesiastical, and cultural history addressed themselves to the human experience of power in the twelfth century. This was not to exclude government (or kingship or justice or finance) as such, merely to enlarge the contexts. Much has been written about government in the twelfth century, surprisingly little yet about power.[1] Participants seemed to have no difficulty recognizing the possibility of a fresh approach to the familiar problem of institutional change by stressing the pretenses, means, sanctions, strategies, words, monuments, norms, and attributes of gender by which people influenced, controlled, or coerced one another in the great century when medieval civilization came of age. But no conceptual test was set, no theoretical agenda. Participants were invited to prepare original studies in several broad areas of substantive competence: aristocracies old and new; images, rituals, commemoration; means and techniques; cultures (literary, legal, scriptural) of power. The somewhat eclectic results,

1. This assertion cannot be fully documented here. Among many other works, see for England William Stubbs, *The Constitutional History of England in Its Development,* 3 vols. (Oxford, 1874–78), 1 (6th ed., 1897); H. G. Richardson and G. O. Sayles, *The Governance of Mediaeval England from the Conquest to Magna Carta* (Edinburgh, 1963); Judith A. Green, *The Government of England Under Henry I* (Cambridge, 1986); and W. L. Warren, *The Governance of Norman and Angevin England (1086–1272)* (Stanford, 1987), who has some corrective remarks, pp. xvi, 1–22. For continental lands the legal histories by Paul Viollet (1890–1903), and García de Valdeavellano (1968) are characteristic. See also Heinrich Mitteis, *Der Staat des hohen Mittelalters: Grundlinien einer vergleichenden Verfassungsgeschichte des Lehenszeitalters* (Weimar, 1941; 8th ed. 1968); for France John W. Baldwin, *The Government of Philip Augustus: Foundations of French Royal Power in the Middle Ages* (Berkeley, 1986). Among comparatively few works anticipating a new approach, see Alexander Murray, *Reason and Society in the Middle Ages* (Oxford, 1978); and M. T. Clanchy, *From Memory to Written Record: England, 1066–1307* (Cambridge, MA, 1979; 2d ed., 1994); also Patrick Geary, "Vivre en conflit dans une France sans état: typologie des mécanismes de règlement des conflits (1050–1200)," *Annales E.S.C.* (1986), 1107–33.

whatever they may lack in theoretical consistency, have nonetheless a larger problematic coherence. They show how diversely power was experienced in those generations when it first assumed protostatist forms; suggest how incomplete a history of twelfth-century government must inevitably be.[2]

For it was arguably an age of little government. Those who corrected and coerced came in time to suppose they were fulfilling purposes externally ordained, but they were born to power and nurtured to dominate personally, affectively, unbureaucratically. The exercise of power—of command or force—was easily and often justified socially, but was commonly, and in lay society almost universally, a mode of self- or familial fulfillment. That is why we begin with the problem of elites. Who were these men and women born to rule in the twelfth century? The four essays in Part I deal with this problem in complementary ways. Theodore Evergates reviews the classic topic of the nature and transformation of the French nobility in light of recent research. One of his questions concerns knights and their access to nobility, which is precisely what Benjamin Arnold seeks to elucidate in German-speaking lands on the basis of an equally comprehensive review of evidence. It remains for Dominique Barthélemy to put this question to the test of a searching study of one small but well documented zone of western France, the Vendômois. The two preceding papers confirm from freshly assembled evidence the famous contrast between nobilities of service and of birth in Germany and France respectively, thereby proving (if proof were needed) that no sociology of power can adequately grasp, let alone explain, how weapons, horses, and castles were deployed to aggrandize and distinguish medieval elites. Evergates stresses, however, the differentiation between nobles and (non- or less noble) knights, while Barthélemy finds that even in France knighthood was an attribute shared by the *barones* and lesser lords. Nevertheless, it was nobility more than knighthood that determined power and limited its diffusion in these societies. The stress on kinship and patrimony in all these essays points to a ubiquitous identification of nobility and power. If one had power, as even families enriched by service did, a presumption of nobility was created.

2. The authors of these studies have addressed power, like culture (see below), as working historians bound by evidence. Several of them develop concepts, such as ritual, social action, and strategy, drawn from social science, but since our collaboration was not directed to theoretical discussion there is no need here to add to their own citations. It is worth editorial remark, however, that Max Weber's concepts of domination and order remain generally applicable to a history from which they were in some part derived, *Economy and Society: An Outline of Interpretive Sociology*, ed. Guenther Roth and Claus Wittich, 2 vols. (Berkeley-London, 1978 [1914–20]). The well-known book of Bertrand de Jouvenel, *On Power: The Natural History of Its Growth*, tr. J. F. Huntington (Boston, 1962 [1945]) is of little use to us, based as it is on a dated conception of medieval institutional practice.

In his essay on "Women and Power" Georges Duby brings us to the essence of the collaborative problem. Only when we cease to take for granted that kings, barons, knights, *ministeriales,* and vavassors who exercised power were men can we comprehend that masculine lordship was part of a natural order in which women were subordinate to the males who alone could fight or coerce. Violent women were either fomenters of disorder or quasi-men. But the representations here obscure a reality that often permitted women of the northern French aristocracy to exploit the contingencies of motherhood and inheritance to wield power. Yet a lady who achieved lordship was ipso facto suspect. Only in the domestic order could the natural division between masculine and feminine tasks bring moral representation into reasonable harmony with lived reality. Educating her children, dominating the servants, allying with her sons, influencing her husband (not least in the marital embrace): in such roles these elite women achieved real power, "for men were persuaded that womanhood was invested with mysterious force." Duby writes of women "participating" in power, for it was a world made and represented by men, who were lords of women along with the rest.

The studies grouped in Part II illustrate some modalities of power, moving us from status and lordship to means and process. Stephen White and Raoul Van Caenegem show how power was related to law in the practice of western France and Flanders in successive generations. Their approaches and evidence are so different that it may be well to stress what they find in common: a tendency in both regions for established law or procedure to be set aside by strategic maneuvering, by interests—by what neither scholar shrinks from dubbing "politics." White deals very concretely with manifestations of power in what has been termed the "disputing process," asking why and with what results so many instances of postponed or cancelled ordeals, forming part of that process, turn up in the records. And often enough it seems that an ordeal could be not only "a legal move in a lawsuit" but also "a strategy of confrontation." It precipitated, changed the options, departed from the strictly procedural model of action, whatever that may have been. On the other hand, judges might propose an ordeal "to intimidate a litigant who was doggedly pursuing a claim with inadequate support." If, as seems to be shown by a dazzling array of evidence, measures to initiate or evade ordeals were virtually "instruments of power" diversely employed, possibly efforts to fix the meaning of the medieval ordeal (in general) are fallacious. In Flanders, too, Van Caenegem discerns some contamination of law with power and interest. The charters defining status and exemption derived from pressures and debate rather than from abstraction. Yet in this area, it is suggested, ordeals had sufficient customary sanction—that is, as a procedural option—to survive till wider constellations of forces combined under Philip of Alsace (1157–91) to abolish it. The substitution of "alderman's truth" (*veritas scabinorum*) shows here again how far from impartial, or abstractly normative, was the making of rules in this twelfth-century society so fertile in instrumental invention. Nevertheless, in seeking to control coercive force and limit violence, the counts of Flanders aspired to a (neo-Carolingian) non-political vision of order. But a lawful order, even so: the count under the law. Van Caenegem concludes by showing how the count was a lord as well as a *princeps,* and argues that in the crisis of 1127 it was not unreasonable to expect a strict application of feudal law, the recognition of the lord-king's suzerainty, to resolve the conflict without politicization of the issues. Here writ large is White's microcosmic tension between law and interests.

The studies by Geoffrey Koziol and Charles Duggan are likewise, though even more diversely, concerned with means and process. Rituals of royalty may seem unlike procedures of incipient papal law, yet both gave expression, the one reflexively, the other administratively, to monarchical ideas of office. A ministerial aura of power suffused the rituals Koziol examines. But he shows too how the knightly ethos overtook Carolingian models of divinely ordained royalty, determining thereby "the most interesting trends in political rituals." And he argues that the English pattern of royal ritual diverged markedly from the French one: the great public rites in England being disrupted by partisan strife, "desacralized"; those in France preserving "the old typologies that held political authority sacred." Koziol raises the question whether this unnoticed difference in recorded ceremonial action corresponds to the constitutional divergence so familiar to an older historiography. With Charles Duggan we are drawn into a new world of written law and proto-bureaucratic command. It is astonishing how easily the judge delegate's "jurisdiction extended to every level and branch of western Christian society, from kings, prelates and magnates to monastic and religious communities, to simple clerks and lay men and women." A dynamic and inexorable logic impelled clerks newly schooled in Gratian, the decretals, and canonist cases to prescribe their procedures, to expect written instructions, and to seek to synthesize their expertise in "judicial process, appeals and (in the words of *Wigorniensis*) the 'instruction of judges in diverse cases.'" Perhaps nowhere among the "cultures" sampled in this volume can we see better how the effectual action of qualified persons created law, or how the (possibly exaggerated) confidence that such law could be executed nurtured a new insistence on the written expression of system. "The Worcester collection" of decretals on procedure "was the work of experienced canonists in the circles of the two most famous judges delegate of the period, Bartholomew of Exeter and Roger of Worcester" and their colleagues. No doubt this micro-history of ecclesiastical procedure has a larger political history (not unrelated to the murder and cult of Thomas Becket) that would help to explain why the English experience looms so large in the later twelfth century. But the new law of the popes can be read in decretals on marriage, election, and so forth everywhere in Christendom, so there can be little doubt that "the creative role of the English judges delegate" was played out on a European stage.

Part III brings together five studies of power in specifically cultural contexts less implicated in process and practice. John Van Engen's thorough inquiry into lordship in clerical thought follows from the papers on aristocracies, for lordship was the prevailing form of noble power. "It was a product of sin," he writes, "and yet divinely sanctioned." This is as much as to say that lordship was, like kingship, a species of that power over human beings ultimately derived from God. *Potestas* was often equated with, as well as attributed to, lay lords; lordship with, and to, kingship: one spoke invariably of the *dominus rex*. Moreover, like kingship, lordship assumed official attributes in clerical thought, a tendency surely encouraged as the ministerial functions of kings and princes were diffused among or claimed by the castellan elites. Assumptions and speculations about tyranny, protection, *dominium,* and so forth, figure in the sources conventionally exploited by historians of what Patrick Geary terms the "high tradition of intellectual history"; yet, as Van Engen shows, these same sources have much to tell us about the rise of lordship as the prevalent category of power.

With John Williams the reading turns from words and events to monuments. His subject is the building of a royal-dynastic pantheon at San Isidoro of León in the mid-eleventh century, with evidence to suggest a programmatic appropriation of early Hispanic royal legitimism. Williams further suggests that the cultural enterprise of Fernando I (d. 1065) marked a conscious effort to organize a capital. And the "capitalizing" of power, so to call it, infused dynastic identity with the translated sanctity of the most widely venerated of Visigothic saints. This is a study which explores the role of prestige in the cultural nurturing of elite power.

Stephen Jaeger reflects on the classic problem of the ideal and the real in literary evidence. He unmasks the "reality" in Peter of Blois' polemic against knightly ways, seeing it as exemplifying a "mimetic fallacy" overlooking the subjective distortion of interest. He argues for a "move of the warrior class from violence to restraint" such as the clergy had long advocated. A conflict of values can be traced in administrative records, but "more abundantly and dramatically" in literary representations; he discerns an enduring "friction zone" of conflict between these social ideas. "Opposite generates opposite," so that the habitual violation of women explains the cult of women in courtly literature. Jaeger proposes certain characteristics of his twelfth-century "friction zone," then sketches the external history of its origin and course. He concludes that courtly literature could well have influenced a refinement in knightly deportment.

Laura Kendrick addresses the problem of literature critical of elites whose lineages and values are alleged to be corrupt. Marcabru's vituperative voice resounds over the great and the *joven*. Here the quality of nobility is at issue, suggesting that in a region—the South—notably afflicted by knightly violence, paternity and legitimacy were considerable issues. Kendrick sees here a potentially political matter, and associates Marcabru's polemics with ecclesiastical interest. His "invective was the vernacular poetic equivalent of excommunication"; he sided with clerics, and notably monks. He "challenges the noble who buys into glorification of his ancestry to live up to an ecclesiastical ideal of secular lordship"—so here, too, a preoccupation with nobility proves to be one of power.

Philippe Buc brings out another zone of "contentious and politicized debate" in which commentators on the Bible underscored the failings of *potestas* and *dominatio*. He contrasts the traditional stress on hierarchical order with the appearance, in the Parisian masters, of resistance to lordship over men. But another strain of exegesis originating at Laon proclaimed the persistence of *prelatio* till the end of time, an equivocal contention that stimulated its own debates. Very curious, Buc shows, is the way violence was taken to be emblematic of power in the exegetes, to the point of clerical and royal cannibalism. Taxation became another crux: legitimate or excessive in essence? Buc discerns a tendency for theoretical levelling in exegetical discourse.

It may not be easy to think of these diverse studies as addressing, let alone defining, a single historical subject. "Power" seems so conceptually vast, so inscrutably inflated, that one instinctively seeks to pluralize the word; there is editorial perplexity in this book's main title. But we intend nothing vague in speaking of "cultures of power," for in either an anthropological or a biological sense we may usefully characterize the interactions of kings and artists in León or of claimant monks in Angevin courts or of scurrilous poets in a capriciously lorded Aquitaine or of English judges delegate or of ritual processions or deference or clerical criticism in royal courts as cultural phenomena. They projected associative meanings, symbolized social realities, distinctly.[3] The biting vernacular of castle-bound knightly singers was a world removed from the procedural discourse of canonist judges. We may even suspect there was something provincial, or even local, about some of these cultures. The *ministeriales* exemplified a concept of status-bound service limited virtually to German imperial lands and borderlands. But our studies also reveal a more pervasive and deeper culture of scriptural and theological moralizing about the exercise of God's power on earth. And there seems no reason to doubt that we may descriptively distinguish between "high" and "low"—or popular—cultures of power thus differentiated. The peasants of Old Catalonia who complained of vicarial brutality in the Ribes valley toward 1165 had no conceptual means of deploring what the learned clerk John of Salisbury would have stigmatized unequivocally as tyranny.[4]

But it would be premature here to project a socially differentiated cultural history. That was no aim as such of our conference, although we had a prospector (Duby) in our midst and although the results of Arnold, Barthélemy, and Jaeger were suggestive of this *piste*. What did concern us was to think of power as situationally distinct, as a proper subject of qualitative description. To think of it as immediate experience, as conventional, traditional, good and bad; to ask how power was felt, imagined, conceived, suffered, as well as institutionalized. This approach might seem to lure us into a perilous swamp of historically documented situations. How many are the regions and topics we have omitted! But it will surely suffice to have approached, without pretending to cover, our subject. A cultural history of medieval power would be even more demanding than the well-tested political-dynastic or constitutional ones. For it is not enough to say what happened to understand how people experienced power, nor can we safely

3. On culture see generally Clifford Geertz, *The Interpretation of Cultures: Selected Essays* (New York, 1973); Pierre Bourdieu, *Outline of a Theory of Practice*, tr. Richard Nice (Cambridge, 1977); and Peter Burke, *Popular Culture in Early Modern Europe* (New York, 1978), Prologue.

4. T. N. Bisson, "The Crisis of the Catalonian Franchises (1150–1200)," in *La formació i expansió del feudalisme català. Homenatge a Santiago Sobrequès i Vidal*, ed. Jaume Portella i Comas, Estudi General, no. 5–6 (Girona, 1985–86), pp. 153–72; John of Salisbury, *Policraticus*, 8: 17, 18 and elsewhere, ed. C. C. J. Webb, 2 vols. (Oxford, 1909), 2: 345–64. On high and low culture, see Burke, *Popular Culture*, pp. 23ff., citing Robert Redfield's model of cultural stratification.

presume to attribute uniformities as easily to cultural as to "political" circumstances. Flanders and Anjou were probably more nearly alike in respect to comital "law and power" in Van Caenegem's terms than were these lands in respect to White's "disputing process." And the findings of Kendrick and Williams only underscore the need, still perhaps more felt than implemented, for historians to attend to visual and literary evidence.

So the title of this volume is descriptive rather than programmatic. The contributions may, or indeed must, be read as they were written, on their own variable terms. They work from several disciplines toward a common problem, their authors mostly sharing an inclination to read evidence closely and critically. And if they are not overly concerned with the developmental history of power, that may not be a bad thing in the present state of our knowledge. People in the twelfth century did not know they were inventing the state.

Part I

Elites Old and New

Theodore Evergates

1. Nobles and Knights in Twelfth-Century France

Marc Bloch could not have imagined the long shadow his discursive essays entitled *Feudal Society* (1939–40) would cast over the historiography of medieval France.[1] Seeking to capture the essence of medieval society for a general audience, he framed a paradigm of social organization that has served as referent ever since. For the period after ca. 1050—what he called the "second feudal age" and precisely the "long" twelfth century of this conference—he adopted two seemingly incongruent propositions from Paul Guilhiermoz's massive study on the French nobility: nobles and knights constituted a single "social class," yet nobility existed in France only when it was recognized by law in the thirteenth century.[2]

Although the weight of evidence accumulated during the past thirty years fails to support either proposition, Alessandro Barbero has recently reopened the debate, reasserting Bloch's formulation and challenging both the findings and methodologies of the regional monographs.[3] We should recall, however, that *Feudal Society* represented only one panel of a triptych on medieval Europe that was to include separate volumes on the economy and government.[4] Moreover, Bloch would certainly have written a

1. Marc Bloch, *La société féodale* (L'évolution de l'humanité, 34–34 bis, ed. Henri Berr), 2 vols. (Paris, 1939–1940), tr. L. A. Manyon, *Feudal Society* (Chicago: 1961). Bloch's appropriation of "feudal" for his volume on medieval society disturbed the series editor, Henri Berr (*La société féodale*, 1: vii–viii).

2. Paul Guilhiermoz, *Essai sur l'origine de la noblesse en France au moyen âge* (Paris, 1902).

3. Alessandro Barbero, *L'aristocrazia nella società francese del medioevo. Analisi delle fonti letterarie (secoli X–XIII)* (Bologna, 1987). Barbero's study was foreshadowed by Giovanni Tabacco, "Su nobilità e cavalleria nel medioevo. Un ritorno a Marc Bloch?" *Rivista Storica Italiana* 91 (1979), 5–25, and in *Studi di storia medievale e moderno per Ernesto Sestan,* 2 vols. (Florence, 1980), 1: 31–55, which fails, however, to account for the regional studies since the 1960s. Critical reviews of Barbero are Jean Flori, "Chevalerie, noblesse et lutte de classes au moyen âge d'après un ouvrage récent," *Moyen Age* 94 (1988), 157–79, and Léopold Genicot, "Noblesse ou aristocratie? Des questions de méthode," *Revue d'Histoire Ecclésiastique* 85 (1990), 334–43.

4. Bloch himself intended to write two volumes on the economy, a subject that preoccupied him in the 1930s; they were announced as volumes 43–44 of the series "L'évolution

different *Feudal Society* had the regional studies, which he long advocated, been available to him: their genealogical and prosopographical approach to social history, which Georges Duby pioneered in *La société mâconnaise* (1953), has become the foundation upon which all generalization must be based.[5]

At this juncture, rather than reviewing a voluminous bibliography on a large and complex subject, I think it would be useful to pose three questions about the nobility in the twelfth century.[6] First, how did contemporaries understand nobility? Second, how did family structure, or lineage organization, account for the circulation of cadets? And third, was the nobility an open elite, accessible to non-nobles?

The Language of Nobility

Modern historians have been reluctant to speak of nobles and nobility for a period in which those terms were seldom employed. Robert Fossier argues that in the twelfth century "noble" was simply "a term of the Church, a learned word that laymen never used to speak of themselves."[7] And in the vernacular imaginative literature, claims Barbero, "noble" neither referred to birth nor designated a social class.[8] It is of course true that when kings, dukes, and counts were quoted directly by their scribes, they did not speak of their nobles but rather of their barons, that is, those who shared in governance; nor did their chanceries characterize their vassals as "noble."[9] Yet

---

de l'humanité": *Les origines de l'économie européenne (Ve–XIIe siècles)* and *De l'économie urbaine et seigneuriale au capitalisme financier (XIIIe–XVe siècles)*. The political volumes were by Louis Halphen, *Charlemagne et l'empire carolingien* (Paris, 1947: written in 1939) and Charles Petit-Dutaillis, *La monarchie féodale en France et en Angleterre (Xe–XIIIe siècle)* (Paris, 1933), tr. E. D. Hunt, *The Feudal Monarchy in France and England from the Tenth to the Thirteenth Century* (London, 1936).

5. Georges Duby, *La société aux XIe et XIIe siècles dans la région mâconnaise* (Paris, 1953), and articles reprinted in *Hommes et structures du moyen âge* (Paris, 1973) [most are translated by Cynthia Postan as *The Chivalrous Society* (London, 1977)]. See also his *Le chevalier, la femme et le prêtre* (Paris, 1981), tr. Barbara Bray, *The Knight, the Lady, and the Priest* (New York, 1983). Bloch's own disinterest in biography and family history is reflected in his uncharitable, three-sentence review of Sidney Painter's *William Marshal: Knight Errant, Baron, and Regent of England* (Baltimore, 1933) in *Annales d'Histoire Economique et Sociale* 6 (1934), 313–14.

6. A similar questionnaire is open for Germany; see John B. Freed, "Reflections on the Medieval German Nobility," *AHR* 91 (1986), 553–75.

7. Robert Fossier, *Enfance de l'Europe*, 2 vols. (Paris, 1982), 2: 965. I, too, have preferred "aristocracy" as a neutral term of analysis; see my *Feudal Society in the Bailliage of Troyes Under the Counts of Champagne, 1152–1284* (Baltimore, 1975), pp. 13, 97.

8. Barbero, *L'aristocrazia*, pp. 27–29.

9. Eric Bournazel, *Le gouvernement capétien au XIIe siècle, 1108–1180: structures sociales et mutations institutionnelles* (Paris, 1975), pp. 151–61, notes the gradual substitution of *barones*

we should not infer the absence of a noble class from the rare usage of *nobilis* in the diplomatic acts and administrative registers. The most systematic and geographically controlled studies of the semantic evolution of *nobilis* and its synonyms from the ninth century demonstrate conclusively that the writers of both narrative and diplomatic texts understood the meaning of nobility and knew who the nobles were.[10] Indeed, Bloch himself was forced to admit a de facto nobility in the twelfth century, since he knew full well that *nobilis* and *nobilitas* shared a long, consistent linguistic tradition that referred to the elite of wealthy, powerful, and endogamous families.[11] By the thirteenth century the term "noble" had triumphed semantically over its synonyms in both Latin and the vernacular to designate those elite families. Laymen in their private acts referred to their parents, spouses, and siblings as noble.[12] The Parlement of Paris conducted inquests to verify the noble descent of petitioners whose noble-ness was not self-evident,[13] and royal letters patent conferred nobility on those who lacked the requisite parentage.[14]

---

for the traditional *optimates* and *proceres,* especially in reference to consultative bodies. For the counts of Flanders, see Ernest Warlop, *The Flemish Nobility Before 1300,* tr. James Bruce Ross, 4 vols. (Kortrijk, 1975–76), 2: 553, n. 2; 554, n. 4. For the use of *nobilis* by princes, see Léopold Genicot, "Une thèse: campagnes et paysans de Picardie jusqu'au XIIIe siècle," *Annales: E.S.C.* (1970), 1476–77 (the count of Ponthieu was quoted as having acted "coram nobilibus patriae mee . . . isti nobiles cum aliis confirmaverunt" [1100], although subsequently he spoke of his "barons"); and Michel Parisse, *Noblesse et chevalerie en Lorraine médiévale* (Nancy, 1982), p. 166 n. 14 (Simon II, duke of Lorraine, affirmed his own succession "cum justo desiderio et vocatione legitima virorum nobilium terre" [ca. 1176]).

10. Warlop, *Flemish Nobility,* 1: chs. 1–2, and Régine Le Jan-Hennebicque, "*Domnus, Illuster, Nobilis:* les mutations du pouvoir au Xe siècle," in *Haut Moyen Age: culture, éducation et société: études offerts à Pierre Riché,* ed. Claude Lepelley et al. (Nanterre, 1990), pp. 439–48, a summary of her unpublished thesis, "Les aristocrates du nord-ouest de la France (IXe–XIe siècles): sémantique du vocabulaire sociale," 2 vols., Université de Paris-I (1983). See also below, n. 93.

11. See Jane Martindale, "The French Aristocracy in the Early Middle Ages: A Reappraisal," *Past and Present,* no. 75 (1977), esp. pp. 10–12, 36; and Karl Ferdinand Werner, "Du nouveau sur un vieux thème: les origines de la 'noblesse' et de la 'chevalerie,'" in *Comptes Rendus de l'Académie des Inscriptions et Belles-Lettres* (1985), 186–200. The precision with which "noble" was employed is amply demonstrated in Jean-Pierre Poly and Eric Bournazel, *La mutation féodale: Xe–XIIe siècle,* 2nd ed. (Paris, 1991), pp. 157–72; tr. (from first edition, 1980) Caroline Higgitt, *The Feudal Transformation: 900–1200* (New York–London, 1991), pp. 88–97.

12. Examples in Jean-Gabriel Gigot, *Chartes en langue française antérieures à 1271 conservées dans le département de la Haute-Marne,* Documents linguistiques de la France (série française), 1 (Paris, 1974).

13. *Actes du Parlement de Paris,* ed. Edgard Boutaric, 2 vols. (Paris, 1863–67): "noble on his father's side" (1:315, no. 9, of ca. 1269); "noble only through his mother" (1:362, no. 419, of 1280).

14. Jan Rogozinski, "Ennoblement by the Crown and Social Stratification in France, 1285–1322," in *Order and Innovation in the Middle Ages: Essays in Honor of Joseph R. Strayer,* ed. William Chester Jordan, Bruce McNab, and Teofilo F. Ruiz (Princeton, NJ, 1976), pp. 273–91.

Since "noble" designated neither title nor office, it seldom occurs in twelfth-century charters which are, for the most part, title-deeds drawn up by the recipient religious houses. Benedictine scribes did occasionally flatter a benefactor by citing his distinguished ancestry but, significantly, not a single charter or pancarte for Clairvaux contains the term "noble" in any form during Bernard's abbacy.[15] As the son of noble parents—his father was lord of the minor castle of Fontaines-lès-Dijon—Bernard understood noble-ness as an attribute of parentage; in fact, it was precisely the advantage of birth that he sought to exclude from his classless monastic community.[16] "In nature," he explained, "no one is inferior, no one superior; no one is placed ahead or behind; and no one is noble or nonnoble, for nature creates us all equal."[17] He stipulated that the Templars, his "new" knights, should ban social distinctions: deference was to be accorded to merit rather than to noble birth.[18] In the same vein Peter Abelard cautioned Abbess Heloise against choosing a noble-born woman as prioress: such a woman, he said, tends to be presumptuous and arrogant because of her birth, and worse, she and her relatives might take over the convent for their own interests.[19]

15. *Recueil des chartes de l'abbaye de Clairvaux*, ed. Jean Waquet et al., fasc. 1–2 (Troyes, 1950, 1982).

16. The *Vita Prima* states that Bernard was born of distinguished parents (*parentibus claris*); the *Vita Tercia* explains that his father Tescelin, one of the *proceres* serving the castle of Châtillon-sur-Seine, was a *vir genere nobilis, posessionibus dives,* a *miles fortissimus,* a companion of his lord (the duke of Burgundy), and a *dominus minoris castri cui Fontanae nomen est,* while Bernard's mother was *ex optimo genere Burgundionum* (*PL* 185: 227, 523–24). Bernard's background is discussed in Jean Richard, "Le milieu familial," in *Bernard de Clairvaux,* Commission d'Histoire de l'Ordre de Cîteaux, preface by Thomas Merton (Paris, 1953), pp. 9–15; Robert Fossier, "La fondation de Clairvaux et la famille de Saint Bernard," in *Mélanges Saint Bernard,* 24e Congrès de l'Association Bourguignonne des Sociétés Savantes (Dijon, 1954), pp. 19–27 (who stresses Bernard's familial ties with several castellan families); and Constance B. Bouchard, *Sword, Miter, and Cloister: Nobility and the Church in Burgundy, 980–1198* (Ithaca, 1987), pp. 329–331.

17. *Sancti Bernardi opera,* ed. Jean Leclercq, C. H. Talbot, and H. M. Rochais, 8 vols. (Rome, 1957–1978), 8B:234 (*Sententiae,* 3): "In natura enim, nullus inferior, nullus superior; nullus anterior, nullus posterior; nemo nobilis, nemo ignobilis; sed omnes aequales nos ipsa natura semper creat." For Bernard's ideal of a classless society, see Jean Leclercq, *Monks and Love in Twelfth-Century France: Psycho-Historical Essays* (Oxford, 1979), pp. 12–13.

18. *Sancti Bernardi opera,* 3:220 (*De laude nova militiae,* 4): "Persona inter eos minime accipitur: defertur meliori, non nobiliori." Yet he recognized the role of noble families in the lay world: in his letter of consolation to Queen Melisende of Jerusalem at the death of her husband, Fulk of Anjou, Bernard encouraged her to persevere because of the glory of her kingdom, her power, and her noble lineage (*lineam nobilitatis*) (8: 297–98 [*Epistolae,* no. 354]).

19. *PL* 178: 269, no. 8, quoted in Alexander Murray, *Reason and Society in the Middle Ages* (Oxford, 1978), p. 326. Around 1152, however, Heloise and the chapter of the Paraclete elected one of their own, a lady Gertrude, *nobilis et honesta femina,* to be the first abbess of La Pommeraye in Sens; see Charles Lalore, *Collection des principaux cartulaires du diocèse de Troyes,* 7 vols. (Paris-Troyes, 1875–1890), 2 (*Cartulaire de l'abbaye du Paraclet*), pp. 71–73, no. 53.

But it is Orderic Vitalis, writing ca. 1127–37, who has left us the most vivid picture of noble society. Orderic relates how Robert Curthose, eldest son of William the Conqueror, was goaded by the high-born young men (*tirones*) in his entourage to seek the duchy of Normany from his father; rebuffed, Robert went into exile complaining bitterly about being treated as a mere hireling (*mercenarius*) dependent on an allowance. In Germany and France he visited the dukes, counts, and castellans who were his noble kinsmen (*nobiles cognates*), and later accepted a castle from King Philip I in the Beauvaisis where he assembled a garrison of common knights (*gregarii equites*). That treasonous act angered his father, but Robert's noble neighbors (*nobiles vicini*), in concert with his father's Norman barons (*proceres*), succeeded in averting open war between Normans and Frenchmen.[20]

Throughout his lengthy account of Anglo-Norman affairs Orderic consistently distinguishes the stipendiary or garrison knights—those who were recruited primarily from non-noble families and who received small rents for their castle service[21]—from the noble-born knights, the "youth" who learned the martial arts in the household of a great baron or relative where they remained until they came into an inheritance and married.[22] One such noble knight whom Orderic knew and admired was Ansold of Maule (d. 1118). As a young man he had served with Duke Robert Guiscard in Italy, then returned home to marry a castellan's daughter and assume the lordship of Maule. Ansold became a local lord very much like the "noble neighbors" of Robert Curthose.[23] Yet only a few of those noble youths ever became castellans; most cadets and those from less wealthy families would settle on modest estates, live in manor houses, and exercise limited rights of lordship.

Recently Jean Flori has marshalled overwhelming evidence for the absolute distinction between nobility (birthright) and knighthood (the profession of arms) through the twelfth century, and even Barbero now accepts that conclusion.[24] Barbero suggests, however, that we pay more at-

20. OV 5, 10 (3:96–113).

21. See Chibnall's remark about the two types of knights in Robert's service, note 8 to OV 8, 1 (4: 119), and her "Mercenaries and the *Familia Regis* under Henry I," *History* 62 (1977), 15–23; see also Olivier Guyotjeannin, *Episcopus et comes: affirmation et déclin de la seigneurie épiscopale au nord du royaume de France, Beauvais-Noyon, Xe–début XIIIe siècle* (Paris-Geneva, 1987), pp. 37–38, 64–65.

22. Georges Duby, "Youth in Aristocratic Society," in his *Chivalrous Society,* pp. 112–22.

23. OV 5, 19 (3:178–82).

24. Jean Flori, *L'essor de la chevalerie, XIe–XIIe siècles* (Paris, 1986); Alessandro Barbero, "Noblesse et chevalerie en France au Moyen Age: une réflexion," *Moyen Age* 97 (1991), 431–37.

tention to the relative nature of nobility, an aspect of nobility to which contemporaries alluded when they designated some personages "more noble" and others "very noble." But it is the *less* noble who are of greatest interest here, those who inhabited the complex world below the level of castellan lords. Again, it is Orderic who best describes that world. The large household of Hugh of Avranches, he says, was "full of the noise of swarms of noble and nonnoble boys" (*nobilium ignobiliumque*), and his court was attended by local lords (*barones*) as well as simple knights (*modesti milites*).[25] Those local lords—recently termed "family barons" or "petits nobles"—who attached themselves to a castellan lord were precisely the noncastellan nobles who possessed allodial estates and a fief or two, and who lived in a manor house rather than a fortified residence.[26] Such a noble was Werric, a widower in 1107 who claimed very noble birth but realized, he said, the vanity and fragility of the world; he decided, therefore, to alienate his entire estate with its tenants to the monastery of Homblières where he and his only son took the religious habit.[27] Another was Bartholomew, the second son of the lord of Sissonne, who in 1163 assigned his wife a dower consisting of his house, allodial property, and three fiefs, two of which he held from monasteries.[28] Such non-castellan nobles, whether eldest sons or cadets, have been practically ignored by modern historians.

Orderic's "simple" or rural knights (*milites pagenses*)[29] were neither noble-born youth nor stipendiary castle knights but rather the more numerous non-noble knights who appear so prominently in the feudal registers of Normandy and Champagne (1170s).[30] They are the textbook "feudal" knights, although we might more properly call them "allodial" knights, as their fiefs only supplemented their hereditary allodial lands.[31] They are difficult to identify before ca. 1150, for in the sources they appear either as

25. OV 6, 2 (3:216–17).

26. Examples in David Crouch, *The Beaumont Twins: The Roots and Branches of Power in the Twelfth Century* (Cambridge, 1986), ch. 4, esp. pp. 115–16 (family barons); Edwin Smyrl, "La famille des Baux," *Cahiers du Centre d'Etudes des Sociétés méditerranéennes* 2 (1968), 65–67 ("petits nobles"); Robert Fossier, *Cartulaire-chronique du prieuré Saint-Georges d'Hesdin* (Paris, 1988), pp. 25–28; and André Debord, *La société laïque dans les pays de la Charente, Xe–XIIe s.* (Paris, 1984), pp. 236–41 (the Bouchard de Tourriers family lacked a castle because its lands were too close to the comital castles).

27. *The Cartulary and Charters of Notre-Dame of Homblières*, ed. Theodore Evergates, with Giles Constable (Cambridge, MA, 1990), pp. 85–86 no. 35 (1106).

28. Laurent Morelle, "Mariage et diplomatique: autour de cinq chartes de douaire dans le Laonnois-Soissonnais, 1163–1181," *BEC* 146 (1988), 247–51.

29. OV 11, 3 (6: 26 and n. 2).

30. On this point, I think Barbero, "Noblesse et chevalerie," p. 443, is entirely correct.

31. Jean Richard, "Châteaux, châtelains et vassaux en Bourgogne aux XIe et XIIe siècles," *Cahiers de Civilisation médiévale* 3 (1960), 444, and Debord, *La société laïque*, pp. 244–46, 253.

allodial proprietors or as knights, depending on the occasion. Although never called lord (*dominus*) in the charters, chronicles, or administrative registers, they probably did exercise some form of lordship on their lands, and in the late twelfth century they usually took their names from villages. Allodial knights were men of some local standing, they patronized nearby monasteries, and they sent their sons into military service and the church, where a few rose to the highest ranks. They lived in simple houses, although the more prosperous among them fortified their residences and came to be called lords of their villages by the end of the century. Except for their non-noble birth, little distinguished these knights from the less wealthy noble-born lords.[32]

Even though the written sources fail to convey the nuances of nobleness expressed by the distinctive clothing, speech, and gestures of the nobles, they do yield a highly consistent picture of the twelfth-century nobility. *Nobilis* expressed a shared understanding of nobility as a quality of birth and lineage; noble families, stratified by wealth, office, and prestige, included non-castellan families whose precise role still remains to be explored. Nobility and knighthood denoted entirely separate characteristics, neither signifying the other; indeed, the knights comprised a remarkably diverse group that included both nobles and non-noble allodial proprietors, as well as impecunious men of all social backgrounds.

Lineage, Primogeniture, and the Circulation of Cadets

Contemporaries saw noble families as the community of well-born from which the highest office-holders, both lay and ecclesiastic, were recruited. But modern historians, by viewing the nobility primarily through those office-holders, especially castellans, have created a simplistic model of the noble family that fails to account for the diverse roles of younger sons and daughters, who did, after all, comprise the greater part of those families. From ca. 1000, it has been argued, noble families restructured themselves into primogenital patrilineages in order to preserve their patrimonies, the material basis of noble standing. Younger sons and daughters were ejected from the paternal household and patrimony: unmarried daughters were placed in convents, while cadets entered the Church, assumed a life of adventure in the retinue of some lord, or set out for the Holy Land. Dynastic

32. Guyotjeannin, *Episcopus et comes*, pp. 151–52 and n. 203.

policy, it is claimed, specifically prohibited younger sons from marrying and founding new lineages until the last decades of the twelfth century, when noble families began to divide their patrimonies among younger sons who were allowed, at last, to marry and found their own lineages. That new practice supposedly led to the systematic fragmentation of noble fortunes in the thirteenth century.[33]

Such a model is not convincing for the twelfth century. A demographic explosion certainly must be counted among the propelling forces of the time,[34] and indeed many noble children *were* placed in the Church. So many women entered convents, in fact, that many institutions by the end of the century had exhausted their meager endowments. In 1196, for example, Celestine III ordered Heloise's convent of the Paraclete to downsize through attrition to sixty nuns; shortly afterward the well-known convent of Avenay was restricted to forty nuns because it was "burdened by debts owed to creditors," a complaint common in the thirteenth century.[35] The Cistercian convent of Fervaques even sought Innocent III's protection from the "nobles and powerful men" who reacted violently when their relatives were refused admission.[36] Yet we should not assume without evidence that the increasing demand for convent placements was simply the result of a desire to preserve patrimonies from division. Unmarried women had a variety of motives for seeking a cloistered life.[37] Moreover, widowed and married women who took the veil for spiritual reasons constituted at least one-quarter of all nuns.[38] To view convents simply as warehouses for excess daughters clearly misconstrues their complex sociological function.

Noble sons, too, flocked to the expanding reformed monasteries and the burgeoning cathedral chapters, where a few were able to attain high

33. The historiographical development of this dynastic model is recounted in T. N. Bisson, "Nobility and Family in Medieval France: A Review Essay," *French Historical Studies* 16 (1990), 597–613. A convincing critique of the core thesis, that the structure of families changed ca. 1000, is in Constance B. Bouchard, "Family Structure and Family Consciousness Among the French Aristocracy in the Ninth to Eleventh Centuries," *Francia* 14 (1986), 639–58.

34. Although it is difficult to measure the exact size of noble families, indirect evidence indicates that they were generally large until reduced by disease, youthful accidents, and war. See Parisse, *Noblesse et chevalerie en Lorraine,* ch. 8 ("L'expansion des familles nobles").

35. Lalore, *Collection des principaux cartulaires,* vol. 2. (*Cartulaire de l'abbaye du Paraclet*), p. 33, no. 20; Louis Paris, *Histoire de l'abbaye d'Avenay,* 2 vols. (Reims, 1879), 2:94, no. 34 (1201: order of the archbishop of Reims).

36. AN, L 239, no. 45 (letter of Innocent III): "nobiles et potentes super receptione sororum vos sepe numero molestare contendunt . . . [he prohibited the nuns] per violentiam aliquorum nobilium aut potentum aliquam in collegio vestro compelli possitis."

37. Penelope D. Johnson, *Equal in Monastic Profession: Religious Women in Medieval France* (Chicago, 1991), esp. pp. 27–34.

38. Jean Verdon, "Les moniales dans la France de l'Ouest aux XIe et XIIe siècles: études d'histoire sociale," *Cahiers de Civilisation Médiévale* 19 (1976), 251–54.

office.[39] Indeed, bishops and abbots were by definition an elite of cadets. Still, only a small percentage of noble sons were absorbed by the Church, perhaps only 15 to 20 percent, and even they were not necessarily forced into the Church by dynastic policy.[40] We should be mindful, too, of diverse family traditions: while some families provided only occasional candidates, others sent a steady stream of sons to create veritable ecclesiastical dynasties in local monastic communities where relatives had already achieved prominence.[41] Of the six brothers of Peter the Venerable, abbot of Cluny, four became abbots.[42] Bernard of Clairvaux, the third son of a minor lord, persuaded all five of his brothers to take the religious habit, including the eldest Guy, who abandoned the paternal lordship to his son-in-law.[43] So persuasive was Bernard, claims his biographer, that mothers hid their sons, wives held back their husbands, and friends restrained one another from following Bernard into the religious life.[44] It is not surprising that a few families even committed dynastic suicide when all the males in their line became celibate.[45] Clearly, the primary motivation for young men to enter the Church was not the preservation of patrimony; indeed, even childhood oblation was in decline.[46] The twelfth century was an age of adult conversion, of individual rather than familial decision.

Genealogical trees mask the fragility of twelfth-century successions in which it was not uncommon for a younger brother, nephew, or cousin to

39. OV 8, 26 (4:324–27) observes that many nobles joined Cistercian communities.

40. Michel Parisse, *La noblesse Lorraine, XIe–XIIIe s.*, 2 vols., thèse, Université de Nancy-II, 1975, 1:339–40, finds that 21 percent of the sons of ducal-comital families and 13.5 percent of the castellan families became ecclesiastics in the twelfth and thirteenth centuries. Bouchard, *Sword*, p. 46, estimates about 15 percent for Burgundian nobles. According to the genealogy established by Lambert of Ardres for the lords of Bourbourg, 25 percent of the men and women entered the Church; see Murray, *Reason and Society*, p. 344.

41. Bouchard, *Sword*, pp. 79–84.

42. They were of the noble family of Montboissier; see Giles Constable, *The Letters of Peter the Venerable*, 2 vols. (Cambridge, MA, 1967), 2:233–46 ("The Family of Peter the Venerable").

43. See Bouchard, *Sword*, pp. 60–62, 329–31. According to the *Vita Prima*, it was Bernard's mother Aleth who dedicated all her children at birth to a religious life (*PL* 185:227); see also above note 16.

44. *Vita Prima, PL* 185:235.

45. Examples in Joachim Wollasch, "Parenté noble et monachisme réformateur. Observations sur les 'conversions' à la vie monastique aux XIe et XIIe siècles," *Revue Historique* 535 (1980), 3–24; Murray, *Reason and Society*, p. 347; and Constance B. Bouchard, "The Structure of a Twelfth-Century French Family: The Lords of Seignelay," *Viator* 10 (1979), 53 (Guy, archbishop of Sens, convinced his brother Bochard to send both of his sons into the Church).

46. John Boswell, *The Kindness of Strangers: The Abandonment of Children in Western Europe from Late Antiquity to the Renaissance* (New York, 1988), pp. 296–321, and Joseph H. Lynch, *Simoniacal Entry into Religious Life from 1000 to 1260: A Social, Economic and Legal Study* (Columbus, OH, 1976), ch. 2. Bouchard, *Sword*, pp. 59–64, reviewing the various motives for conversion, rejects the notion that dynastic policy was the driving force behind noble conversion.

preserve the lineage. The county of Soissons, for instance, which passed through five hands in the course of the century, went only once to an eldest son but twice to a younger brother (and once each to a nephew and a cousin). In that same period the lordship of Nesle passed only twice to the eldest son (and once each to a cadet and a nephew). Of the nine peaceful transfers of Soissons and Nesle—none resulting from confiscation or financial exigency—only three (one-third) went to an eldest son.[47] That same percentage holds for the castle of Bruges, where between ca. 1060 and 1200 the eldest son succeeded in only three of the nine transfers.[48] The lordship of Beaujeu, one of the best documented in Burgundy, passed only once to the eldest surviving son and once to a grandson who designated his sister as heir.[49] In the more turbulent Normandy under Henry I, almost half of the baronies passed to someone other than the eldest son.[50]

Rarely can we recapture the human drama involved in indirect transfers. A mortal battlefield wound, for example, prompted Baldwin VII, the childless count of Flanders, to designate his cousin Charles as his successor (1119).[51] And it was the suspicion that his wife's infant son might not be his own that induced Count Hugh of Champagne to transfer his lands (1125) to his nephew Thibaut, count of Blois (himself a second son whose mother, Countess Adela of Blois, promoted him over his older brother).[52] Both Baldwin and Hugh selected as successors relatives with whom they had already developed close bonds.

Lambert of Ardres tells the story of another count, Manasses of Guines (1100–42), whose only child, a daughter, died leaving a sickly infant daughter.[53] The count was desolate, as his three younger brothers had predeceased

47. Soissons: eldest son Renaud III (ca. 1115); younger brothers Jean (ca. 1108) and Ralph I (1180); nephew Conon (1178); cousin Ivo II (1141). Nesle: eldest sons Ralph (early 12th century) and Ivo II (1131); brother Jean I (1180); nephew Conon (1178). See William Mendel Newman, *Les seigneurs de Nesle en Picardie, XIIe–XIIIe siècle,* 2 vols. (Philadelphia, 1971), 1:59–65, genealogical table at 289.

48. Eldest sons Robert (ca. 1087), Walter (1110), Conon (1160); younger son Jean II (1200); younger brother Jean I (1180); uncle Didier Hacket (1115) (his possible restoration in 1130 is ignored here); "new" men were Erembald of Veurne (ca. 1060), Gervaise of Praat (1127) and Ralph of Nesle (1134). See Newman, *Les seigneurs de Nesle,* 1:59–65, 288, and Warlop, *Flemish Nobility,* pp. 721–27.

49. Humbert III (1137–92) was the sole surviving son; since both of his own sons predeceased him, Beaujeu passed to his grandson Guichard (1192–1216) who in his 1195 testament designated his sister as heir. See Bouchard, *Sword,* pp. 289–95.

50. Charlotte A. Newman, *The Anglo-Norman Nobility in the Reign of Henry I: The Second Generation* (Philadelphia: 1988), pp. 116–18.

51. Galbert of Bruges, *The Murder of Charles the Good, Count of Flanders,* tr. James Bruce Ross, rev. ed. (New York, 1967), pp. 14–15.

52. Henri d'Arbois de Jubainville, *Histoire des ducs et des comtes de Champagne,* 7 vols. (Paris, 1859–69), 2:135–36.

53. Duby, *The Knight,* ch. 13, recounts the story.

him without issue. With great difficulty Manasses found his granddaughter a husband, but when she divorced after a brief marriage, the count decided to adopt his sister's grandson at the baptismal font (1141).[54] About the same time the childless count of Soissons, gravely ill with leprosy, asked his feudal lord, the bishop of Soissons, to determine by inquest which of the five claimants to his lands was his closest heir in order to prevent, as he put it, cupidity from disturbing his lands. The choice fell to his cousin Ivo II, lord of Nesle (1131–78), a powerful neighbor with close ties to the royal seneschal, the count of Vermandois.[55] But fifteen years later, after six years of childless marriage, Ivo designated his own brother's son as heir to Nesle and Soissons.[56]

We have underestimated not only the frequency of collateral transfers but also the role of individual choice and circumstance in the evolution of twelfth-century lineages. When great lords like Ivo II of Nesle and Hugh of Broyes delayed marriage for twenty years after succeeding to their lordships, we must be skeptical about an inherent dynastic imperative ascribed to noble families.[57] Even such a powerful count as Thibaut of Blois (1107–1152), who succeeded at fifteen years of age, ruled his lands vigorously and at considerable risk for fifteen years before marrying, and then only after being dissuaded from taking the monastic habit.[58] Thibaut's eldest son, Count Henry the Liberal of Champagne (1152–1181), followed a similar pattern: betrothed at twenty-one years of age while on the Second Crusade, he did not marry until he was thirty-seven, after twelve years of rule.[59]

A case presented to Count Henry's High Court in 1166 illustrates the variety of attitudes and ambitions regarding lineal descent within noble families.[60] When Guy III, lord of Possesse in the Marne, mortgaged his castle to Count Henry and left the county ca. 1162, perhaps for the Latin East, his younger brother Jean succeeded to the lordship (without its mort-

54. Lambert of Ardres, "Historia comitum Ghisnensium," c. 47, ed. J. Heller, *MGH SS* 24:584–85: "in filium recepit adoptionis." The boy was named Baldwin after the count's own father.

55. Texts in Newman, *Les seigneurs de Nesle,* 2:29–33, no. 6 (1140); 51–53, no. 19 (1147).

56. Newman, *Les seigneurs de Nesle,* 2:84–86, no. 30 (testament of 1157/58).

57. For Ivo, see Newman, *Les seigneurs de Nesle.* He married Yoland of Hainaut in 1151 after two earlier marriage proposals failed to materialize (1:61–2, n. 13). For Hugh, see Georges Poull, *La maison ducale de Bar* (Rupt-sur-Moselle, 1977), 1:103–4.

58. Arbois de Jubainville, *Histoire,* 2:263 n. 1. The "Vita S. Norberti," *HF,* 14:229–30, recounts how Norbert persuaded the count of his responsibilities, then found him a wife.

59. See my "Louis VII and the Counts of Champagne," in *The Second Crusade and the Cistercians* ed. Michael Gervers (New York, 1992), pp. 109–17.

60. Text published in Henri d'Arbois de Jubainville, "Document sur l'obligation de la résidence imposée aux barons par le droit féodal champenois au douzième siècle," *Revue Historique de Droit Français et Etranger* 7 (1861), 68–70.

Genealogical Table 1

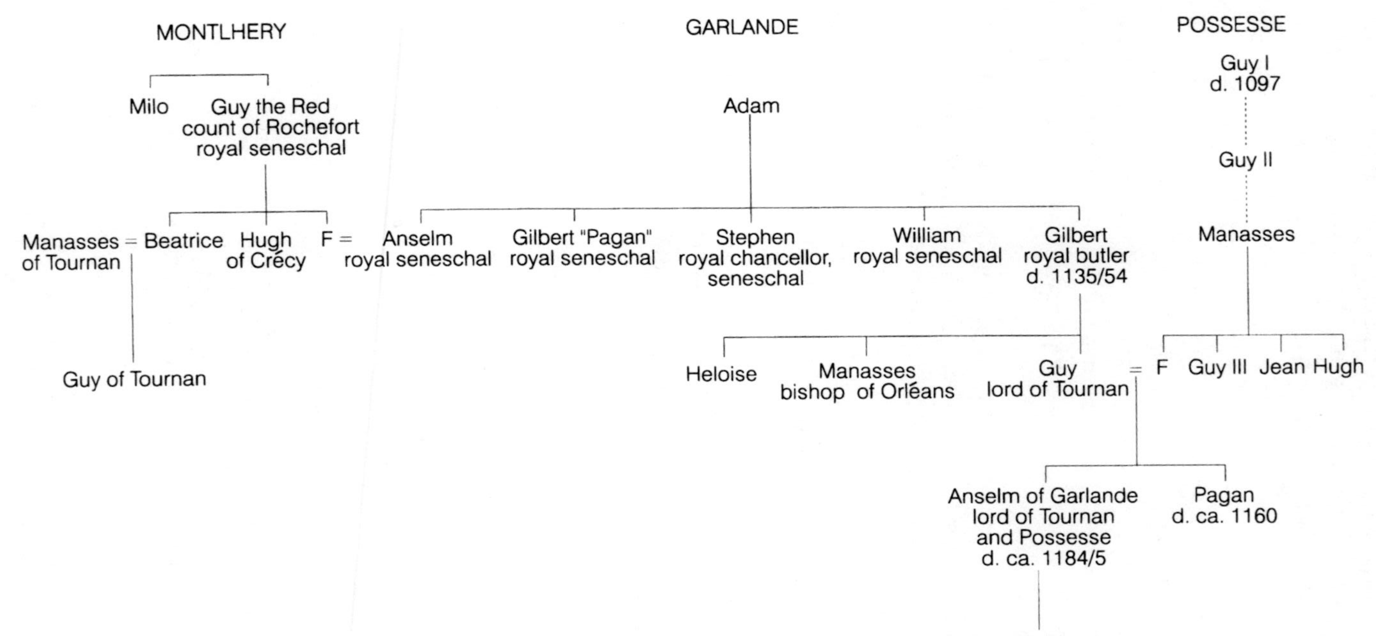

gaged castle).[61] But in 1165 Jean decided to join the Cistercians; he gave substantial gifts to the Templars and five Cistercian houses, founded a hospital in Possesse to serve travelers and the poor, and then entered Clairvaux.[62] At the same time his younger brother Hugh placed his share of Possesse under Count Henry's protection and departed for the Holy Land, never to return, for on reaching Calabria he married and settled there. Thus ended the first house of Possesse when three brothers in succession, for different reasons, abandoned their hereditary land and castle.[63]

At this point their brother-in-law, Guy of Garlande, brought suit claiming Possesse by hereditary right on behalf of his deceased wife's son (Genealogical Table 1). Guy belonged to a powerful noble family that had risen to prominence through royal service: his father Gilbert, the royal butler, was a fifth son whose four older brothers had succeeded one another as seneschal under Philip I and Louis VI.[64] After Gilbert fell from royal favor in 1127/28, he retired to his estates in Brie which, despite lacking a castle,

61. Little is known about the lords of Possesse before the mid-twelfth century. William of Tyre cites Guy I of Possesse twice: (1) among those who took the cross in 1096 who were neither counts nor "distinguished and noble men" but rather "greater men who were not however counts," and (2) as a "vir nobilis de regno Francorum" who died at Nicaea in 1097 (*Willelmi Tyrensis archiepiscopi chronicon*, ed. R.B.C. Huygens, 2 vols. [Turnhout, 1986], 1:138–39, 157, 159). Guy's grandson Manasses (c. 1126–c. 1141) was a baron of Count Thibaut II; see Arbois de Jubainville, *Histoire*, 157 n. 9, and Michel Bur, *Vestiges d'habitat seigneurial fortifié du Bas-Pays Argonnais* (Reims, 1972), p. 85.

62. Texts in: AD, Marne, 53H 91, no. 1 (to the Templars: all his possessions in Morcourt "except the fiefs of knights"); Edouard de Barthélemy, *Diocèse ancien de Châlons-sur-Marne. Histoire et monuments*, 2 vols. (Paris, 1861), 1:402–3 (foundation of the hospital); and J. Delaville le Roulx, *Cartulaire général de l'Ordre des Hospitaliers de S. Jean de Jérusalem (1100–1310)*, 4 vols. (Paris, 1894–1906), 1:239 (arable, fishing rights, and pasture rights to the Cistercian granges of Montiers-en-Argonne, Cheminon, La Chalaude, Haute-Fontaine, and Troisfontaine). Jean was still alive in 1192 when Anselm II of Garlande referred to him as "dominus Johannes, Clarevallensis monachus, predicte [Possesse] quondam dominus, cognatus meus" (AD, Marne, 53H 6, no. 6).

63. Perhaps the brothers objected to the recent imposition of the count's *mouvance*. Possesse was nominally within the empire but effectively independent within a frontier zone between France and Germany until 1162, when Frederick II transferred *mouvance* over nine castles there, including Possesse, to Count Henry the Liberal (Bur, *La formation du comté de Champagne, v. 950–v. 1150* [Nancy, 1977] pp. 406–7).

64. See Bournazel, *Le gouvernement capétien*, pp. 35–40 and genealogical table, based in part on Joseph Despont, "Une famille seigneuriale aux XIIe et XIIIe siècles: la famille de Garlande," unpublished thèse, Ecole des Chartes, 1924; and Robert-Henri Bautier, "Paris au temps d'Abélard," in *Abélard et son temps*. Actes du Colloque International Organisée à l'Occasion du 9e Centenaire de la Naissance de Pierre Abélard (Paris, 1981), pp. 53–77. Although the Garlande are usually taken as a knightly family that rose to success through royal service, when they first appeared in the late eleventh century they were lords with knights of their own near Lagny in Brie (*Recueil de chartes et documents de Saint-Martin-des-Champs*, ed. Joseph Depoin, 5 vols. [Paris, 1912–21] 1:96–98, no. 60; 100–101, no. 62). The evidence presented by Bournazel, who classifies them as "royal knights," accords better with "noble" than "knight," even though they are not associated early with a castle of their own.

must have been substantial,[65] for his son Guy was able to purchase the castle of Tournan-en-Brie from a cousin, with the approval of the bishop of Paris from whom it was held in fief.[66] Guy had already married into the Possesse family, which the Garlande had known since the First Crusade,[67] and he must have counted as a person of some standing by virtue of his brother Manasses, bishop of Orléans (1146–85), and Heloise, abbess of the Paraclete (1129–64), who was perhaps his half-sister.[68] Guy appeared among Louis VII's barons and was well known to Count Henry long before he petitioned the count's High Court in 1166.[69] The court recognized Guy's right to Possesse and notified the absent Hugh of Possesse of the impending transfer, failing his return within one year. Hugh did not return, Guy redeemed the mortgage, and Guy's son Anselm I became lord of Possesse.[70] Thus Guy of Garlande, the eldest son of a non-castellan cadet and endowed with both personal drive and financial resources, acquired two castellanies from his noble relatives and founded a castellan dynasty that survived for another century.[71]

65. Gilbert had lands near Tournan; in 1138 he appeared as a local witness to Count Thibaut II's donation to the nearby priory of Celle-en-Brie (BN, MS latin 5541, vol. 1, p. 61).

66. In a charter dated to ca. 1155 (Bournazel, p. 60), the bishop of Paris allowed Guy of Tournan to mortgage his castle to lord Guy of Garlande (the closest male heir) for 640 *l.* cash, redeemable in two years (BN, MS latin 5441, vol. 1, pp. 62–63). Guy of Garlande's sons Anselm I and Pagan (who died before 1166) witnessed. The loan might have been a disguised sale.

67. William of Tyre twice mentions Guy I of Possesse in the company of a Garlande, as if they were fast companions, on the First Crusade; see above n. 61.

68. Bautier, "Paris au temps d'Abélard," pp. 58, 71–72, 76–77, suggests that Heloise was a Garlande through her mother by an irregular union; such a relationship, claims Bautier, would explain Suger's expulsion of the nuns from Argenteuil where she was prioress.

69. *Recueil des chartes de l'abbaye de Saint-Germain-des-Prés,* ed. René Poupardin, 2 vols. (Paris, 1909–30), 1:188–90, no. 127.

70. In accepting payment (after Christmas 1165, probably in 1166), Count Henry I recalled that Guy III of Possesse had mortgaged the castle to him for 260 *l.,* money of Provins, and 12 *l.,* money of Châlons; text in Henri d'Arbois de Jubainville, "Recueil des chartes inédites émanées d'Henri le Libéral," in J. Carnandet, *Le trésor des pièces rares et curieuses de la Champagne et de la Brie,* 2 vols. (Chaumont, 1863), 1:295–96. Anselm I was first noted as lord of Possesse in 1171/72 when Alexander III complained to the archbishop of Reims that the "nobilis vir" Anselm had burned down a church and entire village after the chapter of Châlons-sur-Marne had complained about his depredations (*PL* 299: 840–41, no. 961).

71. In 1175 Guy apparently wished to assure his heirs of Tournan by having both his son Anselm and his grandson Anselm II give homage to Maurice, bishop of Paris (AN, J 165, n. 12 = Despont, "Une famille," act no. 6 of 1175). After Anselm I died ca. 1186, Guy asked the bishop to accept Anselm II's homage for Tournan (*Cartulaire de l'église de Notre-Dame de Paris,* ed. Benjamin Guérard, 4 vols. [Paris, 1850], 1: 70, no. 72). Tournan and Possesse passed through a single line until 1287, when a childless Anselm of Garlande divided his lands between the two sons of his deceased brother; in 1334 Jean, the last Garlande lord of Possesse, exchanged that lordship with Anselm, lord of Joinville, for Vaucouleurs; *Documents relatifs au comté de Champagne et de Brie (1172–1361),* ed. Auguste Longnon, 3 vols. (Paris, 1901–1914), 1:136, no. 3697.

Younger sons, too, could acquire powerful lordships, often in distant lands during political realignments. In the general purge of Flemish castellans after the assassination of Charles the Good, Count Thierry appointed Ralph, the younger brother of Ivo II of Nesle, as castellan of Bruges (1134).[72] Count Thierry, himself a cadet who had successfully claimed his mother's inheritance,[73] must have selected Ralph of Nesle in part for his military virtues but primarily for his familial ties since Ralph's wife, Gertrude of Montaigu, was Thierry's niece or cousin.[74] In those same years King Fulk of Jerusalem, the former count of Anjou, attempted to reorganize the baronage of his realm by appointing new, loyal castellans wherever he could.[75] One beneficiary was Raymond of Poitiers, second son of William IX of Aquitaine, who was living in England on a pension from King Henry I; Raymond accepted an invitation to marry the infant heiress of Antioch and became its prince in 1136.[76] Another cadet by the name of Fulk, the second son of the count of Guines, had accompanied his father and three brothers on the First Crusade, then stayed on to become lord of Beirut (1110–ca. 1125), although he failed to establish a lineage there.[77]

72. Ralph succeeded Gervais of Praet (1127–1130) (see below, n. 97) and perhaps Didier Hacket, Erembald's son and former castellan (1115–27) who escaped implication in Count Charles's assassination and might have returned as castellan from 1131 to 1134; see Warlop, *The Flemish Nobility* 1:210, and Newman, *Les seigneurs de Nesle,* 1:63–4, nos. 15, 19, 21, 23, and genealogical table (p. 289).

73. Thierry was in fact the eldest son of his father's second marriage to Gertrude of Flanders, daughter of Count Robert the Frison of Flanders; after the murder of her nephew, Charles the Good, she had the closest claim to her father's lands. A brief biography of Thierry is in Thérèse de Hemptinne, "Thierry d'Alsace, comte de Flandre: biographie et actes," *Annales de l'Est* (1991), 83–108.

74. Gislebert of Mons refers to that familial relationship three times, once calling Gertrude the *neptis* of Count Thierry. She was the daughter of Lambert, count of Montaigu, an important vassal of the bishop of Liège, and probably the granddaughter of Thierry's brother Simon, duke of Lorraine. See *La chronique de Gislebert de Mons,* ed. Léon Vanderkindere (Brussels, 1904), pp. 56, n. 7; 124, n. 6; 142, n. 4. Count Thierry might also have been related to Ralph of Nesle through the Vermandois line: Count Charles the Good's wife, Adele, was the sister of Ralph of Vermandois, the royal seneschal (1117–52), and Simon, bishop of Noyon-Tournai (1123–46). It was Simon who used ecclesiastical sanctions to pursue his brother-in-law's assassins in 1127. The treasurer of Noyon, from ca. 1130, was Ralph of Nesle's youngest brother Thierry (see Newman, *Les seigneurs de Nesle,* 1:63, no. 17). Although the exact relationship between the houses of Vermandois and the Nesle is not clear, the fact that they shared the name Ralph suggests a familial tie (perhaps in a distant cadet lineage) as well as a feudal one.

75. Hans-Eberhard Mayer, "Angevins *versus* Normans: the New Men of King Fulk of Jerusalem," *Proceedings of the American Philosophical Society* 133 (1989), 1–15, and "The Wheel of Fortune: Seignorial Vicissitudes Under King Fulk and Baldwin III of Jerusalem," *Speculum* 65 (1990), 860–77.

76. Jonathan P. Phillips, "A Note on the Origins of Raymond of Poitiers," *EHR* 106 (1991), 66–67.

77. Alan V. Murray, "The Origins of the Frankish Nobility of the Kingdom of Jerusalem, 1100–1118," *Mediterranean Historical Review* 4 (1989), 288.

Normandy under Henry I was especially unsettling for noble families. Incessant armed clashes, confiscations, and reassignments of castles dominated Henry's rule until ca. 1130: disloyal barons were punished severely, says Orderic, and were deprived of their honors and wealth without regard for their kinship or noble birth, and many perished in prison unable to ransom themselves.[78] Most castles were reassigned to relatives, so that individuals, not lineages, paid the price of disloyalty. The most significant opportunity for cadets, however, occurred in 1120, when many barons accompanying the royal heir on the White Ship perished in the Channel. Henry "gave their wives and daughters and nieces, together with their inheritances, in marriage to his [noble-born] knights (*tirones*) and in this way generously raised and rewarded many with unlooked-for dignities."[79]

Obviously not all younger sons married heiresses, received escheated lordships, or entered the Church. What became of the other non-succeeding sons: were they deprived of an inheritance? Certainly illegitimate and late-born sons might be excluded from a landed inheritance, but strict primogeniture was rare in the twelfth century when only offices and castles, not property, were indivisible. While eldest sons ordinarily retained the paternal office and chief residence, younger sons shared the family's possessions in varying proportions and daughters received dowries. In a few cases a cadet might even take the paternal inheritance when an older brother preferred the maternal properties. André of Roucy did so in 1102, taking his father's lands of Ramerupt after his older brother Ebles elected to take the more important maternal lands of Roucy.[80] Count Stephen of Blois likewise was assigned his father's lands in 1152, while his older brother Henry took his uncle's more promising lands in Champagne. But the norm in most of the realm, from Picardy and Normandy in the North to Aquitaine and the Midi, was the creation of subsidiary lineages and lordships on paternal lands; indeed, family segmentation must be counted among the more important processes operating within noble families in the twelfth century.[81]

Family segmentation is not easy to trace before ca. 1150 because noble

78. OV 11, 2 (6:18–19).

79. OV 12, 28 (6:308–9).

80. See Bernard Guenée, "Les généalogies entre l'histoire et la politique: la fierté d'être capétien, en France, au moyen âge," *Annales: E.S.C.* (1978), 450–77. Ramerupt passed first to André's only surviving son Ebles, bishop of Châlons-sur-Marne, then to his oldest daughter Alice. Alice's son and daughter later divided the lordship: each half of Ramerupt went to a cadet (a fourth and a second son respectively).

81. See Robert Fossier, *La terre et les hommes en Picardie, jusqu'à la fin du XIIIe siècle*, 2 vols. (Paris, 1968), 2:584 (partible inheritance was the rule before 1200); Guy Devailly, *Le Berry du Xe au milieu du XIIIe siècle* (Paris-The Hague, 1973), pp. 318–19. For Normandy,

lands were still largely allodial and thus readily divisible among family members without external approval and documentation. Indeed, the persistence of allodial estates is a major finding of the regional monographs and one that requires a substantive revision of Bloch's depiction of "feudal" society.[82] In 1133, for instance, when Thomas of Marle's two sons divided his patrimony, the eldest, Enguerran II, took his father's castles in the Laonnois, while the cadet Robert took his grandfather's estate of Boves—though not in feudal tenure—to begin a new lineage.[83] In 1190, when Thomas of Marle's grandson Ralph of Coucy drew up his testament, the eldest son again retained the major castles of the lordship, but four other children were also endowed: two sons received fiefs, an unmarried daughter was assigned a large cash dowry, and the youngest son, a cleric, was left a generous annuity.[84] Thus both lords of Coucy with more than one surviving son produced cadet lineages.[85]

When castles were constructed on undeveloped allodial lands, entirely new lordships were created, as was the case at Châteauvillain in Champagne. Hugh III, lord of Broyes, acquired the land as his wife's dowry (ca. 1143), and twenty years later built a castle there. After her death Hugh remarried and assigned Châteauvillain with its castle to his eldest son Simon by his second wife; that son later held the fief in liege from his older half-brother who inherited the paternal lands at Broyes.[86] As with the Coucy and many other families after 1150, it became normal practice

---

see David Herlihy, *Medieval Households* (Cambridge, MA, 1985), pp. 95–96; and Crouch, *The Beaumont Twins*, pp. 124–26. For the South, see Paul Ourliac's comments in *La France de Philippe Auguste: les temps des mutations* (Paris, 1982), p. 717; R. Aubenas, "La famille dans l'ancienne Provence," *Annales de l'Histoire Économique et Sociale* 8 (1936), 523–24 (the lordship of Châteauneuf was fragmented into 24 parts by the early thirteenth century); Martín Aurell, *Une famille de la noblesse provençale au moyen âge: les Porcelet* (Avignon, 1986), pp. 54–56; and Hélène Débax, "Stratégies matrimoniales des comtes de Toulouse (850–1270)," *Annales du Midi* 100 (1988), 131–51.

82. *La société féodale*, 1:264–66, 379: allods were "very rare" in northern France in the twelfth and thirteenth centuries. It is now clear that nobles retained substantial allodial lands through the twelfth century; see, among others, Warlop, *Flemish Nobility*, 1:289–90; and Robert Boutruche, *Une société provinciale en lutte contre le régime féodale: l'alleu en Bordelais et en Bazadais du XIe au XIIe siècle* (Rodez, 1947); and Fossier, *Cartulaire-chronique*, pp. 15, 25.

83. Dominique Barthélemy, *Les deux âges de la seigneurie banale . . . Coucy (XIe–XIIIe siècles)* (Paris, 1984), pp. 122–123, and Newman, *Les seigneurs de Nesle*, 1:94–99.

84. Barthélemy, *Les deux âges*, p. 405.

85. For the cadet lineages of the counts of Angoulême, see Debord, *La Société laïque*, pp. 208–9, 234–35.

86. Hugh named the eldest son of each marriage Simon; thus Simon the Younger held Châteauvillain from Simon the Elder, lord of Broyes. See Poull, *La maison ducale de Bar*, 1:103–5, and G. Guenin, "Les origines féodales et les premiers seigneurs de la terre d'Arc and de Châteauvillain," *Annales de la Société d'histoire, d'archéologie et des beaux-arts de Chaumont*, 5 (1921–30), 107–18, 248–65.

for younger sons to take their inheritance shares as fiefs from their oldest brothers.[87]

Family segmentation was not a new process in the late twelfth century, only a more visible and dangerous one, as feudal ties reinforced familial ones. State-building princes viewed such coalitions of brothers, nephews, and cousins as inimical to their authority. Philip Augustus tried without success to dismantle those familial-feudal networks on his lands by commanding all rear-tenants to become his liegemen.[88] The counts of Champagne employed a more effective strategy of purchasing the *mouvance* of the more powerful cadets, who in many cases preferred to hold their inheritances from older brothers: the already mentioned Simon of Châteauvillain was one of those who resisted becoming the count's diect liegeman until he was offered a sizeable rent.[89]

Circulation and segmentation were two processes by which noble cadets exercised their birthright as members of the landed elite. When they assumed distant lordships by escheat, purchase, or marriage, they did so with the consent of their new feudal lords. When they received maternal dowries or inheritances, recently acquired lands, or shares of paternal lands from which they carved out new lordships, they did so with the consent of their older brothers. To view lineage in its most restricted sense as descent and inheritance only through the eldest son of the patrilineage is to miss the extraordinary diversity of traditions, attitudes, and fates of noble families in the twelfth century, when primogeniture was still only preferential, not exclusionary. Moreover, female descent played a significant role in both the preservation of lineages (through a sister's children) and the circulation of cadets (who assumed their wives' inheritances). In sum, a broader conception of lineage that sees all noble-born children as entitled accords far better with the families reviewed here.[90]

87. See also André Chédeville, *Chartes et ses campagnes, XIe–XIIe siècles* (Paris, 1973), p. 279; Bouchard, *Sword*, pp. 279–84 (Bourbonne appears to have been created from allodial land before segmenting from the Aigremont family); and H. de Faget de Casteljau, "Recherches sur la maison de Choiseul. II. Les seigneurs de Bourbonne," *Les cahiers Haute-Marnais* 110 (1973), 154–63.

88. Pierre Petot, "L'ordonnance du 1er mai 1209," in *Recueil de travaux offerts à M. Clovis Brunel*, 2 vols. (Paris, 1955), 2:370–80.

89. *Layettes du Trésor des Chartes*, ed. Alexandre Teulet et al., 5 vols. (Paris, 1863–1909), 1:320, no. 848.

90. The broad and narrow senses of lineage are discussed in Dominique Barthélemy, "L'état contre le 'lignage': un thème a développer dans l'histoire des pouvoirs en France aux XIe, XIIe et XIIIe siècles," *Médiévales* 10 (1986), 37–50.

An Open Elite?

In his classic article on social mobility among the nobles in thirteenth-century Forez, Edouard Perroy concluded that new men continually replenished the nobility because noble families in their male lines lasted, on average, only from three to six generations.[91] Perroy suggested that his findings might well reflect a fundamental characteristic of medieval nobilities in other regions and periods. While the regional studies have confirmed a high rate of lineage failure from the late twelfth century, the limitations of the sources have made it impossible to document the rise of non-nobles into the nobility at that time, especially of those to whom Perroy ascribed an important role in restocking noble families in Forez: the household retainers of great princes, the agents of monasteries and secular lords, prosperous merchants, and rural proprietors who married into the less wealthy noble families.[92] The task is further complicated by the fact that Perroy's most visible category of "new" men consists of those whom we would today classify as recirculated nobles: the noble-born sons who established lineages in neighboring provinces or who restored failed lineages by marrying heiresses.

The best known cases of new men within noble families of the twelfth century are of ordinary knights who became castellans. The lord of Parthenay in Poitou, for example, granted the escheated honor of Lamairé to one of his knights, Bucard (ca. 1150), after forcibly expelling the nephews of its deceased lord, Geoffroy Gilbert. The scribe relating the incident comments bitterly that the legitimate heirs of "a most noble man" had been dispossessed by a "certain knight" (whose background, unfortunately, is obscure).[93] In Normandy, writes Orderic Vitalis ca. 1135, Henry I "ennobled (*nobilitavit*) men of non-noble origin (*de ignobile stirpe*) . . . who had served him well, raised them, so to say, from the dust, and heaping all kinds of favors on them, stationed them above earls and famous castellans."[94] Re-

91. Edouard Perroy, "Social Mobility among the French *Noblesse* in the Later Middle Ages," *Past and Present,* no. 21 (1962), 25–38.

92. For example, Fossier, *Picardie,* 2:663–667, finds that old lineages disappeared from the 1190s and new ones rose in the thirteenth century, but the three twelfth-century examples he offers of non-noble ascension into the nobility are based on fragile evidence.

93. George T. Beech, *A Rural Society in Medieval France: The Gâtine of Poitou in the Eleventh and Twelfth Centuries* (Baltimore, 1964), pp. 78–79 and n. 30. The fact that the scribe was moved to comment on the social standing of Geoffroy Gilbert, who was called a *nobilissimus vir* (an unusual expression in the local charters [p. 83, n. 42]), confirms that *nobilis* and its cognates were rare in diplomatic acts only because of scribal convention, not because of the absence of the term in common parlance or the absence of noble families.

94. OV 11, 2 (6:18–19).

cent analysis of the Anglo-Norman magnates, however, has identified only a few men whose royal service and patronage propelled them into the nobility; when it came to reassigning confiscated or escheated noble lands, Henry favored the noble-born relatives of the previous tenants.[95]

In Flanders a castle knight named Erembald murdered the castellan of Bruges (ca. 1060) in complicity with the castellan's wife in order to marry her. Erembald and his two sons and grandson (who were partly noble-born) were accepted as castellans of Bruges for over sixty years, and their numerous progeny virtually appropriated the administration of Flanders.[96] Their non-noble origin would not have mattered, claims Galbert of Bruges, had they not acted so arrogantly. After the assassination of Count Charles the Good (1127), King Louis VI and Count William Clito replaced Erembald's son, Didier Hacket, as castellan of Bruges with Gervais of Praet, the murdered count's household knight and chamberlain who was the first to avenge the count's death. Gervais was not a "new" man, however, for he seems to have been a "noble" knight descended from the very castellan of Bruges murdered sixty years earlier by Erembald himself.[97] Although the Erembald clan had successfully married into the nobility, Count Thierry (1128–68) replaced them and the barons implicated in the assassination by *bona fide* nobles, like Ralph of Nesle, and for the rest of the century the Flemish baronage remained a closed elite.

Benedict of Peterborough reports another well-known case of "a certain knight named André of Chauvigny" who after acquiring renown on the Third Crusade received from Richard the Lionheart the strategically located castle of Châteauroux in Berry with its heiress, Denise of Déols.[98]

95. C. Warren Hollister, "Henry I and the Anglo-Norman Magnates," *Anglo-Norman Studies* 2 (1979), 99–100, reprinted in his *Monarchy, Magnates and Institutions in the Anglo-Norman World* (London, 1986); Newman, *Anglo-Norman Nobility,* ch. 5; and Ralph V. Turner, *Men Raised from the Dust: Administrative Service and Upward Mobility in Angevin England* (Philadelphia, 1988), esp. ch. 1, which reviews the entire question.

96. Jan Dhondt, "Medieval 'Solidarities': Flemish Society in Transition, 1127–1128," tr. Frederic L. Cheyette, in *Lordship and Community in Medieval Europe: Selected Readings,* ed. Fredric L. Cheyette (Huntingdon, NY, 1968), pp. 276–79. Galbert calls Erembald a *homo et miles,* while the *Passio Karoli* calls him a *dapiferus* (Warlop, *Flemish Nobility* 3:457 n. 3); in 1089 Erembald and his eldest son Robert were listed as witnesses among the *nobiles* (Warlop, 1:116). See also R. C. Van Caenegem, "Galbert of Bruges on Serfdom, Prosecution of Crime, and Constitutionalism (1127–28)," in *Law, Custom, and the Social Fabric in Medieval Europe: Essays in Honor of Bryce Lyon,* ed. Bernard S. Bachrach and David Nicholas (Kalamazoo, MI, 1990), pp. 89–101.

97. The comital chamberlains were noble-born since the 1070s. Gervais served as castellan until 1130 but was still alive ca. 1147; his heirs were called noble. See Warlop, *Flemish Nobility,* 1:159–60, 236; 2:414, n. 100; 4:1070.

98. Denise's two older brothers had predeceased their father Ralph VI, lord of Déols (d. 1176)—the king's richest baron in Berry, according to Benedict—leaving her as sole heir-

Their splendid wedding was celebrated at Salisbury in July 1189 in distinguished company.[99] But André was no ordinary knight. His father, a familiar of the count of Poitou, had managed the episcopal lordship of Chauvigny for the bishop of Poitiers, and his mother was the daughter of the viscount of Châtellerault and sister of Ainor, the mother of Eleanor of Aquitaine (Genealogical Table 2). Not only was André a first cousin of Eleanor—her "dearest friend and relative," as she later put it[100]—he was also distantly related to his wife Denise.[101] Thus familial ties allowed André, a fourth son, to enter Richard's service from which he vaulted to the castellan level. Another, more famous, fourth son was promoted in those same days before Richard's coronation: William Marshal, a knight in service to the royal family for over twenty years, received the heiress and lordship of Striguil.[102] But like André, William was "new" only in the degree of his success, since the Marshals were already a minor baronial family.[103]

Joinville recounts the presumption of another "new" man, a trusted

---

ess at three years of age. Over the protest of her uncle, Henry II had her sent to England where she was married in 1178 to Baldwin of Rivers, lord of the Isle of Wight. He apparently never visited her castle, which may have lain in partial ruin since being damaged in 1152 by Louis VII. Henry II restored the castle in 1187, but Philip Augustus managed to capture it in 1188, only to return it by the Treaty of Bonmoulins (November 1188). Denise was widowed that same year at sixteen years of age, but the king died before he could marry her to Baldwin of Béthune. Richard instead gave her to André of Chauvigny. See Devailly, *Berry*, pp. 373–79, 409–13, 423 n. 3; and Eugène Hubert and Jean Hubert, *Le Bas-Berry: Histoire et archéologie du département de l'Indre* (Paris, 1930), pp. 71–80.

99. Devailly, *Berry*, pp. 423–24, 438–41.

100. This relationship was first proposed by Eugène and Jean Hubert, "L'origine de la parenté entre la famille de Chauvigny et les Plantagenêts," *Revue du Berry et du Centre* (1927), 38–40. André's father had married Haois, the youngest of three daughters and two sons of Aimery I, viscount of Châtellerault; see E.H.E. Beauchet-Filleau et al., *Dictionnaire historique et généalogique des familles de Poitou*, 4 vols., 2nd ed. (Poitiers, 1891–1912), 2:314–320. The older sisters, Mabile and Ainor, married respectively Vulgrin II, count of Angoulême, and William IX, count of Poitou. But why would William X, an only son, marry the daughter of a viscount? Perhaps William's father was making amends for a long-standing and public liaison with the viscount's wife, Maubergeone (thesis of Charles-Claude Lalanne, *Histoire de Châtelleraud et du Châtelleraudais*, 2 vols. [Châtellerault, 1859], 1:175). The count's wife Hildegard, deeply offended, told her story to the Council of Reims (1119) where she addressed the prelates "in a loud and clear voice," explaining how her husband had abandoned her and how the viscountess had become her *surrogata;* her husband, summoned to explain, failed to attend the council feigning illness; see Mansi 21:239.

101. On his return from the Third Crusade, André became involved in a bitter dispute with the abbot of Déols, who succeeded in having the bishop of Bourges excommunicate André and annul his marriage on the grounds of consanguinity. André went to Rome where he explained to Innocent III that he had been happily married for fifteen years and had five children; the pope agreed that such a solid marriage should not be dissolved; see Devailly, *Le Berry*, pp. 438–41 and *PL* 214:1048.

102. David Crouch, *William Marshal: Court, Career and Chivalry in the Angevin Empire, 1147–1219* (London, 1990), chs. 2–3 and genealogical table (pp. 220–21).

103. Crouch, *William Marshal*, p. 11, and Painter, *William Marshal*, pp. 3–4.

Genealogical Table 2

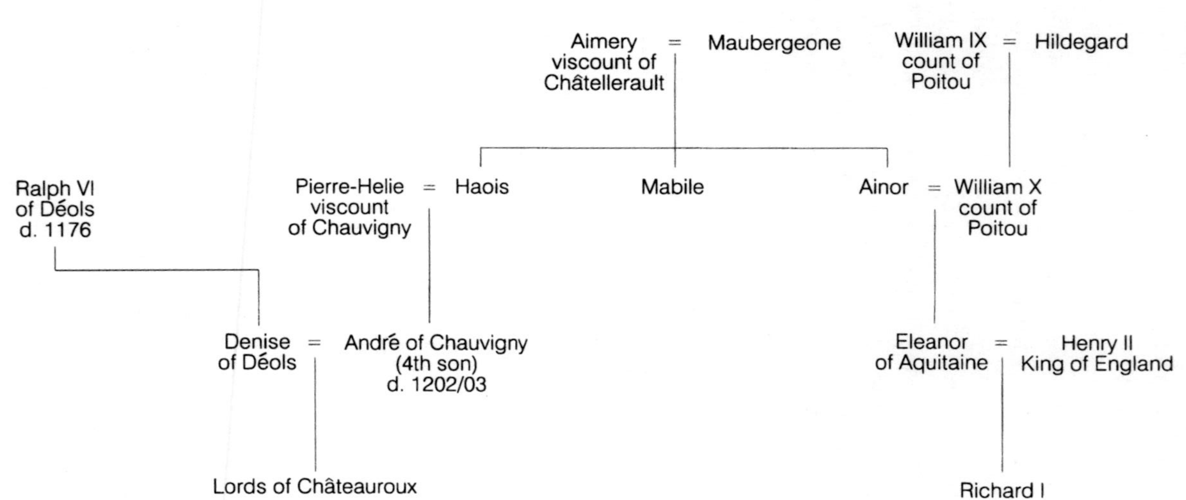

adviser of Count Henry the Liberal by the name of Artaud, who in a well-known incident fended off a poor knight who had approached the count begging for dowry money to marry off two daughters. The count had been so generous, replied Artaud, that he had nothing left to give. "Lord villain, you are incorrect to state that I have nothing to give," retorted the count, "for I have *you*. Take him, lord knight, for I give him to you." The knight, grabbing Artaud by the collar, extracted 500 *l.* before releasing him.[104]

This story is often taken to illustrate a lord's absolute right to dispose of a "serf," but is nothing of the sort. Rather it is an amusing anecdote of the comeuppance of an administrative officer whose impertinence cost him a ransom. As the count's chamberlain (*camerarius*) for over forty years, Artaud regularly witnessed comital acts and was richly rewarded for his services. Although Joinville calls him a townsman (*borgois*), Artaud was actually a knight who owed castle guard for several fiefs he held from the count.[105] Artaud's most notable achievement, according to Joinville, was to build a castle at his own expense. We know—as perhaps Joinville did not—that Artaud built it ca. 1170 at Nogent-sur-Marne on allodial land next to property belonging to Saint-Germain-des-Prés. The monks later protested that Artaud had built not only a tower, but also walls, a moat, an oven, a winepress, and—with the count's permission—had established a Friday market within the castle. In effect, Artaud had created an entirely new lordship. No doubt it was with great pride that he assigned it to his noble-born wife, Hodierne of Nangis, as her dower.[106] Artaud had become a lord (*dominus*), and was so listed in the count's feudal register and in the obituary of a local convent.[107]

Poitou, Normandy, Flanders, and Champagne—four quite different regional societies—afford scant evidence for new men, specifically non-noble knights such as Bucard, Erembald, and Artaud, rising to the castellan

104. *Jean, sire de Joinville, Histoire de Saint Louis,* ed. Natalis de Wailly (Paris, 1874), p. 52, par. 90–91.

105. Arbois de Jubainville, *Histoire,* 3:126–28, 220; *Layettes* 5:23, no. 66 (gift from the count, 1171). Artaud's fiefs are listed in the comital registers; see Longnon, *Documents,* 1: nos. 934, 1600, 1749, 2002. See also note 107.

106. *Layettes* 5:23–24, nos. 67–68, of 1171: letters from Count Henry and Countess Marie, the latter one presumably handed over to Hodierne. In 1178 Count Henry granted Artaud the market rights at Nogent (*Layettes* 5:25, no. 73). Only after the count's death were the monks able to strike against Artaud: in 1182 the count's brother William, archbishop of Reims, awarded them half the revenues of the oven, winepress, and market of Nogent (Poupardin, *Recueil des chartes,* 1:278–79, no. 198).

107. Obituary of Notre-Dame-aux-Nonnains of Troyes in *Obituaires de la province de Sens,* 1, *Diocèse de Sens et de Paris,* ed. Auguste Molinier, 2 vols. (Paris, 1902), 1:925: "obiit dominus Artaudus, miles de Nogent." See also note 106.

level, at least in the twelfth century when an ample supply of cadets obviated the need to promote non-nobles to the highest offices. Other forms of upward social mobility seem to have been more prevalent, although they have yet to be satisfactorily documented. How often, for example, did a non-noble woman marry a noble man? Thomas of Marle, after repudiating his second wife, the sister of the count of Hainaut, married the wife of "a certain knight of the Amienois," and Gerald, lord of Las Tours, married the daughter of a castle knight, to the displeasure of the chronicler Geoffroy of Vigeois.[108] But these cases seem as exceptional as the marriage of non-noble men (such as Erembald and Artaud) to noble-born women.

We would expect such mixed marriages to have occurred more frequently among the less wealthy, although such unions are difficult to detect in the sources. The increasing feudalization of noble lands must have facilitated intermarriages, for the non-noble knights who were capable of performing military service became acceptable husbands of noble women who received inheritance shares, dowries, and dowers in fief.[109] In terms of tenure and lifestyle in the countryside, little distinguished the well-to-do knights from the less wealthy noble women and cadets. Mixed marriages at this tenuous divide between noble and non-noble would account for the numerous charter references to the noble wives of seemingly ordinary knights. By 1200 children of mixed parentage in Flanders were recognized as noble, and slightly later the Parlement of Paris likewise conceded noble descent through one parent.[110] By the fourteenth-century detailed inquests were required to establish noble descent in the face of patently non-noble means and lifestyle.[111]

* * *

In conclusion, we can say that, while Barbero has sharpened our focus on the French nobility, a significant body of evidence weighs against his revival of Bloch's model for the twelfth century. Contemporaries clearly understood the nature of nobility and accepted the role of noble families as ruling elites, elites that remained essentially closed because the availability and circulation of noble cadets obviated the need for new men in leader-

108. Barthélemy, *Les deux âges*, pp. 75–76, and Debord, *La société laïque*, p. 235.

109. See Morelle, "Mariage et diplomatique."

110. Warlop, *Flemish Nobility*, 1:318–19, and above, note 13.

111. See Marie Thérèse Caron, *La noblesse dans le duché de Bourgogne, 1315–1477* (Lille, 1987).

ship positions. Although we do not yet fully understand the dynamics of noble families in the twelfth century, a dynastic model based on strict primogeniture does not accord with the evidence reviewed here. First-born sons naturally were favored, but their siblings ordinarily shared the family's assets in the form of dowries and settlements. We know best the cadets who rose to spectacular heights through familial connection, talent, and circumstance; now we must secure a better understanding of the more numerous non-castellan noble men and women whose resources and lifestyle brought them closer to the prosperous allodial knightly familes with whom they intermarried. If the landed elite was permeable, it was primarily by marriage at that non-castellan level.

Benjamin Arnold

2. Instruments of Power: The Profile and Profession of *Ministeriales* Within German Aristocratic Society, 1050–1225

In the last of the illuminations that decorate the Bern manuscript of Peter of Eboli's *Liber ad honorem Augusti,* Emperor Henry VI is depicted in triumph over his enemies, seated on a throne flanked by his principal counsellors: Conrad of Querfurt, bishop of Hildesheim and chancellor of the Empire; Markward of Annweiler, duke of Ravenna and imperial seneschal; and Henry of Kalden, marshal of the imperial court.[1] Conrad of Querfurt was born into a powerful family of free Saxon lords who were hereditary burgraves of Magdeburg. Henry of Kalden and Markward of Annweiler, on the other hand, were ascribed by birth as *ministeriales* of the imperial household. They were knights in military and administrative function but unfree in legal status, their families being attached over the generations as hereditary dependents of the crown. However, Provost Burchard of Ursberg reported that as a reward for his remarkable successes in subjecting Italy and Sicily to Henry VI's authority, the seneschal was granted free status in 1195 when he was created duke of Ravenna with rule over the Romagna, the march of Ancona, and the counties of the Abruzzi.[2] In the struggles for power which followed the emperor's death in 1197, the duke was eventually able to seize control of the island of Sicily and of the person of Frederick II. Pope Innocent III, who claimed the regency for himself, went so far as to proclaim a crusade against Markward, who died undefeated in 1202.[3]

1. *Liber ad honorem Augusti di Pietro da Eboli,* ed. Giovanni Battista Siragusa, Fonti per la storia d'Italia (Rome, 1906), pp. 150 ff; Sigfrid H. Steinberg and Christine Steinberg-von Pape, *Die Bildnisse geistlicher und weltlicher Fürsten und Herren,* part 1, Die Entwicklung des menschlichen Bildnisses (Leipzig and Berlin, 1931), 3: plate 150.

2. *Die Chronik des Propstes Burchard von Ursberg,* ed. Oswald Holder-Egger and Bernhard von Simson, *MGH SRG* 16 (2d ed., Hanover, 1916): 72 ff.

3. Thomas C. van Cleve, *Markward of Anweiler and the Sicilian Regency* (Princeton, NJ: 1937), and his *The Emperor Frederick II of Hohenstaufen: Immutator Mundi* (Oxford, 1972), pp.

Marshal Henry of Kalden's achievements are equally well attested. He was one of Emperor Frederick Barbarossa's most accomplished generals and was responsible for the successful assault upon Skribention during the Third Crusade.[4] Apart from his services to Henry VI in the subjection of Sicily, he was extremely influential in Germany during the conflict over the throne in the years after 1198. He was interested in reconciliation, and arranged an unsuccessful conference between Otto IV and Philip of Swabia near Cologne in 1206.[5] Once Philip had been assassinated in 1208, the marshal decided to hand over the castles in his custody to Otto IV, and then tracked down and executed the murderer, Count Palatine Otto VIII of Wittelsbach, in 1209.[6] It is not perhaps surprising that Peter of Eboli compared such military commanders to the martial gods of antiquity:[7]

> *Hic Marcualdus, cui se Neptunus ad omne Velle dedit, cui Mars se dedit esse parem.*
>
> Here is Markward, to whom Neptune concedes his powers and with whom Mars admits equality.

One of the most controversial problems in current medieval studies is the relationship between knighthood and nobility, both in concept and in social reality. Karl Ferdinand Werner reviewed the literature in 1985, followed by two other historians with divergent views, Jean Flori and Alessandro Barbero; the continuing debate, assisted by Georges Duby and Fredric Cheyette, took up much of the first session of the conference presented in this volume.[8] My view is that in Germany the *ministeriales* of the twelfth century came to occupy the central position in the world of knighthood, and that the application of the label *nobilis* or noble to them represents more than ecclesiastical rhetoric, if not yet a legal status. The reasons were practical: the operation of knighthood as an instrument of power within the governing structure of Germany. In this sense the rise

38–49; Elizabeth Kennan, "Innocent III and the First Political Crusade," *Traditio* 27 (1971), 229–49.

4. *Quellen zur Geschichte des Kreuzzuges Kaiser Friedrichs I.*, ed. Anton Chroust, *MGH SS* n.s. 5 (Berlin, 1928): 45, 141.

5. *Chronica regia Coloniensis. Annales maximi Colonienses*, ed. Georg Waitz, *MGH SRG* 18 (Hanover, 1880): 224.

6. *Ottonis de Sancto Blasio Chronica*, ed. Adolf Hofmeister, *MGH SRG* 4 (Hanover, 1912): 84.

7. *Liber ad honorem Augusti*, lines 1560–61.

8. Karl F. Werner, "Du nouveau sur un vieux thème. Les origines de la 'noblesse' et de la 'chevalerie'," *Comptes rendus de l'Académie des Inscriptions et Belles-Lettres* (Paris, 1985), pp. 186–200; Jean Flori, *L'essor de la chevalerie* (Geneva, 1986), pp. 343–67; Alessandro Barbero, *L'aristocrazia nella società francese del medioevo* (Bologna, 1987), pp. 334–59.

of *ministeriales* in the Empire is paralleled by the increasing significance of knights everywhere in western Christendom since the eleventh century.

The rise of new retinues of *ministeriales* or servants in the households of the German magnates was broadly established in the eleventh century, and in some cases in the tenth.[9] But the name *ministerialis* indicating a ministry or service goes back to the late Roman Empire, and subsequently was applied to counts and bishops in the Carolingian Empire as well as to menial servants.[10] The transmission of the name and its exact meaning are problematical. The main purpose of this paper is to explain why the focus of service among the new retinues of German *ministeriales* was becoming more distinctly chivalric after 1050, and what political consequences stemmed from this. So we need to examine the ways in which the economic and legal status of the *ministeriales* coalesced with their military and administrative occupations, to form them into a nobility of service under the crown, the princes, and the bishops who held the reins of power.[11]

In spite of literary eulogy, Markward of Annweiler and Henry of Kalden represent the summit of the most numerous knightly group in Germany in the twelfth century, the hereditary and professional order labelled in the Latin sources as *ministeriales*. But like all the militias of European knights in the twelfth century, the German *ministeriales* exhibited wide

9. See John B. Freed, "The Origins of the European Nobility: the Problem of the Ministerials," *Viator* 7 (1976), 211–41 and Josef Fleckenstein, "Die Entstehung des niederen Adels und das Rittertum" in *Herrschaft und Stand. Untersuchungen zur Sozialgeschichte im 13. Jahrhundert,* ed. Josef Fleckenstein, Veröffentlichungen des Max-Planck-Instituts für Geschichte 51 (Göttingen, 1977), pp. 17–39. For the tenth century see Gerhard Flohrschütz, "Die Freisinger Dienstmannen im 10. und 11. Jahrhundert," *Beiträge zur altbayerischen Kirchengeschichte* 25 (1967), 9–79 and John B. Freed, "The Formation of the Salzburg Ministerialage in the Tenth and Eleventh Centuries: An Example of Upward Social Mobility in the Early Middle Ages," *Viator* 9 (1978), 67–102.

10. In his *Mediae latinitatis lexicon minus* (Leiden, 1954–64), the lexicographer Jan Frederik Niermeyer gives eleven meanings for *ministerialis* at pp. 684–87. For discussion see Karl Bosl, "Vorstufen der deutschen Königsdienstmannschaft" in his *Frühformen der Gesellschaft im mittelalterlichen Europa* (Munich and Vienna, 1964), pp. 228–76 and Benjamin Arnold, *German Knighthood 1050–1300* (Oxford, 1985), pp. 29–32.

11. There is an extensive secondary literature on the German *ministeriales,* the main work being Karl Bosl's monumental *Die Reichsministerialität der Salier und Staufer: Ein Beitrag zur Geschichte des hochmittelalterlichen deutschen Volkes, Staates und Reiches,* Schriften der MGH, 10 (Stuttgart, 1950–51). In Germany the traditional method of medieval historiography results in the regional monograph, many of which are cited in the notes that follow. For examples in this genre well worth reading, Johanna Reimann, "Zur Besitz- und Familiengeschichte der Ministerialen des Hochstifts Würzburg" and "Die Ministerialen des Hochstifts Würzburg in sozial-, rechts- und verfassungsgeschichtlicher Sicht," *Mainfränkisches Jahrbuch für Geschichte und Kunst* 15 (1963), 1–117; 16 (1964), 1–266; Gerhard Flohrschütz, "Machtgrundlagen und Herrschaftspolitik der ersten Pfalzgrafen aus dem Haus Wittelsbach" in *Die Zeit der frühen Herzöge: Von Otto I. zu Ludwig dem Bayern,* Beiträge zur Bayerischen Geschichte und Kunst, 1, ed. Hubert Glaser (Munich and Zurich, 1980), pp. 42–110.

variation in wealth, authority, and practical status,[12] from powerful servants of the crown with numerous fiefs, castles, and vassals of their own, down to the local garrisons of *ministeriales* whose principal task was to defend the households, fortifications, and manors of abbots, counts, bishops, margraves, and dukes from their numerous enemies. The social breadth of such an order of *ministeriales*—the expression was already in use in the eleventh century[13]—motivated Eike von Repgow, the Saxon legist writing in the 1220s, to claim that it was impossible to generalize about *ministeriales* because "under every bishop and abbot and abbess the *ministeriales* have differing rights."[14] It is true that not many written rules or custumals survive for the retinues of the monasteries and the cathedral churches,[15] but Eike von Repgow's assertion is belied by a number of authentic charters which did attempt to standardize the rights and obligations of *ministeriales*. In 1135 Emperor Lothar III declared that one rule was valid for four different retinues in Saxony. These retinues belonged to the crown; to the abbots of Wildeshausen and of St Michael's at Lüneburg; and to Lothar's son-in-law, Duke Henry the Proud of Bavaria, a group of *ministeriales* inherited from his mother, the Saxon heiress Wulfhild Billung.[16]

In 1140 King Conrad III confirmed that the right or *libertas* of the bishop of Freising's *ministeriales* was equivalent to the rules for "*ministeriales* of the realm and of other churches."[17] The royal charters already assume that the rules for ecclesiastical and imperial *ministeriales* were well known

12. Paul Kluckhohn, *Die Ministerialität in Südostdeutschland vom zehnten bis zum Ende des dreizehnten Jahrhunderts*, Quellen und Studien zur Verfassungsgeschichte des deutschen Reiches in Mittelalter und Neuzeit, 4, part 1 (Weimar, 1910), and Richard Mortimer, "Knights and Knighthood in Germany in the Central Middle Ages" in *The Ideals and Practice of Medieval Knighthood*, ed. Christopher Harper-Bill and Ruth Harvey (Woodbridge and Dover, NH; 1986), pp. 96ff.

13. *Briefsammlungen der Zeit Heinrichs IV.*, ed. Carl Erdmann and Norbert Fickermann, *MGH*, Die Briefe der deutschen Kaiserzeit 5 (Weimar, 1950): "Weitere Briefe Meinhards von Bamberg," no. 18: 211 (1063).

14. *Sachsenspiegel Landrecht*, ed. Karl A. Eckhardt, *MGH*, Fontes iuris, n.s. 1, pt. 1 (2d ed.) (Gottingen, 1955): 223 (III, 42, 2).

15. See Karl Bosl, "Das ius ministerialium. Dienstrecht und Lehnrecht im deutschen Mittelalter" in his *Frühformen der Gesellschaft*, pp. 277–326; Arnold, *German Knighthood*, pp. 76–99; Franz-Josef Jakobi, "Ministerialität und 'ius ministerialium' in Reichsabteien der frühen Stauferzeit" in *Sprache und Recht: Beiträge zur Kulturgeschichte des Mittelalters: Festschrift für Ruth Schmidt-Wiegand*, ed. Karl Hauck et al. (Berlin and New York, 1986), 1: pp. 321–52; Knut Schulz, "Reichsklöster und Ministerialität. Gefälschte Dienstrechte des 12. Jahrhunderts. Ursachen und Absichten" in *Gesellschaftsgeschichte: Festschrift für Karl Bosl zum 80. Geburtstag*, ed. Ferdinand Seibt (Munich, 1988), 2: 37–54.

16. *Die Urkunden Lothars III. und der Kaiserin Richenza*, ed. Emil von Ottenthal and Hans Hirsch, *MGH Diplomata* 8 (Berlin, 1927), nos. 73, 75: 112–17.

17. *Die Urkunden Konrads III. und seines Sohnes Heinrich*, ed. Friedrich Hausmann, *MGH Diplomata* 9 (Vienna, etc., 1969), no. 46: 78. For the Freising *ministeriales* at this time, see Gerhard Flohrschütz, "Die Freisinger Dienstmannen im 12. Jahrhundert," *Oberbayerisches Archiv* 97 (1973), 32–339.

at the beginning of the twelfth century. In 1114, for example, Henry V referred to the rights of those "who are called in German *dienestman* or servant" without further comment.[18] But a charter confected just about this time and then ascribed to Emperor Conrad II did reveal something of the superior status of imperial knights attached to the royal manor of Weissenburg im Sand in Franconia: the grants in cash and kind which they received to sustain military service upon expeditions to Italy; their hunting rights in Weissenburg Forest; and their extensive fiefs consisting of at least three royal *mansi,* square measures of productive land.[19]

In spite of their personally unfree status within the *familiae* or entourages of their lords,[20] the knightly functions of the German *ministeriales* assured them a social profile defined by the aristocratic image by the end of the eleventh century. Wilhelm Störmer has written convincingly about the deliberate identification of *ministeriales* with aristocratic practices. He stresses that "already in the eleventh century a strong adaptation on the part of the *ministeriales* to the norms of the older aristocratic stratum was taken in hand," in matters of military and administrative service, in the visible symbolism of clothing and arms, in social attitudes, and above all, in the sphere of personal and family nomenclature of which Störmer has made special study.[21] All this was possible because the unfree status of *ministeriales* was not associated with serfdom and its labor obligations or with head taxes as owed by *censuales* and other social categories. From such liabilities *ministeriales* were explicitly exempted.[22]

Unless they were deliberately released by their lords, *ministeriales* were not free to leave the *familiae* into which they had been born, their ascription being to the retinue of their mothers' lords. In this single respect the devolution of their unfree status in the maternal line did resemble that of serfdom. As a royal charter dealing with the status of a *ministerialis* belonging to Duke Frederick IV of Swabia set it out, "the sanction of the law

18. *Mainzer Urkundenbuch,* 1. *Die Urkunden bis zum Tode Erzbischof Adalberts I. (1137),* ed. Manfred Stimming, Arbeiten der Historischen Kommission für den Volksstaat Hessen (Darmstadt, 1932), no. 459, p. 367.

19. *Constitutiones et acta publica imperatorum et regum inde ab a. DCCCCXI usque ad a. MCXCVII (911–1197),* ed. Ludwig Weiland, *MGH Constitutiones* 1 (Hanover, 1893), no. 451: 678 ff.

20. See Arnold, *German Knighthood,* pp. 53–75.

21. "Adel und Ministerialität im Spiegel der bayerischen Namengebung (bis zum 13. Jahrhundert). Ein Beitrag zum Selbstverständnis der Führungsschichten," *Deutsches Archiv* 33 (1977), 84–152, here p. 145.

22. See, for example, the series of Würzburg charters on these issues: *Monumenta Boica* 37 (Munich, 1864), no. 73: 33–34 (1104); no. 78: 40–41 (1131); no. 89: 55–56 (1140); no. 178: 181–83 (1211).

has and serves this purpose, that children follow the mother's condition, and where the mother belongs, the children belong also."[23] The immediate explanation for this principle is that the status of *ministerialis* originated in servile dependence within the lord's household or *familia*,[24] but German custom had probably not been influenced by Roman laws on slavery in this respect.[25]

In all other respects the rules for *ministeriales* resembled those of vassalage as applied to knights everywhere.[26] But the usage of writing offices preferred *ministerialis* to *miles* largely in order to make unfree status obvious, since there were *milites* who were free men in Germany, and sometimes they were called *milites liberi* or free born knights.[27] By contrast *ministeriales* were *homines proprii* or owned men[28] whose lords possessed proprietary right over them. This was made plain in 1123 when a free born family of Saxons, "rendering up the temporal freedom of the body to the ownership and service of the Church . . . gave themselves as property to the church of Paderborn with rights as *ministeriales*."[29]

The legal language is clear about *ministeriales*' unfree status just as the rare social descriptions are clear about their knightly functions which opened to them the use of aristocratic customs and imagery. In his recent book *L'essor de la chevalerie* Jean Flori also asserts the importance of their chivalric status to explain the rapid rise of the German *ministeriales*, pointing out "above all the role which armed service played in this ascent. In the Empire, knighthood finds its origins amongst the *ministeriales*."[30] Actually, our knowledge of *chevalerie* in this sense in Germany goes back well before 1100, and is best illustrated by the custumal for *ministeriales* inserted

23. *Die Urkunden Friedrichs I.*, ed. Heinrich Appelt et al., 5 parts, *MGH Diplomata* 10 (Hanover, 1975–90), no. 153: 264 (1155–56).

24. Thomas Zotz, "Die Formierung der Ministerialität" in *Die Salier und das Reich* 3, *Gesellschaftlicher und ideengeschichtlicher Wandel im Reich der Salier*, ed. Stefan Weinfurter (Sigmaringen, 1991), esp. p. 7; legal confirmation in *Constitutiones et acta publica imperatorum et regum inde ab a. MCXCVIII usque ad a. MCCLXXII (1198–1272)*, ed. Ludwig Weiland, *MGH Constitutiones* 2 (Hanover, 1896), no. 279 (ch. 7): 393 (1222), ". . . quod servi per stipitem et parentelam ex parte matris provenientem sunt retinendi . . ."

25. Jane F. Gardner, *Women in Roman Law and Society* (London, 1986), p. 139: "The child of a slave woman was a slave, and belonged to her owner at the time of birth."

26. Arnold, *German Knighthood*, pp. 100–161.

27. *Urkundenbuch zur Geschichte der mittelrheinischen Territorien*, ed. Heinrich Beyer, Leopold Eltester, Adam Goerz, 2 (Coblenz, 1865), no. 54: 94 (1182).

28. E.g., *Wirtembergisches Urkundenbuch* 2 (Stuttgart, 1858), no. 337: 61 (1152); *Die Traditionen des Hochstifts Passau*, ed. Max Heuwieser, Quellen und Erörterungen zur bayerischen Geschichte, n.s. 6 (Munich, 1930), no. 745: 266 (1180–1220).

29. *Regesta Historiae Westfaliae accedit Codex Diplomaticus*, ed. Heinrich A. Erhard, 1 (Munich, 1847), no. 192, p. 150 (1123).

30. Flori, *L'essor de la chevalerie XIe–XIIe siècles*, p. 264.

into a charter drawn up for Bishop Gunther of Bamberg (1057–65) which already indicates what the military and administrative obligations as well as the legal rights of the *ministeriales* of a great cathedral church were like in the mid-eleventh century.[31] The Bamberg *ministeriales* were sustained by heritable fiefs in exchange for their military services as cavalry, and should a *ministerialis* not be able to procure such a fief from the bishop, then he was at liberty to seek the rewards of service elsewhere, *militet cui vult,* "he may serve whom he wishes." Military duties extended to campaigns south of the Alps, for which the bishops provided extra resources. In the episcopal administration the *ministeriales* were obliged to serve only in the four household offices of butler, chamberlain, marshal, and seneschal, or in the office of master of the hunt, a significant post given the extensive woodlands possessed by the see of Bamberg. Their legal rights of compurgation, wergeld, and inheritance were also laid down.

A century later the monastic chronicle of Ebersheimmünster in Alsace expanded a little upon this chivalric picture of the *ministeriales*' functions.[32] The chronicle fancifully ascribed the establishment of *ministeriales* in Germany to Caesar, the mythic source of several medieval institutions. He is supposed to have commended, before his departure for Rome, the lesser knights, *minores milites,* to the princes to serve them as though they were *domini ac defensores,* lords and champions. The use of the aristocratic predicate *dominus* for *ministeriales* in the twelfth century is indeed authentic.[33] The chronicle goes on to explain that the highest position in the bishop of Strasbourg's *familia* therefore belonged to the *ministeriales:* they made up the entourage "which furthermore is plainly called military, so noble and warlike that it is rightly comparable with free status."[34] Joachim Bumke is quite justified, even too cautious, in observing that "although there were great social differences within the class of *ministeriales,* one would be al-

31. *Monumenta Bambergensia,* ed. Philipp Jaffé, Bibliotheca rerum Germanicarum 5 (Berlin, 1869), pp. 51–52. On this retinue, Franz Joetze, "Die Ministerialität im Hochstifte Bamberg," *Historisches Jahrbuch* 36 (1915), 516–97, 748–98; Erich von Guttenberg, *Die Territorienbildung am Obermain,* Berichte des Historischen Vereins zu Bamberg 79 (Bamberg, 1927), pp. 299–358, 395–456.

32. *Chronicon Ebersheimense,* ed. Ludwig Weiland, *MGH SS* 23 (1925 reissue): 432–33.

33. *Mainzer Urkundenbuch,* 2, *Die Urkunden seit dem Tode Erzbischof Adalberts I. (1137) bis zum Tode Erzbischof Konrads (1200),* part 1, ed. Peter Acht (Darmstadt, 1968), no. 159: 292–97 (1151) for Conrad of Hagen and Arnsburg; *Die Urkunden Friedrichs I.,* no. 796: 365 (1180) for Werner II of Bolanden; *Die Traditionsnotizen des Klosters Raitenhaslach,* ed. Karlheinrich Dumrath, Quellen und Erörterungen zur bayerischen Geschichte, new series 7 (Munich, 1938), no. 24: 22 (1180–90) for Engelram of Hohenstein; *Die Traditionen des Klosters Oberalteich,* ed. Cornelia Mohr, Quellen und Erörterungen zur bayerischen Geschichte, 30, part 1 (Munich, 1979), no. 104: 216–20 (1188) for Liebhard of Falkenstein.

34. *Chronicon Ebersheimense,* p. 432.

lowed to say that already in the time around 1200 the more important *ministeriales* were hardly to be differentiated in their lifestyle from the old aristocracy."[35]

The sources from Bamberg and Ebersheimmünster thus project an authentic picture of the *ordo* of *ministeriales* aspiring to an aristocratic status which was essentially chivalric.[36] Even the lineages of relatively poor *ministeriales* in obscure provinces appear to have been familiar with wielding aristocratic apparatus, or at least it was ascribed to them under the form *nobilis* or nobleman in twelfth-century charters and codices.[37] But it is difficult to generalize because we know so little about individual lineages of *ministeriales* in the twelfth century. Even the large entourage of imperial *ministeriales* still remains in principle a list of names drawn from the witness lists of charters. In his recent convincing study of royal resources in twelfth- and thirteenth-century Germany, Andreas Christoph Schlunk has counted up just over 500 families of imperial *ministeriales* by the last decade of the twelfth century.[38] It is alarming to realize that even for this retinue, only the small upper rank is well researched, "whereas the lower levels (if at all) are at best testified in their very existence by single references alone."[39]

The *ministeriales* constituted an aristocracy created by military and administrative service, not by blood and descent. No one confused them with *ingenui* or free born noblemen, but they were liberally accredited with the less specific adjective *nobilis* in twelfth-century German sources because

35. *Höfische Kultur: Literatur und Gesellschaft im hohen Mittelalter,* 2 vols. (Munich, 1986), 1: 51.

36. Jean-Pierre Ritter, *Ministérialité et chevalerie: dignité humaine et liberté dans le droit médiéval* (Lausanne, 1955), p. 115: "La dignité chevaleresque fut, pour les ministériaux, le véhicule de leur ascension juridique"; and Störmer, "Adel und Ministerialität," p. 145, where the *ministeriales* "suchte sich vielmehr rasch als miles-Schicht zu identifizieren, ohne sich freilich vom Adel abzugrenzen."

37. E.g., *Traditionen des Hochstifts Passau,* no. 120: 97 (1121–38); *Urkundenbuch des Landes ob der Enns,* 2 (Vienna, 1856), no. 116: 174 (1134); "Codex Augiensium," ed. Johann Mayerhofer, in *Drei bayerische Traditionsbücher aus dem XII. Jahrhundert,* ed. Hans Petz et al. (Munich, 1880), no. 145: 117 (before 1182); *Urkundenbuch der Vögte von Weida, Gera und Plauen,* ed. Berthold Schmidt, 1, Thüringische Geschichtsquellen, n. s. (Jena, 1885), no. 28: 10 (1188); *Urkunden- und Regestenbuch des Herzogtums Krain,* ed. Franz Schumi, 1 (Laibach, 1882), no. 157: 139 (1191). See also Otto von Dungern, "Comes, liber, nobilis in Urkunden des 11. bis 13. Jahrhunderts," *Archiv fur Urkundenforschung* 12 (1932), 200.

38. Andreas Christoph Schlunk, *Königsmacht und Krongut. Die Machtgrundlage des deutschen Königtums im 13. Jahrhundert und eine neue historische Methode* (Stuttgart, 1988), p. 92.

39. *Königsmacht und Krongut,* p. 70. The chief guide to the imperial retinue remains Bosl's *Reichsministerialität.* See also Dietrich von Gladiss, *Beiträge zur Geschichte der staufischen Reichsministerialität,* Historische Studien, 249 (Berlin, 1934); Karl Bosl, "Die Reichsministerialität als Träger staufischer Staatspolitik in Ostfranken und auf dem bayerischen Nordgau," *Jahresbericht des Historischen Vereins für Mittelfranken* 69 (1941), 1–103; Schlunk, *Königsmacht und Krongut,* pp. 69–92; in English, Arnold, *German Knighthood,* pp. 209–24.

it was appropriate to their chivalric status as *milites* or knights. As Josef Fleckenstein has succinctly expressed it, the *ministeriales* "are in the eleventh century and finally in the twelfth *milites* . . . and socially constitute, without prejudice to their exceptional legal status still being current, fully valid members of a mutually inclusive *militia*. And since this received its most intense character through the *nobiles*, it was valid for the *milites* collectively that they operated and lived *more nobilium*, 'in the noble manner.'"[40] This is why charters of the bishops of Eichstätt call their *ministerialis* Rüdiger of Affental *miles nobilis* in 1185, and Merboto of Pfünz *nobilis ecclesie nostre ministerialis*.[41]

In 1188 we find a clerk using the expression *nobiles viri* or noblemen to denote the *ministeriales* listed after the Saxon counts and before the townsmen of Goslar in an imperial charter.[42] Although such usage was acceptable, it must have been confusing because families of free born lords without comital titles of their own were also decorated in the charters by the epithet *nobilis*.[43] The word was nevertheless considered appropriate for nobility of service as well as nobility of free birth. Long ago Wipo's biography of Conrad II had furnished the reasons in cultural terms: "For just as valor ennobles very many common men, so nobility without the virtues disgraces many a nobleman."[44] Valor was more or less a professional qualification of *ministeriales* on active service as in the description of "the dreaded and serried array of *ministeriales* and other chosen knights" who had assembled for the Third Crusade.[45] Modern scholarship has reflected this idea in the neologism *Dienstadel* or "aristocracy of service."[46]

Since a significant proportion of German *ministeriales* originated from

40. "Über den engeren und den weiteren Begriff von Ritter und Rittertum (miles und militia)" in *Person und Gemeinschaft im Mittelalter. Karl Schmid zum 65. Geburtstag*, ed. Gerd Althoff et al. (Sigmaringen, 1988), p. 386. On p. 384 he firmly proclaims *miles* and *ministerialis* as synonyms since the eleventh century.

41. *Monumenta Boica* 49 (Munich, 1910), no. 19: 43 (1185); no. 25: 56 (after 1195).

42. *Die Urkunden Friedrichs I.*, no. 978, p. 259; on Saxon *ministeriales* generally, see Erich Molitor, *Der Stand der Ministerialen vornehmlich auf Grund sächsischer, thüringischer und niederrheinischer Quellen*, Untersuchungen zur deutschen Staats- und Rechtsgeschichte 112 (Breslau, 1912).

43. *Die Urkunden Konrads III.*, no. 74, p. 132 (1142); *Die Urkunden Heinrichs des Löwen*, ed. Karl Jordan, *MGH*, Die deutschen Geschichtsquellen des Mittelalters 1, Urkundentexte (Stuttgart, 1949), 52: 73–76 (1162); *Urkundenbuch für die Geschichte des Niederrheins*, ed. Theodor J. Lacomblet, 1, *779–1200*, new ed. (Aalen, 1966), no. 433: 302 (1169); *Monumenta Boica* 49, no. 13: 35 (1180).

44. *Die Werke Wipos*, ed. Harry Bresslau, *MGH SRG* 61, 3d ed. (Hanover, 1915): 4.

45. *Quellen zur Geschichte des Kreuzzuges Kaiser Friedrichs I.*, ed. Chroust, p. 22.

46. Robert Scheyhing, "Dienstadel" and Karl-Heinz Spiess, "Reichsdienstmannen" in *Handwörterbuch zur deutschen Rechtsgeschichte*, ed. Adalbert Erler and Ekkehard Kaufmann (Berlin, 1970–90), 1: cols. 736–38; 4: cols. 557–61.

families of free born vassals, is it possible that the concept or tincture of aristocracy was transferred through them to the large corps of newly established families of *ministeriales*? Free born families accepted status as *ministeriales* in exchange for new fiefs, offices, and castles as well as security of tenure, or as a result of marriages between *ministeriales* and free persons.[47] At one time it was widely argued that a substantial proportion, even the majority, of all *ministeriales* originated in social classes or groups of free status,[48] but such theories did not prevail against the view that *ministeriales* were projected essentially out of the unfree *familiae* and entourages of the lords.[49]

Although the *ministeriales* obviously come forward in the sources with gathering force in the eleventh century, we are not often provided with any precise information about their genealogical background.[50] Shortly before 1025 Bishop Burchard of Worms drew up an elaborate custumal aimed at preventing disorders within his extensive urban and rural *familia* in which the word *ministerialis* is used for some of his servants and dependents. The custumal also mentions the possibility of promoting *fiscalini* to the offices of chamberlain, butler, seneschal, constable, and *ministerialis*,[51] and this is usually taken to mean that in the Rhineland the *fiscalini* who owed services and renders to the Empire and to the bishoprics also provided a social substratum for the *ordo* of *ministeriales* there. It is certain that free vassals were also transferred into the status of *ministerialis*,[52] and probably more than 10 percent of the bishops of Eichstätt's retinue was recruited in this manner in the twelfth century.[53]

Another instructive example concerns the Saxon *homo liberae conditionis* (a man of free condition) Werner of Leiferde, who transferred himself,

47. See Hans-Jürgen Rieckenberg, "Leben und Stand des Minnesängers Friedrich von Hausen," *Archiv für Kulturgeschichte* 43 (1961), 163–76.

48. Discussed in Arnold, *German Knighthood*, pp. 41–44.

49. Zotz, "Die Formierung der Ministerialität," pp. 6–22 for a recent restatement of this.

50. Arnold, *German Knighthood*, pp. 29–46.

51. *MGH Constitutiones* 1, no. 438: 639–44. See Thomas Zotz, "Bischöfliche Herrschaft, Adel, Ministerialität und Bürgertum in Stadt und Bistum Worms" in *Herrschaft und Stand*, ed. Fleckenstein, pp. 95–96, 100–101.

52. *Die Traditionen des Hochstifts Regensburg und des Klosters S. Emmeram*, ed. Josef Widemann, Quellen und Erörterungen zur bayerischen Geschichte, new series 8 (Munich, 1943), no. 804, p. 380 (1141); *Urkundenbuch des Hochstifts Hildesheim und seiner Bischöfe*, ed. Karl Janicke, part 1, Publicationen aus den königlich preussischen Staatsarchiven 65 (Leipzig, 1898), no. 274: 256 (1151); Flohrschütz, "Machtgrundlagen und Herrschaftspolitik," pp. 49–53.

53. Benjamin Arnold, *Count and Bishop in Medieval Germany: A Study of Regional Power* (Philadelphia, 1991), pp. 66–67, 81–82.

his brothers, and his property into the *potestas* or lordship of Duke Henry the Lion *iure ministerialium,* that is, according to the rules for *ministeriales.*[54] But such examples of the sacrifice of free born status are not numerous enough to provide us with a convincing general case for a large scale entry of *liberi* into the order of *ministeriales.* When Conrad III confirmed Abbot Wibald of Corvey's privileges in 1147, it was ascertained that *liberi homines,* free men, might transfer themselves into the property of Corvey Abbey as *ministeriales,* but the abbot also possessed the authority to make *ministeriales* out of unfree persons of low status, *de infimo ordine.*[55] The charter therefore reflects the methods of social recruitment from above and below which are validated by other sources, but it appears that in general the monastic churches of Germany relied more regularly upon recruitment from below for their *ministeriales,* as in the cases of Siegburg Abbey in the Rhineland and Weissenburg Abbey in Alsace.[56] The impression that recruitment "from lower status," *de infimo ordine,* was normal for *ministeriales* would make it difficult to prove that the entry of free men into the status of *ministerialis* was the channel whereby the norms of aristocratic existence were transmitted to the new *ordo.*

Their military duties as cavalry, their enjoyment of the rules of vassalage, their extensive ownership of lands and castles, and their membership of militias which also consisted of free knights[57] appear to have been enough to assure the *ministeriales* of their place as an aristocracy of service in German society, as influential instruments of power employed by the crown, the Church, and the secular princes. In 1128, when Lothar III gave extensive property in the royal forest of Dreieichenhain to the im-

54. *Annales Stederburgenses,* ed. Georg H. Pertz, *MGH SS* 16 (Hanover, 1859): 217. On the *ministeriales* of Henry the Lion, Otto Haendle, *Die Dienstmannen Heinrichs des Löwen. Ein Beitrag zur Frage der Ministerialität,* Arbeiten zur deutschen Rechts- und Verfassungsgeschichte 8 (Stuttgart, 1930).

55. *Die Urkunden Konrads III.,* no. 181, p. 328. See *Urkundenbuch des Hochstifts Halberstadt und seiner Bischöfe,* ed. Gustav Schmidt, part 1, Publicationen aus den königlich Preussischen Staatsarchiven 17 (Leipzig, 1883), no. 123, pp. 85–86 (1106) where Heidenreich and Conrad, sons of Thiethard, "cum essent homines liberi, in nostre ecclesie se mancipaverunt servitium" under Abbot Erkenbert of Corvey.

56. *Urkunden und Quellen zur Geschichte von Stadt und Abtei Siegburg,* ed. Erich Wisplinghoff, 1 (Siegburg, 1964), no. 8, pp. 12–16 (1075) with the revision at no. 95, pp. 198–201 (1223); *Die Urkunden Heinrichs IV.,* ed. Dietrich von Gladiss and Alfred Gawlik, 4 parts (Hanover, 1941–78), 2, no. 473: 642–44 (1102) taken with the reworked charter in *Diplomata regum Francorum e stirpe Merowingica,* ed. Karl A. F. Pertz, *MGH Diplomata* 31 (Hanover, 1872): 149–50.

57. E.g., *Osnabrücker Urkundenbuch,* ed. Friedrich Philippi, 1, *772–1200* (Osnabrück, 1892), no. 272, p. 217 (1146) for "quicunque de militia Osnaburgensis curie sive liber sive ministerialis."

perial *ministerialis* Conrad of Hagen, the stated motive was "on account of his great and assiduous devotion and maintenance of the most faithful service."[58] From him were descended the chamberlains of Münzenberg whom we know from later evidence to have been entrusted with the administration of resources belonging to the imperial fisc, including the mint at Frankfurt and the county of the Wetterau.[59] In his report of the negotiations in 1184 by which Count Baldwin V of Hainaut was to inherit lands from his uncle, Count Henry the Blind of Luxemburg, Gislebert of Mons recorded that the emperor was advised by Cuno of Münzenberg, who was "rich and shrewd, and possessed many castles of his own, lands, and the homages of knights." Of Werner II of Bolanden, probably the richest of all the imperial *ministeriales* in Frederick Barbarossa's time, Gislebert was slightly more explicit: he was "the most sagacious of men, enriched by seventeen castles of his own and many manors, and commanding the homage of eleven hundred knights."[60] Even if these assertions are exaggerations, then the sense of the importance of the *ministeriales imperii* at court is not. In Frederick II's time, Werner II's descendants were seneschals of the Empire, and one of their administrative instruments to have survived, the Bolanden book of fiefs drawn up after 1250, was probably based upon late twelfth-century materials not now recoverable.[61]

By the beginning of the thirteenth century there are other examples of remunerative imperial bailiwicks entrusted to *ministeriales*. They include the *officium* of Neuburg on the Danube and its district enfeoffed to Marshal Henry of Kalden in 1197;[62] the procuration of lands on the Rhine and the Mosel entrusted to Gerhard of Sinzig, burgrave of Landskron, be-

58. *Die Urkunden Lothars III.*, no. 14, p. 17.

59. *Urkundenbuch der Reichsstadt Frankfurt*, ed. Johann F. Böhmer and Friedrich Lau, 1, *794–1314*, new ed. (Frankfurt, 1901), no. 33, p. 17 (1194); no. 44, pp. 21–22 (1216).

60. *La Chronique de Gislebert de Mons*, ed. Léon Vanderkindere, Commission royale d'histoire. Recueil de textes (Brussels, 1904), p. 162.

61. See the discussion in Wolf-Heinz Struck, "Aus den Anfängen der territorialen Finanzverwaltung. Ein Rechnungsfragment der Herren von Bolanden um 1258/62," *Archivalische Zeitschrift* 70 (1974), 1–21 and Albrecht Eckhardt, "Das älteste Bolander Lehnbuch. Versuch einer Neudatierung," *Archiv für Diplomatik* 22 (1976), 317–44. See also Bosl, *Reichsministerialität*, pp. 260–74 and Wolfgang Metz, *Staufische Güterverzeichnisse: Untersuchungen zur Verfassungs- und Wirtschaftsgeschichte des 12. und 13. Jahrhunderts* (Berlin, 1964), pp. 52–76. Metz's argument for a procuration over Rhineland fisc exercised by Werner II of Bolanden (pp. 70–72) cannot now be sustained because the essential evidence turns out to be an eighteenth-century forgery; see Ferdinand Opll, "Das kaiserliche Mandat im 12. Jahrhundert," *Mitteilungen des Instituts für österreichische Geschichtsforschung* 84 (1976), 303, note 102.

62. *Die Regesten des Kaiserreiches unter Heinrich VI.*, ed. Johann F. Böhmer and Gerhard Baaken, Regesta Imperii, 4, part 3 (Cologne and Vienna, 1972), no. 605: 245–46 (1197).

fore 1216;[63] the procuration of royal lands and other resources in Swabia assigned to Seneschal Eberhard of Waldburg and Butler Conrad of Winterstetten before 1222;[64] and the colonial Pleissenland where Hugo of Wartha is attested long before the end of the twelfth century, although the source crediting him as "judge of the land of Pleissen" is a thirteenth-century forgery.[65]

Apart from holding numerous castles and operating under multiple allegiances, Werner II of Bolanden can also be taken to illustrate another important respect in which the German *ministeriales* matched the free born aristocracy, that is, in the possession of real fiefs. Eike von Repgow, who was fond of preserving information about custom long fallen out of practice, claimed that *ministeriales* were not entitled to real fiefs taken by homage,[66] but instead received from their lords a category of fief widely known as *hovelen* or house fief.[67] However, this distinction had ceased to correspond with reality as soon as *ministeriales* took fiefs from lords other than the heads of their own *familiae,* that is, in the eleventh century. And so in 1166 Werner II of Bolanden could give Haboudange Castle to Bishop Dietrich of Metz and receive in exchange some valuable fiefs which were to be held by hereditary right in both lines, *ius beneficialis* and *hereditarium ius* with all the details spelled out. These terms are very similar to those under which Frederick Barbarossa conferred possession of Annone Castle in Italy upon a free born German lord, Arnold of Dorstadt; ". . . to him and to his legitimate heirs both female and male, as real fief following German custom."[68]

Another source, the *Codex Falkensteinensis* compiled for the counts of

63. *MGH Constitutiones* 2, no. 55: 66–67 (1216) and Volker Rödel, "Die Entstehung der Herrschaft Landskron," *Jahrbuch für westdeutsche Landesgeschichte* 6 (1980), 43–67.

64. *Codex diplomaticus Salemitanus: Urkundenbuch der Cisterzienserabtei Salem 1134–1266,* ed. Friedrich von Weech (Karlsruhe, 1881–83), no. 125: 162–63 (1222) and *Chronik des Propstes Burchard von Ursberg,* ed. Oswald Holder-Egger and Bernhard von Simson, pp. 114–15.

65. See Walter Schlesinger, "Egerland, Vogtland, Pleissenland: Zur Geschichte des Reichsgutes im mitteldeutschen Osten," in his *Mitteldeutsche Beiträge zur deutschen Verfassungsgeschichte des Mittelalters* (Göttingen, 1961), pp. 188–211, 477–79; Herbert Helbig, "Verfügungen über Reichsgut im Pleissenland" in *Festschrift für Walter Schlesinger* 1, ed. Helmut Beumann, Mitteldeutsche Forschungen 74, part 1 (Cologne and Vienna, 1973), pp. 273–85; František Kubů, "Die staufische Ministerialität im Egerland," *Jahrbuch für fränkische Landesforschung* 43 (1983), 59–101; Dieter Rübsamen, *Kleine Herrschaftsträger im Pleissenland. Studien zur Geschichte des mitteldeutschen Adels im 13. Jahrhundert,* Mitteldeutsche Forschungen 95 (Cologne and Vienna, 1987), pp. 323–29; *Die Urkunden Friedrichs I.,* no. 1065: 393–96 (dated 1172).

66. *Sachsenspiegel Lehnrecht,* ed. Eckhardt, pp. 81–82 (63, 1).

67. See Arnold, *German Knighthood,* pp. 113, 115 (n. 80), 127–28.

68. *Die Urkunden Friedrichs I.,* nos. 517, pp. 455–57 (1166) and 522, pp. 462–63 (1167).

Falkenstein in Bavaria between the 1160s and the 1190s, simply lists Count Siboto IV's vassals "who have done homage to him for various fiefs,"[69] and more than half of them appear elsewhere in the codex as *ministeriales*. Enactments of the royal court also confirmed that *ministeriales* might hold fief by the same rules as for free born vassals.[70] In another case, Archbishop Gerhard II of Bremen insisted upon the abolition of *hovelen* throughout the country of Stade in 1219 and their replacement by real feudal tenure for *ministeriales*. The motive was to compel Count Palatine Henry of Brunswick, the archbishop's tenant for the county, to recognize that Stade was not an allod but a fief from Bremen in which the *ministeriales* should therefore be the archbishop's rear vassals. The *ministeriales* were required to swear fealty to the archbishop, "and the lands which hitherto they had held from the palatine by *ministeriales'* right they now received from him by feudal right." Eighty-two such tenants were then listed as having sworn fealty to Bremen as rear vassals.[71]

The function of the German *ministeriales* as a knightly aristocracy of service or *Dienstadel* is plain to discern. One of Henry V's captains who is usually considered to have been the progenitor of the marshals of Kalden and Pappenheim[72] was appointed before 1116 to the burgraviate of Meissen,[73] a perilous post held in the midst of the emperor's Saxon enemies. It was his descendant, Marshal Henry of Kalden who was, as we have seen,[74] entrusted in 1197 with a large portion of the imperial fisc in Bavaria, and these crown lands with other resources were subjected to a survey in the second decade of the thirteenth century.[75] The households of the bishops, dukes, abbots, margraves, and counts of the German Empire were served by their own *Dienstadel* of *ministeriales* generally employing the four household titles of seneschal, butler, chamberlain, and marshal.[76] In order to

69. *Codex Falkensteinensis. Die Rechtsaufzeichnungen der Grafen von Falkenstein,* ed. Elisabeth Noichl, Quellen und Erörterungen zur bayerischen Geschichte, new series 29 (Munich, 1978), no. 106: 68–70.

70. *MGH Constitutiones* 1, no. 367, p. 516 (1195) and 2, no. 279, pp. 392–93 (1222).

71. *Hamburgisches Urkundenbuch* ed. Johann M. Lappenberg, 1, 2nd ed. (Hamburg, 1907), nos. 432 and 424, pp. 375, 377–79.

72. Gustav Beckmann, "Die Pappenheim und die Würzburg des 12. und 13. Jahrhunderts," *Historisches Jahrbuch* 47 (1927), 1–17, 56–62.

73. Gerold Meyer von Knonau, *Jahrbücher des deutschen Reiches unter Heinrich IV. und Heinrich V.* 6, Jahrbücher der deutschen Geschichte, new ed. (Berlin, 1965), p. 277.

74. See note 62 above.

75. Wilhelm Kraft, *Das Urbar der Reichsmarschälle von Pappenheim,* Schriftenreihe zur bayerischen Landesgeschichte, 3 new ed. (Aalen, 1974); Metz, *Staufische Güterverzeichnisse,* pp. 77–93; Meinrad Weikmann, "Königsdienst und Königsgastung in der Stauferzeit," *Zeitschrift für bayerische Landesgeschichte* 30 (1967), 328–31.

76. See the material in Arnold, *German Knighthood,* pp. 184–203.

promote the grandeur of the Welf dynasty, the author of the *Historia Welforum* writing in the second half of the twelfth century supposed that in former times their household had been "regulated in regal fashion, so that each of the household offices, that is, the obligations of seneschals, butlers, marshals, chamberlains, and standard bearers were carried out by counts or their equals."[77] But by the later eleventh century the active officers were nearly always *ministeriales,* even in the royal household.[78]

The information we would like to possess about the rise of this kind of administration in the hands of the *ministeriales* is inadequate before the thirteenth century. From the investigated fragments of careers, and from the meaning of the household titles, it is fair to infer that the household offices combined judicial, military, and fiscal duties, but there is not much in the way of administrative record to substantiate their functions.[79] However, the custumal about the Cologne *ministeriales* drawn up for Archbishop Rainald of Dassel about 1165 explained that the chamberlain of Cologne collected the revenues from the tolls and mints, and that this duty exempted him from attending expeditions to Italy.[80] He was also responsible, with the advocate, for locking up homicidal *ministeriales,*[81] incidentally introducing us to another official with wide administrative powers in the households of princes. At Cologne the advocate outranked all other *ministeriales.* He was in charge of the archiepiscopal manors and collected their revenues, and also appointed the bailiffs for twelve manors under his own direction, in his "power and care" or *potestas et procuratio.*[82] Like the chamberlain, the

77. *Historia Welforum,* ed. Erich König, Schwäbische Chroniken der Stauferzeit 1, new ed. (Sigmaringen, 1978), p. 4.

78. On this point see Irmgard Latzke, "Hofamt, Erzamt und Erbamt im mittelalterlichen deutschen Reich," inaugural dissertation (Frankfurt am Main, 1970), pp. 134–46. For the organization of the royal household and its officials, see Julius Ficker's classic "Die Reichshofbeamten der staufischen Periode," *Sitzungsberichte der phil.-hist. Classe der kaiserlichen Akademie der Wissenschaften* 40, part 4 (Vienna, 1862), 447–549; Paul Schubert, "Die Reichshofämter und ihre Inhaber bis um die Wende des 12. Jahrhunderts," *Mitteilungen des Instituts für österreichische Geschichtsforschung* 34 (1913), 427–501; Wilhelm Kraft "Das Reichsmarschallamt in seiner geschichtlichen Entwicklung," *Jahrbuch des historischen Vereins für Mittelfranken* 78 (1959), 1–36; 79 (1960–61), 38–96.

79. Metz, *Staufische Güterverzeichnisse,* pp. 140–43; Johannes Fried, "Die Wirtschaftspolitik Friedrich Barbarossas in Deutschland," *Blätter für deutsche Landesgeschichte* 120 (1984), 212–20.

80. *Quellen zur deutschen Verfassungs-, Wirtschafts- und Socialgeschichte bis 1250,* ed. Lorenz Weinrich, Ausgewählte Quellen zur deutschen Geschichte des Mittelalters. Freiherr vom Stein-Gedächtnisausgabe 32 (Darmstadt, 1977), p. 268.

81. *Quellen,* p. 272.

82. *Quellen,* pp. 268–70. On the Cologne advocates, Wilhelm Pötter, *Die Ministerialität der Erzbischöfe von Köln vom Ende des 11. bis zum Ausgang des 13. Jahrhunderts,* Studien zur Kölner Kirchengeschichte 9 (Düsseldorf, 1967), pp. 71–85.

advocate was exempted from Italian expeditions in order to carry out fiscal duties at home. In 1169 Archbishop Philip of Heinsberg turned the office into a hereditary appointment, and the *ministerialis* Gerhard of Heppendorf was enfeoffed with this advocacy in exchange for real homage.[83] The advocate was also the chief magistrate for the archiepiscopal household, retinue, and *familia:* "Of all the *ministeriales* of St Peter [Cologne's patron saint], no one may pronounce judgement for the archbishop except the advocate of Cologne."[84] If he was absent, then the archbishop might delegate the task to another *ministerialis*.

By the standards of the surviving evidence, our knowledge of the duties of the Cologne chamberlains and advocates in the twelfth century is exceptional. However, in the adjacent imperial dominion of Aachen with its palace, manors, forest, and monasteries, we also find the offices of advocate and chamberlain operated by *ministeriales* in the twelfth century.[85] It is clear that the imperial *ministeriales* stationed at Aachen wielded considerable political influence in lower Lotharingia, which irritated the dukes of Brabant and the archbishops of Cologne who were in any case rivals for the ducal privilege of supervising the general peace and the profitable *conductus* or right of safe-conduct on the roads in the large region between the Meuse and the Rhine. But the sources indicate that towards the end of the twelfth century the custody of that region, including the supervision of *conductus* and of peace keeping, were in the hands of the imperial *ministerialis* Hugo of Worms operating from Aachen "whom the emperor [Henry VI] at that time had placed in command of Lotharingia."[86]

* * *

The hints from Cologne and Aachen about the political as well as the administrative value of the corps of *ministeriales* point broadly to their utility as instruments of power in the service of the crown, the Church, and

83. *Urkundenbuch des Niederrheins,* ed. Lacomblet, 1, no. 434, p. 304 (1169); in no. 445, p. 312 (1173) he was called *ministerialis* and *advocatus curie nostre*.

84. *Quellen bis 1250,* ed. Weinrich, p. 270.

85. *Die Urkunden Konrads III.*, no. 64, p. 113 (1141) for Dietrich *advocatus* and *Die Urkunden Friedrichs I.*, no. 639, p. 139 (1175) for William *camerarius et advocatus Aquensis*. See Bosl, *Reichsministerialität,* pp. 278–82; Dietmar Flach, *Untersuchungen zur Verfassung und Verwaltung des Aachener Reichsgutes von der Karlingerzeit bis zur Mitte des 14. Jahrhunderts,* Veröffentlichungen des Max-Planck-Instituts für Geschichte 46 (Göttingen, 1976), pp. 244–80; Fred Schwind, "Reichsvogteien" in *Handwörterbuch zur deutschen Rechtsgeschichte* 4, cols. 810–14.

86. *Vita Alberti episcopi Leodiensis,* ed. Johannes Heller, *MGH SS* 25 (Hanover, 1880): 151; *La chronique de Gislebert de Mons,* ed. Vanderkindere, p. 231.

the secular princes in Germany. "As managers of central court administration in the incipient territories, as guardians of princely castles, as commissioners of the princes in the towns, the *ministeriales* had a substantial share in the extension of territorial domination; and also in the provinces their influence and their authority increased together with their responsibilities."[87] The *ministeriales* constituted a *Dienstadel*, but the immediate cause for their early assimilation to the established norms of aristocratic society in Germany was the rise of vassal knighthood everywhere in eleventh- and twelfth-century Europe. In other words the militias of *ministeriales* represented for Germany the leading example of the chivalric phenomenon. This is why it is not fruitful to press analogies between German *ministeriales* who were unfree in law and the military elites of servile status in other societies, such as the ghulams, mamluks, and kapikulus of Islam. Closer analogies are provided by the "servants of the king," *pueri regii*, of the Merovingian realms as described by Gregory of Tours[88] and by the *caballarii* of the Carolingian Empire,[89] without such elements having provided concrete institutional antecedents for the *ministeriales* of later times in Germany.[90] Western European and crusading knighthood, of course, exhibited many variations upon the northern French paradigm which remains close to the center of our thinking about medieval chivalry.[91] Apart from the *ministeriales* of Germany one could cite the monastic knighthood of Palestine, the *caballeros villanos* of Castile, and the towns of Lombardy which conferred the apparatus of knighthood upon "young men of inferior condition or even workers pursuing the contemptible mechanical trades," much to the surprise of Bishop Otto of Freising.[92]

We do not have to wait for the literary work of the thirteenth-century

87. Bumke, *Höfische Kultur,* 1, pp. 50–51. As Hans K. Schulze puts it for the march of Brandenburg in "Territorienbildung und soziale Strukturen in der Mark Brandenburg im hohen Mittelalter" in *Herrschaft und Stand,* ed. Fleckenstein, pp. 263–64: "Mit der Entstehung der Landesherrschaft eng verbunden war die Herausbildung eines landsässigen niederen Adels. Die Territorialfürsten bedurften einer besonderen Schicht zur Übernahme der wichtigsten militärischen und verwaltungsmässigen Funktionen, und sie förderten daher den Aufstieg der Ministerialität."

88. Gabriele von Olberg, "Puer regius" in *Handwörterbuch zur deutschen Rechtsgeschichte* 4: col. 100.

89. *Capitularia regum Francorum,* ed. Alfred Boretius and Victor Krause, 2 vols., *MGH Legum sectio II* (Hanover, 1883–97) 1, no. 49, p. 136 (about 807); no. 75, p. 168 (804–11).

90. Arnold, *German Knighthood,* pp. 37–41.

91. Georges Duby, *Hommes et structures du moyen âge: recueil d'articles* (Paris, 1973), pp. 145–66, 213–25, 267–85, 325–41, 395–422.

92. *Ottonis et Rahewini Gesta Friderici I. Imperatoris,* ed. Georg Waitz and Bernhard von Simson, *MGH SRG,* 3d ed. (Hanover, 1912): 116.

Styrian *ministerialis* Ulrich of Liechtenstein to discover the ethos of chivalry ingrained in his class.[93] Apart from Wilhelm Störmer's convincing equation of the aristocratic and the knightly with the *ministerialis* of the eleventh century, Josef Fleckenstein has emphasized the importance of Frederick Barbarossa's courts for revealing the chivalric profile of the *ministeriales* as an aristocratic social group in Germany. In 1184 a great festival was held at Mainz in order to dub the emperor's sons, King Henry VI and Duke Frederick V of Swabia. In 1188 another court called the *curia Ihesu Christi* was summoned back there to make preparations for the Third Crusade.[94] These courts deliberately proclaimed the secular and spiritual glory of knighthood avowed and practised by the entire German aristocracy, from the personnel of the imperial court down to the *ministeriales* generally, as a single chivalric community.[95] As Fleckenstein goes on to point out, the sources explicitly conflated the members of the two gatherings, clerics excepted, as *milites* and as a *militia,* applying the epithet *miles* to named individuals, be they dukes or landgraves, counts or *ministeriales,* as well as to the emperor's sons, characterized by Gislebert of Mons as *novi milites* or "new knights."[96]

The evidence for the courts of 1184 and 1188 underlined the chivalric integration of the *ministeriales* into the German aristocracy of which they made up by far the greater part, but more lies behind this. Other royal court meetings bear witness to the legal functions of the imperial *ministeriales* as judges alongside the princes,[97] and as guarantors for royal acts. At the court held in Nuremberg Castle in December 1186 (possibly 1188), Frederick Barbarossa passed significant legislation aimed against the prevalent nuisance of incendiarism during feuds "with the support and counsel of the princes and others of our faithful men, *fideles* both free born and *minis-*

93. See Reinhold Bechstein, *Ulrichs von Liechtenstein Frauendienst* 2 vols., Deutsche Dichtungen des Mittelalters 6–7 (Leipzig, 1888). For the meaning of texts in relation to German knighthood, Joachim Bumke, *Studien zum Ritterbegriff im 12. und 13. Jahrhundert,* Beihefte zum Euphorion 1 (Heidelberg, 1964) and Hans G. Reuter, *Die Lehre vom Ritterstand: Zum Ritterbegriff in Historiographie und Dichtung,* Neue Wirtschaftsgeschichte 4 (Cologne and Vienna, 1971). In *Ministerialität und Ritterdichtung: Umrisse der Forschung* (Munich, 1976), Bumke shows that there is not much to connect twelfth-century chivalric literature with the *ministeriales,* hence the reference to Ulrich of Liechtenstein as a more secure proposition.

94. Josef Fleckenstein, "Friedrich Barbarossa und das Rittertum. Zur Bedeutung der grossen Mainzer Hoftage von 1184 un 1188" in *Festschrift für Hermann Heimpel zum 70. Geburtstag,* 3 vols. Veröffentlichungen des Max-Planck-Instituts für Geschichte 36 (Göttingen, 1972) 2, pp. 1023–41.

95. Fleckenstein, "Friedrich Barbarossa," pp. 1027–30.

96. *Chronique de Gislebert de Mons,* ed. Vanderkindere, p. 156.

97. E.g., *Die Urkunden Konrads III.,* no. 210: 377–79 (1149); *Chronique de Gislebert de Mons,* ed. Vanderkindere, p. 254.

teriales."[98] About forty years earlier Conrad III had celebrated one of his Christmas courts at Aachen amongst "many of our trustworthy nobles and *ministeriales,*" the latter including Conrad of Hagen, Anselm and Rüdiger of Düren, and Louis of Hammerstein.[99] Perhaps the most striking example of curial duties enforcing the aristocratic condition of *ministeriales* is provided by the Treaty of Constance in 1183 between Frederick Barbarossa, Henry VI, and the Lombard League. Since it was not the custom for kings to swear oaths personally, sixteen of the "princes and nobles of the court" came forward to swear to the treaty.[100] They include four prelates, three dukes, two margraves, three counts, and four *ministeriales* of the Empire: Chamberlain Rudolf of Siebnach, Werner of Bolanden, Cuno of Münzenberg, and Butler Conrad of Wallhausen or Schüpf. As imperial *fideles* the *ministeriales* had indeed arrived.

The royal courts and their business may have provided a vehicle for the social ascent of some of the German *ministeriales,* but the fundamental reason for their emergence as an aristocracy of service must remain in the central need for competent military retinues in the disturbed political milieu of medieval Germany. The sources agree that the War of Investitures (1076–1122) as a species of inner civil conflict was fought on a larger scale and with a ferocity formerly unknown, although the Empire was by no means innocent of previous discords under arms. As the anonymous author of the *Annolied* put it: "After this began the dreadful struggle in which many a man lost his life, as under the fourth Henry [1056–1106] the Empire was thrown into disorder. Killing, brigandage and arson destroyed Church and land from Denmark to Apulia, from France to Hungary" and so on.[101] These cruel events were quickly followed by the widespread hostilities of the reigns of Lothar III and Conrad III and by Frederick Barbarossa's bloodstained campaigns in Italy. The significance of the *ministeriales* for these phases of warfare in the Empire is illustrated by the practice of commemorating the fallen by gifts to monasteries. During Conrad III's reign when struggles were occurring for control of the duchy of Bavaria, Diessen Abbey received a donation of land from the counts of Wolfratshausen in

98. *Die Urkunden Friedrichs I.*, no. 988: 273–77; see Elmar Wadle, "Der Nürnberger Friedebrief Kaiser Friedrich Barbarossas und das gelehrte Recht" in *Wege europäische Rechtsgeschichte. Karl Kroeschell zum 60. Geburtstag,* ed. Gerhard Köbler, Rechtshistorische Reihe 60 (Frankfurt am Main, etc., 1987), pp. 548–72.

99. *Die Urkunden Konrads III.*, no. 142: 256–57 (1145).

100. *Die Urkunden Friedrichs I.*, no. 848: 68–77.

101. *Das Annolied,* ed. Max Roediger, *MGH Deutsche Chroniken und andere Geschichtsbücher* 1, part 2 (new ed.) (Dublin-Zürich, 1968): 129.

memory of their *ministerialis* Magenso, killed at the siege of Valley Castle in 1140; and Liutold of Hausen, one of Count Berthold of Andech's *ministeriales* killed on campaign, was commemorated by a gift from his brother.[102] On the Italian campaigns Frederick Barbarossa commented in 1185 that at the difficult siege of Crema in 1159 "there we lost our enfeoffed noblemen, *ministeriales* and servants in arms, for whom it is difficult to compensate."[103]

The same point about the importance of war and defense in explaining the rise of the *ministeriales* is implied in a charter of Conrad III for Lorsch Abbey issued in 1147. The charter states that of old the vassals and *ministeriales* of the abbey had held fiefs in return for military service.[104] We happen to know that in 1065 and 1066, when Archbishop Adalbert of Bremen had tried to take over Lorsch for himself, the abbot's vassals, *ministeriales* as well as free born noblemen, had taken to arms and built fortifications for the abbey's defense.[105] In the eight decades which lie between these intelligences about Lorsch, the German *ministeriales* took hold as a *Dienstadel* chiefly by means of the powerful chivalric mechanism at work within European society. This is why a charter from the Rhineland dated 1139 could include in one *ordo* of knights a duke and two counts from the old aristocracy and five prominent *ministeriales* of the archbishopric of Cologne from the new.[106]

102. *Die Traditionen und Urkunden des Stiftes Diessen 1114–1362,* ed. Waldemar Schlögl, Quellen und Erörterungen zur bayerischen Geschichte, n.s. 22, part 1 (Munich, 1967), no. 6: 9–11 (1140); no. 9: 13–15 (1137–47). On this custom see Karl Schmid, "Salische Gedenkstiftungen für fideles, servientes und milites" in *Institutionen, Kultur und Gesellschaft im Mittelalter: Festschrift für Josef Fleckenstein,* ed. Lutz Fenske, et al. (Sigmaringen, 1984), pp. 245–64.

103. *Die Urkunden Friedrichs I.*, no. 895: 146.

104. *Die Urkunden Konrads III.*, no. 167: 302–4. On this house, see Hans-Peter Wehlt, *Reichsabtei und König dargestellt am Beispiel der Abtei Lorsch mit Ausblicken auf Hersfeld, Stablo und Fulda,* Veröffentlichungen des Max-Planck-Instituts für Geschichte 28 (Göttingen, 1970).

105. *Codex Laureshamensis,* ed. Karl Glöckner, 1, Arbeiten der Historischen Kommission für den Volksstaat Hessen (Darmstadt, 1929), p. 393.

106. *Urkundenbuch des Niederrheins,* ed. Lacomblet, 1, no. 330: 220–21.

Dominique Barthélemy

3. Castles, Barons, and Vavassors in the Vendômois and Neighboring Regions in the Eleventh and Twelfth Centuries

It is Georges Duby who first sketched the portrait of those *milites* who found a place in the elite by sitting in a castellan's court, thereby sharing in a more elevated sociability than that of the village. He cited Guigonnet de Germolles as an example of such a knight.[1] Other historians also found such examples and in 1960 Jean Richard provided the fullest description of them in an article entitled "Châteaux, châtelains et vassaux en Bourgogne aux XIe et XIIe siècles," a title I draw on here. Richard's model attributed two notable traits to knights of the castle.

(1) The distinction of two groups among them: lords of the countryside and knights of the castral family. The latter, of lesser standing, sometimes bore sobriquets, but both groups exhibited a certain spirit of caste while inclining to endogamy.

(2) A perceptible tendency toward 1200 for the castral knights to be transferred to the countryside, or at least those among them who had not found their way into the "patriciate" of those little towns that had formed in the castles.[2]

There is not much to add to these two Burgundian models, based as they are upon a richer documentation than is available for other regions of northern France. That is why so little new work has been done since 1960 to carry on this discussion. The fine study of Michel Parisse does not descend to the second circle of the Lotharingian nobility; Parisse finds too

1. Georges Duby, *La société aux XIe et XIIe siècles dans la région mâconnaise,* 2d ed. (Paris, 1971), pp. 327–28: "Guigonnet est un paysan qui, de temps en temps, vit mieux."

2. Jean Richard, "Châteaux, châtelains et vassaux en Bourgogne aux XIe et XIIe siècles," *Cahiers de Civilisation Médiévale* 3 (1960), 433–47. See also Richard, *Les ducs de Bourgogne et la formation du duché du XIe au XIVe siècle* (Paris, 1954); and "Le château dans la structure féodale de la France de l'est au XIIe siècle," *Probleme des 12. Jahrhunderts,* Vorträge und Forschungen, 12 (Stuttgart, 1968), pp. 169–76.

little evidence of that group in the sources and refrains from a synthesis that might prove "illusory."[3] The work of Theodore Evergates, using the lists of champagnard feudatories which begin in 1172, is valuable, but too late for the present purpose.[4] Finally, Eric Bournazel makes a good deal of the *milites civitatis* in the Ile-de-France under Louis VI;[5] while my own work has argued for two ages of castellan elites at Coucy, La Fère, and Marle according to the Burgundian model.[6] But do these two latter studies move us beyond impressions? Like Parisse and Evergates, we suffer from a serious shortage of evidence before 1150.

Such is not at all true, however, of the new terrain which has occupied me since 1983: the Vendômois[7] and its border-lands. For here the sources are abundant enough to rival those of Burgundy, notably those from Marmoutier (the Cluny of the West!). They point to a society rather similar to that of the Mâconnais, yet with a somewhat different appearance. During the period 1050 to 1250 the feudal structures stand out more clearly, as does the evolution of castellan justice or that of gifts to saints, matters dealt with by Stephen White in his pioneering studies.[8]

What is offered in these pages is a research study in counterpoint to those of Duby and Richard. The material is assuredly limited in territorial space, but perhaps it will serve to suggest some tendencies of wider significance.

3. Michel Parisse, *Noblesse et chevalerie en Lorraine médiévale: les familles nobles du XIe au XIIIe siècle* (Nancy, 1982), p. 12: "le niveau inférieur d'une chevalerie en changement permanent et dont la connaissance précise est illusoire."

4. Theodore Evergates, *Feudal Society in the Bailliage of Troyes Under the Counts of Champagne, 1152–1284* (Baltimore, 1975). See also John W. Baldwin, *The Government of Philip Augustus: Foundations of French Royal Power in the Middle Ages* (Berkeley, 1986), pp. 294–303.

5. Eric Bournazel, *Le gouvernement capétien au XIIe siècle, 1108–1180: Structures sociales et mutations institutionnelles* (Paris, 1975), notably chapter 2.

6. Dominique Barthélemy, *Les deux âges de la seigneurie banale: pouvoir et société dans la terre des sires de Coucy (milieu XIe–milieu XIIIe siècle)* (Paris, 1984), ch. 2.

7. Dominique Barthélemy, *La société dans le comté de Vendôme, de l'an mil au XIVe siècle* (Paris, 1993). On the nobility, knighthood and the renewal of feudal elites, see notably pp. 507–623, 749–63, 905–1001.

8. Stephen D. White, "*Pactum legem vincit et amor judicium*. The settlement of disputes by compromise in eleventh-century France," *American Journal of Legal History* 22 (1978), 281–308; idem, *Custom, Kinship and Gifts to Saints: The "laudatio parentum" in Western France, 1050–1150* (Chapel Hill, NC, 1988).

Barons and Vavassors from 1050 to 1250

Castellan Barons and Lordship

Let us take Anjou in the time of Geoffrey Martel and his successors—that is, to at least 1109. The work of Olivier Guillot[9] is, on our question, at once enlightening and incomplete; how is nobility there defined?[10]

Around the count we find the *barones;* they form his *curia* and bear as a rule, but not always, the name of the castle they hold. So, for example, Alard de Château-Gonthier, Geoffroi de Preuilly, or Robert the Burgundian were all castellan lords.[11] Here, in these men, is the quintessence of the nobility. They exercise power in this land jointly with the count. But let us note two important points.

(1) A problematic turning on the independence of castellan lordship hardly makes sense. For what does it mean to speak of "independence"? Here as in the Catalonia of Thomas Bisson, feudal structures do not prevent the maintenance of some measure of public order; indeed, they *are* that order. There is no master of a castle who does not owe the count of Anjou military aid or who totally neglects his justice. Moreover, the ties of kinship are such as to require us to define the aristocracy as a network of horizontal relations;[12] its conflicts do not break France into pieces, nor tear the social fabric, but serve on the contrary to define, remodel, even reactivate the ties.[13] It hardly matters whether the title *dominus* turns up in a *cartula* or not;[14] in so accidental a documentation, silence means nothing.

9. Olivier Guillot, *Le comte d'Anjou et son entourage au XIe siècle,* 2 vols. (Paris, 1972).

10. Léopold Genicot raised this question in a (generally favorable) review: "Rois, ducs, comtes, évêques, moines, seigneurs: forces et jeux politiques dans l'Anjou du XIe siècle" (1973), reprinted in *La noblesse dans l'Occident médiéval* (London, 1982), p. 109.

11. Only a few examples can be given here, with others to be found in my *La société.* For "noble barons" around Geoffrey Martel, see *TV,* 1, no. 16; similar profiles, but with the epithets *fideles* and *nobiles, TV,* no. 35.

12. As Michel Bur has written, "l'aristocratie est un système ramifié à l'intérieur duquel circulent des noms et des biens, des droits et des prétensions," *La formation du comté de Champagne (v. 950–v. 1150)* (Nancy, 1977), p. 278.

13. In this sense, Patrick Geary, "Vivre en conflit dans une France sans Etat: typologie des mécanismes de règlement des conflits (1050–1200)," *Annales E.S.C.* 51 (1986), 1107–33; nevertheless, the notion of a stateless France in the eleventh century needs to be nuanced. Fredric Cheyette would place "the invention of the state" in Gregorian times, *Essays on Medieval Civilization,* ed. Bede K. Lackner and Kenneth R. Philp (Austin, TX, 1978), pp. 143–78. Only the nobility, in my view, had a certain freedom with the law, even as they imposed it on non-nobles; the facts so well described by those concerned with legal anthropology are chiefly traits of nobility. Besides, Fredric Cheyette and Stephen White seem to underestimate the impact and diffusion of the written act.

14. Olivier Guillot makes it a criterion for the "independence" of castellan lordship, *Le comte d'Anjou,* 1:305 and passim; in reality *dominus* and *possessor* are perfectly synonymous and

(2) The nobility so defined is not differentiated from a "knighthood" (*militia*) which would form the lower stratum of the aristocracy. The barons who were lords of castles are not only noble but the quintessence of knighthood. Such we learn from the fine circumlocutions of certain acts of La Trinité of Vendôme.[15] In lands of Anjou and Blois every *dominus* bears individually the title *miles,* appearing, in monastic verbiage, as *seculari militie deditus* or *militari gladio accinctus.* As Jane Martindale well saw, nobility is a matter of lineage, birth being the most useful element of kinship.[16] Knighthood perfects it as a realization of noble power and in expressing that individual energy without which the members of any ruling class, whatever their initial socio-cultural advantages, could not maintain itself.[17] That rite of passage which can well be called dubbing (even if the exact term is *miles fieri*) determined access to adulthood in this milieu; it qualified one to a special place in feudal society, namely at once lord (ruling knight) and vassal (serving knight).[18] In other words, and just as in Duby's

---

refer to local power, not the absence of suzerainty. See, for the Vendômois, this expression from the middle of the eleventh century: "qui dominus et possessor est alodii et per se ipsum districtor et judex forisfacti," *MV,* no. 122. Besides, almost all "allods" in the eleventh-century Vendômois were held in fief, even probably the one cited above; the words *dominus* and *possessor* were applied in the 1060s to the lords of Château-Renault, which they held of the count of Anjou or the count of Blois.

15. *TV,* no. 301 (1081): "Lancelinus, castri Balgiacensis dominus, homo quantum quidem ad natalium spectat generositatem, parentum nobilitate clarissimus, quantum vero ad proprie virtutis laudem, tam militaris strenuitatis potentia, quam rei familiaris honesta sollicitudine procurande industria famosissimus." Also *TV,* no. 342 (1092): "extitit quondam sane predives homo, nobilis suo tempore, pre multis potentia famosus, nomine Goffridus qui cognomine de Meduana dicebatur; hic itaque licet seculari militie deditus." The sense of these circumlocutions is simultaneously to bring out a whole cluster of qualities rather than one in particular to indicate position in the highest elite, and to envisage a complementarity of nobility (or of *generositas*) which concerns identity, of birth and kinship, and of knighthood (*militia,* or of *potentia*), which is force in action attested by a more individualised reputation. On the question of *nomen* and *cognomen,* see Dominique Barthélemy, "Le système anthroponymique en Vendômois (Xe–XIIIe siècle)," in *Genèse médiévale de l'anthroponymie moderne,* ed. Monique Bourin, 2 vols. in 3 parts, Publications de l'Université de Tours (Tours, 1989–92), 1:36–37.

16. Jane Martindale, "The French aristocracy in the early Middle Ages: a reappraisal," *Past & Present,* no. 75 (1977), 5–45 (at p. 16).

17. In any case there was no break with the system of values inherited from Carolingian times. In this sense, Karl F. Werner, "Du nouveau sur un vieux thème: les origines de la *noblesse* et de la *chevalerie,*" *Comptes-rendus de l'Académie des Inscriptions et Belles Lettres,* (1985), 186–200, although this writer, at the other extreme from Cheyette and Geary, exaggerates the majesty and regularity of the state and of public order in the early Middle Ages!

18. See the fine account of the lordship of L'Ile-Bouchard toward 1060, *TV,* no. 399: there we see one "Burchardus autem puer, supradicti Hugonis filius jam adultus, quem comes Tetbaldus militaribus armis ornaverat" who thereupon "castellum suum sicut justus heres . . . recuperavit." Other examples in my "Note sur l'adoubement dans la France des XIe et XIIe siècles," *Les ages de la vie au Moyen Age,* ed. Henri Dubois and Michel Zink (Paris, 1992), pp. 107–17. It was not quite enough to be noble to hold an *honor,* one needed some minimum of

Mâconnais,[19] there was only one class, at once noble and knightly.

It had, even so, its different levels. The "system" shown by our sources seems as follows: the nobility of *barones* gleams with special luster,[20] while in the lower levels the light flickers unsteadily. One of this sort will have a "noble funeral,"[21] another will figure in a group of witnesses collectively termed *nobiles,* something of lesser import than an individual title. As for knighthood, one need only read the chroniclers to see that, just as with *puissance,* it presents two or three distinct levels.[22] From top to bottom, a scaling of nobility and knighthood is what we observe, and what contemporaries could manipulate; but the symbolic stakes are the same at all levels. Variable in its forms, the hierarchy is intangible in its principle. One of the most commonly employed pairs of opposition is that of *barones/vavassores.*

The Distinction Between Barons and Vavassors

This distinction turns up most commonly and pertinently in the Loir region, although it is hard to find it justified as a differentiation of feudal ranks or types of service. At Château-du-Loir in the twelfth century, twelve barons and twenty vavassors owed two months of ward.[23] At Vendôme records of La Trinité for the period of "notices" (about 1060–1230) reserve the term "baron" for members of certain families: those happy few who are likewise referred to individually as "noble." What is there concretely to explain the distinction?

(1) Richer and more powerful than the others, the baronial families do not all possess castellan lordships (even if a "new" castle is attributed only to one of this group).[24] In any case, barony is itself a relative notion: castellan lords were barons of Anjou and some of their vassals were barons of

---

proofs: see Bernard Bachrach, "Enforcement of the *Forma fidelitatis:* the techniques used by Fulk Nerra, Count of the Angevins (987–1040)," *Speculum* 59 (1984), 796–819.

19. Georges Duby, "Lignage, noblesse et chevalerie au XIIe siècle dans la région mâconnaise: une révision," *Hommes et structures du moyen âge: recueil d'articles* (Paris, 1973), pp. 395–422.

20. Not caste-like, but with prestige particular to each family, whence the use of comparatives (*nobilior*) and superlatives (*nobilissimus*). It would be wrong to see in these a system of defense by "old" nobles against "new" ones, for it merely refers to normal practice, to a "pecking order" in a society in open and permanent competition.

21. E.g., *MV,* no. 102; *TV,* no. 374.

22. Some examples in Martindale, "French Aristocracy," p. 14.

23. *Cartulaire de Château-du-Loir,* ed. Eugène Vallée, Archives Historiques du Maine 6 (Le Mans, 1905), nos. 71, 72.

24. This is so, in the Vendômois, of the *castrum* of Lisle (first half of the twelfth century). This point has been well addressed, for other regions, by Jean Richard, "Châteaux, châtelains et vassaux," pp. 437–49, and by Theodore Evergates, *Feudal Society,* pp. 102–6.

the castellanies of which they themselves were masters.[25] What makes the baron is the *curia,* but since that was hardly a rigid or abstract institution, the baron had to accomplish socially distinguishing work to maintain and confirm his rank.[26] Moreover, being knight baron in several castellanies, often under different names, was an even better advantage for maintaining rank.

(2) No less important was to have a fief that was an honor. This word, by no means extraordinary nor extra-feudal, was connected in usage with the practice of associating the eldest son with his living father, the Capetian practice,[27] and so to an effort clearly to favor the indivisibility of the barony. So a practice more distinctly *lignagère* here distinguishes the holder of an *honor* just as was true, in the Mâconnais, of the castellan lord.[28]

(3) Finally, it seems that only barons exercised in their lands, without necessarily having a castle, the four cases of high justice, or as one might better say before the thirteenth century, reserved justice.[29]

(4) On the other hand, we must give up Jean Richard's view that all who bore sobriquets were castral knights, and thus vavassors.[30] Between barons and vavassors, the monks who wrote letters or charters established a curious differentiation. Is the count of Vendôme pillaging la Trinité's lands in the Gâtine? He is accompanied by *vavassores.*[31] However, when he goes to do penance or make concessions in the abbey, he is said to be in the company of *barones,* following their counsel.[32] They hastily charge the

25. At Vendôme, the *barones pagi* were grouped, *TV,* no. 143; at Château-Renault the *barones* of the castle, *MV,* no. 172. In Picardy we find the term *pares,* fully synonymous with *barones:* cf. P. Feuchère, "Pairs de principauté et pairs de château," *Revue Belge de Philologie et d'Histoire* 31 (1953), 973ff., and Barthélemy, *Les deux âges,* pp. 153–57.

26. This remark follows from the good studies of Stephen White, cited above, note 8. Just as the relations of kinship had to be maintained and chosen with care, so the solidarities that defined the baronage required constant vigilance.

27. This is clear in three cases of Vendôme and Anjou that we have encountered: *TV,* nos. 51, 298, and especially, for the count of Vendôme, *Cartulaire de Marmoutier pour le Dunois,* ed. Emile Mabille (Châteaudun: Sociéte-Dunoise 1874), no. 163. Thus the Capetian practice finely described by Andrew W. Lewis, *Royal Succession in Capetian France. Studies on Familial Order and the State* (Cambridge, MA, 1981) was fully consistent with common baronial practice.

28. Georges Duby argues indeed that familial policies advantageous to the eldest or non-division between relations were first adopted by the *domini,* "Lignage, noblesse et chevalerie," p. 420.

29. The model of A.C.F. Koch, "L'origine de la haute et moyenne justice dans l'Ouest et le Nord de la France," *Revue d'Histoire du Droit / Tijdschrift voor Rechtsgeschiedenis* 21 (1953), 420–58, works perfectly in the Vendômois; from this writer we may borrow the expression "reserved justice" for the "four great misdeeds."

30. Richard, "Châteaux, châtelains et vassaux," 444.

31. So wrote Abbot Geoffroi de Vendôme in a letter, *PL* 157:104.

32. *TV,* nos. 247, 320, 328, 400.

vavassores with all the sins of knighthood, while too easily absolving a baronial group with which the monks have deep and abiding ties. The image here, toward 1100, is rather different from that found in the later twelfth century in courtly literature, where we encounter the "good vavassors" contrasted with "bad seneschals."[33] Could it be that the rank of vavassor acquired a new legitimacy during the twelfth century? An act of the abbey of Ronceray of Angers suggests that it did.[34] But the romances and especially the customals persist in differentiating between *barons* and *vavasseurs*.

No passive and objective witness to "society" is to be found in the social vocabulary; what it presents, on the contrary, is a field of rivalries. Certain words serve to link the two strata of aristocracy symbolically[35]: thus "knight" (*chevalier*) goes with *courtoisie*. On the other hand, certain oppositions, like baron/vavassor, preserve a distinction in variable concrete situations. As for "noble," a rather rare term found in Latin texts, it can serve either to associate or to exclude. After 1250 everywhere in France, knighthood came to be reserved to members of the baronial class, with some exceptions.

But this final stage does not concern us here. There is plenty to occupy us regarding the evolution, real or apparent, in the twelfth century.

33. B. Woledge, "Bons vavasseurs et mauvais sénéchaux," in *Mélanges offerts à Rita Lejeune,* 2 vols. (Gembloux, 1969), 2:1263–77. Undoubtedly, courtly literature stresses the quality of undifferentiated nobility, associating its strata, despite sometimes contradictory interests, from the angle of ideology. This should not oblige us, however, to espouse the views and terms of Erich Köhler, who at times maintains the irresistible ascent of the lower stratum ("Observations historiques et sociologiques sur la poésie de troubadours," *Cahiers de Civilisation Médiévale* 7 [1964], 27–51), sometimes the end of knighthood in general (*Ideal und Wirklichkeit in der höfischen Epik,* 2d ed. [Tübingen, 1970]; tr. *L'aventure chevaleresque* [Paris, 1974]). In reality, there need not be a direct relation between the readings of social history and the fortunes or misfortunes of literary fashions. Quite simply, the dissatisfaction of poor knights looks like a structural fact of feudal society; every lord was at odds with his vassals over his inability to give from his obligation of largesse all they might wish. The problem became increasingly acute in the courtly societies of princes and great barons in the twelfth century. The *romans* suggest some hierarchical differentiation between barons and vavassors, without insisting on a clear contrast: e.g., *La Queste del Saint Graal,* ed. A. Pauphilet (Paris, 1923), speaks of "li baron et li chevalier" (p. 25), then of "les chevaliers et les vavasors" (p. 49); *chevalier* would seem here the common denominator between two different dignities. But above all, the vavassor was a knight of ripe age, settled, and committed to give just counsel, while the barons were knights in the associative exercise of noble power around a king, a peerage. So the opposition of the terms loses pertinence; both bear the meaning of legitimacy.

34. *Archives d'Anjou,* ed. Paul Marchegay, 3 vols. (Angers, 1843–54), 3, nos. 47 (before 1080) and 344 (c. 1110) for the identity of baronage and nobility in feudal courts; cf. also no. 31 (1160), but at that moment (no. 184, c. 1154) Count Geoffroi Plantagenêt had also a *curia* composed of "legales vavassores" (Brissac).

35. On this point one can only cite Georges Duby's admirable words of introduction to "La diffusion du titre chevaleresque sur le versant méridional de la Chrétienté latine," in *La noblesse au Moyen Age,* ed. Philippe Contamine (Paris, 1976), pp. 39–41.

Evolution to 1230: Two Ages of Castellan Elites?

Renewed Elites?

Let us borrow from Pareto the term "renewal" of elites. Philip Jones applied the model fairly precisely to Italian cities in the thirteenth century. In feudal France, the expression alone may be useful, although for lack of a true dynamic of opposition, the social drama, if there is such, takes other forms.

For baronial lineages the problem was how not to degenerate in face of pressures to give to churches.[36] In this milieu, cadets, bastards, and, in general, descendants through women were at risk of losing status. They were much more numerous than new castles available to them.

What about the vavassors? Newcomers are often mentioned, risen from the shadows or from ministerial service (as in the Empire). And it is true that with respect to *famuli,* mayors, and provosts of churches—these would be the French colleagues of the German *ministeriales,* although less definite in status—we often find them in process of social ascent.[37] From the middle of the eleventh century, the monks of Marmoutier were alarmed by the arrogance of Ascelin, son of Ohelme, who held a mayorship in the Dunois. There had already been trouble with his father before his marriage with a free woman (perhaps of a knightly family?) gave him the support of a considerable kindred. The new couple was given the choice between submitting, thereby recognizing their servitude to Marmoutier for their descendants as for themselves, or giving up their charge.[38] The same thing happened several times in the middle of the twelfth century; perhaps it was by then a well tested scenario.

Although we can be sure that the situation of *famuli* was not unique to churches for which we have documentation, we know little of the relations of castellan lords with their *vicarii.* But it looks as if many of the self-surrenders of the eleventh century, perhaps the majority of those reported by the celebrated *Liber de servis* of Marmoutier,[39] may be viewed as

36. Whatever the political and ideological profit of noble gifts to churches, or the symbolic capital they improved, I now find it harder to justify them than I did in 1984 (*Les deux âges,* pp. 129–36). The guilty consciences of barons caused them to lose something, really to waste their riches and power. For reaction in this sense, tending to regard religious facts as religious, see Constance Bouchard, *Sword, Miter, and Cloister. Nobility and the Church in Burgundy, 980–1198* (Ithaca NY 1987).

37. This problematic was introduced for France by Marc Bloch, "Un problème d'histoire comparée: la ministérialité en France et en Allemagne" (1928), reprinted in *Mélanges historiques,* 2 vols. (Paris, 1963) 1:503–28.

38. *Cartulaire de Marmoutier pour le Dunois,* no. 17.

39. *Le Livre des serfs de Marmoutier,* ed. A. Salmon and C. de Grandmaison, Publications de la Société archéologique de Touraine 16 (Tours, 1864).

the consequence of discipline meted out to notable *famuli* like Ascelin son of Ohelme. But what about their "social origin"? For a hard-up lineage of vavassors, would not a spell in *familia* be a useful means of recovering?[40] "They stoop to conquer." Moreover, as in many conflicts of the eleventh century, the one which opposed Ascelin to his lords, the monks of Marmoutier, sought chiefly to redefine a relationship; yet even so a rupture was envisaged as possible. In this case, the *famulus* with his relations went away and changed his surname; in a word, he escapes us. Chance alone enabled us to find out that, at the end of the twelfth century, the squire of Chavigny, in the Soissonais, was the son of a provost of the castle of Coucy.[41]

So for us the social and genealogical relations between knights of vavassoral status and the ranking *famuli* who figure as witnesses to charters remain mysterious. There must have been some mobility of persons and lineages, but without change in the social structure, without troubling the equilibrium between "barons" and "vavassors," and by a dynamic in which good and loyal service, or deception, must have played a greater role than the conflict dear to the nineteenth century and to Pareto. The criticisms Constance Bouchard made of K. F. Werner's method of utilising *Leitnamen*,[42] if we accept them, hardly affect other considerations. One never finds absolutely *homines novi*, always complex cases.

It is equally important to consider the arguments for the ascent of "knighthood" (our vavassors) opposed to "nobility" (our baronage) when such arguments depend on waves of new names and hereditary surnames from 1070 to 1130. In the Vendômois, where the later eleventh century is well documented, one finds the ancestors of "Roupenon" and of "Fromond Turpin" among the better endowed *milites*; these eponyms of baronial lineages (in Vendôme, that is, for all baronage is relative) were hardly upstarts such as might have been thrown up by unprecedented "seigneurial violence."[43] And, to repeat, the sobriquet does not refer exclusively to vavassors or *famuli* brought up and residing in the castellan's entourage.

40. For André Debord, speaking of the eleventh and twelfth centuries, "même l'ascension réelle de certains ministériaux . . . ne va pas au-delà de la concrétisation de leur situation sociale de fait," *La société laïque dans les pays de la Charente, Xe–XIIe siècles* (Paris, 1984), p. 253.

41. Barthélemy, *Les deux âges*, p. 402.

42. Constance Bouchard, "The Origins of the French Nobility: A Reassessment," *AHR* 86 (1981), 501–32.

43. This theme of seigneurial violence unleashed in the eleventh century, in relation to a hypothetical "shock" created by castellan lordship, seems to me to have been exaggerated by French historians in the past twenty years. See the lucid critique by Alain Guerreau, "Lournand au Xe siècle: histoire et fiction," *Le Moyen Age* 96 (1990), 536. The year 1000 was probably not a turning-point everywhere. More than ten years have passed since Georges Duby professed to prefer the expression "révélation féodale" to that of "révolution."

Displaced Elites?

In Burgundy as in Picardy,[44] it has been possible to see that in the later twelfth century knights often cease to be designated "of such a castle" and become "of such a village" or "hamlet." This denomination by village or hamlet was uncommon toward 1100; it became the rule after 1200, driving out the former practice and coexisting only with a variety of sobriquets and of *nomina paterna*. The same phenomenon is found in the history of lineage in the Vendômois. The leading family "of Vendôme" became that of the lords "du Bouchet" (in Crucheray) after 1160; their cousins "de la Tour" (the tower of Vendôme, which they probably guarded) became "de Lisle" (from the name of a *Wasserburg* then developed in a little isle of the Loir); as for the descendants of Joscelin *de rua vassalorum* (the lower court of the castle, in which figured houses of the *milites castri*), we find them under the names "d'Azé" and "de la Jousselinière."

But was that not simply a consequence of changed patterns of naming? Was the displacement of elites quite as illusory and uncertain as their renewal? Here, in fact, we must introduce some nuances to the "models" of Rougemont and Noyers (Burgundy) and Coucy (Picardy).

(1) In the eleventh century, one and the same man might be designated diversely.[45] To be "from Vendôme," especially vis à vis strangers in the county,[46] did not mean that one belonged to the castle entourage, but only that one had property in the castellany on that account and some regular place in the *curia*. Several *milites* already had virtual local lordships: Hugh, son of Archembaud of Vendôme, was *dominus* at Courtiras.[47] In several cases, the transition to the denomination "of such village" or "of such hamlet" was thus a purely formal evolution.[48] Even so, for several lineages, the change of name corresponded to the development of sites on the edge of woodland (La Jousselinière) or between two parishes (Le Bouchet).[49]

(2) A second adjustment to the model is more important. We should not fall into the trap of imagining a strongly allodial regime of nobility

44. Jean Richard and Dominique Barthélemy, as cited in notes 2 and 6.

45. It seems important, in fact, to distinguish between *désignation* and *dénomination*, as I have done in "Le système anthroponymique," p. 37.

46. This is evident in the *Livre des serfs* of Marmoutier. There the *dénommé* "Hamelin son of Avesgaud" is *désigné* as being "Hamelin of Vendôme" (no. 109).

47. *MV,* no. 21. This had to do with a noble provost, from the third baronial family of Vendôme with the "du Bouchet" and "de Lisle."

48. We glimpsed this at Coucy: Barthélemy, *Les deux âges,* p. 229.

49. The development of the latter site possibly followed the loss of rights on the *ecclesia* of Crucheray. The Gregorian demand for "restitution" of churches held by the laity encouraged local dominations to reorganize around borderline sites, where tallage became the weapon of lordly demand.

to begin with, in an anti-feudal sense, certainly not for the local barons. "Allod" in the eleventh century meant local lordship, lordship of command, while by no means excluding tenure in "benefice" from the count of Vendôme. The charters before 1060 refer mostly to "allods," but those who give them to churches and who bear no title should not be taken for a petty peasantry remolded by a seigneurial reaction;[50] they were, on the contrary, rural elites, implicitly noble, masters of the land, ones for whom the castle meant nothing more than a place of meeting among peers, where essentially villagist dominations were realized.[51] Already thoroughly feudal, knighthood in the twelfth century could hardly become more so! Nevertheless, the relations of lord and castellan vassals underwent a gradual evolution. The feudal aid was increasingly commuted into money, replacing active service in the host and in courts.

These nuances hardly abolish the Burgundian-Picard model, but they oblige us to reconsider the extent of mutation in the second half of the twelfth century. The seigneurial order reproduced itself in adapting to transformations of the relation between town and country. Things changed for knighthood in two ways:

(1) In the village or hamlet, local lordship in the thirteenth century was the child of that of the eleventh, although reinforced in the Vendômois, in three respects. First an agricultural domain (*réserve*) was constituted or reconstituted called the *mestairie* or *gaignerie,* and often exploited by means of farming or sharecropping. Next, justice over larceny became a case for vavassors, recognized as such, before 1273, in the *Usages de Touraine-Anjou;*[52] only the other three cases of high justice remained a baronial monopoly.[53] Finally, ditched lodgings now formed, like the strong houses of Burgundy, the symbolic seat of local lordships.[54] The diffusion of the seigneurial title in records of the thirteenth century closely followed that of the denomination "of such village" or "of such hamlet"; they were two

50. The myth of "petits alleutiers" is often associated with that of cataclysm (denounced above, note 43); see to the contrary, C. Duhamel-Amado, "L'alleu paysan a-t-il existé en France méridionale autour de l'an Mil?" *La France de l'an Mil,* ed. Robert Delort (Paris, 1990), pp. 142–61.

51. Therefore it is not necessary to suppose that castellan lordship, appearing or revealed in the eleventh century, provoked a major rupture. Did not the cities and centers of *pagi,* prior to the tenth century, have the same function of articulation?

52. These *Usages* form the first book of the *Etablissements de Saint Louis,* ed. Paul Viollet, 4 vols. (Paris, 1881–86). On the vavassor's justice, see 2:59–64; the "baron" 's control and view, as lord of the castellany and *chief seignor,* are important.

53. *Etablissements* 2, 37–38. On high justice, see Koch, "L'origine."

54. A notable article for the history of aristocratic residences is J.-M. Pesez and F. Piponnier, "Les maisons-fortes bourguignonnes," in *Château-Gaillard* 5 (Caen, 1972), 143–64.

expressions of the same phenomenon, two different revelations, no doubt, but not without meaning. The time of the small farm, the gallows, and the *salle* was at hand.

(2) The center of the castellany was henceforth a town (*ville*) rather than a castle. At Vendôme as at Noyers-sur-Serein (Bourgogne), the street where the houses of the *milites castri* were located disappeared toward 1200.[55] No noble vavassor was called "of Vendôme" any more; those bearing this surname belonged either to the count's family or to the common inhabitants of the place. But can one say precisely that a new elite emerged from the local population?

With or without commune or "institution of peace," local patriciates began to prosper ever more widely in the time of Philip Augustus. Jean Richard saw in them the integration of certain knights with capital;[56] a case of the same order is that of the Lancelin in Montoire, Lavardin, and Trôo, three towns of the Bas-Vendômois. But the influence and prestige of these rich townsmen did not upset the old social hierarchy. Nobles and knights, barons as well as vavassors of the countryside, retained rentals and even banal rights in the town, but they seem to have been slow to allow the ennobled townsmen to acquire seigneurial land outside the near suburban space of Vendôme. They remained an elite of the castellany, for whom, after 1230, the titles of "sire" (of the village) and of "squire" compensated for the weakening of knighthood.

* * *

When a romance of the 1220s evoked the deliverance of the "virgins' castle," it was this elite of the castellany that reestablished order; the command was given to "les chevaliers et les vavasors de ci entor, car ils tiennent lor fiez de cest chastel."[57] We do not know where they reside, but it was for them to maintain and reform the customs. Let us not jump to the conclusion that this was a knightly literature devised to conceal, for the moral comfort of its public, the power and novel force of the "bourgeoisie."[58]

55. See the information gathered by Gabriel Fournier, *Le château dans la France médiévale: essai de sociologie monumentale* (Paris, 1978), pp. 333–37.

56. Richard, "Châteaux, châtelains et vassaux," p. 446.

57. *La Queste del Saint Graal*, p. 49: "et lor fetes jurer, a aux et a toz cels de ceanz, que ja mes ne maintendront cest costume." In the romances of Chrétien de Troyes, the vavassors of good counsel live either in the castle or in the open country.

58. For a good example of a historian's use of literature, see J. W. Baldwin, "Jean Renart et le tournoi de Saint-Trond: une conjonction de l'histoire et de la littérature," *Annales E.S.C.* 95 (1990), 565–88.

The charters of customs in the Ile-de-France already point to this collegiality of noble legislative power around 1200.[59] Would the situation of the eleventh century have been so different? There were already authentic castral garrisons, but the castle had not yet become the locus of articulation of localised seigneurial powers beneath the castellans.

So a study of the Vendômois confirms what Jean Richard and I had found in other regions while introducing some adjustments to our model. Certainly the descent of the castral knights toward the countryside during the twelfth century is a "notably remarkable fact."[60] But more than a "rupture" of the castellany, it marked an adjustment of a deeply ingrained system of noble and knightly lordship; rather than a major "mutation" it signified a simple turning of feudal history. Must medieval France explode once a century? On the contrary, what is striking about the seigneurial order is its aptitude to reproduce itself down to the thirteenth century, sometimes simply, sometimes by enlargement; this was not at all a "cold society" of the sort studied by ethnologists, but very much a warm one.

And undoubtedly it warmed up progressively in the twelfth and thirteenth centuries! Social mobility tended to increase, even if not to the point of veritable "social change." After 1230 the nobility underwent the partial and periodic renewal of its members while maintaining the principles of its social superiority. In this process of warming, the changes of the grand twelfth century, in the broad sense of this conference (1050–1225), should neither be exaggerated nor underestimated.[61]

59. See Brigitte Bedos, "Innovation ou adaptation, conflit ou conjonction d'intérêts? La charte de franchises de Montmorency," *BEC* 137 (1979), 5–17; see also my remarks, *Les deux âges*, pp. 335–6. See further Brigitte Bedos, *La châtellenie de Montmorency, des origines à 1368* (Pontoise, 1980).

60. Richard, "Châteaux, châtelains et vassaux," p. 446.

61. This study was written late in 1991. Since then my reflection on the subject of knighthood has only deepened. A more complete refutation of mutationist arguments about *milites* may be found in "Note sur le titre chevaleresque, en France au XIe siècle," *Journal des Savants* (1994), 101–34; and a more constructive perspective in "Qu'est-ce que la chevalerie, en France aux Xe et XIe siècles?" *Revue Historique* 290 (1994), 15–74.

Georges Duby

4. Women and Power

The word "power" (*pouvoir*) is vague in French. Let it be clear that I shall not be speaking of all kinds of power, but only of that expressed by the Latin term *potestas* in records of the period we have chosen to study. That is, the power to command and to punish. My question is this: in what measure did women share in this power?

It is a difficult problem. I have my own idea about it. Some of our medievalist colleagues do not agree with me; often I found myself in debate with K. F. Werner, formerly Director of the German Historical Institute of Paris, who did me the honor of attending my seminar. Our disagreement arose partly from the fact that Werner insisted more than I on the letter of the documents, and I more than he on mental representations, but also because Werner tended to think primarily of imperial lands while I had the kingdom of France chiefly in view. Look at the abbesses of the great German monasteries, Werner would say: they are imperial princes, who exercise *potestas* fully. Yes (I would say), but in France feminine monasticism was much less developed. Yes, but in France (and the same is true in Germany) abbesses wielded *potestas* by means of a substitute, an *advocatus*. Moreover, the monastic world was a world apart where the position of women in particular, brides of Christ, was very singular. Hence a further limitation. Having already said that I shall not speak of all powers, I add now that I shall not speak of all women. I shall consider women who remained in the world, married women, wives of one with power, of a *dominus*. I shall speak of *dominae*, of "dames." My question becomes a little more precise: to what extent and in what ways did ladies, the wives of the aristocracy, in northern France from 1050 to 1235 take part in the power of command and of punishment?

In seeking to answer this question, I rely mainly on two types of documents: the admonitions of men of the church to women, and more especially on what remains of the genealogical literature, that genre which flourished so vigorously in this region of Christendom, notably in the second half of the twelfth century. My intention is to examine behavior as really lived. Yet I must begin with a word about the rules and mental representations that determined this behavior, that imposed conduct on people, the conduct of men and women of this social milieu.

* * *

The rules are those imposed by custom, the unwritten law; they appear with less precision in northern France than in the southern regions. They are nonetheless clear enough for us to discern the principal elements. In northern France, by contrast with the Empire, *potestas* in the twelfth century was fully incorporated in the patrimony. "Honors" had long since ceased to be conferred by the king or his agent; they were transmitted by inheritance. But this incorporation of the public power to command and punish was accompanied by a transformation of the structures of kinship. On a royal model the families possessed of this power were organised in lineages, which is to say that the rules of succession were based on the primacy of boys over girls and of the elders over younger sons. Normally, sons prevailed over their sisters and inherited the *potestas*. But if it happened that there were no sons, it was a woman, the eldest of the girls, who inherited. This is an important point.

Important because, by virtue of this fact, the daughters of the *dominus* had great value: their right on the inheritance. They were coveted. They represented, in the hands of the men on whom they depended—their father who had begotten them; their father's heir, their brother; or the partners in their father's power, the "barons," the "knights of the castle" which was the seat of the *potestas,* of the "honor"—a desirable and desired property which these men traded in ceding these women (with their consent, say the texts of the later twelfth century, for on this point the requirements of the church had triumphed) in marriage. *Cum ea,* these texts also say, "with this woman," the husband received the rights she held: that is, with the other girls, a dowry consisting of that part of the familial fortune reserved for the women. But the primary right was their claim to the *dominium,* to the lordship. If the males who blocked them from possession of this *dominium* happened to disappear, or if such a condition were already fulfilled, and if she chanced to be an orphan without a brother, then the husband gathered up with her the power of which she was the legitimate holder.

So much for the law, the juridical rules. Let us now consider the mental representations, taking account of two models which then impressed themselves on everyone. First, a general model. According to the will of the Creator, the universe was a hierarchy, a providential scale of beings in which the feminine was subordinated to the masculine. All the men whose thought we can know were convinced that woman by nature is weak, that she is dangerous (and this idea found justification in the text of Genesis) and that she must therefore be subjected to the man. By her marriage the woman passed from submission to the men of her house to that of her husband, who became her *dominus* and before whom the ritual of marriage obliged her to prostrate herself. The writings of moralists addressed to women all recalled to them this duty of submission. For example, Anselm of Canterbury enjoined them "to obey their husband in all subjection and all love"[1]; and Jacques de Vitry, in a sermon to married couples early in the thirteenth century, repeated the injunction, explaining that women owe such obedience because, being *vagae*, *lascivae*, if left to themselves they would slide toward evil. Jacques also elaborated on the complaints of husbands who judged their partners indocile: if in the conjugal couple the wife assumes command, the world is in disorder and all is upset.[2]

The other model was borrowed from the royalist ideology as forged in the Carolingian period and appropriated by the aristocracy in that dispersion of regalian attributes we speak of as feudalization. In the ninth century the clergy had described the perfect order of the royal household. In the center was the sovereign, but at his side a woman, his own. She was adorned with the king's title, but in the feminine form, *regina*; she was his associate, *consors*. Although assuredly inferior to him, she dominated the rest of the household. Deputed to the "economy," in the etymological sense of this term, she had the task of maintaining domestic life in good order and, in particular, of supervising its reserves of wealth. Finally and above all, whatever power she enjoyed was bound to the obligation that was hers only, the obligation of maternity. It was as *mater regis*, mother of the future king and of all his progeny to the end of time, that she was celebrated.

This model left its mark first on the princely houses, then on those of all holders of *potestas*. In the twelfth century a man, himself alone, headed these houses, as in the royal house. Beside him a woman, herself alone, his wife. For in these houses there was only one conjugal bed, only one place of licit, legitimate, manifest copulation. When the present master's mother, widow of the former master, was still living, she did not live there as a rule.

1. *PL* 159; 190.
2. Sermon 66 ("*ad conjugatos*"), BM, Cambrai, MS 534.

She was driven out. Or else she remarried, given over to another man, as was for example the widow of King Henry I, or Yolande, widow of Count Baldwin III of Hainaut.[3] Or else, retired in the women's monastery annexed to the house, like Emma, widow of Count Manassé of Guines,[4] she was thereby transported into that other society where the women were brides of Christ, who, as I have said, are not of concern to me here. She could even, at the end of the twelfth century, be installed on her own dower, like the widow of the count of Flanders, Philip of Alsace.[5] It is partly for this reason that the dower existed, to liberate the new lord's house from the presence of his mother, so that he would have by him only his wife.

This wife bore her husband's title, in the feminine: *comitissa, castellana,* or simply *domina*. She is associated with him, *consors*; and in the solemnities, in the ceremonial of political power, her husband showed her off at his side bespangled in the emblems of his glory, seated by him in the hall, sometimes even in the private part of the dwelling, in the chamber. A charter of the abbey of Andres[6] shows a feudal tenant of the count Manassé of Guines coming in 1117 to ask his approval of the donation he had just made from his fief to the monastery. Which the count did, says the charter, with the countess Emma, "the two of them seated on their bed." The bed: it was like a conjugal throne, and this image evidently corresponds to that carved in the porches of cathedrals half a century later, showing Christ associating his Mother, seated beside him, in his power.

It was the bed of childbirth. For the married woman, the countess or the lady, like the queen, held the power of her womb, that womb which the holder of *potestas* came to fertilize in the chamber so as to assure the dynasty's future. Whence the wife's prestige. She was held in the domestic memory for that, for having given birth to the master. The genealogical literature I have employed retained the names of wives going back to the most distant past; these were all the names of mothers, the mothers of successive lords. Let me add that this literature places at the mythical origin of the lineage the representation of a woman, a womb, that is; a matrix whence all the glory, all the *potestas,* the power of the dynasty has issued.

So there is a feminine presence in the foundation myths, symbolic of the role of women in building political power. But it is also, in the very

3. *La chronique de Gislebert de Mons,* ed. Léon Vanderkindere (Brussels, 1904), c. 32, pp. 57–58; ed. W. Arndt, *MGH SS* 21 (Berlin, 1869): 507.

4. Lambert of Ardres, *Historia comitum Ghisnensium,* ed. Ioh. Heller, *MGH SS* 24 (Hanover, 1879), c. 51 (p. 586).

5. Lambert, c. 153 (p. 641).

6. *Willelmi chronica Andrensis,* ed. Ioh. Heller, *MGH SS* 24: 693.

narration of the familial destiny, proof that from generation to generation the splendor and wealth of the lineage have been enriched by the contributions of grandmothers, one by one, the wives won by successive lords who thereby procured for their progeny blood often better than their own, more noble, and sometimes, when these ladies chanced to inherit an honor, an enormous increment in prestige. In these ways the *domina* was established in her position of distinction, via genealogical memory when she had passed from this world, and in the exhibitions of power while she was living.

I say exhibition advisedly, for it was a matter of façade, of what one should show, a dramatization of what the documents first tell the historian, of a demonstration the historian can accept. But the historian cannot stop there. He must try to discover, under this blanket, under this representation, the reality. Here let me repeat my question: to what extent was the lady really a partner in power? Properly to answer we must distinguish between the *res publica* and the *res familiaris,* between what pertains to the public sphere and what to the private.

* * *

By nature, because she was a woman, the woman could not exercise public power. She was incapable of exercising it. For Léopold Genicot, it was a matter of law, the notion of "incapacity" being, indeed, a juridical notion, although an abstract one. But what abstract juridical notions could there have been in northern France in the twelfth century? I prefer to evoke a concrete image, a symbolic object, the better to enter into the thought of the men of whom I speak, to look at the world with their eyes. This object is the sword. *Potestas,* the power to command and to punish, the duty of preserving peace and justice, was exercised by the sword such as one solemnly entrusted to the lord's son when he came to power and held unsheathed before him when he fulfilled his function.

A woman could not take sword in hand. It is true that some chronicles refer to women who took up arms in defense of the rights of their husbands or sons. But this seemed abnormal, even scandalous. Consider how the poets Wace and Benoît de Sainte-Maure, in transposing the narration of Guillaume de Jumièges for Henry Plantagenet, related the courage of the *pugnatrices* of Coutances who defended the city against the English: they spoke of these women as "savages," "disheveled"; indecent, that is, disrespectful of customs requiring that a virtuous woman not show her hair in public. They were said to be like "delinquent women," like prostitutes.[7] Normally the woman did not brandish the sword. A masculine arm was required to do so for her, in her name. If she possessed power by birth it was for a man, when she was lady to her husband, to exercise it for her, in her name and in that of the children she had carried in her womb; him to whom she had transmitted this power with her blood while these children were too young to wield this power themselves.

When the husband took possession of his wife's body, her part of the power came into his hands. So it was that when Baldwin, son of the count of Flanders, married Richilde, widow of the count of Hainaut, he took the *comitatus cum ea,* together with her, and exercised the comital power henceforth *per eam,* for her. So at least in principle. In reality, this husband was not entirely free in the exercise of his wife's power, and all the less free when this power was great. He had to reckon with the male relations of this woman who watched over her, who often begrudged him who had grasped this power with her, who waited on her husband's early death, who sometimes killed him, and who were not above pressing on him, alive, for compensation of one sort or another. Thus the brothers-in-law, the lady's brothers, were generally the prime enemies of the husband. This said, the fact remains that it was he who wielded his wife's power, not she. She was merely at his side when he exercised it. She had to be there, in token of adhesion, of assent, of association.

Yet it could happen accidentally, when she was *desolata,* when her husband was not there, that the lady would have to exercise these rights herself, or by means of an agent, like abbesses, whose husband likewise was absent. Together with her own rights, she exercised her husband's powers by virtue of *consortium*. This happened temporarily when the husband was off on a distant expedition. The wife of Thierry of Alsace, count of Flanders, acted in this way when he was in the Holy Land: she received the homages in his place.[8] It happened more durably in widowhood.

As for the widow's power, three possibilities presented themselves.

(1) She had no son. In that case she was returned by her husband's collaterals to her father's house with her share of the inheritance; with regard to the dower they negotiated, discussed, came to agreement. She was entitled to keep it. Generally, they compromised. Restored to her family,

7. *Le roman de Rou,* ed. A. J. Holden, 3 vols. (Paris, 1970–73), v. 1175.
8. Lambert of Ardres, *Historia, MGH SS* 24, c. 137 (p. 630).

she fell under the power of men who remarried her or exercised such rights as she might have.

(2) The widow had sons of legal age. In that case, if suitably aged, she might decide to retire in the familial monastery which she had enriched from her dower. It was not that the abbatial function fell to her; the community had an abbess. But she was truly the patron: nothing was done without her. Or she might live on her dower, often considerable, especially when she had brought much upon marrying. Clémence, widow of Count Robert II of Flanders, was mistress of much of the county, of twelve castles held of the count.[9]

(3) Finally, if the sons were minors, the widow might remarry and her new husband exercise the *potestas* while the boys grew to majority: such was the case of Baldwin, count of Hainaut, by his wife Richilde, and of Arnoud of Ardres, count of Saint-Pol, by his wife.[10] Or else, living alone as a dowager or as a wife temporarily without husband, she would possess the power.

It seems worth pointing out that the authors of the texts I have used generally regarded such a situation, that of the *domina* effectively dominating, as abnormal. Indeed, such a woman figured in the genealogical literature as virtually a usurper. Since it is notably evocative of political power exercised by a woman, let me take the case of Richilde, countess of Hainaut, as seen by the anonymous author of the *Flandria generosa*[11] by Gislebert of Mons,[12] and by Lambert of Ardres[13] in his history of the counts of Guines. *Flandria generosa* eulogizes this lady at the end of her life, in her widowhood. She is praised for the marvelous penance she inflicted on herself in service of the poor and the lepers, bathing these sick people, sharing their bath, crucifying her body (and in this text of 1164 we can predate by a century those forms of charitable mortification of the flesh known to have developed in this region in the burst of feminine spirituality). But that was a purification rendered necessary by the malice exhibited by this woman in the course of her life. The fact is that Richilde, niece of Pope Leo IX and scion of a very high lineage, left a young widow by the count of Hainaut with a son and a daughter of minor age, held the county with

9. Lambert, c. 153 (p. 641).
10. Lambert, c. 114 (p. 615).
11. Ed. L. C. Bethmann, *MGH SS* 9 (Hanover, 1851): 320–23.
12. *Chronique,* ed. Vanderkindere, pp. 2, 4 (*MGH SS* 21: 490, 492).
13. Lambert of Ardres, *Historia, MGH SS* 24, c. 27 (p. 574).

the title of *comitissa tam jure dotalicii* (by reason of her dower) *quam de procuratione puerorum suorum* (as well as through tutelage, or nurture, of the children). Count Baldwin V of Flanders secured it for his eldest son Baldwin, who, as I have said, had the county "through her." The male relations of Richilde tried to prevent the marriage, alleging incest (Baldwin being *cognatus* of Richilde), but the pope authorized his niece to persist in conjugal life on condition of abstaining from carnal union with her husband. Richilde permitted her husband to disinherit the children of the first marriage (because she had disregarded the prohibition, had known this husband, had given birth by him to two boys, whom she favored over the first children, according to Gislebert of Mons). Here the malice began. Richilde, a bad mother, was, like all women, carried away by her *libido* and induced her second husband to sin. This second husband dead, the eldest of her sons, Arnoud, inherited Flanders from his father and in his name Richilde undertook to govern the county. But the paternal uncle survived: Robert the Frisian, brother of the late count. Despite his oaths, he reclaimed the *regnum paternum,* supported by King Philip I of France, his first cousin, and by his mother, dowager of Flanders and paternal aunt of the king of France, who, according to the *Flandria generosa,* preferred her second son Robert to the elder. Richilde resisted. As spouse she controlled reserves of money. She paid Philip I to change sides in her favor. War followed, then battle at Cassel, in 1071. Robert was the conquerer, Arnoud was killed. Robert became count in spite of his oaths and contrary to hereditary right, given the survival of a second nephew. And yet, in the *Flandria generosa,* it is Richilde who was called usurper. She had exceeded her womanly function in wishing to exercise the comital power. Robert had risen against her "tyranny." He had "liberated" Flanders, which had been crushed, humiliated, by the *muliebris insolentia,* by the *crudelitas mulieris* (says the text), by what came from a woman and was insufferable. When Robert tried to talk with her, to negotiate, he found this woman *rixosa* (quarrelsome), *callida* (sly). She was ready in her lust to sleep with a third husband to make an ally. Finally, she was carried away by madness, by the *furor* feminea. The intolerable thing, after all, was what was feminine: power was a man's affair.

Of this reprobation we find an echo in Lambert of Ardres. The taxes Richilde had wished to levy remained illegitimate in the collective memory: she had usurped the right to ask for financial aid. Lambert reported another incident, this too well remembered: at the Battle of Cassel, he says, "this woman prepared an enchanted powder which she threw by hand;

however, by God's will the wind changed and the powder spilled over her and her people."[14] When she took power into her hands, the woman did not use the sword as a man would, but rather witchcraft; she resorted to those perverse, demoniac weapons familiar to women, poisonous, all out of the sorcerer's bag. Lambert similarly dramatizes the dowager countess of Flanders, widow of Philip of Alsace. Like Richilde, she levied unwarranted taxes. Like Richilde, she inflicted an army on the country, *barbarico impetu*. Like Richilde, she was overcome thanks to Heaven and obliged to renounce her arrogance.[15]

Clerical moralists were also convinced that a woman exceeds her estate, the condition in which God gave her birth, when she exercises power. Let me refer to two such who sought in their letters to direct the conduct of princesses. First, Hildebert de Lavardin, bishop of Le Mans, addressing Countess Adèle of Blois, daughter of William the Conqueror.[16] It was a fawning letter. The bishop flatters the princess because he needs her; she holds power; her husband, Count Stephen, is on crusade. Exclaims Hildebert: what a marvel! You are alone and you assume the management of the *comitatus,* all the more difficult (*laboriosor*) in your husband's absence, and "you conduct your sex in glory." Why? Because Adèle is doubly victorious. First, over her femininity: although attractive, she remains chaste and wins thereby the esteem of "her man." Next, over the pride of those who rule, because, says the bishop, "you temper the power, you repress in yourself (no longer the woman, but) the countess insofar as you bring clemency to the exercise of power," and thus you win popular approval. These two victories, however, were miraculous. It was not nature that permitted them, but divine grace, which upset the order of things in Adèle's favor, giving her the strength to suppress normal tendencies: first, what is bad in the feminine by restraining the feminine in her, but also by retaining enough of the feminine to limit what there is of masculine badness in the exercise of power.

The other letter of direction comes from Saint Bernard of Clairvaux.[17] It was written to Melisende, Queen of Jerusalem, who was in the same situation as Adèle. Bernard has the queen speak, has her complain: "I am a woman, hence of weak body and unstable heart. [So that's what renders the woman incapable.] I have no counsel, I am not trained for all this." The

14. Lambert, c. 27 (p. 574).
15. Lambert, c. 153 (p. 641).
16. *PL* 171, c. 144–146.
17. *PL* 182, c. 557.

charge is *supra vires meas et supra scientia scientiam meam*. That is true, replies the abbot. It is not normal for a woman to wield *potestas*: if by lineage, by what she owes to her ancestors, she is endowed with power, it falls to the man to whom she has been entrusted to exercise it. When the man is gone, then the woman must overcome her nature, must be a man's equal. *In muliere exhibeas virum*. The strength she finds not in her own body, let her find it in her spirit, and by the grace of God.

Here is revealed the power of the ideological model. There is a division of tasks between the masculine and the feminine. To the former belongs command. To assume this command a woman must cease to be a woman, must take on masculinity, must change in gender. All of which is miraculous, requiring divine intervention. However, the feminine has its good side. Here is what Hildebert de Lavardin said: through softness and flexibility it can remove the harshness of power. This is what the spouse, the lady, can do without departing from her place beside the *dominus*, using the ascendance she has over him, no slight force.

This force flows from the valor she represents and which depends on her blood, the more so in case of real inequality in the couple, when the wife is of higher nobility than the husband. Arnoud, lord of the castle of Ardres in the county of Guines, had received from his patron, the count of Boulogne, the widow of the count of Saint-Pol. It was a superb gift from which he drew the greatest profit, not to the extent of despoiling this woman's children, but by seizing all the revenues of the "honor." Lambert of Ardres said of him: "in everything and everywhere he venerated this wondrous spouse, he did her reverence and service (*reverentia*, that is, what the lesser owes to the greater and what normally in marriage the wife owes to the husband), not as to his wife but as to his lady, and he obeyed her and humored her."[18] The power of the rich heiress over the husband to whom she brings wealth and power could even become unbearable. There is no lack of evidence of husbands burdened by a wife who always said no. Yet in the moralising literature, one hears more of another power, specifically feminine, *insidiosus*; of the power of seduction. Churchmen appealed to this power, renewing an old theme much stressed in late Antiquity when the barbarian princes were converted, a theme that found support in a passage from the Epistles of Paul. Letters of direction are full of references to this duty of women to incline their husbands to do good. So for example a letter of Anselm of Canterbury to the Countess Clémence of Flanders,

18. Lambert, *Historia*, c. 114 (p. 615).

urging her to influence her husband *opportune et importune.*[19] Most of these letters to the end of the twelfth century are placets, requests for favor. One addressed the lady rather than the lord, and here again we are led to suppose some direct exercise of power by women, seeing that it is only their intercession that is sought, quite as one seeks that of the Virgin with her Son.

The clergy went so far as to suggest that this power of intercession was never stronger than in the bed, in the "embraces of love." According to Orderic Vitalis, Adèle of Blois induced her husband to return to the Orient *inter amicabilis conjugii blandimenta.* This was to anticipate the model later proposed by Thomas of Chobham in his *Summa confessorum,*[20] counseling confessors to impose on wives the penance of nagging their husbands, since no one can soften a man's heart except his female friend. And how should this be done? "In the bed, in the course of embraces, by caresses." So here we have the *domina* proposed as mediator between the holder of powers, and notably of those he wields in his name, and the people who depend in whatever manner on these powers. The *domina* is called upon to introduce *mansuetudo* to the mechanisms of lordship. I take another example from Lambert of Ardres.[21] He tells in passing of a tax or exaction still levied here and there in the county of Guines on dependent persons, "culverts," men and women. It happened that this tax was levied on a free woman when she married. She protested, defending her cause in justice, but it was dismissed. In despair, she turned to the countess Emma of Guines. *Virago nobilis,* Emma was moved by the infamy imputed to women by this case. She spoke to the count, she "took her husband in her arms," she wept. The count, "thus rendered sympathetic," condescended to the request of "his wife and of this woman who supplicated." One wonders if the *domina* was not generally the protector, the accredited mediator with the husband, of the feminine segment of the population subject to the public power. They participated in power, then, but by way of charm. And it is here, I suspect, that one could introduce a whole aside on the game of courtly love. For as I have elsewhere suggested, one may suppose that the woman was carrying out a function of education and of domestication of the masculine youth gathered in the house under her husband's control.

19. *PL* 159, c. 93.
20. Ed. F. Broomfield (Louvain, 1968), 8.2.15.
21. Lambert, *Historia,* c. 36 (pp. 579–580), 21.

* * *

Within the house. This brings me now to the *res familiaris,* to power over the private. Private life was women's business. The interior of the house was normally placed, according to the Carolingian model, in the responsibility of the lady who maintained order. It was for her, the preachers repeated in the early thirteenth century, *regere domum suam.*

To rule. The lady, this time in conformity with worldly order, reigned; she did so notably over the women's rooms, over the chamber or "ladies' chamber," and over the women there quartered. This was her realm. There she dominated the daughters of good birth, her own and those also of the vassals who commended them to her. She was charged with their instruction. Adam of Perseigne sent the countess of Chartres some edifying texts in Latin which she was to have read to her pupils with the help, should some difficulty of interpretation arise, of her chaplain and of a lettered nun.[22] The lady had her say, too, when it was time to marry these girls. John of Marmoutier put into the genealogy of the counts of Anjou he reworked toward 1180 an invented story telling of a king of France who wished to marry the orphan-daughter of a count, his vassal, to his chamberlain. Humiliated, the girl refused, whereupon the king turned her over to his wife, sequestered in the ladies' chamber, to persuade her. This, says the author, did not take long.[23] Such was the lady's power, tyrannical and sometimes cruel, over the lower part of domestic society. Here is another anecdote from Lambert of Ardres,[24] regarding a female ascendant of his lord who was higher blooded than her husband and arrogant. She gloried in her nobility and, through haughtiness of words and gestures, wished to elevate herself yet higher, to dignify herself, and by disordered appetite, vice, and covetousness, to amass riches. Using her economic power, she organized a sheepfold and forced her subjects to place their animals in a common flock. Her servants demanded a lamb from a poor woman who had only children. She offered to deliver one of these to the lady, if she would agree to "put him in pasture." So the lady "adopted the child in place of the lamb." It was a girl, note well: these are stories of women, the lady, the poor woman, the little girl; all takes place in this world apart, which is the feminine domain. When this girl became marriageable, the lady "coupled her to a man," like

22. *PL* 211: 685.

23. *Chroniques des comtes d'Anjou et des seigneurs d'Amboise,* ed. Louis Halphen and René Poupardin (Paris, 1913), pp. 135–136.

24. Lambert, *Historia,* c. 129 (p. 625).

a good shepherd, for the increase of the domestic flock, but "putting her, her and her descendants, into the state of servility." And one sees how the lady's power over the feminine population of the lordship became more intense over those women who were incorporated in the *familia*. They became serfs of the *virago*. And Lambert continues. In the household lived a pretty girl whom the lady had brought from Flanders when she married, along with many other free servants (they were her dowry in moveables). Many men had played with this girl, then had cast her aside. There was one boy of the household, he too a Fleming. She wanted him for a husband. He refused. So she enserfed herself to the lady by the ritual of hands, trusting to the patroness's power, which effectively obliged the man to marry her.

The lady of Ardres, like the countess Emma, was acting here as the protectress of violated women. She coupled this other girl of her ménage. To marry the servants, or rather to give a husband to a female domestic, was an "economic" function of the lady. Thus ordaining the domestic sexuality, her role was analogous to that of her husband when he married off the daughters of his deceased vassals. In this role she was autonomous; just as in the arranging of the sheepfold, she was acting within the *res familiaris*. In this respect the lady was exercising an absolute power over the chamber maids. And if Lambert criticizes the *severitas* of this lady, that is only because she was reducing to servitude the men she mated to her servants and because, when Lambert was writing his history, servitude was regarded a vestige of outmoded barbarism. Yet there was no concern to question the *domina*'s power.

When the lady had fulfilled her function, when she had given children to the husband, her power, this power she wielded in private, increased at a stroke. Alongside the chamber within the women's space was located that room where the young children were mothered. They were cared for by the servant-women, but under the mother's domination. The first duty of the mother was to educate them, as the preachers toward 1200 reminded her. The daughters quite especially. But also the sons, until that early moment when, at the age of six or seven, they were withdrawn from the women to carry on their education among men, in the circles of future clerks or future knights. Between the mother and her son were wrought close affective bonds during this early childhood, ties that suffered rupture at his departure from the ladies' chamber; indeed, it was a traumatic wrenching with apparently considerable repercussions on the psychology of noblemen at this time. On this affection, much warmer and more vital than that binding the wife to her husband, was founded the essence of the power held by ladies of this age. It permitted them to stand up to their *dominus* with the support of their growing sons, who were in this society the natural enemies of their father, whose presence blocked their own access to power. Women drew force from their sons, especially from their second sons, who were naturally jealous of the first-born. The allusions to such connivence in the genealogical narrations are of quite special interest. So, according to the *Flandria generosa,* in the house of Flanders the countess Adèle preferred the cadet Robert to his brother Baldwin; preferred, that is, the son named for ancestors in her lineage to the one named for his father.[25] During the troubles after the murder of Charles the Good, the countess Clémence, dowager widow of Robert II, favored the bastard son of a cadet, William of Ypres, who was related by marriage, against the near kin of the assassinated count.[26]

Moreover, the lady of the twelfth century attained the plenitude of such power as a woman could hope to enjoy in this society when, widowed and rid of her *dominus,* she withdrew on her dower to her own house. There she held, in relation to her eldest son, now head of the house, the position she merited and that the ceremonial induced to believe she had held in relation to her husband, the role of counsellor, serene, shrewd, respected.

Such a situation is illustrated by a portrait of a lady, a matron, that I find in the history of the lords of Amboise composed by a canon of Tours toward 1155. It has to do with the mother of the lord Sulpice II,[27] who had died in prison from mistreatment he had suffered as a captive of his enemy the count of Blois. She was a woman of very good blood. She had been given to Hugh of Amboise with a very large *maritagium* by her half-brother Geoffrey Martel the Young, son of Count Fulk Réchin of Anjou. She immediately proved herself useful, giving her husband three boys as well as an unlikely inheritance, the lordship of Jaligny in the Bourbonnais, which her father had held and which fell to her by the unexpected deaths of her brothers. Whence in time the marriage of a son was supported. Isabelle, for so she was called, demonstrated her character at once in these circumstances. Her distant inheritance was disputed by those of her male kin who remained there. It was up to her husband to go and defend the rights of his wife and her sons. He evaded the task, preoccupied with the defense of his ancestral lands. It was Isabelle herself who went to the Bourbonnais

25. *MGH SS* 9: 321.

26. Galbert de Bruges, *Histoire du meurtre de Charles le Bon, comte de Flandre (1127–1128),* ed. Henri Pirenne (Paris, 1891), p. 76.

27. *Chroniques des comtes d'Anjou,* p. 112.

to fight against her rivals. With her husband's permission, it is true, yet acting, relates our text, "like a man." This is an example of political action taken directly by a woman. However, the affair seemed strange. It created a sensation. It could only be explained—the tone of the narration proves it—as the case of a woman overcoming her femininity to assume maleness.

For in the gallery of portraits found in this record, the figure of Isabelle stands out from the ordinary. Among all women, wrote the author (and he knew her well, for she had just died and he may have lived in her entourage), she was endowed beyond measure. *Fortunata.* There follow four Latin words expressive of how men viewed the feminine condition: *fortunata genere,* or ancestry, the quality of blood, bearer of that value which as a girl she had brought to the house where her marriage drew her; *forma,* or the quality of her body, which counted in a woman; *viro,* by the husband she had received, for a girl existed only in her wifely identity; *liberis,* by the children she brought into the world, for a woman's value is multiplied tenfold by maternity. To all that the eulogy adds one exceptional quality, which assured the singularity of Isabelle of Jaligny: audacity, and the author adds an epithet: "virile." What distinguished this woman was that she was, in reality, a man. *Viriliter,* she took over as widow when her husband, after five years of marriage, went away to die in Jerusalem. She had promptly assumed the struggle against her eldest son, Sulpice, who had seized the power, all his father had held, and refused to give it up. Isabelle relied partly on her second son and partly on Sulpice's lord, Count Geoffrey Plantagenet of Anjou.

It is interesting to see how the author viewed Isabelle at this point in her life. His admiration ceased. He became critical. This woman had in effect become a woman again, seized by the demon, *irata,* inflamed by madness, like another Richilde. She had gone too far, exceeding what is permitted to women. She was, as so often in women, what they must hold in check, a fomenter of disorder. But from another source, the history of Geoffrey Plantagenet written by John of Marmoutier a quarter century later, we learn why Isabelle struggled. For her dower. She had brought suit to the count of Anjou, lord of the fief, *super dotalitii sui diminutione.*[28] She won her case. Her son Sulpice had to give up his part to her, in particular Amboise, where she had her house, next to the church of Saint-Thomas. Mother and son made their peace, reconciled by people of the house. Then, fifteen years later, Isabelle came again to the fore, when, according to the

28. *Chronique des comtes d'Anjou,* p. 210.

Gesta of the lords of Amboise, Sulpice threw himself into unbridled conflict against his other lord, the count of Blois, leading to disaster. Isabelle was thrust into her role as mother. Here are the words the writer attributes to her, the discourse she directs to her son[29]: "Why have you started this war without consulting me? Because I am decrepit you think I am insane, but in my old skin the *animus* is enduring. You could not find better counsel. What can be compared to maternal *affectus*?" Counsel, then, but dictated by affection, by that timeless, immaterial force that linked the two beings. And this brings me to my conclusion.

* * *

By reason of their physical constitution, of the nature of their body, and the sex which defines them, women were deemed incapable of exercising the power of command, *potestas*. They nevertheless succeeded in participating in this power by using another power, that of immaterial order, which attached to their sex: the love which their sons bore them and which secured respect for them and the assurance of being heard in their old age; the desire they instigated in men, and which softened men; the fear also which they evoked, for men were persuaded that womanhood was invested with mysterious power, that women maintained touch with invisible forces.

One fact strikes me about the region and period of which I speak: the place held by feminine figures in piety, well before the moment at the very end of the twelfth century when the texts bear witness to a veritable explosion of new and specifically feminine forms of spirituality. There is the figure of the Virgin, of course. From the start of the eleventh century, the immense majority of new religious foundations were placed under the patronage of Our Lady. But also the figures of holy women. In Christendom as a whole, our period produced few new saints, and still fewer female ones. Yet I note the appearance of a good many women, more exactly wives, ladies, whom the *vox populi,* popular fervor, proposed to elevate on altars after their deaths; and I further discern in genealogical memory a strong tendency to render cult to ancestresses, *venerabiles,* who come in fact to be venerated by their descendants. When we ask about the real power of women, we must evidently take account of this propensity to attribute supernatural value to women who had not remained virgins, who had been

29. *Chroniques des comtes d'Anjou,* p. 127.

given over to husbands; the tendency to celebrate their virtues, to endow them with the power to cure the sick. A power they owe either, as in Saint Godelive of Ghistelle, to their resistance to a husband's persecution; or on the contrary, as in Saint Ida of Boulogne, to their docility, to their generous surrender to the power of this man who came to join them in bed, who was tamed in their arms, acceded to their petition, rekindled his piety in theirs, and finally deposited in them the seed of their boys, of those males who, because they were males, would be the future possessors of *potestas,* of the power to command and to punish.

Part II

Strategy, Means, Process

Stephen D. White

5. Proposing the Ordeal and Avoiding It: Strategy and Power in Western French Litigation, 1050–1110

> Every strategy of confrontation dreams of becoming a power relationship.
>
> —Michel Foucault[1]

Introduction

In around 1060, a *famulus* called Bunghole[2] became entangled in a lawsuit with the abbey of Saint Vincent of Le Mans when, with the support of his lord, Richard of Loupfougère, he challenged the monks' right to a tithe in the village of Puizieux. In response, abbot Hugh arranged a meeting to discuss the dispute in the court of count Roger of Montgomery at Luerzon. There, in the count's absence, Bunghole offered to support his challenge against the monks by undergoing the ordeal of hot iron. On the barons' advice, abbot Hugo accepted the offer. But when he and the barons returned to Luerzon at the time appointed for the ordeal, both Bunghole and his lord Richard were absent. The barons, judging Bunghole's challenge unjust, decided that the disputed tithe "belonged fully and quietly to Saint Vincent." Even so, when Richard later quitclaimed the same tithe to the abbey, the monks reciprocated by including him in their prayers.[3]

Bunghole's decision to avoid an ordeal was not unusual.[4] In one way

1. "The Subject and Power," *Critical Inquiry* 8, 4 (summer 1982), 777–95, here 794.
2. *Pertusus*.
3. *V* 769 (1056–68). For a key to the abbreviations used in the notes, see the end of this essay.
4. The following modern discussions of trial by ordeal are particularly important for the present argument, even though none of them focuses on cancelled ordeal cases: Dominique Barthélemy, "Diversité des ordalies médiévales," *Revue Historique* 280 (1988), 3–25; Barthélemy, "Présence de l'aveu dans le déroulement des ordalies (IXe–XIIIe siècles)," *L'aveu:*

or another, participants in recorded lawsuits involving western French monasteries between 1050 and 1110 usually avoided the unilateral ordeal of hot iron or boiling water, as well as the bilateral ordeal of battle, and they commonly did so even after an ordeal had been proposed.[5] The reason, however, for examining cancelled ordeals—that is, ordeals proposed but then avoided—is not just that they evidently outnumbered completed ones, but also that they sometimes illuminate distinctive political strategies of confrontation in late eleventh-century litigation and, by extension, the micro-economies of shifting power relations that underlie court hearings.[6] Treating the study of medieval politics broadly as the study of power relations, I follow Foucault in assuming that "the analysis of power relations cannot be reduced to the study of a series of institutions, not even to the study of all those institutions which would merit the name 'political.'"[7] Instead, if "power relations are rooted deep in the social nexus" and are not simply "reconstituted 'above' society as a supplementary structure,"[8] then the study of them should not only cover the domain of politics, as conventionally defined, but should also focus, as Foucault argues, on many

antiquité et moyen-âge, Collection de l'École française de Rome 88 (Rome, 1986), pp. 191–214; Robert Bartlett, *Trial by Fire and Water: The Medieval Judicial Ordeal* (Oxford, 1986); Yvonne Bongert, *Recherches sur les cours laïques du Xe au XIIIe siècles* (Paris, 1949), esp. pp. 211–51; Peter Brown, "Society and the Supernatural: A Medieval Change," *Daedalus* 104 (1975), 133–51, reprinted with additional notes in Brown, *Society and the Holy in Late Antiquity* (Berkeley, CA, 1982), pp. 302–32; Olivier Guillot, "La participation au duel judicaire de témoins de condition serve dans l'Ile-de-France du XIe siècle: autour d'un faux diplôme de Henri Ier," in *Droit privé et institutions régionales: études historiques offertes à Jean Yver* (Paris, 1976), pp. 345–60; Paul R. Hyams, "Trial by Ordeal: The Key to Proof in the Early Common Law," in *On the Laws and Customs of England: Essays in Honor of Samuel E. Thorne*, ed. Morris S. Arnold et al. (Chapel Hill, NC, 1981), pp. 90–126; Margaret H. Kerr, Richard K. Forsyth, and Michael J. Plyley, "Cold Water and Hot Iron: Trial by Ordeal in England," *Journal of Interdisciplinary History* 22 (1992), 573–96; William Ian Miller, "Ordeal in Iceland," *Scandinavian Studies* 60 (1988), 189–218; Charles Radding, "Superstition to Science: Nature, Fortune and the Passing of the Medieval Ordeal," *AHR* 84 (1979), 945–69; Stephen D. White, "Inheritances and Legal Arguments in Western France, 1050–1150," *Traditio* 43 (1987), 55–103, here pp. 56, 78–82.

After the present article was completed, the cases it discusses from the Vendômois (from *MB, MV*, and *TV*) were treated more ably by Dominique Barthélemy, whose thorough, lucid study of dispute-processing in the eleventh-century Vendômois supplements my own. See *La société dans le Vendômois dans le comté de Vendôme de l'an mil aux XIVe siècle* (Paris, 1993), pp. 652–80.

5. Between 1040 and 1149, for example, proposals to hold ordeals are mentioned only about 50 times in almost 500 disputes recorded in *A, C, MB, MP, MS, MV, N, TV*, or *V*. Although there are significant differences between unilateral and bilateral ordeals (Bartlett, *Trial*, pp. 2, 113–26) and among different kinds of unilateral ordeals (Barthélemy, "Diversité des ordalies"), different kinds of ordeals are still worth studying concurrently for certain purposes (Hyams, "Trial," pp. 92–93).

6. See Foucault, "The Subject and Power."

7. "The Subject and Power," pp. 792–93.

8. "The Subject and Power," p. 791.

different "situations of confrontation" and on the procedures or "strategies" used in them "to deprive [an] opponent of his means of combat and to reduce him to giving up the struggle."[9] In considering later eleventh-century western French society,[10] where power relations at every level were in the process of being reconstituted through innumerable confrontations in every social sphere but had yet to become as highly institutionalized[11] as they later became, it is particularly instructive to examine some of the ways in which trial by ordeal was incorporated into the political strategies of participants in documented lawsuits.

To pursue this approach, I shall treat trial by ordeal as a flexible political process that could alter power relations. Because in cancelled ordeal cases the notorious ritual of deciding a lawsuit by ordeal was never held, we certainly cannot represent it—as other modern studies do—as "a form of proof"[12] or as a "reassuring" ritual.[13] Instead, the ordeal ritual figures in cancelled ordeal cases as something less tangible: as a worrisome procedural possibility, as a threat or instrument of power, which influenced the course of a lawsuit, whether or not the ordeal was actually held. I therefore focus on the entire ordeal process, which began with a proposal to hold an ordeal; ended with a judgment, a concord, or renewed hostilities; and included, in between, complicated maneuvering centering on the invisible processes of imagining where the proposal to hold the ordeal might lead. While restricting the analysis to a period when state institutions were relatively weak and to a particular type of litigation, I take it for granted that, being a highly malleable process, the ordeal must have figured in different strategies when used in either different political formations or different types of lawsuits. But because records of eleventh-century monastic litigation are unusually rich in narrative detail, they provide a rare opportunity to examine the political uses of a ritual that must always have been something more than a legal institution.

To develop this approach, I shall first show that, in several crucial respects, the ordeal process was flexible enough to leave considerable room for political, as well as juridical, strategizing. For one thing, the process

9. "The Subject and Power," p. 793.

10. On the region where most of the disputes considered here arose, see Olivier Guillot, *Le comte d'Anjou et son entourage au XIe siècle*, 2 vols. (Paris, 1972); and Barthélemy, "Le Vendômois," pp. 659–1506.

11. Or "governmentalized": Foucault, "The Subject and Power," p. 793.

12. See, e.g., Bartlett, *Trial*, p. 153.

13. Brown, "Society," p. 313. Brown also represents the ordeal as an "instrument of consensus" to "contain disruptive conflict" (p. 311).

could be started in different ways at different junctures of a lawsuit and could bring the case to several different outcomes, including definitive judgments, compromise settlements, and renewed litigation and feuding. The process could be influenced, moreover, by many kinds of participants at a *placitum* (or court hearing), including the judges (on whom previous scholarship mainly focuses); the litigants; and even witnesses, probands, and onlookers. All of these participants could try to use the ordeal process to alter the procedural and political possibilities of a lawsuit, even though none of them could ever control the process fully. The ordeal was such a versatile instrument, I argue, partly because in western French monastic litigation it was not restricted to a narrow range of legally defined cases, and was, in fact, proposed in lawsuits that were distinguished less by the evidentiary or substantive legal issues they raised than they were by the political intensity with which they were contested. Finally, the ordeal process was flexible because it did not necessarily result in an ordeal ritual, which could be cancelled at many different junctures of the process by any of those people whose participation was essential.

Having suggested that the ordeal process left room for political as well as for legal strategizing, I shall then suggest that proposing the ordeal, accepting it as proof, and, finally cancelling it were all tricky and dangerous but potentially effective bargaining ploys that different participants in a court hearing could use as instruments of self-empowerment to move an unusually protracted and embittered lawsuit toward a politically favorable and workable settlement. I shall also argue, however, that these ploys worked differently—and took on different meanings—in different political contexts. Sometimes, for example, they were executed from positions of great strength; at other times, they were acts of desperation. Sometimes they worked, and sometimes they backfired.

Although the reconstruction of these strategies is inevitably a speculative enterprise, we can control our own speculations somewhat by noting that what is a hermeneutic exercise for us was, for the participants, a matter of power[14]: in the first instance, the power of an individual litigant, judge, or witness to secure the political support of others in a lawsuit by imposing on them his or her interpretation of the conflict; second, the power of lords over property or peasants or conversely, the power of peasants to be free of certain seigneurial powers; and finally, the power of judgment that medieval people sometimes attributed—somewhat uneasily, I think—

14. See William I. Miller, *Bloodtaking and Peacemaking: Feud, Law, and Society in Saga Iceland* (Chicago, 1990), p. 13.

to God. So instead of assuming, as legal historians sometimes do, that participants in cancelled ordeal cases simply organized their strategies around procedural and substantive rules of law, I shall argue that they also used the ordeal process, in the short run, to alter power relations at a *placitum* and, in the long run, to secure at least the partial objectification of these new power relations in the form of a judgment or a concord.

To understand strategies at work in cancelled ordeal cases, it is important to note that the ordeal process always formed part of an even lengthier and more flexible disputing process,[15] which could proceed, moreover, without any mention of the ordeal and, indeed, without any resort to a *placitum* where an ordeal might be proposed. Because any such dispute was always potentially resolvable by non-adjudicatory methods (such as bilateral negotiation or third-party mediation), the adjudication of a dispute at a *placitum* presupposes that other means of processing it had failed or had been bypassed for strategic reasons that surely colored the subsequent process of adjudication.[16] Because adjudication, moreover, usually led to either a judgment or a concord without any mention of the ordeal, any decision to propose an ordeal involved the rejection of alternative adjudicatory procedures, again for strategic reasons that must have had bearing on the subsequent ordeal process. In short, because ordeal cases constitute only a small subset of my sample of lawsuits, we can account for decisions to propose ordeals by positing the existence of strategies.

Even when the ordeal was proposed, there was still considerable room for strategic maneuvering. If the proposal did not lead an agreement to hold an ordeal at a later meeting, then the dispute would usually be terminated at the initial *placitum* by a judgment or concord. But if the proposal was accepted, then the initial *placitum* would end (as it did in Bunghole's case) with an agreement to hold the ordeal on a specified day at a particular location.[17] Even then, participants retained until the very last instant the

15. On "dispute processing," see Laura Nader and Harry F. Todd Jr., eds., *The Disputing Process—Law in Ten Societies* (New York, 1978); John L. Comaroff and Simon Roberts, *Rules and Processes: The Cultural Logic of Dispute in an African Context* (Chicago, 1981); and *Disentangling: Conflict Discourse in Pacific Societies,* ed. Karen Ann Watson-Gegeo and Geoffrey M. White (Stanford, CA, 1990). On medieval dispute-processing see Patrick J. Geary, "Vivre en conflit dans une France sans état: typologie des mecanismes de règlement des conflits (1050–1200)," *Annales E.S.C.* 41 (1986), 1107–1133; and Geary, "Moral Obligations and Peer Pressure: Conflict Resolution in the Medieval Aristocracy," in *La perception du monde médiéval,* ed. C. Amado and G. Lobrichon (to appear).

16. On negotiation, mediation, and adjudication in eleventh-century Western France, see White, "Inheritances," pp. 64–70.

17. The place designated for the ordeal was not always identical with the one where the initial *placitum* was held, e.g., *A* 404. The same agreement also specified what the ordeal would test.

option of cancelling the ordeal, in which case either one party would default or else the two of them would make a concord. If the ordeal ran its full course, the judges would terminate the lawsuit with a judgment favoring one party or the other, unless the ordeal's outcome was disputed,[18] in which case the lawsuit would probably end in compromise, or unless the loser disputed the judgment based on the ordeal, in which case the conflict would simply begin all over again.[19]

If trial by ordeal can be represented, for certain purposes, as an "instrument,"[20] then it was a very versatile one that could be used by a variety of people playing different roles in a lawsuit. In a region where no ruler monopolized the legitimate use of force, no one fully controlled the use of this recognized instrument of legitimation. The judges could either tell one party to undergo a unilateral ordeal or decide that the two parties or their champions should fight a battle. In addition, either party, his witness, or his warrantor could propose to support an oath by means of either a unilateral ordeal or a battle against the opposing party. Among the litigants and witnesses who proposed ordeals, moreover, we find people occupying different social positions, including abbots and other monks,[21] knights,[22] peasants or servants,[23] a priest,[24] and a craftsman;[25] serfs[26] as well as free people; and one woman[27] as well as many men. Further complicating the procedural and political dynamics of the ordeal process was the fact that not everyone who proposed the ordeal was obliged to undergo it personally. Because an alleged *collibertus* had to undergo the ordeal himself whereas monks, knights, and lords could do so by proxy, the status of the person proposing an ordeal significantly influenced the proposal's meaning.[28]

The process of initiating an ordeal was also flexible and unpredictable because there was no single time during a *placitum* when this maneuver

18. On disputed outcomes of ordeals, see Brown, "Society"; Radding, "From Superstition to Science"; Hyams, "Trial"; Bartlett, *Trial,* esp. pp. 39–41; and White, "Inheritances," pp. 78–82 (on a case in which the disputed outcome of a unilateral ordeal was to be resolved by a battle, which was later cancelled so that the parties could make a concord).

19. See, e.g., *MB* 93.

20. Or "device." Brown uses both metaphors ("Society," p. 311), while both Hyams ("Trial by Ordeal," p. 95) and Bartlett (*Trial by Fire and Water,* p. 36) use the second.

21. *A* 325, 878; *MD* 10, 16; *MV* 9.

22. *TV* 189, 257.

23. *A* 194; *MS* 11, 109, 127; *MV* 119; *V* 769.

24. *V* 315.

25. *N* 154.

26. *A* 194; *MS* 11, 109, 127; *MV* 159.

27. *MS* 127.

28. The implications of this procedural peculiarity for the bargaining process are hard to calculate, but well worth exploring.

had to be executed. The lay litigant could propose an ordeal when first stating his claim,[29] or else a monk[30] or warrantor[31] could make the proposal when responding. Later on, either the litigant[32] or the litigant's witness[33] could also propose the ordeal during subsequent exchanges between the opposing parties. The judges, too, could propose an ordeal after hearing the arguments of both sides.[34] Even after a judgment, the losing party or even the judges could still propose an ordeal to test the judgment's justice.[35] Whenever it was made, the proposal marked the dramatic highpoint

29. After invading land at Draché that Rainaldus the Young had previously given to Noyers, Natalis de Draché offered at a *placitum* to prove by ordeal that he held the land rightfully: N 146. In separate disputes with La Trinité, Petrus Cadebertus (*TV* 189) and Landricus de Bolone (*TV* 257) each undertook to support his claim by battle. See also discussions below of *MV* 159, *A* 137, 387, *MS* 127.

30. After Hamelinus de Langeais justified his challenge about some vineyards in the Dunois by alleging that the monks of Marmoutier were holding them without his authorization, even though they formed part of a fief held from him, the monks responded that a man of theirs would prove by the ordeal of hot iron that the vineyards formed part of their allod at Chamart: *MD* 10. In a dispute with Girardus son of Hubertus de Beaugency over the property of two former serfs of Marmoutier who were descended from an *ancilla* of Girardus's wife's grandfather, the monks undertook battle: *MD* 16. In a *placitum* held in Vendôme, monks from the same abbey undertook battle with Tetbaldus de Vendôme to acquit various properties about which he had made a challenge: *MV* 9. In the dispute between the lord of Malicornant and Saint Aubin, the abbot of Saint Aubin proposed an ordeal when responding to Waldinus's claim that because the monks had acquired their property in Arthèze from his ancestors, they should acknowledge him as their lord with respect to these holdings: *A* 325.

31. See the case of Constantius de Adquadratus (*A* 189), discussed below.

32. See the case of Girardus de Blanco Furno (*A* 878), discussed below.

33. In a dispute between Martinus Evigilans Canem and Saint Aubin over property at Montreuil-Bellay, Wido son of Laurentius, whom abbot Archembaldus brought to the court of Berlaius, lord of Montreuil-Bellay, offered to prove by battle that Martinus had previously granted the disputed property to Saint Aubin: *A* 144. In a dispute between Marmoutier and *ministri* of count Geoffrey Martel about a house in Rilly Ulricus undertook at a *placitum* to defend the monks' rights by battle: *MB* 26. In a *placitum* held at La Roche before a lord called Tetbaldus, Turbatus's claim that he was not a serf of Marmoutier was answered by his kinsman, Joscelinus de Rupeculis, who undertook battle against him: *MS* 11. The battle fought to resolve the dispute already mentioned between Marmoutier and Constantius de Ranay may have been proposed by the abbey's witness, Fulbertus: *MB* 87. See also the case of Mauritius (*MS* 53), discussed below. For a case in which an ordeal was proposed by a witness whom the monks had not brought to court and whose support they had not counted on, see *V* 315.

34. After Malrannus, brother of Archembaldus, had seized a mill from Noyers, the monks contended at a *placitum* that Archembaldus had given it to them with the approval of Malrannus, from whom Archembaldus had previously bought the plot (*arca*) for the mill. Because Malrannus asserted, however, that he had not sold, but had merely mortgaged, the plot to Archembaldus and had never approved his brother's gift to Noyers, it was decided, probably by the judges, that Malrannus should prove his allegations about the mill by battle: *N* 24. At another *placitum,* it was decided that Landricus should prove by the ordeal of hot iron his claim to some vineyards and other lands held by the monks of Noyers at Beaulieu: *N* 154. See also discussions below of *MB* 126, *A* 404, and *A* 388, where a litigant who failed to present proof that he had previously offered to provide was later ordered by the judges to undergo an ordeal.

35. See Roaldus's case (*A* 203), discussed below.

of a *placitum,* but because it could be made at different junctures of such meetings, the dramatic rhythms of ordeal cases varied substantially.

Although trial by ordeal sometimes played a role in halting a dispute, it was both a potentially costly procedure for all participants and a highly uncertain one, which could not, by itself, bring peace.[36] Even a victorious litigant sometimes incurred significant costs, including a reward for his champion or proband,[37] gifts to a recalcitrant loser and his kin,[38] and even the trouble of waging or enduring renewed hostilities.[39] The loser's costs, moreover, were potentially greater than those he would have incurred in making even an unfavorable concord, since he risked losing his claim forever, incurring shame and dishonor,[40] becoming liable for various fines, and forgoing the concessions such as money and prayers that lay litigants often received when they made concords with monks.

If the costs of a completed ordeal were potentially significant for all participants, its benefits were questionable. When both parties had the will and political resources necessary to sustain a protracted conflict and when the court lacked the power to enforce its decisions, a legally definitive judgment based on an ordeal might be less valuable than a politically workable settlement. In theory, trial by ordeal injected certainty into an otherwise unpredictable disputing process by insuring that the case would be decided by God's judgment; in practice, it might only intensify the uncertainties of litigation.

Given these costs and uncertainties, why did anyone ever propose an ordeal? Were they simply following established rules of legal procedure? Or were conventions of pleading flexible enough to leave room for political strategizing? If the ordeal were simply a legally regulated mode of proof, then the most obvious hypothesis is that people proposed it simply because the law required them to do so. This hypothesis needs careful consideration since the ordeal is represented in eleventh-century records of monastic litigation as a means of achieving one of at least four different legal purposes. It could be proposed to prove a statement of "fact," on which the judges could then base their judgment; to prove concurrently a factual statement and a normative conclusion based on that statement; to test a disputed

36. I use "cost" in the sense employed by F. G. Bailey in *Stratagems and Spoils: A Social Anthropology of Politics* (New York, 1969; reprinted Oxford, 1985).

37. See *A* 94.

38. See *MB* 93.

39. See the Saint Florent case mentioned above and discussed in White, "Inheritances."

40. On the dishonor incurred by the loser of a battle, see, e.g., *La mort le roi Artu: roman du xiiie siècle,* ed. Jean Frappier (Geneva and Paris, 1964), ch. 84, line 40 (p. 106).

claim about the legal implications of an uncontested fact; and finally, to establish in more general terms which litigant had "right" on his side.[41]

The simplest cases are the ones in which an ordeal was proposed for the explicit purpose of resolving a factual disagreement. When Sibilla initiated a dispute about a mill held by the monks of Marmoutier on the grounds that her father had given it to the monks without her consent, and when the monks responded that Sibilla had, in fact, approved her father's gift, an ordeal was proposed, presumably by the judges, to resolve this factual dispute.[42] Similarly, when Waldinus, lord of Malicornant, challenged properties of Saint Aubin in Arthèze on the grounds that the monks had acquired them from his ancestors, the abbot proposed, as he had previously done in another *placitum,* an ordeal to prove the veracity of a charter allegedly showing that his community had received the disputed properties from kings of France.[43] In a lawsuit between Mauritius and Marmoutier about a serf named Hermandus whom Mauritius's father Gelduinus had previously given to Saint Martin, Mauritius asserted that "he had not approved the gift of his father," while Hermandus's brother Godevertus eventually "prepared himself to make law, to bear *judicium* that Mauritius had approved the gift of his father."[44]

Whereas these cases show that one legal reason for holding a trial by ordeal was "to reveal a specific fact" to which the law could then be applied,[45] a lawsuit between Marmoutier and Constantius de Ranay illustrates

41. Published formulae—which seem more appropriate to criminal than to civil cases—never make distinctions of this kind. Instead, they simply represent the ordeal as a means of distinguishing an innocent (*innocens*) man from a guilty (*culpabilis atque reus* or *obnoxius*) one (*Formulae Merowingici et Karolini aevi,* ed. Karl Zeumer. *MGH* [Hanover, 1886]; 605), as well as truth from falsehood (Zeumer, p. 615). Several texts also suggest that soliciting God's judgment was a means of learning about "*secreta*" (Zeumer, p. 612), because God was the "*scrutator occultorum cordium*" (p. 608).

42. *MB* 126.

43. *A* 325.

44. *MS* 53 (1032–64). In other lawsuits ordeals were proposed for the purpose of answering the following factual questions. Did Albericus, now deceased, give some land at Alleuds, now held by Saint Aubin, to the monks' present adversary, Galterius de Meigné, in return for a horse (*A* 404)? Did Malrannus mortgage, rather than sell, the mill-site of the mill of Grautel to his brother Archembaldus (*N* 24)? Did the vineyards held by Marmoutier and challenged by Hamelinus de Langeais form part of the latter's fief, rather than part of the monks' allod (*MD* 10)? Did the land of Cré belong to Saint Aubin *before* Otgerius married Emelina (*A* 878)? Had Martinus Evigalans-Canem previously granted to Saint Aubin the property at Montreuil-Bellay that he now challenged (*A* 144)? Was the alleged serf Vitalis born before his father and mother became serfs of Marmoutier (*MS* 127)? Under an agreement made at Beaugency between Radulfus Toaredus and two monks of Saint Aubin, was the former entitled to an especially opulent form of hospitality when he visited the monastery with his men (*A* 387)?

45. Bartlett, *Trial,* p. 79.

a second legal rationale for the ordeal. Here, a battle was scheduled (and actually held) to test not only the factual allegation of the monks' witness Fulbertus that when he had held the mill of Ranay, he had never paid the custom that Constantius was now demanding from the monks—who had succeeded Fulbertus as tenants of the mill—but also Fulbertus's normative contentions that *by right, he ought not to have done so* and, by implication, that the monks ought not to pay this rent to Constantius.[46] Another case involving the same abbey shows that an ordeal could be proposed for a third legal purpose: to establish the legal implications of an uncontested factual allegation. After marrying an *ancilla* of Saint Martin, a free man named Stephanus Dog-Leg became a serf of Marmoutier. "But when she died and he took as a wife another woman who was free, he denied that he was a serf of Saint Martin and undertook to do battle with [the monks] about this matter." Instead of arguing that Stephanus had misrepresented the facts of his case, the monks evidently maintained that he had drawn the wrong juridical conclusion from them. In their view, his remarriage to a free woman did not make him free.[47] Finally, a case involving the abbey of Noyers shows that a fourth purpose could be attributed to trial by ordeal. When Otbertus de la Montée proposed to undergo an ordeal in his dispute with the abbey of Noyers, he did so in order to prove that "the monks had no right to the land" he claimed.[48] Here, God was asked to assess only a general legal conclusion whose legal and factual bases went unspecified.[49]

Nevertheless, although the cases just considered clearly specify legal purposes that the ordeal could serve and therefore constitute important evidence about what was sayable about the ordeal at a *placitum,* they do not rule out the possibility that ordeals were proposed for other purposes that no participant in a lawsuit would openly avow at a court hearing. In fact, there are several reasons for not excluding this possibility, and thus for skepticism about the hypothesis that both trials by ordeal and proposals to hold them served *only* judicial functions. First, even if everyone involved in the disputing process firmly believed that trial by ordeal was a potentially legitimate and effective means of ascertaining God's judgment, no experienced participant in a lawsuit could have disentangled the process

46. *MB* 87.

47. *MV* 159 (1032–84). Factual and normative questions were also merged in *A* 189.

48. *N* 147.

49. According to Milsom, "Proof was not a matter of establishing the facts so that rules could be applied . . . . the unanalyzed dispute is put to supernatural decision by ordeal or the like. A blank result settles the dispute but can make no law. What if the beating was accidental or the debt forgiven? The questions cannot be asked as legal questions until the supernatural is replaced by a rational deciding mechanism" (*Historical Foundations of the Common Law,* 2d ed. [Toronto, 1981], p. 4).

of predicting the legal outcome of a lawsuit in which an ordeal might be held from the process of assessing the political climate in which it would be proposed and possibly held. Instead, he would surely have understood the crucial bearing of human politics, as distinguished from God's judgment, on the outcome of the disputing process. He would have known that a unilateral ordeal could be rigged; that because its physical outcome might be open to conflicting interpretations, friendly judges were preferable to hostile ones; that he could not necessarily count on the opposing litigant's willingness to accept an unfavorable judgment based on defeat in a duel; and, finally, that even if he himself were fully prepared to act on the unshakable conviction that trial by ordeal would actually lead to a just outcome, others, including his own supporters, might view it differently. Given the crucial significance of such essentially political considerations, no one could have proposed an ordeal with much confidence that it would actually serve its alleged juridical function.

Second, a purely juridical model of trial by ordeal cannot fully explain why the ordeal was proposed only in certain cases and not in others. The most obvious answer to this question is that participants in the total sample of monastic lawsuits generally followed a procedural rule that restricted the use of ordeals to limited classes of disputes raising distinctive evidentiary or substantive issues. Thus, trial by ordeal may have been legally necessary or permissible, for example, "only when other ways of discovering the truth were not available."[50] But in several well-documented cases, ordeals were proposed at least partly for the purpose of resolving normative, not factual, questions; in other cases cited, ordeals were proposed when one litigant simply challenged the other's oral or documentary evidence. In fact, since the alleged purpose of many ordeals was to support the testimony of people claiming to have direct knowledge of a crucial factual issue in a lawsuit,[51] one can argue that, frequently, the legal purpose of an ordeal was not to supplement the available evidence but to strengthen some of it.

To account for some of the case evidence, one could argue that the procedural rule followed in our cases permitted ordeals not only when the written or oral evidence was utterly lacking, but also when it was somehow defective and therefore in need of corroboration.[52] But when a litigant or warrantor concluded his opening *narratio* by proposing an ordeal, he could

50. Bartlett, *Trial,* p. 26; see also pp. 37, 38, 79, 101–2, 153.

51. See, in addition to many of the cases discussed below, Bongert, *Recherches,* pp. 213, 221–22.

52. Bartlett argues that it was "a universal principle that some deficiency in human testimony was necessary before recourse could be had to the ordeal" (*Trial,* p. 28); see also Bongert, *Recherches,* p. 219.

not have known for certain what evidence his adversary would present. In certain lawsuits, moreover, the only apparent flaw in one party's evidence was that the other party rejected it. Now, if a litigant could unilaterally brand his adversary's evidence as defective, then a rule allowing ordeals only when other evidence was unavailable or defective could hardly have limited significantly the use of ordeals; on the contrary, it would have allowed the ordeal, if not required it, in scores of cases in which it is not mentioned. Furthermore, the hypothesis that ordeals were permitted only when the available evidence was defective in no way accounts for cases in which the ordeal was represented as a means of settling a question of "right," not "fact."[53] To meet these objections, one could argue that ordeals were permitted *either* in cases where the available evidence was somehow defective *or* in limited sets of lawsuits raising certain substantive, as opposed to procedural, issues. The second part of this hypothesis, however, is not supported by a comparison of cases in which ordeals were proposed with those in which this procedure went unmentioned. In each group of cases, litigants seem to have raised identical substantive issues.[54]

Third, the hypothesis that ordeals were proposed only for purely legal purposes is undercut by the finding that, in practice, they hardly ever served those purposes. Unless samples of recorded lawsuits are so hopelessly skewed that they inexplicably exclude numerous monastic victories in the ordeal, as well as monastic defeats, or unless participants in these cases

53. Although the finding that some ordeals were proposed to answer disputed questions of fact while others were proposed to resolve broader issues of right may show only that the ordeal served one kind of judicial function in some cases and another judicial function in others, the same evidence may indicate that, at least in certain cases, the outcome of an ordeal was potentially open to several different interpretations. Unless every participant in an ordeal was somehow bound to interpret its outcome in accordance with the stated purpose of the ordeal, then the ordeal could sometimes be construed *either* as a means of ascertaining God's judgment on the truthfulness of a specific oath sworn on behalf of a litigant *or* as a method of determining how God judged the justice of that litigant's cause. If so, then the ordeal must have been seen as a treacherously ambiguous ritual, not simply because a unilateral ordeal, at least, could be rigged or could yield an ambiguous physical outcome, but also because the normative significance of even a clear outcome of a unilateral or bilateral ordeal was open to conflicting interpretations. Even if everyone acknowledged that God spoke through an ordeal, who could be sure precisely what he had said about a complex lawsuit? Imaginary ordeal cases in several Arthurian romances (e.g., Frappier, *La mort le roi Artu*] and various versions of the Tristan story) are constructed in such a way as to suggest that medieval story-tellers were acutely conscious of the problems involved in interpreting the outcomes of ordeals. This issue is treated but not satisfactorily resolved in Lynette R. Muir and R. Howard Bloch, "Further Thoughts on the 'Mort Artu,'" *Modern Language Review* 71 (1976), 26–30; and R. Howard Bloch, *Medieval French Literature and Law* (Berkeley, CA, 1977), chapter 1.

54. For example, charters in the collections cited on p. 122 record many disputes that turned on the question of whether a lay challenger had approved his kinsman's or his feudal tenant's gift to an abbey. But ordeals were proposed in very few of these cases.

knew even less than modern historians do about how such cases usually proceeded and were repeatedly thwarted in their sincere efforts to settle lawsuits by ordeal, hardly anyone—and certainly not an experienced abbot, bishop, or lay lord—could ever have proposed an ordeal with any confidence that it would actually be held. A decision to propose an ordeal must be sharply distinguished from a decision to hold one.

If a proposal to hold an ordeal was not strictly regulated by legally binding rules of evidence and was made by people who did not necessarily want to settle a lawsuit by this means, then it cannot be treated simply as a legal move that a litigant, his supporter, or a judge was sometimes legally required to make either to achieve a legal victory or render a just judgment. In addition, if people proposed the ordeal in order to gain an advantage in a lawsuit, then to treat it solely as a means of meeting the "needs" of lordship or community is, at best, misleading. An alternative hypothesis is that a proposal to hold an ordeal was understood as *both* a legal move in a lawsuit *and* a political bargaining ploy or strategy of confrontation. This hypothesis is speculative, but surely no more so than the underlying assumption of previous writers that the ordeal was either a "reassuring and peace-creating"[55] method of solving social "problems"[56] or "a way of obtaining a [judicial] result in peculiarly intractable cases."[57] Instead of proposing the ordeal because they were obliged to propose it, believed in it, or thought it would bring peace, they proposed it because, as William Miller puts it, "the ordeal was there to be used in a pinch"[58] by participants in what Hyams terms "quasi-political" episode.[59]

What kind of pinch? Although it is difficult to show, without circular argumentation, that ordeal cases were unusually embittered but not so embittered as to make war the only way of settling them,[60] there is certainly evidence to support this conclusion. For one thing, the mere fact that these lawsuits had arisen out of *calumniae* that monks had chosen to contest, instead of "lumping it," and that were not subsequently settled by negotiation or mediation before a *placitum* was arranged, suggests that they were both lengthy and hotly contested. Just as "a *judicium* actually performed meant obstinate litigants, a quarrel that might yet revive,"[61] a *placitum*

55. Brown, "Society," p. 313.
56. Brown, "Society," p. 317.
57. Bartlett, *Trial,* p. 37.
58. Miller, "Ordeal," p. 196.
59. "Trial," p. 94.
60. On war as a means of settling disputes, see Fredric L. Cheyette, "*Suum Cuique Tribuere,*" *French Historical Studies* 6 (1970), 291.
61. Hyams, "Trial," p. 98.

actually held meant disputants who had already spurned or avoided opportunities to make peace. In addition, accounts of these lawsuits frequently mention the length of the dispute,[62] the lay litigant's vehemence in pressing his claim,[63] angry altercations,[64] *clamores,*[65] and excommunications,[66] and, finally, the most confrontational forms of secular "self-help," including the seizure of land[67] and movable property,[68] burning,[69] and homicide.[70] Some of the disputes involved multiple hearings in different courts;[71] others were ones in which courts were reluctant to intervene and had trouble summoning the lay parties. Furthermore, many such disputes were really segments of "extended cases," some of which related to long-term economic changes,[72] while others involved either repeated disputes between an abbey and a single contentious litigant[73] or successive representatives of the same kin group,[74] or else a conflict with an abbey that had arisen out of an intense dispute among laymen.[75]

At a *placitum* convened to discuss a dispute, no one would even consider proposing an ordeal unless he believed that by doing so he could attain a more favorable outcome than he could reach simply by arguing for his case, presenting oral and written evidence to support his claim, or proposing a compromise settlement. In lawsuits in which ordeals were proposed, there were sometimes good reasons for seeking an alternative to these routine procedures of dispute processing not only because these lawsuits had previously been hotly contested, but also because the meetings where they were discussed were themselves marked by discord. A *miles* called Fulcradus showed such vehemence and violence in challenging the *vicarietas* of some allods previously given to the abbey of La Trinité that a

62. *A* 388 (1082–1106): "frequently moving a quarrel against the monks, [Walicherius of Brion] finally came to a *placitum*."

63. *TV* 57: "tantaque instantia praestitit, ut et inde bellum indiceret judicio comitis Gaufridi." *A* 387: Radulfus Toaredus tried to impose "a very evil custom" on the monks of Saint Aubin.

64. *A* 387: the "good men who had convened from each side began to denounce" the lay litigant.

65. *A* 203; *A* 325.

66. *A* 203.

67. *N* 146; *N* 206.

68. *MB* 28.

69. *MS* 127.

70. Constantius's case: *MB* 93.

71. *A* 325; *A* 388.

72. See *A* 144; and Constantius's case (*MB* 93), which, as his second quitclaim shows, was closely connected to disputes about two other neighboring mills.

73. See *MV* 9, which records one of many disputes between Marmoutier and Tebaldus of Vendôme: *MV* 1–8, 10–12.

74. See *N* 24 and 151; *MS* 127, 108, 118.

75. *N* 24.

duel was arranged,[76] and in their dispute with Tebaldus of Vendôme, the monks of Marmoutier proposed a battle only when they had been "provoked to this."[77] When attending a meeting at Varenne about a dispute with Saint Aubin over vineyards that Constantius Adquadratus had given to the abbey, Constantius's kin gathered "many powerful men" to join the meeting with them, presumably because they expected trouble, and initially contested Constantius's efforts to warrant his gift to the monks.[78] At La Pélerine, the monks of Saint Aubin agreed to a battle with Giraudus de Blancofurno only after he "strongly contested" the words of their witness, whom they knew to be telling the truth.[79] Similarly, in a dispute between Marmoutier and Mauritius son of Gelduinus over various serfs at Fontinetum, the monks' witness "prepared himself to make law, to bear *judicium*" only after Mauritius had "resisted" his testimony and after "a great struggle on both sides" ensued.[80] A "great *altercatio*" broke out at a *placitum* when a man of Marmoutier named Benedictus Blanchardus said he was ready "to bear the hot iron" in order to disprove the claim of Godefredus of Blois to Engelricus *sartor*.[81] The intensity of the same abbey's dispute with Hamelinus of Vendôme over a serf called Guarinus is revealed in the fact that after the monks had won a victory by having their man Teelus offer to undergo an ordeal, Hamelinus then initiated another questionable *calumnia*, this one concerning Guarinus's mother Helena.[82]

As several previously cited examples suggest, a distinctive feature of many *placita* where ordeals were proposed was a sharp dispute between the opposing parties about a specific fact, along with one party's insistence on using an ordeal to validate his own version of critical events. When Mauritius son of Gelduinus claimed Hermandus from Marmoutier on the grounds that he had not approved his father's gift of this serf to the abbey, Hermandus's brother Godevertus "rose up, making himself a witness that Mauritius had granted [Hermandus] to Saint Martin" when Gelduinus had given him; and "when Mauritius contested this, Godevertus prepared himself to make law, to bear *judicium* that Mauritius had approved the gift of his father; and . . . there was a great struggle on both sides."[83] The *ratio* of

76. *TV* 57. See Barthélemy, "La société," pp. 676–77.
77. *MV* 9. See Barthélemy, "La société," p. 677.
78. *A* 189.
79. *A* 878.
80. *MS* 53.
81. *MS* 102.
82. *MS* 101.
83. *MS* 53.

Hamelinus's challenge against Marmoutier about Engelricus *sartor* and the other sons of Guarinus was that "Gundacrus of Vendôme . . . had given him not as a *servus* but as a *collibertus*," whereas the monks' man Teelus "would prove by oath and the judgment of God that, previously, Gundacrius had possessed Guarinus [the brothers'] father by the "law of serfs" and that, later, "we possessed Guarinus as a serf by the gift of Gundacrius."[84]

In an angry debate about an embittered conflict that no one had yet found a way of resolving, a proposal to hold an ordeal did far more than initiate an established judicial procedure. For one thing, it modified the substance of subsequent discussion because, in quick-freezing what had previously been a relatively fluid debate about a multi-faceted dispute, it forced everyone involved to focus intently on the specific issue or issues that the proposed ordeal would test. At the same time, the proposal transformed the procedural possibilities of the case by insuring that, instead of being processed through more commonplace forms of adjudication, mediation, or negotiation, it would now follow one or another of the unusual procedural tracks outlined above, each of which involved a critical strategic decision about whether to continue or cancel the ordeal process. In addition, the proposal altered the tone, the pace, and the possible meanings of subsequent litigation, as the participants began using a discourse distinguished from other forms of debate by formal oaths, denials, prayers, and appeals to supernatural power as they approached the time when the proband might actually fight or grasp the iron. In the short run, the pace of the lawsuit quickened, as other participants were obliged to formulate an immediate response to the proposal. In the long run, however, the proposal, if accepted, slowed down the pace of litigation, because a preliminary agreement to hold an ordeal would leave the participants with several weeks for further strategizing and maneuvering. Finally and most important, because several of the procedural paths that the dispute might now follow led to total defeat for one party or the other and because defeat in the ordeal entailed dishonor as well as material loss, the proposal to hold the ordeal also transformed the politics of the lawsuit, increasing for everyone the political risks involved in the complex bargaining process that the proposal would initiate. Paradoxically, the proposal to settle the lawsuit by ordeal could serve to intensify the dispute: instead of initiating a "reassuring and peace-creating" process through which violence would be channelled into ritual, the proposal not only dramatized the litigants' un-

84. *MS* 101.

willingness to make peace, but also threatened to reintroduce violence, in ritualized form, into a *placitum* where the ritual of adjudication had briefly replaced the violence of self-help as a method of dispute processing.[85]

For all these reasons, a proposal to hold an ordeal can be interpreted as a strategy of confrontation, as a means of issuing a political threat, designed to put an adversary on the defensive. In the simplest cases, a proposal to hold an ordeal, when made by a litigant or litigant's supporter, was meant to break a political and legal impasse in the case by intimidating the opposing party to the point where he would either default or accept a relatively unfavorable compromise; when made by a judge, the proposal could be a signal to one party or the other that he had nothing to gain and everything to lose by continuing his suit. In either case, however, if the second litigant rightly or wrongly interpreted the proposal to hold the ordeal as a bluff or if he wished, for some other reason, to continue the ordeal process, then he could accept the proposal to hold the ordeal, leaving his adversaries and the judges with the problem of deciding whether he was merely bluffing and would sooner or later cancel the ordeal process. Even though the proposal was intended to be read as a "theatrical device"[86] of self-righteous self-dramatization, there must have been times when the proposer's audience read it as an act of stupidity or desperation. Finally, because the ordeal process that the proposal initiated was so flexible that it allowed for different sequences of responses and subsequent moves and gave all the participants room to change their tactics, and because no participant's public posture ever coincided with his actual intentions, the relationship between the initial proposal to hold an ordeal and the final outcome of the lawsuit is sometimes difficult to fathom. The ordeal process could vary, depending on such factors as the proposer's social position and legal role in the case, the type of ordeal he proposed, the legal and factual issues raised by the case, the experience and skill of the litigants and judges, and, above all, the political strength and cohesiveness of the proposer's party relative to that of other groups involved in the case.

The considerations involved in deciding whether to propose an ordeal or how to meet an adversary's proposal were so complex that people facing these choices must have resorted to improvisation.[87] As we have seen, con-

85. Brown, however, thinks that "the ritual itself was . . . peace-creating" ("Society," p. 313).

86. Brown, "Society," p. 311.

87. On improvisation, see Pierre Bourdieu, *Outline of a Theory of Practice,* translated by Richard Nice (Cambridge, 1977), p. 17; and Renato Rosaldo, *Culture and Truth: The Remaking of Social Analysis* (Boston, 1989), pp. 102–5.

ventions governing the use of ordeals in civil cases were so flexible that no one could be certain whether such a proposal would be made, who might make it, what form it would take, or where, once made, it might lead. What made such proposals disquieting was not that everyone either believed or doubted that the ordeal could reveal the truth, but that no one could be sure how the case would now proceed. Would the ordeal even be held? If held, what outcome would it have? And how would that outcome be interpreted? In a battle, unless the champions could be identified in advance and were clearly unequal in skill and strength, no one could be sure who would win.[88] The unilateral ordeal was even more unpredictable not only because the ritual itself was open to tampering, but also because its outcome was sometimes disputed. Finally, either a battle or a unilateral ordeal might serve as the basis for a judgment that the loser would ignore. In practice, an ordeal's outcome might not be any more predictable than that of a modern jury trial, which experienced practitioners commonly regard, in Miller's words, as "a crapshoot."[89] But the ordeal differed profoundly from other games of chance because even a clear outcome would not necessarily bring victory. For all these reasons, participants in lawsuits may well have believed that the best way of controlling the ordeal was to avoid it whenever they could.

Like a proposal to hold an ordeal, a decision to avoid one could be made at several different junctures of a lawsuit. Sometimes the proposal was immediately rejected in favor of another method of settling the dispute.[90] On other occasions, the parties reached agreement during the interval between the first *placitum* and the day set for the ordeal.[91] A third possibility was that one litigant would simply fail to appear for the ordeal.[92] Finally, if both parties appeared for it, one or both of them could initiate its cancellation before it began or even after it had commenced.[93]

Because monastic scribes did not preserve records of their abbeys' most ignominious defeats in litigation, it is hardly surprising that in most recorded cases, it was the lay litigant who avoided the ordeal.[94] But scribes

88. The commonplace that the outcome of battle was uncertain appears in *TV* 57.

89. Miller, "Ordeal," p. 189.

90. *A* 325, 387; *MS* 11, 101, 102; *N* 147, 151; *V* 315.

91. *MV* 159; *N* 484; *V* 597.

92. *A* 404; *MB* 26, 28; *N* 529; *V* 769. Lawsuits in which monks defaulted may well have gone unrecorded.

93. *MB* 126; *MS* 53, 109, 127; *MV* 9; *N* 124, 126; *TV* 157, 189, 257.

94. *A* 189, 203, 325, 388, 404, 878; *MB* 26, 28; *MV* 159; *MS* 11, 101, 109, 127; *N* 24, 146, 151, 484, 529; *TV* 57, 189, 257; *V* 597, 315, 769.

still recorded cases in which the monks avoided battles[95] or unilateral ordeals.[96] In many cases, one party's proposal to hold an ordeal was sooner or later followed by the other's decision to avoid or cancel it.[97] But just as frequently, the party who had proposed the ordeal eventually backed out of it.[98] In two other cases, the decision to avoid the ordeal was mutual.[99] When judges, rather than litigants, proposed an ordeal, monks[100] as well as lay litigants[101] sometimes avoided it.

Why did lay people and monks avoid trial by ordeal? Although the reasons they supposedly gave for doing so vary from case to case, several of them appear so frequently and accord so well with accounts of agreements reached in other lawsuits[102] as to suggest that the process of withdrawing from an ordeal, like the process of proposing one, was stylized, even ritualized. Once a lawsuit had been transposed into a new key by a proposal to hold an ordeal, it would remain in that key until one or both parties could effect another modulation by sounding a familiar sequence of chords. To shift the image, in a society where posturing was an integral part of political life and where dramatic changes in posture were acceptable and sometimes even obligatory,[103] people could stop the ordeal by assuming the proper postures. This conclusion implies, in turn, that a litigant's public justification for avoiding an ordeal need not have coincided with his real reasons for doing so, any more than a litigant's or judge's proposal to hold an ordeal communicated a sincere wish to employ this procedure. The same conclusion also implies that experienced participants in lawsuits knew, even before anyone proposed the ordeal, that this procedure, if proposed, could be aborted. For all participants, therefore, the subtext of the lawsuit was just as important as the text.

Certain passages purporting to explain why particular litigants avoided ordeals point toward the comforting conclusion that trial by ordeal was really an effective method of dispute processing because widespread belief in its efficacy as a divinely sanctioned test of truth deterred liti-

95. *A* 144; *MB* 126; *MV* 9.
96. *A* 137; *MD* 10; *MS* 53, 102; *N* 147.
97. *A* 137, 878; *MB* 26, 28; *MS* 11, 101; *N* 147, 151; *V* 315, 597.
98. *A* 144; *MD* 10; *MS* 53, 102, 127; *MV* 9, 159; *TV* 189, 257; *V* 769.
99. *A* 204; *MD* 16.
100. *MB* 126.
101. *A* 203, 388, 404; *N* 24, 529; *TV* 57.
102. On agreements, see Geary, "Vivre en conflit" and the literature he surveys.
103. See Geoffrey Koziol, *Begging Pardon and Favor: Ritual and Political Order in Early Medieval France* (Ithaca, NY, 1992).

gants from pursuing unjust causes to the bitter end. According to a scribe of Noyers, "when the *probi homines* acting on behalf of Saint Mary were ready for the battle . . . Malrannus, acknowledging before the many people present that he had not undertaken battle rightfully, gave up the challenge he had unjustly undertaken."[104] Similarly, after undertaking battle against the same abbey to support a claim to free status, Theovinus and Amalvinus first acknowledged before the day of battle that "they had undertaken [battle] wrongly" and then restored themselves to the lordship of Saint Mary.[105] Landricus gave up his challenge against La Trinité of Vendôme because, knowing it to be unjust, he did not dare to fight the monks' champion.[106] Just before a battle with a champion of the same abbey, Fulcradus decided that it was wrong to litigate about God's land, especially when he knew his claim to be unjust. Impelled by the fear of God, he gave up his challenge.[107]

Fears of a similar kind supposedly led Otbertus the Shoemaker to avoid an ordeal that he himself had proposed to undergo in support of his claim to some vineyards held by Noyers: "When Otbertus came to swear and to undergo *judicium* and saw that the . . . monks were intent on receiving this proof, then, fearing that on account of the disinheritance of the church [of Saint Mary], from which he wished to take away property, the holy mother of God would be opposed to him, and being terrified of swearing God's word on the relics of the same church, he did not wish to undergo *judicium*. Instead, he gave up the vineyards and lands about which the quarrel had arisen, so that they would be held by the monks." Even though this passage emphasizes, as the primary reason for avoiding an ordeal, the litigant's fear of supernatural retaliation by his monastic adversary's patron saint, it also suggests, at least implicitly that he also avoided this procedure in the belief that if he followed it by swearing "God's word," he would be revealed as a perjurer.[108]

Whereas the conventionalized passages just cited all suggest that people avoided the ordeal in the belief that it would reveal the truth about an oath, other common and equally conventionalized passages about avoid-

104. *N* 24.

105. *N* 484.

106. *TV* 257. See Barthélemy, "La société," p. 677.

107. *TV* 57. See Barthélemy, "La société," pp. 676–77.

108. *N* 154. The same belief may also explain both the failure of litigants or probands to appear for ordeals and last-minute decisions to avoid the procedure: see *A* 325, 388; *MS* 127, 192.

ance of ordeals implicitly articulate reservations about the same procedure, mainly by associating it with violence or discord, rather than with peace. One commonplace method of explaining and obliquely justifying withdrawal from the ordeal was to express a general preference for amicable compromises over judgments.[109] In a culture where sudden shifts in political posture from enmity to amity were commonplace, a scribe could easily impute this preference to fellow monks who had previously been engaged in relentless litigation. Glossing a decision by abbot Girardus of Saint Aubin to compromise with Hugo, who was ready to undergo a unilateral ordeal to prove his claim against the abbey, a scribe claimed that his abbot "wished to deal with men peaceably."[110] Similarly, a monk of Marmoutier who compromised with Godefredus of Blois just as the abbey's man was about to undergo a unilateral ordeal, did so supposedly because he "preferred to seek right (*rectum*) by peace rather than strife (*jurgium*)."[111] A scribe of the same monastery gave a more complex, yet highly conventionalized explanation for his brothers' decision to avoid a duel proposed by the judges in the lawsuit with Guarnerius *bisolius*: "When our man and his were prepared for battle, a concord was made justly or unjustly. Even though we trusted in the justice of our cause, we preferred buying time to wasting time on litigation and did not want human blood to be spilled on our account."[112]

In several instances, responsibility for a party's decision to avoid an ordeal was assigned to others who counseled him to take this step. On the day of battle between the champions of Marmoutier and Tetbaldus de Vendôme, the monks "were called upon by [their] *amici* to terminate the dispute by peace rather than by strife."[113] Under generally similar circumstances, the friends of Petrus Cadebertus advised him to settle "amicably" his dispute with La Trinité.[114] Occasionally, third parties joined a litigant's friends in pressing him to avoid an ordeal. At a meeting convened to consider a dispute between Noyers and Otbertus de Montigny, abbot

109. See Michael T. Clanchy, "Law and Love in the Middle Ages," in *Disputes and Settlements: Law and Human Relations in the West,* ed. John Bossy (Cambridge, 1983), pp. 47–67; and Stephen D. White, "'*Pactum . . . Legem Vincit et Amor Judicium*': The Settlement of Disputes by Compromise in Eleventh-Century Western France," *American Journal of Legal History* 22 (1978); 281–308.

110. *A* 137; see also 144.

111. *MS* 102.

112. *MB* 126.

113. *MV* 9.

114. *TV* 189.

Stephanus and his monks were helped by "good men," as well as their own friends, to reach a concord with Otbertus, who had proposed to undergo an ordeal.[115] As these and other passages suggest, the intervention of *amici* to stop ordeals and promote concord was so conventionalized as to support the hypothesis that litigants who publicly committed themselves to participate in ordeals did so with the knowledge that their friends might well extricate them from this predicament.

By assuming one or another of the postures just described, a litigant in a civil dispute could evidently avoid an ordeal, whether or not he really felt certain of losing it, or truly feared God's wrath, or suddenly saw the injustice of a dispute he had been waging for months or years, or felt a new-found preference for peace, or was persuaded by the wiser counsel of friends. Moreover, if a litigant avoided an ordeal by publicly assuming the posture of a God- and saint-fearing penitent, a peace-lover, or a man receptive to the wise counsel of friends, he would probably not emerge from the dispute empty-handed. Although the mere fact that litigants often gained something tangible after avoiding ordeals hardly shows that they avoided the ordeal for this reason and not for ones that scribes imputed to them, it suggests that scribal accounts of what were obviously stylized ceremonies were, at best, incomplete. Along with the motives that scribes customarily ascribed to them, litigants had other good reasons for avoiding the ordeal.

In lawsuits that would not have been recorded, monks may have secured no land at all when they avoided the ordeal. But in recorded cases, monks who took this step invariably secured quitclaims from their lay adversaries,[116] who also surrendered their claims in cases where the decision to avoid the ordeal was mutual.[117] When a lay litigant initiated the cancellation of an ordeal, the monks often granted him such things as money,[118] a partial interest in the disputed property,[119] the privilege of confraternity,[120] burial rights,[121] a place as a brother in the monastery,[122] a partial pardon for offences committed during the dispute,[123] and the right to keep plunder he had taken from the monks' lands.[124]

115. *N* 147.
116. *A* 137, 144; *MD* 10; *MS* 53, 102; *MV* 9; *N* 147.
117. *A* 204; *MB* 126; *MD* 16.
118. *A* 189; *MS* 101; *N* 24, 151; *TV* 189; *V* 597.
119. *A* 144; *N* 146, 154.
120. *A* 137; *MD* 16; *TV* 57; *V* 769.
121. *TV* 57.
122. *A* 878.
123. *MD* 16.
124. *A* 325.

Not every litigant, however, could gain something tangible by avoiding the ordeal, and even when he did so, the extent of his gains would vary. The outcomes reached after ordeals were cancelled were sometimes discernibly influenced by the relative strengths of the two parties' bargaining positions. Because the only litigants who received nothing at all when they avoided the ordeal were either free people who defaulted rather undergo the ordeal personally or by proxy[125] or alleged serfs who could have proved their free status only by undergoing the ordeal themselves,[126] there are certainly grounds for thinking that litigants with hopelessly weak cases avoided ordeals simply because they feared the physical process of undergoing the ordeal or the judicial, political, and religious consequences of losing it. Whereas these litigants withdrew from ordeals in an effort to cut their losses, others who exercised the same procedural option under different political circumstances may have done so in the belief that their bargaining position, though weaker than that of their adversary, was not so weak as to prevent them from gaining anything at all from litigation. When an ordeal was cancelled at the monks' initiative or by mutual agreement, the payment made to the lay litigant in return for his quitclaim to the monks was usually considerably higher in value than it was when he initiated cancellation of the ordeal.[127]

Within limits, there may also have been a rough correlation between how strong a free litigant considered his bargaining position to be, how long he would persist in his suit, and how favorable an outcome he could secure for himself. Alleged serfs were clearly in a distinctive position, because as parties to disputes in which compromise was evidently unthinkable, they probably had less to lose by pursuing a lawsuit all the way to a judgment based on an ordeal. Up to a point, the longer a free litigant pursued his claim the better his chances would be of achieving a favorable outcome. If he immediately rejected a proposal by the judges or the monks to hold an ordeal, he might well get nothing[128] and would certainly go empty-handed if he defaulted by failing to appear for a scheduled ordeal.

125. *A* 404; *N* 529.

126. *MS* 109; *MS* 159; *N* 529. For cases in which litigants gained nothing when they avoided ordeals at an earlier stage of a lawsuit, see *A* 388; *V* 315.

127. *Cancellations by monks*: 100 *solidi* (*A* 137); 50 *solidi* (*A* 144; *MD* 10); 40 *solidi* (*MV* 9); 30 *solidi* (*MS* 102); 10 *solidi* (*MS* 53). *Mutual cancellations*: 120 *solidi* (*MD* 16); 45 *solidi* (*MB* 126); 15 *solidi* (*A* 204). *Cancellations by lay litigants*: 30 *solidi* (*TV* 189); 25 *solidi* (*A* 189); 20 *solidi* (*N* 24, 171); 10 *solidi* (*V* 597; *MS* 101). It may also be significant that three of the largest payments in the first two kinds of cancellations were accompanied by either a grant of confraternity (*MD* 16; *A* 137) or a grant of a partial interest in the disputed property (*A* 144).

128. *A* 388.

If he initially agreed to a proposed ordeal, the monks might well propose a compromise, especially if he actually appeared for the ordeal. However, a litigant who obstinately pursued a claim instead of picking an opportune time to compromise could lose everything he had been trying to gain by unduly prolonging the lawsuit.

The cancelled ordeal process assumed many different forms because, like the completed ordeal process, it involved "a myriad of variables,"[129] including when the proposal to hold the ordeal was made, who made it, what type of ordeal was proposed, whether it was offered or demanded, who bore the burden of undergoing it, what the ordeal was supposed to prove, where it was to be held, who cancelled it, when it was cancelled, and what form the cancellation took. Cases in which the judges proposed the ordeal, for example, differed significantly from those in which the proposal was made by a monastic or lay litigant; cases in which a litigant proposed the ordeal at the outset of a *placitum* differed from those in which the judges or one of the parties proposed the same procedure only after the lawsuit had been extensively debated. Lawsuits in which battle was waged differed from those in which a unilateral ordeal was proposed.

Although the cancelled ordeal process assumed so many different forms that virtually every example of it followed a distinctive course, it is possible to divide examples of the process into a few groups by focusing on three critically important procedural variables. First, was the proposal to hold the ordeal made by the judges or by one of the litigants? Second, did the proposal induce the litigant who did not make it to avoid the ordeal and accept either an adverse judgment or a compromise? Third, was the ordeal cancelled before or after it commenced? In the first set of cases discussed below, the judges' proposal to hold an ordeal sooner or later induced one of the litigants to abandon his claim (Roaldus, Galterius, Walicherius). In a second set of cases, after one litigant proposed an ordeal his adversary decided to settle the case by compromise (Hugo, Otbertus, and the relatives of Constantius). In a third set of cases, however, after one party's proposal to hold an ordeal was accepted by the other party (Radulfus, Bunghole, Pletrudis), the first party sooner or later avoided the ordeal and then either defaulted or made a compromise with the other party. In one final case, a litigant who had accepted his adversary's proposal to hold an ordeal cancelled the ordeal after it was underway (Giraudus).

In interpreting the procedural moves made in these examples of the

129. Miller, "Ordeal," p. 199.

cancelled ordeal cases, it is important to consider not only the many procedural options that were open to the participants and the legal issues, both substantive and evidentiary, that were explicitly raised in the lawsuit, but also such factors as the "identity of the parties [and judges], their past relations, their relative status,"[130] and their respective skills in negotiating the ordeal process. Although we will never know for certain why the judges, the litigants, and the litigant's supporters acted as they did in any particular case, we can assume that their actions were the products of strategies that were based, for better or worse, on their own assessments of the political context of the lawsuit. Certain litigants, for example, were probably confident that by proposing an ordeal they or the judges could intimidate their adversaries into accepting unfavorable judgments or settlements, while other litigants may have believed that their only hope of winning a case lay in successfully undergoing the ordeal. Judges of important courts in major centers of power such as Angers were probably more successful in using the ordeal as an instrument of power than were the judges of lesser courts. Certain litigants were probably successful in predicting how a cancelled ordeal case would proceed, while others may well have stumbled through the process without any clear sense of where it would lead. Speculative as such assumptions are, they provide our only means of explicating lawsuits whose procedural twists and turns are otherwise opaque.

* * *

In several cancelled ordeal cases, the judges apparently used a proposal to hold an ordeal as means of intimidating a litigant into avoiding the ordeal and either defaulting or accepting a compromise. It is probably no accident that these lawsuits were all settled in Angers, rather than in some outlying lordship of the region. When Roaldus of Luigné, a village lying about 24 kilometers southeast of Angers, travelled to Angers to confront the monks of Saint Aubin at a *placitum* in the court of bishop Gaufridus, he probably had little hope of winning his claim to some land in Alleuds (4 kilometers closer to Angers than Luigné) which he had previously seized from the monks on the grounds that "it pertained to his right." The meeting had taken a long time to arrange, probably because Roaldus was reluctant to attend it; when it finally convened, he and five supporters faced four monks and five monastic *famuli* in the presence of nine clerics

130. Miller, "Ordeal," p. 199.

and nineteen laymen, who were there to act as judges or witnesses. After the abbot had made his complaint about Roaldus's unjust invasion of the monks' property, Roaldus may have displayed some uneasiness about his chances of securing a favorable judgment when he said he would make no response to the abbot's complaint unless the bishop first promised to do right to him in his dispute with the monks. Roaldus's caution was probably warranted since many of the judges were close associates of his monastic adversaries. After the bishop made this promise, the judges first listened to Roaldus's narration of his claim and the abbot's response and then deliberated on each part of what was evidently a complex case. They then decided that the monks ought not to enter into further litigation about land that was known to have been given to them long ago. Having resolved the legal issues in the dispute to their own and the monks' satisfaction, the judges still had to confront the political problem of inducing the loser to accept their judgment. Roaldus protested it; in response, bishop Gaufridus and archdeacon Marbodus both undertook to swear on the gospels that the judgment was just and in accord with "ancient custom." This proposal neither mollified nor cowed Roaldus, who continued to protest. Finally, two of the lay judges, Babinus de Raies and Girardus son of Andefredus, declared: " 'Our lord bishop and lord archdeacon Marbodus wish to show by swearing that the judgment that we, along with them, made is right. We laymen wish to do the same by fighting, if there is anyone against whom we should prove this.' " Upon hearing this challenge, Roaldus and his five supporters apparently wanted to prove by fighting that the judges had judged the case falsely. But none of them spoke. In theory, Roaldus could still have undergone a battle to support a claim of false judgment. But at that moment, he was faced with a practical political problem, surrounded as he was by more than two dozen powerful men who were now openly supporting his adversaries. He must have realized that it would be politically inexpedient (and possibly dangerous as well) to accept a duel with Babinus or Andefredus, whose proposal to hold a bilateral ordeal had clearly intimidated him, just as they had presumably intended for it to do.[131]

Under slightly different circumstances, a knight called Galterius of Meigné was intimidated by the prospect of undergoing a unilateral ordeal proposed by the judges, and defaulted rather than appearing for it. Galterius had initiated a challenge about some land at Noyau, which the monks of Saint Aubin had received as a gift from Albericus of Vihiers and his

131. *A* 203 (1082–1101).

wife Adela and had allegedly held for a long time. At the court of the same bishop Gaufridus who judged the monks' lawsuit with Roaldus, Galterius was interrogated about his claim, not by the judges, by the bishop, or by archdeacon Marbodus (who was also present), but by Albericus, who was evidently assuming an obligation to warrant his and his wife's gift to Saint Aubin. When, in reply to Albericus's questioning, Galterius said that in return for a horse he had received the disputed land at Noyau from Albericus's ancestor, also named Albericus, the judges declared that he should prove this allegation by the ordeal of hot iron. When someone (perhaps Galterius himself) asked where the ordeal would be held, the response came, not from the judges, but from Albericus, who continued to exercise his influence on the court's proceedings by proposing to hold the ordeal at his own estate in Vihiers, about twenty kilometers south of Angers. Doubtless unnerved both by the substance of Albericus's proposal and by the judges' deference to the abbey's warrantor, Galterius was not yet ready to abandon his claim completely but still began to excuse himself, indicating that he did not dare go to Vihiers for the ordeal. But instead of thereby inducing the judges to name another site for the *judicium* they had proposed, Galterius merely secured from Albericus a promise of safe-passage to Vihiers and back. By now, Galterius should have seen that his lawsuit was doomed. But instead of giving in at once and seeking something by way of compensation for quitclaiming the land at Noyau, he agreed to go to Vihiers. At the appointed time for the ordeal, Albericus expressed his confidence about its outcome by saying to abbot Girardus of Saint Aubin: "Send whomever of your monks you wish to see the ordeal and to see how I shall acquit your land to you." Meanwhile, Gualterius and the three friends who had associated themselves with his *calumnia* simply decided, not surprisingly, to spare themselves a trip to Albericus's estate, with the result that no one appeared to undergo the ordeal at Vihiers. Although their decision to default may have been due to their conviction that the ordeal would reveal the injustice of what they now knew to be a spurious claim, it can be attributed to a more general and well-grounded fear that, in one way or another, the journey to Vihiers would turn out badly for them.[132]

Like Roaldus of Luigné and Galterius of Meigné, Walicherius of Brion was intimidated, in a dispute with Saint Aubin, by the judges' proposal that he undergo an ordeal. But he gave up less quickly than did the other two

132. *A* 404 (1082–93).

litigants. According to Walicherius, a vineyard the monks held at Brion lying about thirty kilometers east of Angers, pertained to him *per parentagium*. When he and the monks attended a *placitum* in the village, the judges asked him how he knew that the disputed vineyard pertained to him. He responded that at a subsequent *placitum* a man named Aufridus would legally warrant the vineyard, as Aufridus was obliged to do. But when, at the appointed time, Aufridus, though present, somehow failed to warrant the land, the judges decided that Walicherius should prove his claim "*per judicium*."[133] Because Walicherius did not dare to undergo the ordeal, the judges judged his claim to be unjust. Even though Walicherius then protested what he represented as an unjust judgment, his fear of undergoing the proposed ordeal ultimately proved fatal to his case when, with support from his lord, Gaufridus of Brion, he revived his claim in Angers. There, in the *auditorium* of Saint Aubin, he again narrated his claim to the vineyard at Brion. A man of Saint Aubin from Brion responded by citing Walicherius's previous failure at Brion to prove the same claim by ordeal. The judges at Angers therefore judged his claim to be unjust.[134]

* * *

In each of the three cases just considered, the judges' proposal to hold an ordeal, made late in a *placitum*, served to intimidate a litigant who was doggedly pursuing a claim with inadequate support. Any one of these litigants could have undergone the ordeal, but each of them must have realized that victory in this process would be either impossible or useless. In three other lawsuits, a litigant's proposal to hold an ordeal also seems to have worked effectively, since the other litigant responded sooner or later by avoiding the ordeal and proposing a settlement. In a dispute with Saint Aubin over a mill and a weir on the Loire near Les Ponts-de-Cé, Hugo, the *nepos* and heir of Teschelina, came to the court of bishop Gaufridus and offered to prove the justice of his claim by the ordeal by hot iron. The abbot of Saint Aubin, however, rejected Hugo's offer, proposing instead to give him 100 *solidi* if he would surrender his claim. Hugo accepted this compromise and, along with his wife, later received the privilege of confraternity at Saint Aubin. Attributing the abbot's decision to settle the case by compromise rather than by ordeal to his desire for peace, the abbey's

133. The text reads "*per juditium contra mortuum*." On the type of ordeal proposed here, see Bongert.

134. *A* 388 (1082–1106).

scribe failed to indicate why his pacificism was not manifested earlier in the lawsuit.[135] In a dispute with Noyers, Otbertus de la Montée offered to prove by ordeal that the monks had no right to the land he claimed. Instead of simply accepting the offer and awaiting the outcome of the ordeal, the abbot and monks made a concord with Otbertus, allegedly because they had doubts about accepting proof by ordeal from such a man and were yielding to the advice of their friends and the "good men" participating in the *placitum* as third parties.[136]

In another Saint Aubin case, after various relatives of Constantius Adquadratus had initiated a challenge about some vineyards that Constantius had previously given to the monks, the two sides met to discuss the dispute in the presence of Heudo, lord of Blazon. First the monks' adversaries explained their claim. Then Constantius warranted his gift to Saint Aubin by declaring himself ready to show by an ordeal undergone by his man that after the death of his father, he had bought the disputed vineyards fully and quietly and had worked them, so that he could do with them as he preferred, whether by selling or giving them away for his own soul, without any just contradiction of challenge by any of his kin. Eventually, after Constantius's man had sworn an oath at his lord's command, Constantius's relatives made a concord with the monks. Accepting from Constantius 25 *solidi*, which they divided among themselves, they all surrendered their challenge.[137]

* * *

Whereas the lawsuits just considered suggest that proposing the ordeal was often an effective means of inducing the litigant who had not proposed it to avoid the ordeal and either default or make a compromise, several other cases show that this tactic was not foolproof. If the proposal to hold the ordeal were accepted, the case could proceed in many different ways, several of which are illustrated by the following cases. In two cases (Radulfus and Martinus), the lay litigant whose proposal to hold the ordeal was accepted by the monks later decided to cancel it and make a compromise with the monks. In a third case (Bunghole), although the lay litigant who had proposed the ordeal lost his case when he failed to appear for it, the monks later made a compromise with his lord. In a final case (Pletrudis), a

135. *A* 137.
136. *N* 147 (1087).
137. *A* 189 (1060).

litigant whose proposal to hold an ordeal was accepted withdrew from the procedural at the last possible moment.

To support his claim that the monks of Saint Aubin were obliged to provide him with unusually opulent hospitality whenever he and his men visited Angers, Radulfus Toaredus angrily attended a *placitum* at Beaugency. Here he undertook battle to prove that the abbey owed him the hospitality he claimed under an agreement he had previously made at Beaugency with two monks of the monastery. To fight on his behalf, Radulfus designated a *famulus* called Haimarus Malspetit, who had allegedly witnessed the disputed agreement and would uphold, by oath, Radulfus's claims about it. The monks, however, presented as their own champion a man of the abbey, who had allegedly witnessed the same agreement and would prove against Haimarus that "what Radulfus had said was false." The battle never took place. While Haimarus and the monks' champion were confronting one another, "the good men who had convened from each side began to denounce Radulfus, saying that he was demanding an unjust and evil thing from the monks." Clearly, Radulfus was still entitled to pursue his claim by insisting that the battle be held. But because he had supposedly been "convinced" by the arguments of the "good men" and by "the testimony of his own conscience," he gave up his claim on the understanding that the monks would grant him and his wife the privilege of confraternity and would render him, on his visits to Angers, as much charity as they customarily rendered to their own visiting brothers.[138] Having overplayed his hand at the outset of the meeting, Radulfus salvaged something from the lawsuit by avoiding the ordeal.

In cases such as Roaldus's, it appears that one party or his supporter proposed an ordeal in the hope that his adversary would avoid it and either abandon his claim completely or accept a relatively unfavorable settlement. But when the second party called the first party's bluff, the latter avoided the ordeal and accepted a settlement less favorable than he had hoped for. The same sequence of tactical maneuvers is also illustrated by an early twelfth-century dispute between Saint Aubin and Martinus Evigilans Canem. Abbot Archembaldus of Saint Aubin came to the court of Berlaius, lord of Montreuil-Bellay, to discuss, among other things, Martinus's challenge to some rocks and a small parcel of land suitable for building houses, all of which the monks supposedly held by a gift or gifts from Berlaius. Accompanying the abbot was Widdo son of Laurentius, who first testified

138. *A* 387 (1082–1106).

that Martinus had previously granted the disputed property to Saint Aubin and then offered to prove this allegation by battle. When Martinus, however, denied Widdo's allegations and agreed to fight him, the abbot, for the sake of peace, proposed an agreement that was relatively favorable to Martinus. The abbot gave him 50 *solidi* and one of the disputed rocks on condition that he would sell it to no one but the monks. Only then did Martinus surrender his entire claim with the approval of his *nepos,* Paganus Beraldi. On the same occasion, Berlaius and his son Giraldus agreed that if a burg were established in any part of the disputed property, the men belonging to it would have the same "liberty" and "custom" as Berlaius had previously granted to the men of another burg at Franchia Villa. Here a small dispute is clearly linked to a larger one.[139]

Whereas Radulfus may have proposed an ordeal because he was arrogantly overconfident about his chances of winning his case against Saint Aubin, Bunghole may have done so either because he expected the proposal to be rejected, in which case he could have gained something from a compromise, or because he saw no other way of gaining anything from what he knew to be a weak claim. Once the ordeal had been scheduled by the judges, who revealed their hostility to Bunghole's case when they advised abbot Hugo to accept Bunghole's proposed proof, Bunghole, like Galterius de Meigné, may have seen no point in appearing for an ordeal he felt certain of losing. However, the fact that Bunghole's lord Richard later secured something from Saint Vincent's in return for surrendering his claim suggests that the tactics of proposing an ordeal could be even more complex than the preceding argument suggests. Perhaps Richard's plan had been for Bunghole to take the lead in aggressively prosecuting the claim to the tithes so that he himself would not be so deeply implicated in the suit as to prevent him from subsequently making a deal with the monks.[140]

If certain litigants or witnesses proposed the ordeal because they were stupidly overconfident or because they were so wily that their maneuvers now seem almost incomprehensible, others may have done so out of sheer desperation. In around 1090, a woman called Pletrudis offered to prove by the ordeal of hot iron that her son Vitalis was not a serf of Marmoutier. This unusual lawsuit formed part of a prolonged conflict between one of the most powerful abbeys of medieval France and a small peasant kin

139. *A* 144 (1107–20).
140. *V* 769.

group. Pletrudis's husband, Otbertus the Shepherd, had once held free status, which he later lost by marrying a female serf of Marmoutier. However, after her death and his own remarriage to Pletrudis, who was free, he withdrew himself from the abbey's lordship, while the monks continued to claim him as their serf. While carrying on his dispute with the monks, he burned down one of their granges; when he could not pay a fine for this offense, he definitively lost his freedom, as did Pletrudis. Years later, when the monks claimed the couple's son Vitalis as their serf, Pletrudis (whose husband was dead by this time) contested the claim on the grounds that Vitalis had been born before his parents had become the abbey's serfs. In proposing to prove by ordeal this critical point—which may well have been complicated by disagreement about when, precisely, Vitalis's parents had become serfs of the abbey—Pletrudis was adopting the only course open to her, because the monks contested her claim and she found no witnesses to support her, and because disputes over personal status, as previously noted, were not considered amenable to compromise. Pletrudis pursued her case through all the preliminary rituals of the ordeal, but when the time came to grasp the iron, she drew back. Unlike knights, lords, or monks who withdrew from ordeals, she gained nothing by doing so. Instead of proposing a compromise, the court ruled against her. Nevertheless, a certain sort of balance was eventually restored in the relations between her kin group and the community of Saint Martin. Her son Vitalis refused for many years to acknowledge the monks' lordship and eventually did so only after burning and plundering the monastery's lands.[141]

* * *

Whereas all the cases considered thus far suggest that litigants were often so uneasy about the mere prospect of having their cases judged by ordeal that they preferred to avoid this procedure completely, one final case reveals that a litigant might base a decision to cancel a battle on his assessment of how well it was proceeding. After Giraudus de Blanco Furno and his kin renewed a claim that they previously made to some land held by the monks of Saint Aubin at Cré, abbot Girardus arranged a *placitum* close to Cré at La Pelérine, which began with an unusually well-recorded narration by Giraudus. He said that one of his mother's two sisters, named Amelina, became the concubine of Otgerius, a serf of Saint Aubin. Her kin

141. *MS* 127 and 108.

threatened to kill Otgerius unless he married her, but for a long time he spurned their threats. He finally married Amelina after her kin agreed to give him the land of Cré *in matrimonium*. At present, according to Giraudus, because there was no survivor from the *genus* of either Otgerius or Amelina to take the land, he himself and his kin were claiming it, "because it moves from us and ought to revert to us." An unnamed woman testifying on the monks' behalf then asserted that Giraudus's *narratio* was false, because, she said, the disputed land of Cré had belonged to Saint Aubin before Amelina's marriage to Otgerius, who did not, in fact, accept it with his wife *in matrimonium*. "What I say, I saw," she said, "and for it I am a witness." Giraudus strongly contested the woman's story. But the monks, who allegedly knew that her words were true, undertook battle against Giraudus and his kinsman Hubertus. They accepted the duel, which was to be held in the "court" of the abbey of Saint Pierre de Bourgeuil. The abbot and his people appeared there for the battle at the appointed time, as did Giraudus, his kin, and his lord Raherius. After the customary preliminaries, including the swearing of oaths, the champions began to fight. But when Giraudus and his associates saw that the fight was going badly for their man, they stopped it and made a compromise with the monks. In return for quitclaiming the disputed land at Cré to Saint Aubin, Giraudus was allowed to become a brother of the abbot and monks of the abbey. He also received the privilege of confraternity at the monastry of Bourgeuil, which the abbot of this community granted him out of love for the abbot and monks of Saint Aubin.[142] Because Giraudus could probably have made a more favorable settlement with the monks if he had simply avoided the battle and instead made a compromise with them, his case suggests that there were risks involved in accepting battle. Nevertheless, the fact that the monks were willing to compromise with him at all instead of pressing for legal victory also shows that a litigant of some standing did not risk everything by accepting a battle.

* * *

In later eleventh-century western France, both proposals to hold ordeals and measures taken to avoid them appear primarily as instruments of power, as tricky, dangerous bargaining ploys that litigants, their supporters, and judges might use to achieve what they considered favorable

142. *A* 878 (1082–1106).

outcomes in disputes. These particular ways of using the ordeal were clearly specific to a particular legal culture in which access to this instrument of power—this method of asserting power over people through the double mediation of acts of submission to God and to a court—remained open to many kinds of people playing different roles in a lawsuit. Because the lawsuits considered in this study come mainly from the troubled reigns of Geoffrey the Bearded (1060–1068) and Fulk Rechin (1067/68–1109), it is tempting to associate the flexible legal culture revealed in western French cancelled ordeal cases with the broader political features of a particularly conflict-ridden society, marked by "internal dissension" and a pronounced decline in comital authority.[143] In any event, it seems clear that in those cultures where access to the ordeal was more restricted and more closely regulated, the ordeal process must have assumed different forms and taken on different meanings. Nevertheless, the present study of the ordeal process in cases of a certain type from one region during a brief period raises questions about previous efforts to establish the ordeal's nature and about the entire enterprise of assigning a single meaning and a single function to this complex procedure. Instead of indicating that the ordeal was a "reassuring," "rational," or effective means of solving legal problems or meeting social needs, evidence of monastic litigation in late eleventh-century western France suggests that well before trial by ordeal began to fall into disuse (whenever that happened)[144] and perhaps throughout its history, participants in medieval lawsuits used it as a chancy, but potentially useful method of settling disputes on favorable terms. Viewing trial by ordeal from many different perspectives, depending on the political position they occupied in a lawsuit, they proposed its use in order to gain a tactical advantage in a relatively small number of cases and, perhaps, threatened to use it in other lawsuits. They also avoided it whenever they could conveniently do so.

In addition to *MV* and *TV* (for which see p. ix of this volume), the following abbreviations are used throughout the notes:

A *Cartulaire de l'abbaye de Saint-Aubin d'Angers,* edited by Bertrand de Broussillon, 3 vols. (Paris, 1903).

C *Cartulaire de Cormery précédé de l'histoire de l'abbaye et de la ville de*

143. Guillot, *Le comte d'Anjou* 1:175.

144. Brown, for example, believes that the ordeal was gradually abandoned during the twelfth century ("Society," p. 310); Bartlett argues that it did not decline at all in this period and that the unilateral ordeal was simply "abandoned" in 1215 (*Trial,* p. 100).

Cormery d'après les chartes, edited by J.-J. Bourassé, Mémoires de la Société Archéologique de Touraine 12 (Tours, 1861).

MB *Marmoutier: Cartulaire blésois,* edited by Charles Métais (Blois, 1889–91).

MD *Cartulaire de Marmoutier pour le Dunois,* edited by Emile Mabille (Châteaudun, 1874).

MM *Cartulaire manceau de Marmoutier,* edited by E. Laurain, 2 vols. (Laval, 1911–40).

MP *Cartulaire de Marmoutier pour le Perche,* edited by Philibert Barret (Mortagne, 1894).

N *Cartulaire de l'abbaye de Noyers,* edited by C. Chevalier, Mémoires de la Société Archéologique de Touraine 22 (Tours, 1872).

V *Cartulaire de l'abbaye de Saint-Vincent du Mans,* edited by R. Charles and Menjot d'Elbenne, 2 vols. (Mamers, 1886–1913).

Geoffrey Koziol

6. England, France, and the Problem of Sacrality in Twelfth-Century Ritual

Historians have long recognized the importance of ritual in communicating the sacred attributes of early medieval kingship. For almost as long they have understood that the power of later medieval monarchies to shape public opinion was the power of political theater.[1] But between the sacred liturgies of pontifical kings and the political theater of statist monarchs lies the twelfth century, whose political rituals we understand scarcely at all. The fundamental difficulty lies in the transitional nature of twelfth-century kingship, which was moving toward the sophisticated administrative apparatuses of the later medieval state while still publicly avowing the political morality of the Carolingians. The result is a discrepancy between ideal and reality that finds its way especially into those histories that try to encompass both. As that transition was sharpest in England and France, so the discrepancy is most visible there as well. Thus D. C. Douglas writing of William the Conqueror, Judith Green writing of Henry I, and W. L. Warren writing of Henry II all dutifully reiterate the traditional beliefs articulated in Carolingian and Ottonian sources: that kings ruled in the image of God and the Old Testament rulers of Israel and that the great ceremony for communicating this typology was the royal anointing. Yet when these historians get down to the real business of Norman and Angevin kingship they describe feudal levies, financial exactions, and judicial reform, with not another word about pontifical kings.[2]

1. See, for example, Geoffrey Koziol, *Begging Pardon and Favor: Ritual and Political Order in Early Medieval France* (Ithaca, NY, 1992); Janet Nelson, *Politics and Ritual in Early Medieval Europe* (London, 1986); Hans Joachim Berbig, "Zur rechtlichen Relevanz von Ritus und Zeremoniell im römisch-deutschen Imperium," *Zeitzschrift für Kirchengeschichte* 92 (1981), 204–49; *Rituals of Royalty: Power and Ceremonial in Traditional Societies*, ed. David Cannadine and Simon Price (Cambridge, 1987).

2. D. C. Douglas, *William the Conqueror* (Berkeley, CA, 1964), pp. 253–59; Judith A. Green, *The Government of England Under Henry I* (Cambridge, 1986), pp. 3–11; W. L. Warren, *Henry II* (Berkeley, CA, 1973), pp. 242–44. Conversely, Robert Folz, *Les saints rois du Moyen Age en Occident (VIe–XIIIe siècles)* (Brussels, 1984), discusses the phenomenon of twelfth-century royal sainthood as if it were identical with its earlier manifestations.

How, then, to judge the changing role of ritual in the political life of the new administrative monarchies? Monographic studies of individual rituals are essential, of course; yet in their need to establish the formal elements of a given ritual, such studies too often lack social and political context, and therefore evade critical questions about the culture in which the rituals occur. Even on formal grounds the definitiveness of such studies can be undermined by the very profusion of twelfth-century sources that makes them possible, since it is difficult to know whether an apparently new ritual really was new, or merely newly recorded. For these reasons, it may be useful to abandon momentarily the practice of studying the formal traits of individual rituals taken in isolation and look at all political rituals together, in order to discern common and distinctive characteristics that point to widespread concerns within the political community. A general overview does have its own limitations. The twelfth century as a whole was so complex, its cultural vectors so contradictory, that any generalization can easily be qualified. More important, a broad overview sacrifices not just the specificity of individual rituals but also the artifice behind individual ritual narratives. For the chroniclers and historians who described these rituals were not neutral observers. All had their own individual programs, leading them in any given instance to accentuate the divisive or the concordant, the sacred or the secular. Although something must and will be said about the overarching patterns that shaped authorial bias, it will not be possible to do full justice to the issue. But if the approach has limitations, it also has the clear virtue of allowing us to see patterns that otherwise become lost in details or occluded by historiographical convention.

The most obvious of these patterns is the overwhelming continuity of twelfth-century political liturgies with earlier rites. The fact would not bear mentioning were it not so unexpected against the backdrop of an ecclesiastical reform movement that was supposedly uncomfortable with the sacrality of kings.[3] Yet twelfth-century kings continued to be anointed, and on high feast days were still ceremonially recrowned before a solemn mass and acclaimed with *laudes*.[4] Penitent rebels still fell before their feet

3. Many of the observations in this paragraph have already been made by Bernhard Töpfer, "Tendenzen zur Entsakralisierung der Herrscherwurde in der Zeit des Investiturstreiten," *Jahrbuch für Geschichte des Feudalismus* 6 (1982), 164–71, and Colin Morris, *The Papal Monarchy: The Western Church from 1050 to 1250* (Oxford, 1988), pp. 226–28.

4. Kurt-Ulrich Jäschke, "Frühmittelalterliche Festkrönungen? Überlegungen zu Terminologie und Methode," *Historische Zeitschrift* 211 (1970), 556–88, here 562, 566; Percy E. Schramm, *A History of the English Coronation,* tr. Leopold G. Wickham Legg (Oxford, 1937), pp. 31–32, 38–39, 56–59, 64–69; Ernst H. Kantorowicz, *Laudes Regiae: A Study in Liturgi-*

and begged for pardon in an unmistakable imitation of penance, as rebels had done ever since the reign of Louis the Pious.[5] Before crossing the channel to fight in Normandy, English kings received a solemn blessing from the archbishop of Canterbury, while Louis VII's departure on crusade was preceded by splendidly sacred gestures, from his caring for the lepers of Paris to his prostration before the altar of Saint-Denis when receiving the oriflamme and his final meal with the monks in their refectory.[6] Even a king as impatient with ceremony as Henry II was happy enough to participate in the translation of Edward the Confessor, bending to a time-honored custom and carrying the reliquary on his shoulders through the cloister of Westminster to its new shrine.[7]

For all Gregory VII's radical desacralization of royal authority in the Empire, in France and England the ecclesiastical reform movement's ultimate impact on political liturgy was minimal. Granted, the polarization of positions during the Investiture Contest could give royal rituals a sharper edge not visible before, particularly in England, as we will see. On the other hand, a variety of factors led the two sides to compromise both their practice and their theory, from the papacy's growing pragmatism after Urban II to the kings' own sincere desire for reform and their discovery that giving up the investiture of prelates did not mean giving up a say in their appointment. The urge for compromise was even stronger within the French and English episcopate, and not only because so many bishops were still the king's men.[8] Bishops also needed the king as an ally for their own ma-

cal Acclamations and Medieval Ruler Worship (Berkeley, CA, 1946); H. E. J. Cowdrey, "The Anglo-Norman *Laudes Regiae*," *Viator* 12 (1981), 39–78.

5. For examples of prostrate supplications for mercy by rebels, criminals, and intercessors making petitions in behalf of rebels and criminals see OV, 11, 3 (6:30–31); 12, 22 (6:278–79); Galbert of Bruges, *Histoire du meurtre de Charles le Bon, comte de Flandre (1127–1128),* ed. Henri Pirenne (Paris, 1891), c. 65 (p. 106), c. 73 (p. 117); Suger, *Vie de Louis VI le Gros,* ed. Henri Waquet (Paris, 1929), cc. 2–4, 8, 15, 18, 19, 25, 29 (pp. 14–20, 24, 40–42, 90, 92, 126, 134, 180–82, 232); *Historia gloriosi regis Ludovici* in *Vie de Louis le Gros par Suger suivie de l'Histoire du roi Louis VII,* ed. Auguste Molinier (Paris, 1887), p. 176; Walter Map, *De nugis curialium,* ed. M. R. James, rev. ed. C. N. L. Brooke and R. A. B. Mynors (Oxford, 1983), 5: 444–45, 462–43; 454–45; *The Chronicle of Jocelin of Brakelond,* ed. and tr. H. E. Butler (London, 1949), p. 23. For the history of these gestures see Koziol, *Begging Pardon and Favor.*

6. Eadmer, *Historia novorum in Anglia,* ed. Martin Rule, Rolls Series, 81 (London, 1884), 4: 97 (and cf. Rufus's rejection of Anselm's blessing before a campaign, 1: 52); Odo of Deuil, *De profectione Ludovici VII in orientem,* ed. and tr. Virginia Gingerick Berry (New York, 1948), pp. 14–19.

7. Richard of Cirencester, *Speculum historiale de gestis regum Angliae,* ed. J. E. B. Major, Rolls Series, 30 (London, 1869), pp. 319–27, here 326; Frank Barlow, *Edward the Confessor* (Berkeley, CA, 1970), p. 283.

8. Martin Brett, *The English Church Under Henry I* (Oxford, 1975), pp. 34, 42–45, 72–75, 104–12; C. R. Cheney, *From Becket to Langton: English Church Government, 1170–1213* (Man-

neuvering within the church, and they learned to use his rituals for their own agendas. William Rufus may have blasphemed against God, plundered the church of Canterbury, and driven its archbishop into exile, but as that archbishop, Anselm was quite happy to use Rufus's royal prerogatives over the English church to fend off unwelcome interference by a papal legate in his own province.[9] In fact, all prelates, whether reformers or not, were more likely to dispute their own rights of precedence in a king's ceremonies than to dispute the sanctity the ceremonies conferred. Thus, coronations and festal coronations became one of the fields on which Canterbury and York battled for the primacy of England, while in France the abbots of Saint-Denis increased their prestige by incorporating the kings into an ever expanding calendar of rituals.[10]

Still more important in drawing churchmen to the king was the fact that their perception of the political world was fundamentally different from the papacy's. To the church leadership of England and France, the emperor was no pressing enemy, and the pope no immediate ally. The real enemies were nearer at home, in upstart communes, rapacious, promiscuous knights, and local lords waging destructive wars. In the face of such evils, the old ideal of cooperation between kingship and priesthood remained eminently serviceable. As a result, even reforming prelates welcomed truces in their conflicts with rulers by returning to normal ritual

---

chester, 1956), pp. 19–41; Warren, *Henry II,* pp. 411–17, 442–55; Marcel Pacaut, *Louis VII et les élections épiscopales dans le royaume de France* (Paris, 1957), pp. 117–21.

9. Sally N. Vaughn, *Anselm of Bec and Robert of Meulan: The Innocence of the Dove and the Wisdom of the Serpent* (Berkeley, CA, 1987), p. 192.

10. Jäschke, "Frühmittelalterliche Festkrönungen?" 557–58; Brett, *English Church,* pp. 69 n. 3, 70; Anne Heslin, "The Coronation of the Young King in 1170," *Studies in Church History,* 2, ed. G. J. Cuming (London, 1968), 165–78. For Saint-Denis see, for example, the reception of Paschal II by Philip I and Louis VI in 1107 (Suger, *Vie de Louis VI,* c. 10, pp. 50–54); the burial of Louis VI's son (c. 31, pp. 266–67); *La chronique de Morigny, 1095–1152,* ed. Léon Mirot [Paris, 1912] 2: 15, p. 57); Louis VI's investiture with the oriflamme and its solemn return for the campaign against Henry V in 1124 (Suger, *Vie de Louis VI,* c. 28, pp. 218–20, 226–28); the burial of Louis VI (cc. 33–34, pp. 272–84); the translation of the relics of Dionysius and his companions and the consecration of their new altar in 1144 (*Abbot Suger on the Abbey Church of St.-Denis and Its Art Treasures,* ed. Erwin Panofsky and Gerda Panofsky-Soergel [Princeton, NJ, 1979], pp. 110–21); and the rites preceding Louis VII's departure on crusade (Odo of Deuil, *De profectione Ludovici VII,* pp. 14–19). I cannot agree with Erlande-Brandenbourg that the royal funerals were either private or merely religious, with no regalian implications. In the hands of Suger there is nothing merely religious about any royal liturgy, and the phrase *more regio* is, in my view, a shorthand formula indicating the presence of regalian rites and emblems. See Alain Erlande-Brandenbourg, *Le roi est mort: étude sur les funérailles, les sépultures et les tombeaux des rois de France jusqu'à la fin du XIIIe siècle* (Geneva, 1975), p. 14. On Suger's propaganda war with Reims and its purposes see especially Eric Bournazel, "Suger and the Capetians," in *Abbot Suger and Saint Denis,* ed. Paula Lieber Gerson (New York: Metropolitan Museum of Art, 1986), pp. 55–72.

practice as quickly as possible, so that no sooner had Henry I settled his quarrels with Anselm than all the old liturgies returned as if nothing had changed: the crown-wearings, archiepiscopal masses for the king, and blessings for his Channel crossings. Indeed, far from trying to dilute the sanctity of kingship, ecclesiastics invented new ceremonies that if anything accentuated it. For example, the late eleventh and early twelfth centuries saw the origin of the royal touch, in which kings cured the sores of the scrofulous with a touch of their hands and the sign of the cross. The rite is well documented in France for Philip I and Louis VI. And though Marc Bloch could find no convincing evidence of subsequent practice until the reign of Louis IX, Philippe Buc has recently filled that lacuna by demonstrating that in the 1160s masters at the University of Paris took it for granted that the rite of anointing conferred the power of healing on the king.[11] To Buc's incontrovertible proof one might also be able to join an odd incident passed over with studied quickness by Odo of Deuil, abbot of Saint-Denis, in his description of the ceremonies attending Louis VII's departure on crusade in 1147. According to Odo, before leaving Paris for Saint-Denis to receive the oriflamme, Louis went to the leper colony outside the city gates and, pointedly leaving his retinue outside, entered the leper house with only two companions. What he did there Odo refuses to say; but having thoroughly piqued his readers' interest by mentioning the incident only to drop it, Odo draws still more attention to its importance by adding that Louis stayed inside the house "for a long time" (*per longam moram*).[12] Granted, if Louis did touch, he was touching for leprosy not scrofula, but at a time when neither disease was symptomatically specific, that may not matter.[13] What does matter is that some 120 years earlier, during a pilgrimage through southeastern France, Robert the Pious had also entered the houses of lepers, and Helgald of Fleury was less reticent than Odo about what the king did inside: he touched the diseased sores, made the sign of the cross on them, and cured the sufferers of their sickness.[14]

11. Marc Bloch, *The Royal Touch: Sacred Monarchy and Scrofula in England and France*, tr. J. E. Anderson (London, 1973), pp. 13–14, 20–21, 69–74; Philippe Buc, "David's Adultery with Bathsheba and the Healing Power of the Capetian Kings," *Viator* 24 (1993), 101–20. See also Frank Barlow, "The King's Evil," *EHR* 95 (1980), 3–27; Jacques Le Goff, "Le mal royal au moyen âge: du roi malade au roi guérisseur," *Mediaevistik* 1 (1988), 101–9. Colin Morris makes the tantalizing suggestion that the basins donated by one of Henry I's chamberlains to a Norman monastery were those in which the king had washed his hands after touching, *Papal Monarchy*, p. 228; Walter Map, *De nugis curialium*, 6: 490–91.

12. Odo of Deuil, *De profectione Ludovici VII*, p. 16.

13. Barlow, "The King's Evil."

14. Helgaud de Fleury, *Vie de Robert le Pieux*, ed. and tr. R.-H. Bautier and Gillette Labory (Paris, 1965), pp. 124–27; Christian Lauranson-Rosaz, *L'Auvergne et ses marges (Velay, Gévaudan) du VIIIe au XIe siècle* (Le Puy-en-Velay, 1987), pp. 442–53.

The setting of the two rituals is too uncannily similar to have been coincidental. Robert and Louis were both on pilgrimage. Both entered leper houses. And both pilgrimages were described by the authors in explicitly christomimetic terms, each, for example, being associated with Easter, while Louis had been marked with the cross in preparation for his crusade. The parallels are too exact for Louis's ritual not to have culminated in a similar healing, all the more so because Odo introduces the scene by telling his reader that he is about to describe "a praiseworthy thing, which few, perhaps no one of his lofty rank, could imitate," a statement that makes most sense if we assume that what no one could imitate was not Louis's virtue in caring for lepers (Theobald of Blois did that, too) but his power to cure them.[15]

Although less famous, another of the century's new rituals demonstrates even more clearly how resilient the old typologies were, and how immune to the demands of radical reformers, for this ritual occurred at the nadir of Henry I's conflict with Anselm and the papacy. In April 1105 Henry landed in Normandy to begin the conquest of the duchy from his brother, Robert Curthose. Easter he celebrated in a small church crammed with the chests and tools of peasants who had gathered them there for safety. Serlo, bishop of Séez, delivered the sermon. Using the peasants' humble possessions to recall a godly ruler's obligation to protect the weak, the bishop spoke of Henry's high purpose and contrasted it to the excesses of Curthose's court, with its whores, jesters, and drunkenness, a maelstrom of godless lasciviousness symbolized for the bishop in the chivalric custom of wearing long hair. The bishop asked that the king set an example for his barons, and upon Henry's agreement took scissors and cut first his hair, then that of all his magnates, who confirmed their resolve by crushing their fallen locks into the ground. Seen in Orderic Vitalis's perfect hindsight, Henry's subsequent victories were inevitable, God's gift to a pious ruler who did God's work.[16]

The story not only illustrates the hold of the belief in the sacredness of

15. Walter Map, *De nugis curialium*, 5, 6: 462–65. Breton of Amboise also made caring for lepers an Angevin virtue, though, like Map, he does not attribute any healing power to the counts, further confirming that touching was recognized as a specifically royal power linked to the anointing: *Chroniques des comtes d'Anjou et des seigneurs d'Amboise*, ed. Louis Halphen and René Poupardin (Paris, 1913), pp. 141–42. Odo of Deuil's reference to others "of lofty rank" is probably a reference to the kings of England, an indication that the issue of whether or not their touch could heal was disputed in the twelfth century, as it is now. See also below, note 54.

16. OV, 11, 11 (6: 62–69), with Chibnall's discussion at p. 66 n.1; also Vaughn, *Anselm of Bec and Robert of Meulan*, pp. 285–87; Gabor Klaniczay, *The Uses of Supernatural Power* (Princeton, NJ, 1990), pp. 60–62.

the royal ministry to conservative ecclesiastics like Serlo; it also points to the specific moral concerns that made the belief so necessary. For to Serlo, short and long hair were only the visible signs of a larger set of moral oppositions: between drunkenness and abstinence; lewdness and continence; gender confusion and gendered order; profanity and sacredness. These, in turn, were mapped onto a specific political opposition more to his (and Henry's) immediate purpose. The incontinent, the lewd, the wanton—these were the knights, the *juvenes* of Curthose's court who oppressed the church and ignored its ethical teachings. The pure, the pious, the responsible—these were the *seniores,* the old men, the great lords who ruled in God's name to protect his church and his faithful. Henry's conquest of Normandy became the victory of a moral and political order maintained by kings over the immoral anarchy threatened by knights.

More than ecclesiastical liberty, knighthood and the ethical code associated with knighthood stand as the single most problematic element in twelfth-century political ritual. Thus, Suger's account of Louis VI's coronation has the initiate king setting aside the "sword of worldly knighthood" (*secularis militie gladius*) to be girded instead with "the ecclesiastical sword for punishing the wicked," and then receiving the royal insignia of crown, scepter, and staff that symbolized his authority to "defend the churches, the poor, and the kingdom."[17] The insignia were the same as in earlier centuries, but their interpretation was not. In the immediate post-Carolingian age "the sword of worldly knighthood" *was* what kings had been invested with to protect the church and the poor. But that was when *militia* had signified a public ministry of service appropriate to kings and counts. By the early twelfth century, in contrast, *militia secularis* had gained the denotation of knighthood as we usually think of it: a way of life associated with members of a youth cohort distinguished not so much by chronological age as by the absence of economic and governmental responsibilities.[18] In Suger's eyes, it is this cohort that Louis leaves behind when he relinquishes the sword of worldly knighthood, for up to this moment Suger had consistently described Louis as an *adolescens* or *juvenis.* After, Louis is simply a king full of majesty, and never again described as a youth.[19] As with Henry at his hair-cutting, so for Louis at his coronation,

17. Suger, *Vie de Louis VI,* c. 14, pp. 84–86.

18. Jean Flori, *L'essor de la chevalerie, XIe–XIIe siècles* (Geneva, 1986), pp. 44, 274–75; Georges Duby, *William Marshal: The Flower of Chivalry,* tr. Richard Howard (New York, 1985); Duby, "Youth in Aristocratic Society: Northwestern France in the Twelfth Century," in *The Chivalrous Society,* tr. Cynthia Postan (Berkeley, CA, 1980), pp. 112–22.

19. Suger, *Vie de Louis VI,* cc. 2, 4, 7, 13, 15; pp. 14, 20–22, 30–32, 82–84, 88; also c. 12, p. 80, where Louis and his retinue are referred to as *fortissimi milites,* contrasted with c. 21,

acceptance of public office required a public ritual in which the ruler formally set aside the badges of knighthood, and with them adherence to the ethos of the *juvenes*.

But twelfth-century polities were nothing if not conflicted, and rituals alert us to their contradictions. The opposition between *juvenes* and *seniores* was therefore crosscut by competing forces that drew the two groups together. The continental principalities offer the clearest illustrations of the trend, most notably Flanders, where a sequence of narrative sources allows us to trace the changing relationship between counts and knights in public rituals. Thus in the eleventh century the counts of Flanders had presided over Peace assemblies where, surrounded by the relics of saints, they enforced decrees that protected the poor and unarmed against marauding knights and castellans. In this way, the Peace of God dramatized the need to subject the crude military power of warriors to the legitimate rule of counts. Like bishops, abbots, and kings, but utterly unlike knights and castellans, the counts possessed an authority sanctioned by God and protected by the saints. In the eleventh century that special ministry was further acclaimed by narratives of their entries into the towns of Flanders, which begin with the counts' ceremonial reception by monks and clerics, who greet them with relics and incense while singing the *Te Deum*.[20] In clear contrast stands Galbert of Bruges's description of William Clito's *adventus* into Saint-Omer in 1126 to receive the townspeople's allegiance. In Galbert's narrative, William was first greeted not by the relics and hymns of the clergy but by a parade of youth (*pueri*) ranged in companies and fighting in mock combat with bows and arrows. William, says Galbert, was all the more pleased by the scene because he himself was a *puer, aetate juventae*; and so he not only allowed the boys "their playful sports," he even participated in them by seizing their standard and banner and laughing and joking. That was the signal for dancing to begin, and the entire troop advanced to the city, William now part of the band, led in joyously by it.[21]

---

p. 160, where he is described as *miles emeritus* and obliquely criticized for behaving as if he still were a *miles* and not *rex*.

20. *Les annales de Saint-Pierre de Gand et de Saint-Amand*, ed. Philip Grierson (Brussels, 1937), p. 89; *Miracula sancti Ursmari*, c. 9, AASS Apr. II, 572; *Une translation de reliques à Gand en 944. Le "Sermo de Adventu Sanctorum Wandregisili, Ansberti et Vulframni in Blandinium,"* ed. N. Huyghebaert (Brussels, 1978), pp. 26–29, 45–46, 49–51; "Cartulary of Saint-Thierry-les-Reims," Reims, BM, MS. 1602, fols. 214–15 (1090); and *Actes des comtes de Flandre, 1071–1128*, ed. Fernand Vercauteren (Brussels, 1938), no. 22 (1096). For other references and a discussion of the meaning of these ceremonies, see Koziol, *Begging Pardon and Favor*, pp. 131–37.

21. Galbert of Bruges, *Histoire du meurtre de Charles le Bon*, c. 66, pp. 106–7. If, as is quite possible, the *pueri* that greeted William were not knights but young warriors, not yet dubbed, training for knighthood, then the opposition to an ecclesiastical *occursus* would have

This absorption of counts into the world of chivalry was especially marked in principalities that were built upon conquest and battle. In these communities lords could not stand apart from castellans and knights while pretending to be transcendent rulers in the image of kings and the King of kings. To rule successfully, they needed to accommodate the powerful leaders of retinues that held castles on marches of tenuous loyalty. In order to garrison castles and raise cavalry quickly, they dispensed fiefs and allowed vassals to subinfeudate in turn to their own vassals. Above all, they needed to fight against their enemies; the ensuing warfare fostered *camaraderie* and a sense of mutual need between rulers and warriors. Wherever these conditions obtained, the undermining of old Carolingian lordship by a chivalric ethos of honor, largesse, and daring was precocious: in Normandy and Blois, therefore, in Flanders to a lesser extent, but above all in Anjou.[22]

It was here that in the first decades of the twelfth century a clerical propagandist wrote a history of the counts' dynasty—or is it a romance? In fact it is both, one of those hybrid romance-histories so popular at princely courts in this period.[23] Thus Thomas of Loches's counts hale from Brittany, land of romances. Indeed, their earliest history is made to intersect with the tales of Breton history popularized by Geoffrey of Monmouth, for the counts' ancestors were among those expelled from Brittany by Arthur's ancestors in the late Empire.[24] By the reign of Charles the Bald the family was among the *novi et ignobiles* who sought fame and fortune by "seeking after martial glory." Torquatius, the dynasty's distant progenitor, became Charles's forester. But Torquatius's son, Tertullus, whom Thomas considers the first real Angevin, was dissatisfied with his humble lot and decided that he was going to try to eke out his meagre fortune by going to

---

been both obvious and intentional, since in monastic *occursus* the young male novices (also called *pueri*) preceded the adult choir monks and initiated the antiphons. See *The Monastic Constitutions of Lanfranc,* ed. and tr. David Knowles (London, 1951), pp. 22–25; also *Liber tramitis aevi Odilonis abbatis,* ed. P. Dinter, Corpus Consuetudinum Monasticarum 10 (Siegburg, 1980), pp. 23, 68–69; Ulrich of Cluny, *Consuetudines Cluniacenses, PL* 149: 653, 670, 744. On the other hand, *pueri* can also be associated with dubbed knights, as in OV 12, 39 (6: 350, 356).

22. The argument is detailed in Koziol, *Begging Pardon and Favor,* chap. 8. See also Dominique Barthélemy, *L'ordre seigneurial (XIe–XIIe siècle)* (Paris, 1990), pp. 207–10.

23. Raymonde Foreville, "La typologie du roi dans la littérature historiographique anglo-normande aux XIe et XIIe siècles," *Etudes de civilisation médiévale, IXe–XIIe siècles: mélanges offerts à Edmond-René Labande* (Poitiers, 1974), pp. 275–92.

24. *Gesta consulum Andegavorum,* in *Chroniques des comtes d'Anjou,* ed. Halphen and Poupardin, p. 26. Compare the more fully developed account of these events in the *Liber de compositione castri Ambaziae,* in *Chroniques des comtes,* p. 9, which probably reflects the scheme of Thomas's lost preface to the *Gesta consulum,* resumed in the *Liber de compositione.*

serve the king. He fought in the campaigns against the Normans among Charles's soldiers (his *viri militares*) and did so well that the king came to love him dearly, and gave him a wife and some land.[25] Tertullus's son, Ingelgerius, was an even better fighter. He was actually knighted by Charles's son (*miles efficitur*) and proved to be "a bold youth" (*juvenis alacer*) and "a great knight" (*miles optimus*), who gained more benefices by dint of his strong arms.[26] Whatever truth may underlie these tales, it is not hard to see that they are also the stuff of romance, the dream not of any ninth-century warrior but of every twelfth-century bachelor: finding a lord to fight for and earning his love, a wife, land. There is even rumor of a good love affair with a noble lady.[27]

If this is what the counts wanted to hear—if this is what the counts wanted their *men* to hear—is it any wonder that rites of sacred authority played so poorly in Anjou? The counts rarely acted the role of lords graced by God. When we see them in rituals in the dynasty's house literature (even in their charters), we see them with knights and as knights: in Jean of Marmoutier's *History of Geoffrey le Bel,* for example, Geoffrey being knighted; Geoffrey eating with knights as one of them; Geoffrey carrying the day in tournaments against all odds; Geoffrey keeping vigil in a church at Le Mans along with his knights and being solemnly received the next morning by them (not by the clergy) in front of the cathedral church.[28] We do not need to appeal to the church's desire for ecclesiastical liberty in order to understand the waning sacredness of political rituals in Anjou. If rituals speak to the community that performs them, then to understand what happened to comital rituals we need only look within the counts' own community of followers.

Kings were not immune either to the realities of castle warfare or to the seduction of chivalric romance, and both caused them, like counts, to draw closer to their knights. To take the realities first, the late eleventh and early twelfth centuries were the time when kings began to rely more heavily than ever before on *milites castri* for military support and administrative aid. Eric Bournazel documented the phenomenon for France in the reigns of Louis VI and Louis VII, but historians have always regarded the French kings with some disdain in comparison with their wealthier,

25. *Gesta consulum,* pp. 25–29.

26. *Gesta consulum,* pp. 29–30.

27. *Gesta consulum,* p. 29.

28. *Historia Gaufredi ducis,* in *Chroniques des comtes d'Anjou,* ed. Halphen and Poupardin, pp. 179, 181–83, 196, 211; Koziol, *Begging Pardon and Favor,* pp. 258–67.

more powerful English rivals and have tended to see their association with knights as a sign of weakness.[29] Yet Henry I was just as dependent on a personal following of knights, perhaps more so. He himself may not have been much of a fighter (or perhaps he was just too hard-headed to risk success in romantic gambits for honor and glory). Yet like any twelfth-century lord, whether castellan, count, or king, Henry took the sons of the powerful under his care, raised them, taught them, and when they came of age personally dubbed them; hence his fury when Hugh of Gournay rebelled against him, for Hugh had been one of his *juvenes*.[30] Contemporaries also recognized that one of the sources of Henry's strength was his retinue of personal fighters, like those *milites pagenses* who shouted down the earls in a public meeting and warned Henry to beware of their treachery. In the days of rebellion, all chroniclers agree that these were the only men he could trust. Without them, he would have had no power at all.[31]

Early twelfth-century kings had not only become more politically and militarily dependent on knights; they had also imbibed enough of the current chivalric ethos to think of themselves as knights, or at least to move in circles that were strongly impregnated with that ethos. After all, old kings had once been young bachelors themselves, and no mere ceremony could have caused a young king to set aside familiar habits and friends. Henry I may have cut his hair when trying to distance himself from the excesses of Curthose's court, but he also surrounded himself with the likes of Waleran of Meulan, the most dashing figure of his generation and the co-dedicatee of Geoffrey of Monmouth's *History of the Kings of Britain*.[32] And there were Henry's own sons and their friends: what could be more knightly than the boorish cynicism towards clerics and the drunken recklessness that brought these *juvenes* to their deaths on the White Ship?[33]

The case of France is more interesting still, for not even Suger's old-fashioned Carolingian rhetoric expounding the king's duty to protect the poor can mask the fact that Louis VI was in love with the image of himself

29. Eric Bournazel, *Le gouvernement capétien au XIIe siècle, 1108–1180* (Paris, 1975); Jean-François Lemarignier, *Le gouvernement royal aux premiers temps capétiens, 987–1108* (Paris, 1965), pp. 133–36.

30. OV 12, 3 (6: 192–95).

31. OV 11, 3; 12, 14, 28; 13, 18 (6: 26–27, 222–23, 308–9, 444–47); Green, *Government of England*, pp. 24–25; J. O. Prestwich, "The Military Household of the Norman Kings," *EHR* 96 (1981), 1–35.

32. David Crouch, *The Beaumont Twins: The Roots and Branches of Power in the Twelfth Century* (Cambridge, 1986), part 1, esp. pp. 15, 22–28.

33. OV 12, 26 (6: 296–99), describing the rowdiness as a matter of *iuventus* and recalling the youths' taunting of the priests who came to bless the ship before its embarkation.

as a heroic knight. He is never without his *tirones,* his *manus militum,* and he himself had visited Henry I's court as a youth to serve as a "distinguished young knight."[34] And that is just how he fights, after his anointing as before: no real tactics, just a gleeful, impetuous rush into battle, whatever the cost. He offers to meet Henry in single combat to determine possession of Gisors.[35] He throws himself into a skirmish by a stream in the Berry, "urging on his horse with his spurs" and knocking an opponent into the water with his lance: Suger is impressed by his bravery, but says that the action little became a king.[36] He decides to attack Henry from an inferior position—overruling the advice of a tested lord like Burchard of Montmorency and heeding instead the taunts of the knights of Chaumont.[37] Nor were Louis's sons any different from Henry's—Philip, for example, dying in a fall from a horse while he was playing in games like a *juvenis.*[38]

Given this change in political culture, it is easy to see that the most interesting trends in political rituals were occasioned not by the Investiture Controversy but by the spell of chivalry. The coronation itself quickly came to reflect the encroachment of knighthood upon kingship with a striking change, indeed, the only clearly verifiable change from the earlier rite: at some point in the early twelfth century, in addition to the traditional insignia of crown, ring, rod, scepter, and sword, English and French kings were given spurs.[39] Suger ignores the innovation, probably because its symbolism contradicted his own interpretation of the ceremony as a repudiation of knighthood; for spurs are clearly a chivalric emblem. They are not the only sign that kings whose entries and anointings had once drawn them close to Christ and bishops were now drawing closer to the mounted warriors who supported them. In the contemporary romance histories by Geoffrey of Monmouth and Geoffrey Gaimar, the liturgical elements of

34. Suger, *Vie de Louis VI,* cc. 1, 2, 5, 7, 11, pp. 8, 14, 16–18, 24–26, 30–32, 70–72, and esp. c. 12, p. 80: "dominus Ludovicus et sui, ut fortissimi milites"; OV 11, 9 (6: 50–51).

35. Suger, *Vie de Louis VI,* c. 16, p. 108. Andrew Lewis, "Suger's Views on Kingship," in *Abbot Suger and Saint-Denis,* pp. 49–54, has also noted that Suger's description of Louis's actions and motivations do not change with the coronation.

36. Suger, *Vie de Louis VI,* c. 12, pp. 78–80.

37. Ibid., c. 26, pp. 196–98, criticizing Louis's *improvidam audaciam*; OV 12, 18 (6: 234–35), on Louis's preference for the advice of the knights of Chaumont to that of Burchard of Montmorency.

38. OV 13, 12 (6: 420–21); Walter Map, *De nugis curialium,* 5: 456–57.

39. H. G. Richardson, "The Coronation in Medieval England: The Evolution of the Office and the Oath," *Traditio* 16 (1960), 111–202, here 118–19. See also Schramm, *History of the English Coronation,* p. 69, and for criticism of Richardson's analysis of the "Third Recension," J. Brückmann, "The *Ordines* of the Third Recension of the Medieval English Coronation Order," in *Essays in Medieval History Presented to Bertie Wilkinson,* ed. T. A. Sandquist and M. R. Powicke (Toronto, 1969), pp. 99–115.

English crown-wearings are thoroughly subordinated to chivalric rituals such as tournaments and dubbings to knighthood.[40] Similarly, descriptions of the lords who served kings at festive meals changed in the same period from the vice-regal governmental officers of the Carolingian and Ottonian empires (dukes and counts, for example) to the military functions of the Capetians and Angevins (constables, marshals, and dapifers).[41] The lure of chivalric romance must also lie behind one of the stranger ceremonies in the history of monastic ritual: the elevation and translation of the bodies of Arthur and Guenevere at Glastonbury in 1191, after a search complete with all the old hagiographic topoi, including helpful visions and cryptic inscriptions. Richard I is said to have attended the translation, Henry II himself to have initiated the search for the bodies. Since its purpose was to prove to the conquered Welsh that Arthur was really and truly dead, and not merely sleeping before awakening to lead them to freedom, the event may say little about the kings' own belief in the Arthurian legends. Nevertheless, the translation still says much about a political climate in which the memory of a romance king had become so powerful a symbol that it shaped a political agenda and transformed a hieratic liturgy for the veneration of saints into a semiparodic ritual for a legendary hero.[42]

* * *

In all these ways, political rituals in France and England shared a common course of development. The fact is hardly surprising, given the intertwined histories of the two countries after the Norman Conquest and their

40. Geoffrey of Monmouth, *Historia Regum,* ed. Griscom, 9: 13–14, pp. 455–58; Geoffrei Gaimar, *L'Estoire des Engleis,* ed. Alexander Bell, Anglo-Norman Texts 14–16 (Oxford, 1960), pp. 192–93, vv. 6076–79. Note also the parody of hair-cutting that occurs in the subsequent lines of Gaimar.

41. Compare, on the one hand, the *Vita Oswaldi archiepiscopi Eboracensis* in *Historians of the Church of York and Its Archbishops,* ed. James Raine, Rolls Series, 71 (London, 1879), p. 438; Widukind of Corvey, *Res gestae Saxonicae,* in *Quellen zur Geschichte der sächsischen Kaiserzeit,* ed. Albert Bauer and Reinhold Rau (Darmstadt, 1971), p. 88; and Notker the Stammerer, *Gesta Karoli magni imperatoris* 2: 11, ed. G. H. Pertz, *MGH SS* 2: 736; with, on the other hand, Achille Luchaire, *Histoire des institutions monarchiques de la France sous les premiers capétiens (987–1180),* 2d ed. (Paris, 1891) 1: 164–72, 177–85; Schramm, *History of the English Coronation,* pp. 66–67. The same offices are found in princely courts of the period: Jim Bradbury, "Fulk le Réchin and the Origin of the Plantagenets," *Studies in Medieval History Presented to R. Allen Brown,* ed. Christopher Harper-Bill et al. (Woodbridge, 1989), pp. 27–42, here 34–35.

42. Geraldus Cambrensis, *Speculum ecclesiae,* ed. J. S. Brewer, *Opera* 4, Rolls Series, 21 (London, 1873), 47–51; Geraldus Cambrensis, *De principis instructione liber,* ed. G. F. Warner, *Opera* 8, Rolls Series, 21 (London, 1891), 126–29; W. A. Nitze, "The Exhumation of King Arthur at Glastonbury," *Speculum* 9 (1934), 355–61.

similar social and economic development. All the more surprising, then, that despite these parallels, the tone of public ceremonies should have been so different. Because the differences were essential to the kingdoms' diverging political cultures, their analysis will repay attention. We will begin with England, or rather, the Anglo-Norman union.

Given the forceful personalities of its kings and the strength of their administrations, we are not used to thinking of England as a fertile field for the development of grand ritual. We think rather of energetic campaigning, sophisticated fiscal administration, and powerful courts. It is therefore somewhat surprising to realize that contemporary sources record an innumerable multitude of public rituals for twelfth-century England, many more than for France in the same period: royal marriages, homages, blessings before campaigns, political trials, and coronations and festal coronations, to name only the most prominent. What is even more interesting, however, is how many of these spectacles must be judged failures, if we take a royalist point of view and assume that their purpose was to display the power of the kings and the cohesiveness of the political community under their leadership. We can begin with William the Conqueror and the riot that broke out at his coronation.[43] We can continue to William's abortive crown-wearing, when a jester mocked his pretensions to God-given kingship by shouting out, "Behold, I see God!"[44] William's funeral was scandalously shameful, from the ransacking of his chamber at the moment of his death to the attempt to force his body into a too-short coffin, causing his bowels to burst and spreading such a stench through the church that everyone ran out, leaving the canons of Saint-Etienne to rush through the ceremony as hurriedly as possible. And at the moment when the archbishop of Rouen asked the assembly to forgive the great duke any injustices he might have done them (a ritually anodyne request if there ever was one), a man stepped forward and made claim to the very spot in which William was being laid, saying that the duke had unjustly stolen it from his father to build his monastery. The bishops had to buy him off with 160 shillings on the spot to be able to proceed with the burial.[45]

Thereafter, the Norman kings (and the Angevin, too, for that matter) were never able to count on their magnates to respect the solemnity of their rites, not even on the bishops they appointed. For example, the

43. Schramm, *History of the English Coronation*, pp. 27–28; Janet Nelson, "The Rites of the Conqueror," *Anglo-Norman Studies* 4 (1981), 117–32, 210–21, at 122–23.

44. Nelson, "Rites," pp. 131–32.

45. OV 7, 16 (6: 100–107).

first crown-wearings after Anselm's death should have provided a moment of relief, if not triumph, for Henry I. Instead, at the Christmas feast the bishop of London and the archbishop of York fell into an ugly dispute over which had the right to crown the king, a dispute that continued right into the festal meal after the coronation, as the two prelates argued over seating precedence.[46] Bishops did not shrink from affronting the king directly. In 1121, on the occasion of Henry's second marriage, the mass was at the introit when the archbishop of Canterbury saw that the king was already wearing his crown. Immediately he removed his insignia and his stole, refusing to continue with the ceremony unless Henry removed his crown and let himself be recrowned. Henry had to agree.[47]

If the greatest prelates were not afraid to disrupt the solemnity of these rituals to enforce their prerogatives, it is not hard to understand the effrontery of barons, lesser clerics, and even ordinary subjects. Once, as Henry I came to London and was heading toward his palace, he was met by two hundred priests marching in barefoot procession, protesting what they saw as his extortionate, manifestly venal fines. Henry had them forcibly driven from his sight, an act that did nothing for his reputation either in England or abroad.[48] During his dispute with Anselm, Henry ordered the archbishop of York to consecrate William Giffard as bishop of Winchester, hoping in this way to break the momentum of Anselm's resistance. The ceremony was going as scripted when at the very last minute, right in the middle of the interrogation, William abruptly refused to accept consecration at all, and the crowd began to shout abuse at Henry's prelates.[49] And so it went in England. Not only was William I's corpse abandoned and pillaged, but also, say the sources, Henry II's and John's; and the only reason Henry I's was not desecrated was because it was never left without a strong guard.[50] Even before Stephen's court became known for the king's habitual violation of safe-conducts, it was known for its milling chaos—"confused and disorderly, as usual," according to the *Gesta Stephani*.[51] In

46. Eadmer, *Historia novorum* 4: 212.

47. Eadmer 4: 292.

48. Eadmer 4: 172–173.

49. Eadmer 3: 152–153.

50. Erlande-Brandenbourg, *Le roi est mort,* pp. 16–17; OV 13, 19 (6: 448–51); *Gesta regis Henrici secundi,* ed. William Stubbs, Rolls Series, 49 (London, 1867), p. 71; Kate Norgate, *John Lackland* (London, 1902), p. 285 (John also being buried with a highly visible guard of mercenaries).

51. *Gesta Stephani,* c. 13, ed. K. R. Potter, rev. ed. and tr. R. H. C. Davis (Oxford, 1976), pp. 24–27; H. A. Cronne, *The Reign of Stephen (1135–54)* (London, 1970), pp. 185–86.

the time of Henry II, some courtiers poisoned the king's mind against his Norman chamberlain, William of Tancarville. Henry began to destroy the man as only an Angevin could, razing his castles and denying him his day in court. So William struck back—through a ritual. During the feast at the royal Christmas assembly in Caen, as an attendant was about to perform the chamberlain's office of washing Henry's hands, William entered unannounced with an armed retinue and strode through the crowd right up to the king. Without saying a word he grabbed the silver basins from the attendant and began to wash the king's hands himself, and the hands of Henry's sons and the duke of Saxony; then handing the basins to one of his own men, he simply sat down. Henry said nothing.[52] The logical culmination of such displays of ritual defiance was not just Magna Carta but also the skepticism that greeted Henry III's solemn translation of a vial of the Savior's blood in 1247, when members of the court stood about openly impugning the relic's genuineness and, by implication, calling attention to Henry's gullibility.[53] Given this tradition of contentiousness and parody, is it any wonder that Henry I and Henry II often preferred *not* to celebrate crown-wearings, or that that while the royal touch is well-documented in twelfth-century France, and though English kings *may* have touched on the Continent, evidence that shows English kings touching in England is rare and ambiguous before the thirteenth century?[54] In fact, the one clear case in which an English king did touch in England produced mixed results, for though Henry II managed to cure a girl's scrofula, she almost

52. Walter Map, *De nugis curialium,* 6: 488–95.

53. Matthew Paris, *Chronica Majora,* ed. H. R. Luard, Rolls Series, 57 (London, 1872–84) 4: 640–45; W. L. Warren, *The Governance of Norman and Angevin England (1086–1272)* (Stanford, CA, 1987), pp. 179–180.

54. For crown wearings and their decline under the Norman kings see Jäschke, "Frühmittelalterliche Festkrönungen?" pp. 562, 566; Schramm, *History of the English Coronation,* pp. 31–32, 38–39, 56–59, 64–69; and especially Martin Biddle, "Seasonal Festivals and Residence: Winchester, Westminster and Gloucester in the Tenth to Twelfth Centuries," *Anglo-Norman Studies* 8 (1985), 51–72. As for the royal touch, all the earliest evidence for Edward the Confessor's thaumaturgy is associated with writers from northern France (in particular, Flanders). William of Malmesbury subsequently locates the practice of Edward's thaumaturgic miracles in Normandy (and in any case disputes thaumaturgy as an attribute of any kings, English or French, by virtue of their anointing). If, as Colin Morris claims, the basins given by Henry I's chamberlain were those in which the king had washed his hands after touching, they were given to a Norman not an English abbey, by a Norman not an English chamberlain. Finally, Peter of Blois was French, studied at Paris (where theologians accepted the thaumaturgical powers of kings), and at the time of his letter suggesting Henry II's thaumaturgical powers had, in fact, spent little time in England. For citations for these sources see the works cited above, n. 11.

immediately became subject to a severe paralysis, as if in punishment for having had recourse to the king.[55]

But how does one explain such contentiousness? The ecclesiastical reform movement was surely partly to blame, insofar as it created a destabilizing environment for royal rites by legitimating the resistance of reformers to kings perceived as unjust. Still, the degree and persistence of contentiousness in England exceeds this single cause, just as the willingness to use rituals to ridicule and confront went beyond the single class of church reformers to encompass laymen, courtier-bishops, and simple priests. Alternatively, one might explain away the contention as an illusion created by biased ecclesiastical sources. Thus Orderic Vitalis used the chaos at William the Conqueror's funeral to illustrate the vanity of worldly power, said to be a conventional monastic topos, while Eadmer's outrage at royal violations of ecclesiastical liberty led him to dwell on events that highlighted the kings' tyranny and the bishops' courage.[56] One could multiply these specific examples, but they would still not add up to an explanation of the general pattern; though each chronicler had his own individual bias, stories of contentious rituals are told by all, both those that supported the kings and those that criticized them. This suggests that the contentiousness was a fact chroniclers had to deal with. They could use it to illustrate their criticisms, take refuge from its implications in a conventional moral, or rearrange the facts to deflect ignominy from the kings they supported, but they could not ignore it, any more than the author of the *Gesta Stephani* could ignore the fact that some fundamental principle of political order had been violated when Stephen arrested the bishops of Salisbury and Lincoln in a public council. He could only shift the burden of guilt onto the bishops and the

55. *Miracula sanctae Frideswidae*, c. 37, AASS Oct. 8: 567–90, here 575–76. The juxtaposition, coupled with the author's implied denigration of the belief in the royal touch ("scrophulis . . . quae contactu regiae manus curari dicuntur"), makes it appear that the paralysis proved the falseness of the belief in the king's curative power. My thanks to Jay Rubenstein for this reference.

56. Above, notes 45, 47–49; below, note 73. On Orderic see Roger D. Ray, "Orderic Vitalis and His Readers," *Studia Monastica* 14 (1972), 17–33, and "Orderic Vitalis on Henry I: Theocratic Ideology and Didactic Narrative," in *Contemporary Reflections on the Medieval Christian Tradition: Essays in Honor of Ray C. Petry*, ed. George H. Shriver (Durham, NC, 1974), pp. 119–34; also Marjorie Chibnall, "Orderic Vitalis on Castles," in *Studies in Medieval History Presented to R. Allen Brown*, ed. Christopher Harper-Bill et al. pp. 43–56. For dismissals of Eadmer's and other chroniclers' hostile judgments on English kings see V. H. Galbraith, "Good Kings and Bad Kings in Medieval English History," *History* 30 (1945), 119–32; Emma Mason, "William Rufus: Myth and Reality," *Journal of Medieval History* 3 (1977), 1–20; Thomas Callahan, Jr., "The Making of a Monster: The Historical Image of William Rufus," *Journal of Medieval History* 7 (1981), 175–185.

king's courtiers, and allege that a rueful king had done penance for the sacrilege. It is yet another case of an English ritual gone wrong. Indeed, it is the archetypal case, since the melée at the council and the arrest of the bishops at once symbolized the loss of a sense of the sacredness of public space in England and helped unleash the anarchy that was the result of that loss.[57]

However, the true distinctiveness of this English pattern emerges only from a comparison with other traditions, notably the French. For French chroniclers also manifest a profound bias towards the liberties and prerogatives of their churches, yet they simply do not tell tales about their rulers. Not that France was an idyll of peace and contentment. There were Louis VI's wars with Henry I and Theobald of Blois, though to a certain extent these were no more than politics as usual. But we also have troubling suggestions of a conspiracy by Queen Bertrade against the life of the young Louis VI and hints of dissatisfaction and perhaps conspiracy upon the accession of Louis VII.[58] And there are more ominous signs still that political consensus was decaying, taking with it the elemental morality that keeps political societies intact: an assassination at Laon on orders of the bishop, soon followed by the assassination of the bishop himself and civil war; the assassination of the count of Flanders, again followed by civil war; and the distant eddies of turmoil within the royal court itself, as supporters of the Garlandes took revenge on their court rivals by murdering the bishop-elect of Orléans and the prior of Saint-Victor.[59] Yet to read the chroniclers, in France the spirit of community survived this crisis, and respect for the sacredness of royal rites survived as embodiments of the spirit. We can therefore compare the troubled coronations and crown-wearings of William Rufus and Henry I with Louis VI's coronation by the archbishop of Sens. After the fact, delegates from the church of Reims arrived to protest, claiming that the prerogative of crowning a king belonged to their church. Had the claim been made in England, the clergy would have destroyed the ceremony if that is what it took to enforce their rights. In

57. *Gesta Stephani*, cc. 34–36, pp. 72–81. On the event and its aftermath see R. H. C. Davis, *King Stephen* (Berkeley, CA, 1967), pp. 31–34; Edward J. Kealey, *Roger of Salisbury, Viceroy of England* (Berkeley, CA, 1972), pp. 182–86; Cronne, *Reign of Stephen*, pp. 38, 93–98; and, in a revisionist vein, Kenji Yoshitake, "The Arrest of the Bishops in 1139 and Its Consequences," *Journal of Medieval History* 14 (1988), 97–114.

58. Suger, *Vie de Louis VI*, c. 18, pp. 122–126; OV 11, 9; 13, 12 (6: 50–55, 422–25); Achille Luchaire, *Louis VI le Gros: annales de sa vie et de son règne* (Paris, 1890), nos. 13, 76, 478; Marcel Pacaut, *Louis VII et son royaume* (Paris, 1964), pp. 39–40.

59. Luchaire, *Louis VI*, pp. xlix–liii, nos. 505, 518–19; OV 13, 12 (6: 422–25).

France, in 1108, the clergy of Reims murmured but bit their tongues and said nothing publicly.[60] Whereas the funeral of William the Conqueror was a scene of riot and desertion, and William's funeral cloth had to be paid for by a simple knight, that of Philip I (no saint himself) went off without a hitch, his own son Louis adorning the body and accompanying it to Fleury while Louis's own ministers carried the bier.[61] During the Norman rebellions of 1118 Henry I slept with weapons at his side, was plagued with nightmares, and suffered at least one documented assassination attempt; but Louis VII slept beneath a tree in the open woods without any guard at all; and when the count of Blois took him to gentle task for such carelessness, Louis replied with a telling slight to the power of the king of England, who enjoyed money but (the implication was) no such security.[62]

This story, of course, is myth-making; but to dismiss the political significance of such stories on that account is to overlook the obvious fact that in the early twelfth century, the French and English were making significantly different myths about their kings. For like their English counterparts, French chroniclers had their biases, none more pervasive than the staunch royalism of the abbots of Saint-Denis, whose writings so thoroughly control our understanding of the Capetians. But even granting that in this early period the tradition of chroniclers at Saint-Denis was already biased towards the French kings, where in the same period was the English equivalent of Saint-Denis? It did not exist, not at Gloucester, nor at Winchester, and certainly not at Canterbury.[63] Yet France had not only Saint-Denis but also the churches of Reims, Fleury, Saint-Martin of Tours, Saint-Valéry, and Saint-Riquier, each at one time or another and for reasons of its own narrow self-interest predisposed to uphold the image of the early Capetians as just and pious rulers.[64] What is still more signifi-

60. Suger, *Vie de Louis VI,* c. 14, pp. 86–88.

61. Suger, c. 13, pp. 82–84.

62. Walter Map, *De nugis curialium* 5: 452–53.

63. *Pace* Dieter Berg, "Regnum Norm-Anglorum und Englisches Königtum: Zur Entwicklung der anglonormannischen Herrschaftsideologie im 11. und 12. Jahrhundert," in *Historiographia Mediaevalis: Festschrift für Franz-Josef Schmale zum 65. Geburtstag,* ed. Dieter Berg and Hans-Werner Goetz (Darmstadt, 1988), pp. 168–80. Misrepresenting Antonia Gransden (*Historical Writing in England, c. 550 to c. 1307* [Ithaca, NY, 1974]), Berg gives Anglo-Norman chroniclers of Henry's reign a sense of mission and organization they did not have. On the contrary, Gransden emphasizes the parochial interests of the chroniclers, who criticized the kings more often than not for their abuse of their own churches' rights.

64. *Abbot Suger,* ed. Gerson; Gabrielle Spiegel, *The Chronicle Tradition of Saint-Denis* (Leyden, 1978); "The Cult of Saint Denis and Capetian Kingship," in *Saints and Their Cults,* ed. Stephen Wilson (Cambridge, 1983), pp. 141–68; Sharon Farmer, *Communities of Saint Martin: Legend and Ritual in Medieval Tours* (Ithaca, NY 1991), pp. 195–205; Bloch, *The*

cant, that image was not very different outside the orbit of royal bishoprics and abbeys. For example, Flemish chroniclers writing in the aftermath of Charles the Good's assassination accepted Louis VI's intervention in the county in spite of the difficulties it caused; and they describe his entries and courts in glowing and hallowed terms, with not even a rumor of dissension, even when these occurred on the threshold of civil war.[65]

It is also too little acknowledged that these differences in rituals and rhetoric are repeated in all facets of the two political cultures.[66] In England, for example, ascetic holy men publicly rebuked kings for the injustices of their administrations. French kings were, if anything, rebuked for being holy men themselves.[67] Although the twelfth century was everywhere the time when writers rediscovered the art of satire, Anglo-Norman political satire tended to be directed against the court of the English kings. In France, it tended to be directed against the church.[68] Finally, it was again Anglo-Norman writers who rediscovered the classical figure of *Fortuna,* blindly lifting men up to the pinnacles of power only to dash them down again, regardless of what they deserved. But in France, even a secular cleric

---

Royal Touch, p. 132; Jäschke, "Frühmittelalterliche Festkrönungen?" pp. 556–57; Thomas Head, *Hagiography and the Cult of Saints: The Diocese of Orléans (800–1200)* (Cambridge, 1990), pp. 62–64; Claude Carozzi, "Le roi et la liturgie chez Helgaud de Fleury," *Hagiographie, cultures et sociétés, IVe–XIIe siècles,* Actes du Colloque organisé à Nanterre et à Paris, 2–5 mai, 1979 (Paris: Etudes Augustiniennes, 1979), pp. 417–32; Carozzi, "La *Vie du roi Robert* par Helgaud de Fleury: historiographie et hagiographie," in *L'historiographie en Occident du Ve au XVe siècles,* Actes du Congrès de la Société des Historiens Médiévistes de l'Enseignement Supérieur Public (Tours, 10–12 juin 1977), *Annales de Bretagne et des Pays de l'Ouest* 137 (1980), 219–35; Karl Ferdinand Werner, "Die Legitimität der Kapetinger und die Entstehung des 'Reditus regni Francorum ad stirpem Karoli,'" *Die Welt als Geschichte* 12 (1952), 203–25, here pp. 213–16. The gathering together of these strands in later medieval France is discussed by Colette Beaune, *The Birth of an Ideology: Myths and Symbols of Nation in Late-Medieval France,* tr. Susan Ross Huston (Berkeley, CA, 1991).

65. Heriman of Tournai, *Liber de restauratione sancti Martini Tornacensis,* ed. Georg Waitz, *MGH SS* 14: 287 (c. 33), 288 (c. 35); Galbert of Bruges, *Histoire du meurtre de Charles le Bon,* c. 55, p. 86; cc. 77–78, pp. 121–22. See also Walter of Thérouanne, *Vita Karoli comitis,* c. 46, ed. R. Koepke, *MGH SS* 12: 558, although Walter acknowledges Louis's difficulties in the face of Henry I's allies in Flanders (cc. 45, 48, pp. 558–59) and is generally less effusive in his praise of his policies.

66. For a later period, however, see Charles T. Wood, *Joan of Arc and Richard III: Sex, Saints, and Government in the Middle Ages* (Oxford, 1988).

67. Karl Leyser, "The Angevin Kings and the Holy Man," in *St. Hugh of Lincoln,* ed. Henry Mayr-Harting (Oxford, 1987), pp. 49–73; Walter Map, *De nugis curialium,* 5: 446–51; Suger, *Vie de Louis VI,* c. 2, p. 14. See also Henry Mayr-Harting, "Functions of a Twelfth-Century Recluse," *History* 60 (1975), 337–53; and David Farmer, "The Cult and Canonization of St Hugh," in *St. Hugh of Lincoln,* pp. 76–77.

68. Ronald E. Pepin, *Literature of Satire in the Twelfth Century: A Neglected Mediaeval Genre* (Lewiston, NY, 1988); Egbert Türk, *Nugae curialium: le règne d'Henri II Plantagenêt (1154–1189) et l'éthique politique* (Geneva, 1977); John A. Yunck, *The Lineage of Lady Meed: The Development of Mediaeval Venality Satire* (South Bend, IN, 1963), pp. 147, 160–66.

like Galbert of Bruges, experienced in the ways of the world, struggled to keep Fortune out of his account of the Flemish civil wars, preferring to see the rise and fall of successive counts as God's reward for virtue and vice. Without any struggle at all Suger fell back on the traditional Carolingian device that interpreted political and military success as a reward for humility, failure as a punishment for pride.[69] Nor do Suger and Galbert think to use a ruler's death to expound on the vanity of worldly power; still less do they describe that ruler's putrefying flesh, stinking and fetid. That was a topos, but one applied primarily to English kings by Anglo-Norman writers.[70]

Something in the Anglo-Norman experience of politics tended to desacralize political authority, rendering it fit for parody and resistance, while in France something made it possible to adapt the old typologies that held political authority sacred. We need, then, not to discount the bias of our sources but to explain it, for eventually the bias became so much a part of the mythology of these two countries that it shaped the perceptions of contemporaries, until even English bishops and chroniclers touted the French king as a model of the *rex christianissimus* and a dying Becket commended his soul to Saint Denis.[71]

69. Emma Mason, "Magnates, Curiales and the Wheel of Fortune," *Anglo-Norman Studies* 2 (1979), 118–140; Jan Dhondt, "Une mentalité du XIIe siècle: Galbert de Bruges," *Revue du Nord* 39 (1957), 101–9; Walter Mohr, "Geschichtstheologische Aspekte im Werk Galberts von Brugge," in *Pascua Mediaevalia: Studies voor Prof. Dr. J. M. De Smet* (Louvain, 1983), pp. 246–62; Suger, *Vie de Louis VI,* c. 19, p. 140; c. 25, pp. 180–82; Gabrielle Spiegel, "History as Enlightenment: Suger and the *Mos Anagogicus,*" in *Abbot Suger and Saint-Denis,* pp. 151–58; Spiegel, "Defense of the Realm: Evolution of a Capetian Propaganda Slogan," *Journal of Medieval History* 3 (1977), 115–33; Koziol, *Begging Pardon and Favor,* pp. 185–86.

70. OV 7, 16 (4: 100–107); Henry of Huntingdon, *Historia Anglorum,* ed. Thomas Arnold, Rolls Series, 74 (London, 1879), pp. 256–57, and "De contemptu mundi," pp. 310–12; Suger, *Vie de Louis VI,* cc. 13, 22–24, pp. 82–85, 266–67, 272–87; Galbert of Bruges, *Histoire du meurtre de Charles le Bon,* cc. 77–78, 119, pp. 121–22, 170–72. See also Heriman of Tournai, *Liber de restauratione sancti Martini,* c. 35, *MGH SS* 14: 288; and Walter of Thérouanne, *Vita Karoli comitis,* cc. 25–27, 30–31, 47, *MGH SS* 12: 548–52, 558, the latter actually attributing miracles and popular veneration to the slain count. On the genre of *contemptus mundi,* both generally and with respect to Henry of Huntingdon, see Dietrich Lohrmann, "Der Tod König Heinrichs I. von England in der mittellateinischen Literatur Englands und der Normandie," *Mittellateinisches Jahrbuch* 8 (1973), 90–107; and Nancy Partner, *Serious Entertainments: The Writing of History in Twelfth-Century England* (Chicago, 1977), pp. 20, 32–36. For reasons similar to those advanced in the text, it is not entirely relevant that stories of English kings' tumultuous and disrespectful burial rites are so common as to seem conventional, because it is the convention itself that is disrespectful. Significantly, the topos is not applied to the burials of French kings in the eleventh and twelfth centuries—not even to Philip I.

71. Walter Map, *De nugis curialium,* p. 442 n. 3; Türk, *Nugae curialium,* pp. 89, 121–24; Raymonde Foreville, "Thomas Becket et la France capétienne," in *Studies in Medieval History Presented to R. Allen Brown,* ed. Christopher Harper-Bill et al. (Woodbridge, 1989),

Assuming that we take these differences seriously, explaining them is a profound and complex problem, but any explanation must take into account the historical conditions peculiar to Norman and Angevin kingship. As William I's jester so indelicately reminded him, he was not born a king, not even born into a royal dynasty or into a people ruled by kings. He was king not by the grace of God but by conquest, and for almost a century every successful king after him had to fight in order to make good his claim to the throne, every one of them facing strong (and legitimate) competitors. At the very least, the harsh struggle required before each king could consolidate his power and forge a group of dedicated supporters must have created a climate of competition and multiple occasions for legal wrangling over confiscated lands and offices.[72] The same constraints certainly caused the Norman and Angevin kings to develop an unusually sophisticated fiscal apparatus to raise the money to finance their wars. The techniques were effective, but they also lay on the margins of traditional political morality. The result was greater material wealth and military power at the risk of respect for the principles of sacred political authority, and disrespect was especially likely to be shown at moments of high ritual, and not just royal ritual. Eadmer was appalled, for example, when on the very day of Anselm's installation as archbishop, after the solemn *occursus* of the monks, clergy, and people of the town and the new archbishop's enthronement, Ranulf Flambard arrived at Canterbury on orders from the king to give notice of a suit against Anselm, "paying not the slightest regard to any considerations of piety or restraint," with "no compunction in disturbing the great rejoicing of the Church," and to the great hurt and indignation of the community.[73]

Did the dictates of conquest further abet the desacralization of kingship by requiring the kings to govern more ruthlessly, even arbitrarily, to preserve their power? Some have thought so, given the Norman and Angevin reputation for stern and angry justice, but others have denied it, pointing out that stern and angry justice is just what contemporaries praised in them. It is not unreasonable to believe that these contradictory judgments reflect the real puzzlement of contemporaries, awed by the

p. 117; Foreville "L'image de Philippe Auguste dans les sources contemporaines," *La France de Philippe Auguste: le temps des mutations,* ed. Robert-Henri Bautier (Paris, 1982), pp. 115–32; Leyser, "The Angevin Kings and the Holy Man," pp. 53–54.

72. James C. Holt, "Politics and property in early medieval England," *Past and Present* 57 (1972), 19–24, with provisos at 30–33.

73. Eadmer, *Historia novorum,* 1: 41–42.

"violent greatness" of kings whose unprecedented power they, like Jolliffe, saw as the only means of reducing a conquered people to submission and taming an unusually fierce baronage.[74] If this was true, then it may also be possible that in trying to work out the paradox, writers were required to look at kingship differently, not necessarily more objectively, but with greater balance and less automatic acceptance of any easy typological solution to the disparity of means and ends.[75] And that would imply less automatic acceptance of the liturgies that communicated the typologies.

France differed in every way. In place of repeated dynastic upheaval, it possessed a stable dynasty whose legitimacy was accepted by even the most powerful counts. In turn, the kings accepted their magnates' vice-regal authority and (at least until Philip Augustus) did nothing to undermine either it or their own carefully cultivated reputation for piety and fair play. Though the kings' material resources were quite traditional, and therefore quite limited, by the same token they were morally acceptable to the church in a way that Henry I's and Henry II's were not. Yet these traits are all renderings of a more fundamental characteristic: the discrepancy between the early Capetians' great moral stature and minimal effective power. The paradox is only superficial; for though the strength and autonomy of the principalities limited the kings' power, it was also within the principalities that respect for political authority was nurtured. Ever since the late tenth century, the counts and dukes of the West Frankish realm had modeled their authority on the king's, borrowing his epithets for themselves, aping his ceremonies, and appropriating his moral standards for their own propaganda. Whatever strains chivalry and ecclesiastical reform had created in this tradition, in twelfth-century France kingship retained its mimetic power.[76] We therefore find the same belief in the sacredness of political

74. J. E. A. Jolliffe, *Angevin Kingship*, 2d ed. (1955); C. Warren Hollister, *Monarchy, Magnates, and Institutions in the Anglo-Norman World* (London, 1986). For examples, see also OV, 7, 15 (4: 82–83), William of Malmesbury, *De gestis regum Anglorum libri quinque*, ed. William Stubbs, Rolls Series, 90 (London, 1889), pp. 473, 486–88; Henry of Huntingdon, *Historia Anglorum*, pp. 208–10, 255–56.

75. Robert W. Hanning, *The Vision of History in Early Britain: From Gildas to Geoffrey of Monmouth* (New York, 1966), pp. 128–35, 138–42; also Partner, *Serious Entertainments*, pp. 26–27. Thus Orderic Vitalis appears to have accepted Henry I's justification for having had two rebels blinded even though they were not his direct vassals; yet he was still troubled enough by the act to have recorded Count Charles of Flanders's objection to the punishment as a violation of the "custom of knighthood" (OV 12: 17, 21, 39 [6: 228–29, 260–61, 352–55]).

76. See Pacaut, *Louis VII et son royaume*, pp. 27–28; Karl Ferdinand Werner, "Kingship and Principality in Twelfth-Century France," *The Medieval Nobility: Studies on the Ruling Classes of France and Germany from the Sixth to the Twelfth Century*, ed. and trans. Timothy Reuter (Amsterdam, 1978), pp. 243–290; Barthélemy, *L'Ordre seigneurial*, chap. 6; Koziol, *Begging Pardon and Favor*, pp. 165–73, 288.

authority within the principalities that we find in the royal domain, and as before, that belief was filtered through the churches. Thus, just as the abbots of Saint-Denis sanctified the royal dynasty, monks of Marmoutier celebrated the lineage of the counts of Anjou with legends extolling their regal wisdom and virtue, while canons of Bruges, Thérouanne, and Tournai praised the holiness of the counts of Flanders, and a canon of Angoulême exalted his little counts with grandiose virtues fit for a great king.[77] The counts and dukes of France also had their own quasi-royal rituals that dramatized these ideals; and though such ceremonies did give greater prominence to knights than once had been the case, relics and incense still had a large place in them. The dukes of Aquitaine, for instance, were inaugurated at Poitiers in the monastery of Saint-Hilaire, where after receiving its lay abbacy they were invested with the ducal insignia of lance and banner, given the ring of Saint Valery, and finally received within the city in a formal procession.[78] In 1096 Fulk le Réchin, count of Anjou, basked in a visit from Pope Urban II, who dedicated the church of Saint-Nicolas and presided over the reburial of Fulk's uncle and predecessor in the nave, effectively sanctifying his dynasty and legitimating his reign.[79] William Clito was welcomed outside the walls of Saint-Omer by troops of knights brandishing weapons, but at the walls themselves stood the city's clerics, waiting with incense, tapers, and hymns to lead the count to the church. In fact, in most ways Galbert's description of William's *adventus* was entirely atypical, since Flemish sources consistently depict the ritual life of the counts of Flanders as a liturgical round, tightly integrated with the churches of his principality.[80]

77. For Anjou, see *Gesta consulum Andegavorum,* ed. Halphen and Poupardin, pp. 140–42; Farmer, *Communities of Saint Martin,* pp. 79–82, 86–88. For Flanders, encomiastic treatments of the counts may be found in Galbert of Bruges, *Histoire du meurtre de Charles le Bon;* Heriman of Tournai, *Liber de restauratione sancti Martini;* and Walter of Thérouanne, *Vita Karoli comitis.* For praise of the counts of Angoulême, see *Historia pontificum et comitum Engolismensium,* ed. Jacques Boussard (Paris, 1957), p. 32. This reflexive deference probably accounts for the puzzle, noted by Beech, that Aquitainian chroniclers advance the same old epithets of piety and virtue when writing of Duke William IX, saying nothing of his unsavory reputation, while Anglo-Norman chroniclers are interested precisely in the tales that constituted that reputation for bawdiness. See George Beech, "Contemporary Views of William the Troubadour, IXth Duke of Aquitaine, 1086–1126," in *Medieval Lives and the Historian: Studies in Medieval Prosopography,* ed. Neithard Bulst and Jean-Philippe Genet (Kalamazoo, MI: 1986), pp. 73–89.

78. Geoffroi de Vigeois, *HF* 12, 442–43.

79. *Chroniques des comtes d'Anjou,* ed. Halphen and Poupardin, pp. 237–38, on which see Bradbury, "Fulk le Réchin," pp. 37–38.

80. Heriman of Tournai, *Liber de restauratione sancti Martini,* cc. 27–28, p. 285; Galbert of Bruges, *Histoire du meurtre de Charles le Bon,* cc. 12, 15, 81, 103; pp. 20–21, 25, 124, 149; Walter

There are no equivalent English rites in English sources because there were no equivalent principalities in England. English politics was royal politics, pursued at the court, around the king. As a result, court rituals became highly politicized, for only by participating in them could magnates publicize their grievances and maintain their positions.[81] In contrast, French rituals probably occurred within political communities that were smaller and more homogeneous: in France, even a royal burial was largely a household affair. The more parochial arena of the rituals therefore truly reflected a more politically fragmented kingdom. Yet this cannot be the whole story, for even when different sectors of the realm gathered around the king, as when fending off the German invasion in 1124, electing a count in Flanders under royal auspices in 1127, or witnessing the king's vow of a crusade in 1147, there still seems to have been a certain willingness to suspend competition momentarily. In this way, the crown and its rituals became a symbol not only for the unity of France but also, and still more fundamentally, for the principle that political authority was sacrosanct, that of the realm's counts, count-bishops, and monastic immunities as well as of the king himself. That, and not the royal touch, may have been the true Capetian miracle. But as with all miracles, the power did not inhere in the rituals but in the community, predisposed to see the miraculous.[82]

---

of Thérouanne, *Vita Karoli comitis,* c. 25, *MGH SS* 12: 548–49; *Actes des comtes de Flandre,* no. 22, pp. 65–67 (1096).

81. Schramm, *History of the English Coronation,* pp. 66–68, 71; see also Warren, *Governance of Norman and Angevin England,* pp. 49–52; Robin Frame, *The Political Development of the British Isles, 1100–1400* (Oxford, 1990), pp. 55, 61–62, 64–65.

82. Geoffrey Koziol, "Monks, Feuds, and the Making of Peace in Eleventh-Century Flanders," in *The Peace of God: Social Violence and Religious Response in France Around the Year 1000,* ed. Thomas Head and Richard Landes (Ithaca, NY, 1992), pp. 239–58, here 247–52.

R. C. Van Caenegem

7. Law and Power in Twelfth-Century Flanders

In the twelfth century the county of Flanders was one of the most famous "territorial principalities" of the kingdom of France.[1] For two centuries it had behaved as an autonomous state—Galbert of Bruges does not hesitate to call it a *regnum* and its count a *princeps*[2]—but legally speaking it was held in fief from both the French and the German crowns. These two parts of the county are known respectively as *la Flandre sous la Couronne* or *Kroonvlaanderen* (almost 90 percent of the total Flemish territory) and *la Flandre Impériale* or *Rijksvlaanderen*; the Scheldt frontier went back to the famous treaty of Verdun of 843, when it separated the lands of Charles the Bald from those of Lothar I. Principalities that belonged to the kingdom of France and were held in fief from the French crown, but behaved in fact as autonomous states, were a well-known feature of the period—the duchy of Normandy, like Flanders, being another familiar example. There is here a contrast between legal and political reality, to which I shall return at the end of this study.

In twelfth-century Flanders there was a lively concern with legal problems. This is clear from the comparative wealth of borough charters, the testimony of narrative sources, such as Galbert of Bruges, and scholarly writings such as Lambert of Saint-Omer's *Liber Floridus*.[3] The county

1. For an authoritative survey of medieval Flanders and its institutions, see F. L. Ganshof, *La Flandre,* in *Histoire des institutions françaises au moyen âge, I, Institutions seigneuriales,* ed. Ferdinand Lot and Robert Fawtier (Paris, 1957), pp. 343–426.

2. *Histoire du meurtre de Charles le Bon, comte de Flandre (1127–1128) par Galbert de Bruges,* ed. Henri Pirenne (Paris, 1891); Galbert of Bruges, *The Murder of Charles the Good,* tr. James B. Ross (Toronto, 1988).

3. For a critical survey of eleventh- and twelfth-century Flemish borough charters, see R.C. Van Caenegem, "Coutumes et législation en Flandre aux XIe et XIIe siècles," in *Les libertés urbaines et rurales du XIe au XIVe siècle* (Brussels, 1968), pp. 245–79; a selection of texts can be found in M. Martens, "Recueil de textes d'histoire urbaine belge des origines au milieu du XIIIe siècle," in *Elenchus fontium historiae urbanae,* ed. C. van de Kieft and J. F. Niermeijer (Leiden, 1967), 1: 281–404. For the legal sections in Lambert's encyclopaedia see F. L. Ganshof, "Droit romain dans le 'Liber Floridus,'" *Tijdschrift voor Rechtsgeschiedenis* 29 (1961), 432–44

therefore provides a good case study for the theme of this colloquium, which has presented a welcome opportunity to develop my views on early Flemish law.[4]

I

As a starting point I would like to make the general observation that legal rules are not so much invented by jurists reasoning in the abstract and deducing norms from axiomata dictated by natural justice, but are to a large extent established as the result of conflicting interests and pressure groups which at a given moment reach a point of equilibrium. This proposition can be illustrated with some examples from twelfth-century Flanders, moving from the more obvious to the more unexpected.

1. The crisis of 1127–1128 was the greatest drama of the century there: the treacherous murder of the childless Count Charles the Good; the ensuing struggle between various pretenders leading to civil war; the death in 1128 of one of the principal candidates for the succession, William Clito; and the consequent recognition of his main rival, Thierry of Alsace, who went on to rule till 1168. Although we are in the presence of a typical and violent power struggle, there is no doubt that legal principles were involved. Indeed, the immediate cause of the drama was the rigorous application of the law of serfdom with all its practical implications. The Erembald clan, which had risen to power and wealth in the counts' service, was of servile origin and its members had, legally speaking, always remained comital serfs. Socially and politically, however, they had outgrown their legal status, and it was when Charles the Good decided to reduce them to their true position, in reality as well as in law, and thus to demean them beyond endurance, that they felt trapped, and resorted to murder and a vain attempt

---

and "Note sur deux textes de droit canonique dans le 'Liber Floridus,'" in *Etudes d'histoire du droit canonique dédiées à Gabriel Le Bras,* 2 vols. (Paris, 1965) 1: 99–116. For Lambert's text, see *Lamberti S. Audomari canonici Liber Floridus,* ed. Albert Derolez (Ghent, 1968).

4. Although the critical study of medieval Flemish law was initiated by L.A. Warnkoenig (1794–1866) more than 150 years ago and was followed by numerous publications on points of detail, there is no modern comprehensive survey of the subject. Fortunately, Flemish private law receives full attention in the authoritative recent book by Ph. Godding, *Le droit privé dans les Pays-Bas méridionaux du 12e au 18e siècle* (Brussels, 1987). Further bibliographical information can be found in John Gilissen, *Belgique et Nord de la France. Introduction bibliographique à l'histoire du droit et à l'ethnologie juridique,* C/3 (Brussels, 1970). Some recent bibliography will be found in P. de Win et al., *Rechtshistorische Bibliografie van België, 1980–1985.* Iuris Scripta Historica, 4 (Brussels, 1991).

to put their man on the throne. After a few days of stunned hesitation the leading men in the country launched a counter-offensive and in a matter of weeks the revolt was put down and the clan exterminated. The first legal problem, which had in fact been concerned with wealth and power, was settled by violence and not, as had been planned, by the judgment of a court of law.[5]

The other legal question concerned the succession to the county and the right of the suzerain, the king of France, to intervene and impose his candidate in the vacant fief. An analysis of the events of those years will lead the observer to the somewhat cynical conclusion that the law in this respect was indeed observed, but only as long as its observance was backed by sufficient political support. At first, in the months following the murder on 2 March, all went according to the rules of the feudal game.[6] The Flemish fief was vacant, the suzerain entered it and, in the absence of a direct descendant, chose among the pretenders to the Flemish inheritance the one he preferred, William Clito, a grandson of William the Conqueror's Flemish queen Matilda. The Flemish barons accepted Louis VI's candidate at Arras on 23 March or shortly after, and soon the new count was received in various Flemish towns, where homage was done to him.[7] Galbert's detailed description of the event in Bruges is among the classic texts on feudal law.[8] However, by February 1128 the political wind had changed and the Flemish towns, led by Ghent and Bruges, went over to Thierry of Alsace, the candidate supported by the king of England, and feudal law gave way to the law of politics; as Clito's military strength collapsed, he—and the law—became the victims of the new balance of power. On 31 March and 1 April 1128 homage was done in Bruges to Thierry of Alsace, whom Galbert at that moment scathingly referred to as the "newly elected Thierry, count only of the people of Ghent and Bruges and their accomplices."[9] All was not lost, however, for legal principle. The castellan of Bruges and

5. I refer to the Introductions to the works quoted in note 2. See also R.C. Van Caenegem, *Galbert van Brugge en het Recht* (Brussels, 1978); and Van Caenegem, "Galbert of Bruges on Serfdom, Prosecution of Crime, and Constitutionalism (1127–28)," in *Law, Custom, and the Social Fabric in Medieval Europe: Essays in Honor of Bryce Lyon,* ed. Bernard S. Bachrach and David Nicholas (Kalamazoo, MI, 1990), pp. 89–112. Galbert and the crisis of 1127–28 also receive extensive treatment in ch. 4, "The Crisis," in Ernest Warlop, *The Flemish Nobility Before 1300,* 4 vols. (Kortrijk, 1975–76), 1: 185–208.

6. I shall return to this point in detail.

7. F. L. Ganshof, "Le roi de France en Flandre en 1127 et 1128," *Revue Historique de Droit Français et Étranger* 27 (1949), 204–28.

8. *Histoire,* c. 56, ed. Pirenne, p. 89.

9. *Histoire,* c. 103, p. 148. Something significant has been lost in Ross's translation of *complices* as "confederates."

eminent leader of the resistance against the Erembalds, Gervase of Praet, who joined Thierry's party in spite of his homage to William Clito, justified his move by invoking the very feudal law he was breaking, or at least by paying lip service to it. In his speech of 2 April he explained as follows why he acted against his previous homage and fealty: "I break completely with Count William . . . because the peers of the land and all the people have condemned the one who is still wandering about the land lawless, faithless, without regard for the justice of God and man."[10] He was clearly referring to the principle derived from the contractual nature of feudalism that a vassal had the right of *diffiduciatio* towards a lord who treated him unjustly.[11] An interesting point remains open to discussion here. Did Gervase refer to a formal condemnation by a law court or was he speaking in terms of a condemnation by public opinion as represented by the people and their leaders without legal proceedings before a court of law? If the former interpretation is correct, could it be that Gervase had in mind the court proposed by Yvain of Aalst in his speech in Ghent on 16 February 1128? There the leader of Thierry's party suggested to Clito that a court should meet at Ypres in the middle of Flanders, where "barons from both sides, and our peers and all the responsible men among the clergy and people" should gather to judge Clito and decide whether he deserved to keep the countship. A very day, March 8, was set for the assembly at Ypres. That this court ever met appears unlikely, considering the political climate and the fact that Galbert makes no further mention of what would have been a most remarkable event. On the other hand, the speech of Gervase of Praet refers to a condemnation by "the peers of the land and all the people," which is close to the formula "the barons . . . and our peers and all the responsible men" of Yvain's proposal (no clergy are mentioned, but they could possibly be included in "all the people"), so that the possibility of a formal condemnation by a court, at Ypres or elsewhere, on the lines of the February proposal cannot be excluded.[12]

2. The waning of serfdom was related to the rise of the towns. It seems

10. *Histoire,* c. 104, pp. 149–50.

11. Walter Ullmann, *The Individual and Society in the Middle Ages* (London, Methuen, 1967), pp. 64–65; Ullmann, *Law and Politics in the Middle Ages: An Introduction to the Sources of Medieval Political Ideas* (Ithaca, NY, 1975), pp. 218–19; F.L. Ganshof, *Qu'est-ce que la féodalité?* 5th ed. (Paris, 1982), pp. 157–61.

12. I owe this suggestion to Dirk Heirbaut, author of an unpublished thesis on feudalism in medieval Flanders, entitled "Graaf en Vazallen. Een institutionele analyse van enkele aspecten van de feodo-vazallitische relaties tussen de graaf van Vlaanderen en zijn vazallen van de meerderjarigheid van Boudewijn IV tot Boudewijn IX (ca. 990–aanvang 1206)" (Ghent, 1988).

appropriate therefore to direct our attention to urban autonomy in twelfth-century Flanders and to three topics in particular: the impact on serfdom, the growing importance of legislation, and the changes in the criminal law.

Although there is no proof of a general observance in Flanders in the first half of the twelfth century of the rule *Stadtluft macht frei* (if it is permitted to use this nineteenth-century phrase), there is no doubt that personal freedom in one way or another was a typical urban asset, and in the thirteenth century increased urbanization would lead to the virtual disappearance of serfdom in Flanders.[13] How sensitive the matter was in 1127 was demonstrated by the incident at Lille on 1 August of that year, so vividly described by Galbert of Bruges. While the yearly fair was being held, William Clito, accompanied by his mainly Norman retinue, turned up and spotted one of his runaway serfs, who was promptly arrested in order to be sent back to till the land to which he was attached. To the count's surprise this normal and lawful step caused a great uproar: the burgesses rushed to arms and chased Clito and his men out of the town. Two legal principles clashed here. The count, acting not as a head of state but as a lord and landowner, wanted his serf back, and the townsmen wanted to preserve their fellow-citizen's newly won freedom, or if he were legally still a serf, to force his lord to resort to a judicial process if he wanted to reclaim him; they may also have been defending the special peace that protected their market and was in fact one of its great attractions. Which of these urban considerations was material is unclear—possibly all three. What is in no doubt is that the outcome of this clash of interests and of legal principles was settled by force of arms, the legitimate use of violence. William besieged the town with a superior army and imposed his solution of the problem by a show of military strength: the town had to submit and was made to pay an *amerciamentum*[14] of 1,400 marks silver.[15]

Legislation is rightly considered an attribute of the monarch.[16] In

13. *The Cambridge Economic History of Europe*, 2d ed. (Cambridge, 1966), 1: 337.

14. Galbert, c. 93, p. 137. On the Norman *amerciamentum* see Le Foyer, *Exposé du droit pénal normand au XIIIe siècle* (Paris, 1931), pp. 245ff.

15. This was a very considerable sum. The relief paid to the king of France in 1127 for the county of Flanders amounted to 1,000 marks; in 1192 it was 5,000 marks, which at that time represented approximately one year's revenue from the Flemish fief held from the French crown (the southern part, the future county of Artois, not included). F.L. Ganshof, "Armatura," *Archivum Latinitatis Medii Aevi* 15 (1940), 192, n. 1. See the tables based on the *Grote Brief* of 1187 in T. Luykx, *De grafelijke financiële bestuursinstellingen en het grafelijk patrimonim in Vlaanderen tijdens de regering van Margareta van Constantinopel (1244–1278)* (Brussels, 1961), pp. 42–47.

16. Sten Gagner, *Studien zur Ideengeschichte der Gesetzgebung* (Stockholm, 1960); Armin Wolf, "Die Gesetzgebung der entstehenden Territorialstaaten," in *Handbuch der Quellen und*

Flanders it was normally exercised by the count. He could issue laws for the whole county, as, for example, the *lex comitum* and the *jus comitis* on serfdom, referred to by Galbert.[17] He could grant borough charters containing various norms and privileges to particular towns. Introducing new law at the burghers' request was one thing, but giving away the legislative authority itself to them was another. The furthest a count would go under normal circumstances was to allow the town authorities to issue local bylaws under his supervision, which is what Philip of Alsace did in art. 20 of his Great Borough Charters of 1165–1177.[18] In the power game of 1127, however, the need of the pretenders to woo the towns was so pressing that William Clito granted to Bruges, as part of the price for his recognition and "in order to make the citizens well disposed towards him," the right "to correct *potestative et licenter* their customary laws from day to day and to change them for the better as circumstances of time and place demanded."[19] This momentous shift in the Flemish constitution was clearly caused by the political tension of the moment. The same can be said of another grant to a town of what was normally regarded as a regalian right: coinage. In order to ingratiate himself with the burgesses of Saint-Omer, William in 1127 went so far as to grant them his mint there: henceforth the revenue was theirs, and so was the responsibility for the quality of the coinage produced by the urban mint.[20] The same charter also revealed the strong pressure the communes could exert to curb existing law by the express recognition of the urban *droit d'arsin* or *Wüstungrecht*. This was the right of the commune to direct an armed expedition against somebody in the countryside, possibly a robber baron operating from a stone castle, who had harmed a burgher and refused to stand trial in the urban law court. Whatever killing, burning, or destruction took place during such a retaliatory expedition was considered legitimate and went unpunished.[21] Urban

---

Literatur der neueren europäischen Privatrechtsgeschichte, ed. Helmut Coing (Munich, 1973–), 1: 517–800.

17. Van Caenegem, "Galbert of Bruges on Serfdom," pp. 94–96.

18. "Kritische uitgave van de *Grote Keure* van Filips van de Elzas, graaf van Vlaanderen, voor Gent en Brugge (1165–1177)," *Handelingen v.de Kon. Commissie voor Geschiedenis*, ed. R. C. Van Caenegem and Ludo Milis, 143 (1977), 254.

19. Galbert, c. 55, p. 87. Ross (p. 204) translates *potestative et licenter* as "freely," thus leaving out the significant *potestative*, "on their own authority"; *potestas* is a weighty concept.

20. Charter of 14 April 1127, art. 14, ed. Georges Espinas, "Le privilège de Saint-Omer de 1127," *Revue du Nord* 29 (1947), 46.

21. Art. 20, p. 47. See on this institution A. Delcourt, *La vengeance de la commune: l'arsin et l'abattis de maison en Flandre et en Hainaut* (Lille, 1930); R. C. Van Caenegem, *Geschiedenis van het Strafrecht in Vlaanderen van de XIe tot de XIVe eeuw* (Brussels, 1954), pp. 175–90; E. Fischer, *Die Hauszerstörung als strafrechtliche Massnahme im deutschen Mittelalter* (Stuttgart, 1957).

power had brought about a change in the law. Indeed, the normal course of events would have been to obtain the condemnation of the contumacious culprit by a law court, either that of the castellany, the *curia comitis,* or even the urban court, which could pronounce a condemnation *in absentia,* followed by the execution of the judgment by a comital officer. The *droit d'arsin* was an innovation and an anomaly, a *Fremdkörper,* imposed by a new power in the state.

3. Twelfth-century Flanders was a feudal society, so it is interesting to see the role played by feudal ideas in the dramatic events described by Galbert of Bruges. I shall limit my observations to one episode only, the speech made by Yvain of Aalst in Ghent on 16 February 1128. In 1127 Count William had abolished various taxes and charges as a sop to the town of Ghent. As they belonged, however, to the castellan of Ghent, Wenemar II, a powerful baron, the count had no right to give them away. So when the castellan refused to accept the loss of revenue caused by Clito's promises and insisted on the old payments, the town revolted against Wenemar, and Count William had to rush to his rescue.[22] It was at this juncture, in the tense atmosphere of a mass meeting, the first recorded in a long chain of protests and revolts in Ghent's market places, that Yvain of Aalst, one of the leaders of Thierry of Alsace's party, addressed Count William. He made an accusation and proposed a line of action. He told the count that he had broken his pledge to the people and was therefore forfeit as lawful ruler. Instead of dealing justly with the citizens of Ghent, he had imposed evil exactions upon them, treating them with hostility instead of protecting them. Clito, Yvain maintained, had "acted contrary to law, and in his own person had broken the oaths sworn on the maintenance of peace and other rights." "You have violated your faith and done injury to ours," Yvain told him. After this blunt and direct accusation the spokesman of the revolt proposed that the decision on the truthfulness of his indictment should be entrusted to a court of law composed of "barons from both sides, and our peers and all the wiser men among the clergy and the people." According to the findings of this assembly, which we might view as a prefiguration of a constitutional court or of a Congress wielding the weapon of impeachment, the count would either continue in office or have to abdicate. If we consider this court as an afforced *curia comitis,* Yvain's reasoning followed established feudal lines: the lord who broke his contract could be sanctioned by the *diffiduciatio* and *exfestucatio* of his men, and his feudal court was competent to deal with possible complaints. However, it soon

22. Galbert, c. 95, pp. 138–41. Cf. R. C. Van Caenegem, "De Gentse Februari-Opstand van het jaar 1128," *Spiegel Historiael* 13 (1978), 478–83.

appeared that right and might were two different things, for Clito refused to submit to the proposed judgment. He "leapt forward and would have thrown back the *festuca* to Yvain, if he had dared do so." Instead, he challenged his opponent to a judicial combat, offering "*bello comprobare*" that he had acted "rightly and reasonably."[23] To try to establish the righteousness of a claim by judicial combat was very acceptable in the twelfth century, and it is interesting to witness here the clash of two approaches to the question of proof, duel, and the trust in God on the one hand, and the rational enquiry, presumably through discussion and the hearing of witnesses and legal experts, on the other. Clito's counter-proposal was probably never taken up, nor did the proposed judicial combat ever take place. Civil war broke out instead, in the course of which Clito was slain. To the contemporary mind, however, his fate amounted to some sort of an ordeal, a judgment of God, as battles were often interpreted as being won or lost *justo judicio Dei.* The question posed on 16 February 1128 was settled therefore by judicial combat after all, but not in the way William had intended; nor was it settled by the judgment of a human court of law, but by the Almighty.

4. So far we have dealt with legal changes and decisions where power had the final word. Is it possible to find other fields where the dictates of law and justice were paramount, and where principles counted for as much as political pressure and more or less legitimate force? Some historians have little feeling or appreciation for the impact of principle and see in every move a political manoeuvre. This was, for example, the criticism levelled at Leopold von Ranke by Lord Acton, who said of the great German historian: "his hand loses its cunning when political motives do not exist, when it has to deal with principles, or with heroes."[24] Let us avoid that snag and look for a clear example of the impact of legal principle, pure and simple. Article 1 of the charter of Saint-Omer of 1127 perhaps fits our bill, as it appears to have arrived at the notion which would nowadays be called the essence of the *Rechtsstaat.* It proclaims that everyone, including the state and its head, ought to operate under the law and be accountable to the courts. All disputes in Saint-Omer, according to article 1, will be settled by the court of the aldermen, and the count will enforce its judgments against everyone, even himself[25]: we are clearly moving towards the "rule of law" in principle and away from power games and politicizing. Yet even here, as will soon appear, the element of power, the use of legitimate force, was

23. Galbert c. 95, p. 139.

24. Herbert Butterfield, *Man on His Past: The Study of the History of Historical Scholarship* (Cambridge, 1955), p. 222.

25. "Privilège de Saint-Omer," 45.

at hand, since the question remained as to who was to enforce a possible judgment against the count and in favour of the townspeople. *Quis custodiet custodes?* The answer was given in an extension of the forementioned article which was added in article 25 of Thierry of Alsace's confirmation on 22 August 1128 of Clito's charter of the previous year. The text says that if need be, the Flemish barons will in case of conflict between count and town take sides in favour of the latter and exert pressure on the former until he gives in and agrees to implement the judgment against him.[26]

5. It is clear that all the provisions we have so far studied were involved with power as much as with law. Let us, however, not too quickly give up hope of finding a field where legal ideas and speculative thought were clearly predominant. Could the great changes in the modes of proof during the twelfth century be the answer to our quest? The first impression is positive. Was not the dramatic eclipse of the archaic ordeals and their replacement by jury and inquest the result of a change in the outlook of a small but influential group of intellectuals who condemned the ordeal as a *temptatio Dei* on theological grounds? The role of the theologians in the preparation of the famous canon of 1215 against clerical involvement with the unilateral ordeals is well known, and nobody should underestimate its impact.[27] But other sections of society were likewise turning their backs on the old modes of evidence, even before the theologians did. Townspeople had shown their aversion by obtaining privileges of exemption, and rulers had made declarations and issued charters and decrees that left their distrust of the old methods of inquiry, and preference for more reliable ones in no doubt.[28] The civilians, moreover, could not help being contemptuous of procedures that were ignored by their newly discovered bible, the *Corpus Juris Civilis*. Western society during the "Renaissance of the Twelfth Century" made enormous strides forward in terms of material, institutional, and intellectual progress, and the changes in the judicial administration of proof can be seen as an aspect of this wider phenomenon.[29]

26. Ed. Georges Espinas, *Recueil de documents relatifs à l'histoire du droit municipal*, I. *Artois* 3 (Paris, 1943), 306.

27. J. W. Baldwin, "The Intellectual Preparation for the Canon of 1215 Against Ordeals," *Speculum* 36 (1961), 613–36.

28. See the recent survey by Robert Bartlett, *Trial by Fire and Water: The Medieval Judicial Ordeal* (Oxford, 1986). For some critical remarks, see R. C. Van Caenegem, "Reflexions on Rational and Irrational Modes of Proof in Medieval Europe," *Legal History Review* 58 (1990), 263–79. See also the survey by Dominique Barthélemy, "Diversité des ordalies médiévales," *Revue Historique* 280 (1988), 3–25.

29. R. C. Van Caenegem, "Methods of Proof in Western Medieval Law," *Mededelingen van de Kon. Acad. voor Wetenschappen van België Academiae Analecta, Kl. Letteren* 45 (1983, 3), 85–127 (with extensive bibliography).

Do we then have an example here of a legal development that belongs entirely to *Kulturgeschichte* and is free from the disturbing effects of *Machtsgeschichte*? Not quite, as I would like to demonstrate by the following considerations.

It was not enough for townspeople to dislike and distrust ordeals in order to get rid of them; they needed the necessary influence in terms of urban wealth and militias to obtain the desired legal changes from their rulers. The *libertas* obtained in 1116 by the town of Ypres from the count of Flanders is a good illustration of this mechanism.[30] Similarly, it was not enough for the theologians to condemn the ordeals, which the Church had administered with much pomp and circumstance for many centuries, in order to eliminate them. It took the prohibition by a pope and an oecumenical council to achieve that. The observance of such canons avowedly depended to some extent on the mental preparedness of public opinion, but also on a powerful ecclesiastical organization capable of enforcing its orders and prohibitions.

Finally, it was not enough for the rulers to distrust the old engrained habits and techniques in order to get rid of them in practice. It was a measure of their effective power if they could issue the necessary instructions and enforce them. Thus the powerful count of Flanders, Philip of Alsace (1157–1191), managed to introduce in the seven major Flemish towns a similar new borough charter, called *lex et consuetudo . . . a comite instituta,* which ignored the archaic ordeals and made the *veritas scabinorum* (*scepenwaerhede, verité de escevins*) the pivotal mode of proof.[31]

The very name of this institution—the "aldermen's truth"—deserves closer attention and justifies, I believe, the following interpretation. *Veritas scabinorum* can and should be understood as an enquiry, a search for the truth, conducted by two or more aldermen. But it can also be understood as the "aldermen's truth," and not someone else's truth. It is a fact of life that the truth seldom occurs in a void; it usually reflects somebody's views and values: various people hold and cherish various truths. The government's truth is not necessarily the opposition's; the laymen's truth does not automatically coincide with that of the clerics. It is not different with the law itself. Legislators' law can be quite different from that of the judiciary.

30. *Actes des comtes de Flandre, 1071–1128,* ed. Fernand Vercauteren (Brussels, 1938), pp. 177–78.

31. Van Caenegem and Milis, "Grote Keure," pp. 207–57. See also R. C. Van Caenegem, *Geschiedenis van het Strafprocesrecht in Vlaanderen van de XIe tot de XIVe eeuw* (Brussels, 1956), pp. 170–79; and Van Caenegem, "Methods of Proof," pp. 109–11.

Various powers in the state create and develop the law, but each has its own vision and approach. Thus in the historic English common law, the judges were so jealous of their control of the law that they did not hesitate to call it *nostre ley,* "our law."[32] Something similar took place in the struggle for the control of the truth in twelfth-century law courts, for the obvious competitor for the "aldermen's truth" was the "clergy's truth." It is clear that the latter's control over the old ordeals, particularly that of hot iron, as documented by the *Registrum Varadinense,* made the truth which they unveiled very much the clergy's truth.[33]

There is no doubt that when a particular social group controls the truth in criminal cases, often a matter of life or death, it occupies a marked position of strength, so that the replacement of clerical by lay control of judicial proof must have constituted a striking shift in the balance of power between laity and clergy. The *veritas scabinorum* signified heightened lay and urban power, to the detriment of that of the clergy. It also signified heightened state-power—*regnum* scoring against *sacerdotium*—since the aldermen were the count's urban judges, who sat on the bench at the behest of his judicial officers. Philip of Alsace's Great Borough Charters introduced a state-supported *ordo judiciarius,* based on inquiry conducted and judgment given by the ruler's judges. They could not be contradicted[34] and were summoned by the count's officials, who also executed their judgments. This system constituted a true, advanced judicial order, even though it was in no way related to the Roman-canonical procedure, nor was the term *ordo judiciarius* used. The system imposed by Count Philip in his principal towns put public order in the hands of his judges, who judged on the basis of the truth as they perceived it, and whose pronouncements were final and brooked no contradiction. This was different from the shapeless village palavers that had often prevailed in the past. There people shied away

32. Thus Martin JCP and Ashton JCP in the time of King Henry VI, Norman Doe, *Fundamental Authority in Late Medieval English Law* (Cambridge, 1990), p. 23.

33. Our best source for the administration of the ordeal of the hot iron by the clergy is the register of Nagy Varad, the basilica where people were sent from all over Hungary to have their cases tested by the canons there: *Registrum Varadinense,* ed. J. Karacsonyi and S. Borovszky (Budapest, 1903). Although it is widely accepted that the clerics who administered the ordeal also gave the verdict on its outcome (see for example, the fundamental work of Hermann Nottarp, *Gottesurteilstudien* [Munich, 1956], p. 265, who calls them the *Ordalpriester*), this does not exclude lay witnesses from playing a role (Nottarp, pp. 233, 256, with texts from Anglo-Saxon England and thirteenth-century Navarre). And there is also the interesting case of the Yorkshire woman who in 1177 underwent the ordeal of hot iron and whose hand was inspected by twelve knights of the county, R.C. Van Caenegem, *English Lawsuits from William I to Richard I,* 2 vols. (London, 1990–91) 2: 558–59, no. 506.

34. Van Caenegem and Milis, "Grote Keure," art. 15, pp. 236, 252.

from clear-cut authoritative pronouncements, preferring to reach a compromise and agreement in talks conducted by witnesses, parties, friends, and the judges themselves, who often enough were known to favour one party above the other.[35] Ordeals could also be conducted as a sort of negotiated judgment, where the weight of public opinion and of local potentates was felt heavily. Even when the clergy controlled the administration of the ordeal of hot iron, for example, the presence of powerful interested laymen could well influence the clerics' verdict on whether the examinee was *justificatus* or *combustus*. There is a brief passage in Galbert that deserves our attention in this respect, even though the author suggests more than he actually says in so many words. In chapter 105 he tells us that on 6 April 1128 Lambert of Aardenburg, who was generally known to have taken part in the conspiracy against Count Charles and later underwent divine punishment for it, "cleared himself by the hot iron of [the charge of] betraying and putting to death the lord Count Charles." Galbert takes the trouble to specify that this was done "in the presence of Count Thierry," and adds, perhaps more significantly, that "Daniel [of Dendermonde] and Yvain [of Aalst] were not present." Could there be a suggestion here that if those two leaders of the Thierry camp (who may have known more about Lambert than Thierry of Alsace) had been present, the outcome of the ordeal would have been different? If the ordeal was possibly administered under the control of the canons of St. Donatian, might there have been a deal that they would let Lambert off the hook for services rendered or to be rendered, but that Daniel and Yvain would have objected to this?[36] If so—and this is no more than reasonable speculation—a political power-element would have again played a role in what was in principle a judgment given by God. But even if this is so, there is one important indication that the struggle for power was not all-pervasive and that considerations of principle did play a distinct role of their own. The Church itself abolished the participation of the clergy in the administration of the ordeals, and, if it had only been interested in maintaining clerical power in the judicial field, this autodestructive measure would have made no sense. Clearly other theological and intellectual considerations were more powerful and tilted the balance

35. On the popularity of this sort of *palavers* in eleventh- and twelfth-century Europe, see R. C. Van Caenegem, *Royal Writs in England from the Conquest to Glanvill* (London, 1959), pp. 41–42. Their role is also discussed in several contributions to *The Settlement of Disputes in Early Medieval Europe,* ed. Wendy Davies and Paul Fouracre (Cambridge, 1986).

36. I would like to thank the students at Harvard who took my seminar on "The Rule of Law in Twelfth-Century Flanders" in the spring term of 1991 and contributed some stimulating remarks when this problem was discussed.

in favour of the prohibition of 1215, even if it was bound to result in a loss of clerical power and control in a field where they had prevailed for many centuries. The idea of forcing God to perform judicial miracles had in fact become intellectually untenable, and therefore it had to be abandoned by the leadership of the Church, that is, Pope Innocent III and the Fourth Lateran Council.[37]

II

Let us now turn our attention to another aspect of our enquiry, the place of the twelfth century in the long-term evolution toward a state monopoly of legitimate force. The earlier counts of Flanders used force of the most violent sort against crime, personally beheading, hanging, and boiling culprits; their starting point was the dynamic notion of the *pax comitis*, a promise of peace and order, given and warranted by the count. It initially protected particular places and occasions, such as markets and trade fairs, before developing into a general principle.[38]

The counts were, however, far from alone in fighting unlawful behaviour and they certainly did not enjoy a monopoly of the use of legitimate force. Self defence and the right of corporal punishment by husbands and fathers remained recognized institutions for centuries to come. The same applies to the right of destruction, known as *arsin et abattis de maison,* in the hands of the towns and their militias. The family feud, the legitimate and often murderous vengeance taken by wronged families and often leading to veritable warfare, was similarly eroded in the course of a long process. The right of feud came under attack from two sides. It was rejected by the urban mystique of peace, which abhorred violence between the burgesses and sought to impose conciliation brought about and supervised by a special body of communal peacemakers. The count and his aldermen had their own way of limiting feuds, by authoritatively imposing a temporary *treuga* or a permanent *pax,* and by monopolizing revenge and punishment in the hands of the state and its judicial machinery (even though the execution of

37. This is the central theme of Bartlett, *Trial by Fire and Water.*

38. Van Caenegem, *Strafrecht,* pp. 244–46; Henri Platelle, "La violence et ses remèdes en Flandre au XIe siècle," *Sacris Erudiri. Jaarboek voor Godsdienstwetenschappen,* 20 (1971), 101–73; Platelle, "Crime et châtiment à Marchiennes: Etude sur la conception et le fonctionnement de la justice d'après les Miracles de sainte Rictrude (XIIe siècle)," *Sacris Erudiri* 24 (1980), 153–202.

the death penalty imposed by the courts might still be left to a volunteering kinsman of the victim).[39]

III

In this context I would like to venture some speculative observations.

For centuries there have existed two views of the law, one cynical and one idealistic. The former was already voiced more than two thousand years ago by the Greek sophists, who pointed out that the laws were made by the powerful and used as tools to consolidate their position (they may have been inspired by Solon's observation that the laws were like "spiders' webs, which stand firm when any light and yielding object falls upon them, while a larger thing breaks through them and makes off").[40] The latter view sees the law as an authority that curbs, and thrones above all people, including the powerful and even the ruler himself; here again we might recall a Greek example, in the *agraphoi nomoi* invoked by Sophocles's Antigone. It is clear that this sort of law, encompassing everyone in its protection and domination, appears preferable in our democratic age and its *Rechtsstaat*.[41] The nagging question remains, however, why, if the rich and powerful control the law, they should ever produce enactments to protect the weak and curb themselves and their associates. Can they be expected to pass laws against their own interests? I shall, of course, not really enter into this vast debate here, but limit myself to a few remarks on the twelfth-century Flemish experience. People had a lively awareness of the law and its importance. I have already referred to Lambert of Saint-Omer and the numerous and detailed borough charters that were granted by the counts. I could also mention, if further proof be needed, the numerous utterances in Galbert of Bruges about people who acted either *jure* and *honeste,* or *contra jus, injuriose, perverse, male,* and *injuste*—the latter sort of person being called *exlex, sine fide, dolosus,* and *perjurus*. The general enforcement of the rule of law was the re-

39. Van Caenegem, *Strafrecht,* pp. 137–229. On the execution by a kinsman of the victim, see Egied I. Strubbe, "Het terechtstellen van den misdadiger door de familie van het slachtoffer in het vlaamsche recht der XIIIe eeuw," *Handelingen Genootschap "Soc. d'Emulation" te Brugge* 71 (1928), 88–91; repr. in Strubbe, *De luister van ons oude recht. Verzamelde rechtshistorische studies* (Brussels, 1973), pp. 534–36.

40. Reported in Diogenes Laertius's *Lives of Eminent Philosophers,* 1: 58, tr. R. D. Hicks (London, 1950) 1: 59.

41. See R. C. Van Caenegem, *Legal History: A European Perspective* (London, 1991), pp. 185–200.

sponsibility of the count, who stood above the conflict between the social groups in his land and, as a true father, did not hesitate to protect the poor and curb and punish the wealthy. In so doing he followed the medieval idea of the Christian monarch. Of this mission Charles the Good was particularly aware. Galbert calls him "a good prince . . . , the supporter of the poor, the protector of the churches . . . , the defender of the fatherland."[42]

Did this somewhat dithyrambic profession of faith in an exalted monarchy mean that the ruler stood above the law? To the Flemish awareness of the period this was certainly not the case, as there existed a manifest expectation that the prince, guarantor of the law, would himself live according to its dictates. This appears, *inter alia,* from the forementioned article 1 of the charters of Saint-Omer of 1127 and 1128. It is also made abundantly clear by the speech of Yvain of Aalst at Ghent in February 1128 which, as we have seen, proposed that a court of law should meet at Ypres and be invested with the highest judicial authority. Yvain, directly addressing the count, put it as follows (as reported by Galbert): "If in the opinion [of that court] you can in the future obtain the countship without violating the honour of the land, I want you to obtain it; if, however, you are one of these lawless and faithless people, deceivers and perjurers, get out of the county, so that we can commend it to some suitable and lawful man."[43] This was, in a nutshell, the twelfth-century formula of the *Rechtsstaat*: all classes under the law, as enforced by the prince, and the prince himself bound by the law, as enforced by a supreme court.

* * *

It is time to formulate some final considerations. It might be a good idea to devote some attention, by way of a conclusion or a postscript, to two seeming contradictions in the position of the count of Flanders. The first concerns his dual position as the vassal of two neighbouring kingdoms and the ruler of his own fully-fledged state, a *regnum,* as Galbert calls it. To the modern mind, a vassal holds a fief from his direct feudal overlord and ultimately from his suzerain. How can this be combined with a position

42. Galbert, c. 1, p. 4; Introduction, p. 3. The reference to the urban rich occurs in c. 3, p. 7, where Galbert talks of "those men of Ghent who had allowed poor people whom they could have fed to die of hunger on their doorsteps."

43. Galbert, c. 95, pp. 138–39. My translation differs from that of Ross (p. 268) on a few points. Thus she renders *discedite a comitatu et eum nobis relinquite* as "give up the countship! relinquish it to us" and *idoneo et legitimo alicui viro* as "to someone suitable and with rightful claims to it."

of head of state? Can a vassal at the same time be subjected to somebody else's rule and himself be a ruler? Can his domain be at the same time a fief, held by him as a tenant, and a *regnum*, an autonomous principality?[44] The elements of this seeming contradiction between feudal subjection and political independence were clearly perceived by contemporaries. Galbert, who in the very first lines of his diary calls Count Charles *naturalis noster dominus et princeps*, knows very well that Flanders is a French fief and he accepts the imposition of the new count by the French suzerain during the vacancy following Count Charles's death—Flanders being at that moment, in the correct description by a modern medievalist, a "fief mouvant de la couronne, vacant et sans héritier certain."[45] And even the Flemings who at a later stage maintained that the king of France had no such right, conceded that he was entitled to the *armatura*, thereby recognizing his position as their feudal overlord and Flanders's status as a French fief[46]: Flemish feudal dependence on France was an old and well-established fact of life. Already Count Baldwin I "Iron Arm" is referred to as *vassallus vester* by Pope Nicholas I to Charles the Bald in 862,[47] whereas Count Baldwin II successively became the vassal of Kings Eudo and Charles the Simple,[48] and generally speaking, one can maintain with Ganshof that the counts of Flanders have always "fulfilled vis à vis the Capetian dynasty their duties as vassals, notably as far as *auxilium* and *consilium* were concerned."[49] Thus they regularly took part in the royal *hostis* from the twelfth to the fifteenth century but, although legally speaking "ils servaient leur seigneur comme vassal," in political terms "les comtes de Flandre agissaient en réalité comme alliés."[50] Count Charles himself took part in several French royal expeditions, and one of his predecessors, Robert II, died in 1111 from a wound received in the incursion led by King Louis VI against Theobald of Blois. His immediate successor, Baldwin VII, met a similar fate, and died in 1119 of a wound incurred in 1118 in French royal service in the battle of Bures-en-Brai in Normandy against the English King Henry I.[51] Inside the county

44. F. L. Ganshof, "Les origines du concept de souveraineté nationale en Flandre," *Revue d'Histoire du Droit* 18 (1950), 136, insists that it is "parfaitement légitime de considérer la Flandre comme un état et d'en user comme cadre pour l'étude d'un problème d'histoire de la souveraineté."

45. Ganshof, "Roi de France," p. 212.

46. Ganshof, "Roi de France," p. 219. I will later return to this point.

47. Ganshof, *Qu'est-ce que la féodalité?* p. 44.

48. Ganshof, *La Flandre,* p. 345.

49. Ganshof, *La Flandre,* pp. 359 and 360.

50. Ganshof, *La Flandre,* pp. 360, 361.

51. F. L. Ganshof, *Vlaanderen onder de eerste graven* (Antwerp, 1944), pp. 45–46; Ganshof, "Roi de France," p. 205 and note 3; Ganshof, "Concept de souveraineté," 136.

of Flanders feudalism was by that time an old and well-established institution.[52]

Did this position of the counts of Flanders, to the modern mind contradictory, also seem contradictory to contemporaries? Feudalism was based on a chain of command, stretching from the king at the top of the pyramid to the last sub-vassal at the bottom. As the position of a tenant in chief differed from that of the lowest vavassor, so did the size and importance of their tenures. The French tenants in chief, the *pairs de France,* might hold great provinces which developed into regional states; some of their tenants were lords of seigniories containing several villages and hundreds of subjected peasants; at the bottom there were feudatories who held manors composed of a fraction of a village or even, through repeated subinfeudation, no more than a few acres. Yet although the difference between a count of Flanders and some obscure minor feudatory was obvious to everyone, they nevertheless both held their land in fief from their respective feudal lords. It is not because the count held his land from the king that he was any less the legitimate ruler of the county, and it was not because a great landowner in Flanders held his seigniory from the count that he was any less the lord of his peasants. And as the count respected the rights of these landowners in their seigniories, so the king respected the rights of the dukes and counts in their principalities, as long, that is, as the rules of the game were followed, that is, homage done, relief paid, and feudal inheritance laws observed. We should not forget that feudalism started as a system of personal obligations: as long as the count of Flanders was loyal to his suzerain, he could manage his fief as he liked. So it had been before the crisis of 1127–28 and so it was again under the counts of the House of Alsace. And so it has been for centuries in the old German Empire.[53] It was only when the French monarchy was no longer satisfied with the status quo and wanted to intervene in the internal affairs of the county—particularly under Philip IV the Fair—that the latent contradiction between the "fief" and the "state," the "prince" and the "vassal," became too visible, and in the end untenable. In the short run the outright annexation of Flanders, which took place in 1300, seemed to solve the problem in a way comparable to the conquest of Normandy in 1204, but this shortlived occupation did

52. See the comments in Ganshof, *Qu'est-ce que la féodalité?* p. 48.

53. In Germany also we can distinguish the three levels: the manors are encompassed by the territorial principality and that in turn by the empire. As Peter Blickle, *Deutsche Untertanen: Ein Widerspruch* (Munich, 1981), p. 20 puts it: "In modellhafter Konstruktion ist Staatlichkeit im Reich hierarchisch gestaffelt: die Guts- und Grundherrschaft wird überdacht von der Landesherrschaft, die Landesherrschaft vom Reich" (the author calls it a *Dreierkonstellation*).

not really solve anything and was followed by years of dispute. The definitive solution of the old contradiction had to wait till the Treaty of Madrid of 1526 confirmed in Cambrai in 1529, when the ancient feudal tie between Flanders and France was dissolved de jure.[54]

The second seeming contradiction concerns the count's dual position as ruler and lord. In the opening lines of his narrative Galbert calls him both: *dominus* and *princeps*, "lord" and "prince." Here again the modern mind would prefer to make a clear distinction. Both the leader of a band of warriors, a *Gefolgschaft*, and the lord of a manor certainly are *domini* who command bodies of men (whether bound to the land or not), but they are in no way comparable to a *princeps*, the head of a *regnum*. The former belong—in Roman-law terms—to the sphere of private, the latter to that of public law. The state is not comparable to any other organization, and its chain of command is of a different nature. However, to medieval man (particularly in pre-Bolognese days) that was far from obvious. To him the lordship of a kingdom and that of a local seigniory showed striking similarities. Both the king and the lord of the manor wielded public authority that went far beyond the private rights of an owner vis à vis his tenants: both legislated, policed their land and its inhabitants, organized justice, imposed taxes, and issued charters. If the king had his *curia regis*, the lords had their own feudal and manorial courts. In that perspective the notion could easily arise that the king was the top-lord, having the whole kingdom as his domain, while the barons governed their own estates, and so down to the possessors of obscure manors with a few dozen peasant families: they all exercised lordship, they were all *domini*, rulers of men, and wielding authority over certain areas of land.[55] The underlying idea was that of the necessary *liens de dépendance*: everybody depended personally on some authoritative figure in the local as well as in the national and even supranational sphere, and these personal relationships, rather than the submission

54. Henri Pirenne, *Histoire de Belgique des origines à nos jours* (Brussels, 1949), 2: 66–70; *Algemene Geschiedenis der Nederlanden* (Haarlem, 1980) 5: 462–63. A recent comprehensive analysis of the Franco-Flemish relationship in general and the role of the Flemish appeals to the Parlement of Paris in particular was undertaken in the unpublished dissertation by S. Dauchy, "De Vlaamse appels bij het Parlement van Parijs: Een rechtshistorisch onderzoek naar de wording van staat en souvereiniteit in de Bourgondische en Habsburgse periode" (Ghent, 1991).

55. As F.M. Stenton, *The First Century of English Feudalism, 1066–1166* (Oxford, 1932), p. 66, explained in graphic language, royal authority was supreme, but the authority of a lord over his vassals, and a landowner over the peasants on his manors was no less real and legitimate. In this view the Norman kingdom of England consisted of numerous "honours," held by greater and lesser barons, whereas the greatest and most eminent honour, that of the crown, was the kingdom itself, which comprehended and surpassed the others.

to the state and its abstract laws, were paramount. There were nevertheless some obvious differences between a king and a manorial lord. Most kings were anointed and wore crowns. More importantly, rulers had responsibilities that went much further than those of mere local landowners. The heads of states were responsible for the protection of the Church, they were "like a father and protector of the churches of God," to use Galbert's phrase, and they felt responsible for the peace of the land in general and the protection of the weak and the poor in particular. Thus Charles the Good shielded the peasants in the Bruges area against their cruel oppressors and curbed the greed of the rich burgesses who tried to profit from a famine. Nor did he hesitate in 1122 to take severe measures against Baldwin III of Aalst, the *advocatus* of the Ghent St. Peter's Abbey in Imperial Flanders, who had abused his position to oppress the abbey's tenants.[56]

There was yet another source of confusion: heads of states were at the same time landlords, usually the largest in the country. Kings and counts had their own demesne lands, from whose income they lived like all landowners. The count of Flanders was the *princeps* of his *regnum,* but he was also an important landowner; he disposed of a small army of officials who administered his lands and received and registered in the comital *spicaria* the rents and farms, in kind and in money, to which he was entitled.[57] It is of some interest to pursue this point and to have a closer look at William Clito's position in this respect. The young count, who had been introduced by the suzerain and accepted by the county, was clearly the new head of state. But he was also a manorial lord, and it is striking that the first nasty incident between him and his new subjects was related to his position as a landowner. In Lille in August 1127, as we have seen, he arrested and detained without judgment one of his runaway serfs. Galbert attaches great political importance to this event, and clearly sees it as the first rumbling of the revolt that led eventually to Clito's downfall. And yet in Lille Count William reacted as any ordinary landlord. He claimed what was his, in the sphere of private law; how could this be related to his position as a ruler in the public sphere? Legally speaking, not at all, but politically speaking it was highly relevant, for in the urban world the issue of serfdom and liberty was very sensitive. Most towns must have contained an important

56. Warlop, *Flemish Nobility,* 1: 199.

57. See Raymond Monier, *Les institutions financières du comté de Flandre du XIe siècle à 1384* (Paris: 1948); Adriaan Verhulst and Maurits Gysseling, *Le Compte Général de 1187, connu sous le nom de "Gros Brief" et les institutions financières du comté de Flandre au XIIe siècle* (Brussels, 1962); Bryce Lyon and Adriaan Verhulst, *Medieval Finance: A Comparison of Financial Institutions in Northwestern Europe* (Bruges, 1967).

percentage of freemen of recent date—one of the reasons, by the way, why the unfree Erembalds enjoyed a surprising measure of sympathy in Bruges, even after their treacherous deed: they were a symbol of what unfree people could achieve.[58] William's acceptable behaviour as an exploitative landlord was not necessarily acceptable as the attitude of the head of a state where the urban element was strongly in the ascendant! The Ghent revolt of February 1128 also was connected, as we have seen, with questions of freedom: its direct cause was the pretention of the castellan to reintroduce the abolished *tallia,* a feudal and agrarian tax.[59] Significantly, the occasion which had led to the conspiracy against Count Charles was also related to the issue of serfdom. Here again an act of exploitative lordship gained great political significance, and the measure taken by a landowner led to the murder of a prince. When Count Charles decided publicly to call back the mighty Erembalds as his serfs, with all the personal and financial consequences involved, he acted as a landlord, and claimed what was his own, just like Clito in Lille in 1128. But as Charles of Denmark, the landowner, was also Count Charles, the action which he intended to bring before a court of law in Cassel was more than a measure of manorial administration. The serfs he claimed had risen to great political importance in the state, so that their social downfall must have meant the end of their political status as well. Thus the role of the landlord was intertwined with that of the leader of the state.[60] The crisis provoked by the count led to his own as well as his opponents' ruin. Who can tell what comparison the Flemish burgesses unconsciously made between the steps which both Charles and William Clito had taken against their "emancipated" or runaway villeins? Liberty was a politically sensitive issue, and any move by a count-landlord to recover his serfs, whether they seemed emancipated and occupied high positions or had fled his manors, was bound to be watched closely and suspiciously by the freedom-loving townspeople.

We have seen that acting legally was not always acting wisely, or in other words, what was good law was not necessarily good politics. So let us have a closer look at the relation between law and politics during

58. During the first week after the assassination the citizens of Bruges kept aloof; only after 9 March was it clear that the conspirators could not count any more on help from the town (which may have had sympathy for William of Ypres, who was involved in the treason), Warlop, *Flemish Nobility* 1: 201. And even after the siege of the conspirators had started, they still had contact with citizens of Bruges (Ganshof, "Roi de France," p. 214), whereas the citizens of Bruges did not hesitate to show their sympathy for Robert the Young, a member of the Erembald clan (Ganshof, "Roi de France," p. 223).

59. Van Caenegem, *Meurtre de Charles le Bon,* p. 36.

60. Van Caenegem, "Galbert of Bruges on Serfdom," pp. 94–100.

the crisis of 1127–1128. Since politics is about the struggle for power, that crisis was obviously and dramatically political. The step that provoked the good count's murder was seemingly legal and judicial—a lord claiming his serfs—but was in fact political, for Count Charles was fighting people who threatened his personal position as well as the social order. The Erembalds were *homines novi* who endangered the prestige of the old, true nobility. What followed the murder was the most typical political syndrome of medieval times, the struggle for a vacant throne. Since for the first time in the history of the dynasty, there was no son or designated relative to succeed the dead ruler, several members of the House of Flanders strove to succeed Charles. All were supported by various interests in the county. Thus Bruges initially felt much sympathy for the son of the countess of Holland, for commercial reasons; the king of France's support for Clito, who was already his vassal for other French territories, was a move in his struggle against King Henry I of England, who for that reason opposed Clito and supported Thierry of Alsace. The crisis led to the worst form of political contest a country can experience: civil war. Finally one of the two most powerful candidates was killed in battle and the uncertainty was over. With remarkable speed the county rallied round Thierry of Alsace, whom even King Louis quickly accepted as his new vassal, investing him with the Flemish fief.[61] Legitimacy was restored, the law again reigned supreme, and politics dropped out of sight.

Could the strict application of the law in Flanders in 1127 have prevented the political conflict? At first sight one is inclined to give a negative answer to this question, as the various candidates were all related to the Flemish dynasty. Both William Clito and Thierry of Alsace, for example, were great-grandsons of Count Baldwin V and had a good claim. There was, however, another element, which we should not overlook. Feudal law, as we have seen, allowed the suzerain to intervene in the succession to a vacant fief, in the absence of a son ready to take it over, and to choose, with the consent of his court, the successor among the other relations of the deceased vassal. This, as we know, is what King Louis did, so that William Clito undoubtedly had the law on his side. Afterwards, however, politics took over and a conflict arose between what was legitimate and what was realistic. It soon appeared that Clito was bound to run into serious trouble, because his rule, based on the hope of an invasion of England and the lib-

61. Galbert, c. 122, p. 176.

eration of his imprisoned father, Robert Curthose, was bound to have a negative effect on Flemish trade and industry.

Can we see the revolt against Clito purely in terms of expediency versus legitimacy? At first sight this seems indeed to be the case, as the new count had received the vacant fief in accordance with the law. Nevertheless, two considerations are appropriate here. First, that King Louis himself had introduced his protégé out of blatant political calculation: Clito was his choice, not because he was the best ruler for Flanders, but because he was supposed to pull the county into a war against England. So it was the king himself who dragged politics into the problem of the succession, and he had only himself to blame if in course of time the Flemings also gave precedence to politics. Second, there was the contention of the Flemings, at a later stage in the crisis (April 1128), that the feudal ties with France did not entitle the king to impose a new count in his Flemish fief.[62]

A comparable though not similar situation had arisen in 1071. Robert the Frisian had not accepted that his older brother, Baldwin VI (†1170), should be succeeded by the latter's young son, Arnold III. Supported by a large part of the country, he rose against his nephew and the latter's forceful mother, Richildis, who had made herself unpopular. In the course of that revolt King Philip I of France intervened *manu militari* in order to save Count Arnold, but to no avail.

At Cassel, on 22 February 1071, Robert was victorious and succeeded Arnold, who was killed on the battlefield.[63] This first French intervention in Flanders since that of King Lothaire in 965 (upon the death of Count Arnold the Great) had ended in total failure. The merits of the Flemish contention in 1128 are difficult to assess. Whereas it is clear that King Louis had the general principles of feudal law on his side in imposing his candidate, it is also true that no precedent for their application could be found in the history of the Flemish fief for more than a century and a half, which to all practical purposes meant "since time immemorial," a weighty consideration in a society dominated by custom and precedent.[64] And to the obvious question

62. Galbert, c. 106, p. 152: "Neque rex habet rationem aliquam ut potestative seu per coemptionem seu per pretium nobis superponat consulem aut aliquem preferat"; all he was entitled to was an *armatura,* that is, a relief of arms, a symbolic survival of an earlier custom by which the arms of the deceased vassal were returned to his lord. See Ganshof, "Armatura" and Ganshof, "Roi de France" 219. A high, arbitrary relief (a "price" in a "sale") would imply that the king could "sell" the county to the highest bidder, that is, freely dispose of it.

63. See the classic study of Charles Verlinden, *Robert Ier le Frison, comte de Flandre: étude d'histoire politique* (Antwerp, 1935).

64. In that light Ganshof's contention that the burgesses maintained "mendaciously" that the king was only entitled to an *armatura* may be somewhat extreme, "Concept de sou-

why the Flemings had accepted Clito the previous year, they not very convincingly replied, according to Galbert, that it was "because the king and the counts of Flanders were formerly joined together by the bond of kinship."[65] Whatever the legal merits of the case, the crisis unleashed in Bruges on 2 March 1127 was a dramatic example of a clash between political will and feudal principle. Unsuspected social tensions surfaced and sectional interests showed their real power. The Erembald clan and its followers as well as the old aristocracy and the towns all pursued their own aims; even within the urban camp there was discord, as towns supported various candidates for purely local reasons. But as soon as the new ruler was accepted and his legitimacy recognized, the dissensions disappeared or at least went underground, and the divergent social forces were again under control: harmony was reimposed by the restored authority of the prince. Thus the crisis of 1127–28 demonstrated once again the essential role of legitimate monarchy in medieval society.

---

veraineté," p. 154. Pirenne in his edition of Galbert calls it (p. 152, note 2) an "affirmation gratuite des Brugeois pour les besoins de la cause." It is useful to distinguish carefully two elements in this discussion: the choice of a new count (by the king or by the people), and the relief due by the new count to the French suzerain (a traditional and symbolic *armatura* or a relief in the form of a substantial and even arbitrary sum of money).

65. Galbert, c. 106, p. 153; cf. Ganshof, "Roi de France," p. 225. The "bond of kinship" refers presumably to the fact that Louis VI's mother Bertha of Holland (first, repudiated wife of King Philip I of France) was a stepdaughter of Robert the Frisian (Verlinden, *Robert le Frison*, p. 30). There may also possibly be an allusion here to the fact that Count Charles and King Louis VI were cousins by marriage: the king had married Adelaide, niece of the Countess Clemence, the wife of Charles's uncle, Robert II (Ross, *Galbert of Bruges*, p. 187, n. 4).

Charles Duggan

8. Papal Judges Delegate and the Making of the "New Law" in the Twelfth Century

The Foundation of the "New Law"

In the exercise of power in twelfth-century Europe, no claims to primacy of authority and jurisdiction equalled those of the papacy in their universality and essentially spiritual nature. The fundamental basis of papal claims to universal jurisdiction lay centuries earlier in the doctrine of Petrine supremacy, the superiority of Peter among the apostles. From the fourth and fifth centuries, following the imperial acceptance of Christianity, this theological concept was interwoven with the jurisprudence and judicial procedures of Roman Civil Law, and from this union flowed the Romano-canonical procedures of the papal curia, and of the canonists and ecclesiastical judges of later centuries. Already in the pontificate of Gelasius I (†496), the judicial primacy of the pope was asserted in the right of all Christians to appeal to him—the origin of the doctrine of the pope as Universal Ordinary—the source of authority to whom every Christian could refer as to his own diocesan bishop.[1] Across the centuries, later popes consolidated and built on these foundations, most decisively in the pontificates

1. The papal assertion of an ultimate authority in matters of jurisdiction, and especially in the receipt and resolution of appeals, was expressed in a letter of Gelasius I (492–96) to the bishops of Dacia, from which a brief excerpt was transmitted to Gratian's *Decretum* (see n. 2), Causa 11, qu. 3, c. 17: "Cuncta per mundum novit ecclesia, quod sacrosancta Romana ecclesia fas de omnibus habet iudicandi, neque cuiquam de eius liceat iudicare iudicio. Siquidem ad illam de qualibet mundi parte appellandum est; ab illa autem nemo est appellare permissus"—excerpt from *Valde mirati,* Philipp Jaffé, *Regesta pontificum romanorum ad annum 1198,* ed. F. Kaltenbrunner (anno 64–590), P. W. Ewald (anno 590–882), and S. Loewenfeld (anno 882–1198), 2 vols. (Leipzig, 1885–88), 1:664, *anno* 493. There are two versions of the letter in Mansi 8:49–71: "Gelasius episcopus urbis Romae ad Dardanos"; cf. cols 54: "Non reticemus," and 66: "Non plane tacemur." Cf. also Frederic W. Maitland, *Roman Canon Law in the Church of England* (London, 1898), p. 104 and nn. 1, 2 and Jane E. Sayers, *Papal Judges Delegate in the Province of Canterbury 1198–1254* (Oxford, 1971), pp. 5–6. Thanks are due to my wife, Dr. Anne Duggan, for exceptional help in preparing this paper.

of Gregory VII (†1085), Alexander III (†1181), and Innocent III (†1216); the evolution of canon law and its codification ran parallel with the development of these doctrines. In this long and complex process, two factors are essential points of reference here: the centralizing and decisive impact of the "Gregorian Reform" from the late eleventh century onward, and the publication of Gratian's *Decretum* (*ex* 1139), which marked the dividing point between *ius antiquum* and *ius novum,* the old law and the new.[2]

On the one hand, the *Decretum* provided an authoritative summary of the old law—the culmination of centuries of development—combining papal, scriptural, patristic and conciliar rulings, texts from Roman law, the laws of secular kingdoms, and many other sources. On the other hand, it became the basis for the development of new law, defined in recent conciliar legislation and, still more significantly, in papal decretal letters addressed to many thousands of recipients throughout Latin Christendom. More than any other book in the history of canon law, it helped to create a new ethos of learned law and to establish new standards of professional conduct in ecclesiastical courts. Although never officially promulgated, it swiftly became the standard work of reference in the courts and in the schools, and provided the theoretical framework and the technical instructions necessary for the conduct of judicial cases throughout the Latin Church. One distinction in part 1, for example, defines the authority of decretal letters and the necessary obedience to papal rulings: decretals have authority even if not included in the canonical corpus; all sanctions of the apostolic see must be observed; whatever the Roman Church decrees must be observed by all; and so forth.[3] And one *quaestio* in part 2 has the character of a judicial handbook *in statu nascendi,* assembling statements of principle, procedure and practical guidance on the proper stages of litigation, supported by both canonical and civilian authorities. The final recension of this section includes decretals attributed to popes from the first century onwards (some in fact retraceable to the ninth-century Pseudo-Isidore), texts from Roman Law, including the Theodosian Code and the Digest,[4] Gratian's own *dicta,*

2. For the most accessible edition, see *Corpus Iuris canonici,* ed. Emil Friedberg, 2 vols. (Leipzig, 1879–81), 1.

3. *Decretum,* Dist. 19, cc. 1, 2, 4 et al.

4. *Decretum,* Causa 2, q. 6. Cf. Stephan Kuttner, *New Studies on the Roman Law in Gratian's Decretum* Canon Law Studies (Washington, DC, 1953, reprint from *Seminar* 11 [1953], 12–50); cf. Gabriel le Bras, Charles Lefebvre and Jacqueline Rambaud, *L'âge classique, 1140–1378: sources et théorie du droit* (Paris, 1965), pp. 119–28: Les additions, 3, Les textes du droit romain; Charles Munier, "Droit canonique et droit romain d'après Gratien et les-décrétistes," in Munier, *Vie conciliaire et collections canoniques en Occident, IVe–XIIe siècle* (London, Variorum Reprints 1987), no. 20.

and passages of precise and practical instruction. Both the basic principle of the right of appeal and aspects of the judicial process are emphasized in Gratian's rubrics—all have the right of appeal to the apostolic see, as if to a mother; the hearing of an appeal belongs to the one to whom it was made; and appeals are permissible before pronouncement of sentence[5]—to which Gratian's own *dictum* gave still further precision: an appellant must make his appeal, and set out to prosecute it within five days. Moreover, following chapter 31 on letters dimissory (*apostoli*: the formal notification issued by the judge from whom an appeal is made to the one who takes cognizance of it), Gratian inserted a series of standard letters relating to various kinds of appeal.

> The form of *apostoli* is this: "I En., bishop of the holy church of Bologna, by these apostoli, send you Roland, priest and chaplain of San Apollinare, to the apostolic see, to which you appealed from my judgment."
>
> The form of appeal is this: "I, Adelinus, unworthy minister of the church of S. Regina, feeling myself oppressed by the lord Walter, archbishop of the holy church of Ravenna, appeal to the Roman see, and request *apostoli*."
>
> The form of appeal after sentence will be: "I, A(delinus), unworthy minister of the church of S. Regina, appeal to the Roman see against the sentence of lord Walter, archbishop of the holy church of Ravenna, unjustly laid on me on Wednesday, 30 April, in the year of the Lord 1105,[6] and request *apostoli*."
>
> If one or two wish to appeal on behalf of several, they shall appeal in this form: "We, G. and P., acting for the canons of the holy church of B., feeling ourselves oppressed (or against the sentence *etc*), appeal to the Roman see, and request *apostoli*."[7]

Compiled in Bologna, the dominant law school in Europe at that time, the *Decretum* established itself immediately as the basis of canonical jurisprudence throughout the Western Church. During the following twenty years or so (1140–60), its ideas were disseminated to receptive ecclesiastical administrators throughout Europe. The *Decretum* was used by John of Salisbury, for instance, in the composition of legal letters for archbishop Theobald of Canterbury in the 1150s.[8] Without the general reception of this law book, recognized as authoritative by teachers and practitioners of

5. *Decretum,* Causa 2, q. 6, cc. 6, 8, 12 and 21. Rufinus (1157–59) prefaced his commentary on this section with a series of questions. "What is an appeal, who can appeal, by whom and to whom should an appeal be made, when and how often, how and within what time?" *Rufinus von Bologna: Summa decretorum,* ed. Heinrich Singer (Paderborn, 1902; repr. Aalen, 1963), pp. 251–53.

6. This date is inaccurate: 30 April 1105 was a Sunday.

7. *Decretum, post* Causa 2, q. 6, c. 31 (ed. Friedberg, p. 478).

8. *The Letters of John of Salisbury,* I: *The Early Letters,* ed. and trans. W. J. Millor and Harold E. Butler (London, 1955; reissued, Oxford, 1986), p. xx note 1.

the law, and of the general principles of jurisprudence which it contained, the remarkable growth of the appellate jurisdiction of the papacy, and the complementary system of judges delegate which supported it, would have been almost inconceivable in the form in which they developed through the second half of the twelfth century.

At the heart of the new law stood the papal decretal. Decretal letters were commissions to judges delegate, or replies to questions submitted to the pope for guidance on points of law or procedure, the resolution of specific disputes or problems, and a host of consultations of all kinds.[9] Gratian had defined the authority of decretal letters as equal to that of conciliar canons,[10] to which the canonist Rufinus (1157–59) simply added "because of the primacy of the Roman Church."[11] Later, in the early thirteenth century, the Bolognese canonist Tancred expressed the matter succinctly: "Rome is the fatherland of all—*patria omnium*—and the pope is judge ordinary for every individual."[12] Decretal letters were therefore the expression of the pope's superior jurisdiction in Christian society and also the means of its execution—with the judges delegate as executors—but they were essentially reactive, issued in response to judicial appeals or requests for clarification of points of law.

The right of appeal to the pope was universal and unrestricted. At any stage in a dispute, with or without an initial process in a local court,[13] an aggrieved party could appeal to the pope, who issued in response a commission to two or more local judges to hear and terminate the case, or bring the parties to an amicable settlement in their presence. Through this procedure, ever widening networks of connexion were established between the periphery and the center, between the curia and the provinces. It is sometimes supposed that the systematic development of the pope's appel-

9. In Stephen of Tournai's familiar definition (c. 1160–1170), "a decretal is a papal rescript to any bishop or ecclesiastical judge, who has consulted the Roman Church on any doubtful matter," *Die Summa des Stephanus Tornacensis über das Decretum Gratiani,* ed. J. F. von Schulte (Giessen, 1891), p. 2: "Decretalis epistola est, quam dominus apostolicus aliquo episcopo vel alio iudice ecclesiastico super aliqua causa dubitante et ecclesiam Romanam consulente rescribit et ei transmittit." Cf. Charles Duggan, *Twelfth-Century Decretal Collections and Their Importance in English History* (London, 1963), p. 32 and note 4.

10. "Decretales epistolae canonibus conciliorum pari iure exequantur," *Decretum,* Dist. 20.

11. *Rufinus,* p. 42, ". . . hic de momento decretalium epistolarum tractat, ostendens eas eiusdem auctoritatis fore, cuius et canones, propter primatum Romane ecclesie." These matters are more fully discussed in Duggan, *Twelfth-Century Decretal Collections,* pp. 34–39.

12. Maitland, *Roman Canon Law,* p. 104 n. 2, citing Cambridge, Gonville and Caius College, MS 85, fol. 7: "ille est iudex ordinarius rei apud quem ille reus domicilium habet. . . . Item Roma est patria omnium [*Digest,* 50.1.33] et dominus papa iudex est ordinarius singulorum, ut ix. qu. iii. cuncta per orbem [*Decretum,* C.9, qu. 3, c. 17]."

13. Sayers, *Papal Judges Delegate,* pp. 5–8.

late jurisdiction was inimical to the traditional rights and jurisdiction of diocesan bishops, but its effectiveness was in fact dependent on the active collaboration of local ecclesiastics such as bishops, archdeacons, deans, abbots, and priors. Some of the English bishops acquired a high reputation as papal judges delegate. Bartholomew of Exeter and Roger of Worcester, for instance, "the twin lights of the English Church" in Alexander III's familiar evaluation, were the most frequently appointed judges delegate of their generation.[14] No fully comprehensive survey of papal commissions to judges delegate is possible for the twelfth century, since the papal registers for the period are mostly lost. But their receipt and transcription are abundantly recorded in local archives, from which many volumes of *Papsturkunden* have been printed, notably for the various regions of France, for England, Spain, Portugal, Germany, and the military orders; a vast number of papal letters of all kinds to Italian recipients are registered in several volumes of the *Italia Pontificia*. The archival records of cathedral chapters and religious houses throughout Europe preserve rich evidence of commissions to judges delegate, their procedures, and judicial settlements. And from these it is frequently possible to trace the origin, process, and outcome of the various stages of litigation and series of disputes through prolonged periods of time. Such records reveal with unusual clarity and completeness the process by which the papal judges were appointed and discharged their duties.

The Standardization of the Process

The papal commissions of delegation empowered the judges to summon the parties, examine witnesses, evaluate the evidence, and reach a judgment by the pope's authority, and mandate the execution of sentence by the local ordinary. On the conclusion of the case, the judges issued letters to the parties and reported all details to the pope. The appeal therefore set in motion an interactive chain of juridical authority, from litigant to pope,

14. In evident recognition of the rapid expansion of delegated jurisdiction in the twelfth century and of the bishops' outstanding share in the process, almost every published biography of English bishops in the period now includes a chapter on the bishop in question, as judge delegate, as well as scattered references to his judicial activities. Cf. Dom Adrian Morey, *Bartholomew of Exeter. Bishop and Canonist: A study in the Twelfth Century* (Cambridge, 1937), esp. ch. 4, "The Bishop as Judge Delegate"; Morey and C. N. L. Brooke, *Gilbert Foliot and His Letters* (Cambridge, 1965), pp. 230–44; Mary G. Cheney, *Roger, Bishop of Worcester, 1164–79* (Oxford, 1980), esp. chs. 4, "The Judge-Delegate," and 5, "The Bishop and the Law"; and Duggan, *Decretal Collections*, passim.

from the pope to the judges, from the judges to the local bishop, and from the judges back to the pope. If difficult or unusual questions were raised in the course of litigation, the judges could seek clarification from the pope. Each stage was conducted in accordance with universally applied norms derived from Gratian and professional commentaries and formularies specifically compiled for this purpose, pervasively influenced by the processes of Roman civil law.[15] Even before the composition of such strictly canonical formularies, handbooks on civilian procedure, like the *pseudo-Ulpianus de edendo,* were widely used by ecclesiastical lawyers in the formulation and presentation of cases in church courts.[16]

The universal reception of the *Decretum* and the adoption of Romano-canonical procedure by the papal chancery, the canonists, and the judges delegate decisively shaped the exercise of judicial authority in the Church. Gratian established general principles of ecclesiastical law which could be applied universally, *mutatis mutandis,* throughout Christendom. The Romano-canonical process created new standards for the conduct of cases, the submission of evidence, and the interrogation of witnesses.[17] Although local customs sometimes remained intact, the new law helped to break down regional barriers and establish a common law, the *ius commune* of the whole Church. Bishops, archdeacons, and local officials could not ignore these developments, for their own local authority and jurisdiction were

15. Sayers, *Papal Judges Delegate,* ch. 12, "The Procedure of the Courts of Judges Delegate"; Wacław Uruszczak, "Les juges délégués du pape et la procédure romano-canonique à Reims dans la seconde moitié du xiie siècle," *Tijdschrift voor Rechtsgeschiedenis,* 53 (1985), 27–41; Ludwig Falkenstein, "Appellationen an den Papst und Delegationsgerichtsbarkeit am Beispiel Alexanders III. und Heinrichs von Frankreich," *Zeitschrift für Kirchengeschichte,* 97 (1986), 36–65; cf. the summary of the formulary "A. B. C. Judices" in the Appendix, below. For a short overall survey, cf. G. G. Pavloff, *Papal Judges Delegate at the Time of the Corpus Iuris Canonici,* Canon Law Studies (Washington DC, 1963). On papal rescripts and the canonists, see now the exhaustive treatment of judges delegate in Harry Dondorp, "Review of Papal Rescripts in the Canonists' Teaching," *ZRG KanAbt,* 76 (1990), 172–253; 77 (1991), 32–109; on judges delegate specifically see 51–60.

16. Francis de Zulueta and Peter Stein, *The Teaching of Roman Law in England Around 1200,* Selden Society, Supplementary Series 8 (London, 1990), p. xli; cf. Linda Fowler-Magerl, *Repertorium zur Frühzeit der gelehrten Rechte. Ordo iudiciorum vel ordo iudiciarius: Begriff und Literaturgattung,* Ius Commune: Veröffentlichungen des Max-Planck-Instituts für Europäische Rechtsgeschichte, Frankfurt am Main, Texte und Monographien, 19 (Frankfurt am Main, 1984), pp. 65ff.

17. Stephan Kuttner, "The Revival of Jurisprudence," in *Renaissance and Renewal in the Twelfth Century,* ed. Robert L. Benson and Giles Constable (Cambridge, MA, 1982), pp. 299–323; Richard H. Helmholz, "Canonists and Standards of Impartiality for Papal Judges Delegate," in Helmholz, *Canon Law and the Law of England* (London, 1987), pp. 21–39; Stanley Chodorow, "Dishonest Litigation in the Church Courts," in *Law, Church and Society: Essays in Honor of Stephan Kuttner,* ed. Kenneth Pennington and Robert Somerville (Philadelphia, 1977), pp. 187–206.

undermined and open to criticism and review if their subjects found them wanting in due process or in the law itself. But the judges delegate were not simply passive agents of papal authority. Their judgments helped to shape the law in their own regions; their questions to the *curia* elicited definitions on difficult or contentious points of law or procedure; and the collections of decretals compiled in the households of notable English judges delegate provided the sources from which the new decretal law of the entire Latin Church derived.

The decretal *Quamvis simus,* addressed by Alexander III to bishop Richard of Winchester in 1177, affords a perfect example both of papal responses to multiple consultations on points of principle and procedure, and their dismemberment and incorporation in professional collections. The letter deals with eight points, later distributed according to subject matter in the systematic collections. In the primitive Bridlington collection (*ex* 1181), the letter is still preserved as an entity under the general rubric *Quot iudicibus et in quibus delegatus possit delegare,* but it is subdivided into eight distinct topics, each with its individual rubric. The first six deal with judges delegate and the judicial process, as briefly summarized here:

(a) *Delegatus condelegato causam delegare potest etiam si hoc in litteris non apponatur, sed non appellatione remota:* a delegate can sub-delegate to one or more others, to hear and resolve the matter at issue, or to hear statements and take evidence, while reserving judgment to himself. Everything is subject to his will and satisfaction, though he cannot delegate a case *appellatione postposita,* even if it was commissioned to him *appellatione remota*—without leave of appeal. And if a case is commissioned to two judges, one of them can commit judgment to his colleague or to another, even if the commission does not state that one can proceed without the other.

(b) *Si quis crimen obicit testi, qui contra eum producitur:* if anyone imputes a crime against witnesses brought against him, of such a nature that he could prevent their bearing witness in a civil case, his objection shall be heard; and if it can be proved in civil process, the witnesses cannot be admitted to give testimony against him, but neither should they be punished because of it.

(c) *Inhibita appellatione, deferendum est appellationi facte ex incidenti questione, sine qua principalis causa non poterit terminari:* the question is: should a case be left undecided, when appeal has been made on an incidental question, even though the principal matter was commissioned without leave of appeal? The pope replies that, if the question arising is such that the principal issue cannot be decided without it, the hearing of the whole case should be intermitted in deference to the appeal, until the superior judge, to whom appeal was made, decides otherwise about the whole affair—*aliter de tota causa disponat.*

(d) *Si diverse littere impetrantur diversis iudicibus, priores preiudicant:* if a litigant secures letters of commission from the apostolic see, and his adversary has the same matter commissioned to other judges, the former should proceed to hearing and settlement, unless the later letters mention the earlier commission. Otherwise, the later letters have no force of law. But if the earlier commission is mentioned in the later, the case is thereby removed from the earlier judges, since the later were not obtained by fraud—*non sint tacita veritate impetrate*. Moreover, if a case is commissioned in the presence and with the assent of the parties, of whom one has the case later committed to another, concealing the earlier commission and not informing his adversary, the party guilty of such deceit and fraud should be condemned to pay the expenses thereby incurred by his opponent.

(e) *Nullus cogitur ad ferendum testimonium:* the Roman Church has not been accustomed (*minime consuevit*) to compel anyone to bear witness to the truth.

(f) *Delegatus potest sententiam executioni mandare, si ordinarius noluerit:* if the diocesan bishop neglects to mandate execution of the sentence imposed by the judge delegate, the latter, by virtue of his delegation by the Roman pontiff, has full power to order its execution.[18]

This letter is of exceptional interest, not only for the precise and technical nature of its juridical instructions and for the light it throws on the process of judicial consultation between bishops and the papal curia, but also for the identity of its recipient. The bishop of Winchester, who had no doubt submitted a list of questions arising from the conduct of delegated jurisdiction, was none other than Richard of Ilchester, who had been foremost among Henry II's secular administrators during and after the Becket dispute, and was engaged in the royal administration of Normandy when he received it.[19] Here is an example of a 'royalist bishop' actively participating in the advancement of canon law in England and beyond. *Quamvis simus* soon entered the canonical tradition: after its appearance in the Bridlington Collection, it appears dismembered in seven parts in the *Appendix* and *Bamberg* collections,[20] and in nine segments in Bernard of

18. Oxford, Bodleian MS 357, fol. 85v (Bridl. 23). For the component parts, cf. *JL* 14156 (parts a, b, d–f, h), 14152 (part c), 14154 (part g). Full details of all decretal collections cited in this essay, their manuscripts, printed analyses and relevant studies are provided in *Decretales ineditae saeculi xii* (cf. n. 30, below).

19. With his former colleagues in the royal administation, John of Oxford and Geoffrey Ridel, he was elected bishop in 1173, and consecrated in 1174: Charles Duggan, "Richard of Ilchester, Royal Servant and Bishop," *Transactions of the Royal Historical Society*, 5th Series, 16 (1965), 1–21, esp. pp. 16–20.

20. The parts are distributed in *Appendix* and *Bambergensis* as follows (in each case, two of the original chapters appear as one): *Appendix* (Mansi, 22: 248–453, 7.8, 8.6, 10.31, 7.9, 8.6, 7.10, 15.6, 39.2); *Bambergensis* (Walter Deeters, *Die Bambergensisgruppe der Dekretalensammlungen des 12. Jhdts.:* Inaugural Dissertation . . . der Philos. Fakultät der Rheinischen Friedrich Wilhelms-Universität [Bonn 1956]: 33.8, 39.5, 42.31, 33.9, 39.5, 33.10, 44.4, 22.1). Cf. Charles

Pavia's *Compilatio prima*,[21] from which four segments were received into the *Decretales* of 1234.[22] In this way the responses to questions raised by one local ecclesiastic came to form part of the general law promulgated by Gregory IX.

The Making of the "New Law": Cases

The canonical developments of the mid-twelfth century were such that very few bishops were unaffected by them. Whether actively or passively engaged in the process, ecclesiastical administrators of all kinds were drawn into the new legal structure as judges or litigants, and a knowledge of the law and expertise in its procedures became essential accomplishments. Not all bishops were trained lawyers, but most found it necessary to recruit *iuris periti* to their households. Archbishop Roger of York, for example, employed the eminent Roman lawyer Vacarius, who played a leading role in the advancement of Roman Law in England. Vacarius himself appears in decretal letters and in litigation.[23]

More than fifty decretals to Roger survive in the collections, their interests ranging from dynastic questions in the English state to the Canterbury-York dispute for primacy in the English Church; the status and rights of churches, clerics, and religious; marriage disputes involving English magnates; religious orders and their houses; and judicial and procedural questions.[24] The York decretals show very clearly the juridically complex and sophisticated nature of the procedures involved in the discharge of papal mandates. The commission *Cum iam pridem* to arch-

---

Duggan, "English Canonists and the *Appendix Concilii Lateranensis*, with an Analysis of the St. John's, Cambridge, MS 148," *Traditio* 18 (1962), 459–68; repr. in Duggan, *Canon Law in Medieval England: The Becket Dispute and Decretal Collections* (London, 1982), no. 8.

21. *1 Comp*. (= *Quinque compilationes antiquae nec non collectio canonum Lipsiensis*, ed. Emil Friedberg [Leipzig, 1882; repr. Graz, 1956], pp. 1–65), 1.21.7, 2.13.13, 2.20.34, 1.2.3, 2.13.13 + 2.14.1, 1.21.8, 3.33.10, 1.20.4.

22. *Corpus iuris canonici*, 2 (cited as *X*), 1.29.6, 1.3.3, 2.38.8, 1.28.3. For this tradition, see below, pp. 184–85. Sections of the letter were entered under three different numbers in Jaffé's *Regesta*, nos. 14156 + 14152 + 14154.

23. Cf. Peter Stein, "Vacarius and the Civil Law," in Stein, *The Character and Influence of the Roman Civil Law: Historical Essays* (London, Hambledon Press, 1988), pp. 167–85; Stein, "Vacarius and the Civil Law in England" and "The Liber pauperum," in de Zulueta and Stein, *Roman Law in England*, pp. xxii–vii and xxviii–xxxvii. Cf. Cheney, *Roger, Bishop of Worcester*, pp. 361–62 n. 87; and below, p. 189 n. 50.

24. Charles Duggan, "Decretals of Alexander III to England," *Miscellanea Rolando Bandinelli, Papa Alessandro III*, ed. Filippo Liotta (Siena, 1986), pp. 85–151.

bishop Roger, Bartholomew of Exeter, and the abbot of Ford (or Rufford) records charges against the prior of Bridlington on grounds of immorality and uncanonical election. The case had been commissioned previously to the bishop of Durham and the abbot of Fountains, who exonerated the prior and reported back to the pope. But the charges were later repeated in person to the pope by canon Walter, who alleged that the judges had not conducted the case in due legal form, and listed various other malpractices. Unwilling to leave the matter in silence or re-open the case once settled, the pope re-commissioned the case with a long and complex series of instructions, ordered the new judges to discover how the earlier judges had proceeded, and laid down the following alternatives:

(a) If they find that the judges absolved the prior before hearing the brothers, they must ensure that Walter's expenses are paid by the church, hear the case in all the matters mentioned and reach a fair judgment.
(b) If they find that the judges received the canons' oath and then absolved the prior, that decision is upheld.
(c) If the prior excommunicated any of the canons after Walter placed them under the protection of the Roman Church and the pope, the sentence is not to hold, unless the prior was absolved by the judges (as they reported to the pope).
(d) If the prior establishes his case, the judges must strictly forbid him to use that opportunity to molest or oppress any of the brothers, and ensure that Walter and his associates remain in peace, unless they have presumed to trouble him again, after he was lawfully absolved.
(e) If the prior refuses to answer or submit to their judgment, they are to suspend him by apostolic authority and forbid the brethren to obey him.
(f) And if the prior wishes to appeal, the judges will hear all the charges and exceptions, hear witnesses, place their sworn testimony under seal, send them to the pope, and fix a term for both parties to appear before him. Sufficient expenses are to be provided from the church for the canons to appear against the prior.[25]

The Bridlington case records appeals by a religious community against their superior. But while the right of appeal could be a protection for the oppressed, it could be used also to evade legitimate authority. In a clear

25. Duggan, "Decretals of Alexander III," p. 123: *WH* (= number assigned by Walter Holtzmann in his projected *Regesta decretalium saeculi XII,* in process of completion by Stanley Chodorow and Charles Duggan), 250; *JL* (= Jaffé, *Regesta Pontificum Romanorum ad annum 1198* 13891, 1161–81 (? 1174–80); pd *Claustr.* (= Ferdinand Schönsteiner, "Die Collectio Claustroneoburgensis," *Jahrbuch des Stiftes Klosterneuburg* ii [1909], 1–154), p. 205; cf. Walter Ullmann, "A Forgotten Dispute at Bridlington and its Canonistic Setting," *Yorkshire Archaeological Journal* 148 (1951), 469–73.

and brief directive, *Relatum est auribus,* the pope condemned in general terms the abuse of the process by persons in the York diocese who launch an appeal to evade the archbishop's jurisdiction, when they have in fact no complaint.[26] The remedy of appeal was devised to relieve the oppressed—*ad oppressorum levamen est inventum.* Therefore, if any of Roger's subjects wish to appeal on any matter, he must compel them by apostolic authority to prosecute their appeal within a year, in person or through a suitable representative, or stand to his judgment, unless they can show clear and reasonable cause for failing to do so. Elsewhere, in *Proposuit nobis G.,* the pope ruled that an appeal in one case does not make the appellant less answerable in others in which an appeal has not been made. But, since the judge seems suspect to the appellant, he should not compel the latter to answer in other cases while the first is still pending, except for a crime so grave and manifest that he may rightly be condemned ipso facto.[27] Again, in *Super eo quod,* in reply to Roger's enquiry about the respect due to an appeal launched by one party in fear of a report that his adversary had secured papal letters, the pope ruled that deference should not be paid to an appeal seemingly launched to frustrate the legal process.[28] And the problem of forgery[29] was the subject of *Si quis obiciat,* a brief fragment which states that if a litigant alleges forgery and wishes to prove it, but claims that his proofs are overseas, he should be allowed deferment, and he can appeal, if it is refused, even if appeal was forbidden on the principal question.[30]

The Making of the "New Law": Decretal Collections

These few examples merely suggest the comprehensive range of the delegates' jurisdiction, and record their initiative in seeking authoritative papal

26. Duggan, "Decretals of Alexander III," p. 141: *WH* 874, *JL*—, 1159–81; pd *Claustr.,* p. 194.

27. Duggan, "Decretals of Alexander III," p. 136: *WH* 749, *JL* 14350, 1159–81; pd *X,* 2.28.4.

28. Duggan, "Decretals of Alexander III," p. 145: *WH* 1009, *JL* 14163, 1159–81; pd *2 Comp., Quinque compilationes antiquae,* p. 77 and Mansi, 21: 1097.

29. Cf. Charles Duggan, "*Improba pestis falsitatis:* Forgeries and the Problem of Forgery in Twelfth Century Decretal Collections (With Special References to English Cases)," in *Fälschungen im Mittelalter,* ed. Horst Fuhrmann, *MGH, Schriften* 33/2 (Hanover, 1988), pp. 319–61.

30. *Si quis obiciat:* Duggan, "Decretals of Alexander III," p. 142: *WH* 914, *JL*—, 1164–81, pd *Decretales ineditae* (= *Decretales ineditae saeculi XII,* ed. et rev. Stanley Chodorow and Charles Duggan, from the papers of Walther Holtzmann, Monumenta Iuris Canonici, Series B: Corpus Collectionum, 4 [Città del Vaticano, 1982]), pp. 128–29 no. 74. The fragment is probably a re-wording of an excerpt from *In eminenti,* to Roger of York: *WH* 552, *JL* 14350, 1164–81, pd. *1 Comp.* 2.20.40.

instructions, definitions, and decisions, thus actively sharing in the judicial process. But the English judges delegate went an important stage further, and played a creative and dominant role in the formation of the first post-Gratian decretal collections. These early collections were essentially a reflection of judge-delegate activity, both recording the commissions of the judges and providing a corpus of precedents for their successors. The first traces of their activities can be seen in the many individual texts of all kinds inserted by canonists in Gratian manuscripts—the so-called *paleae,* and the creation of early *Dekretanhänge,* or appendices to Gratian, which were compiled as small independent supplements to the *Decretum.*

The practical and professional purpose of these early additions is evident. The earliest extant primitive collection is the short *Wigorniensis altera,* composed in the household of Roger of Worcester, one of the most famous judges delegate of Alexander III's pontificate. At least three of its texts are found also in earlier *Dekretanhänge,* and only one is dated *post* 1174.[31] From the same source came the crucially important Worcester collection itself (*Wigorniensis,* 1181).[32] No decretal collection records more clearly the appointment, functions and procedures of judges delegate in the period. It is a large, professionally organized compilation of 274 numbered items, arranged by subject matter in seven books, and provided with numerous rubrics, summarizing the essential points of canonical interest in the subsections of the longer decretals. It lacks only the principle of decretal dissection to make it fully systematic, but the apparatus of rubrics compensates for that deficiency. The first four books deal respectively with marriage questions, the status and privileges of religious, of the clergy, and of churches. Of exceptional significance are the last three books, directed specifically to the work of judges delegate, the judicial process, appeals, and "instruction of judges in diverse cases," as their titles and contents make clear:

31. Duggan, *Twelfth-Century Decretal Collections,* pp. 69–71; analysis, pp. 152–154 and plate I: an emended analysis of the collection is in preparation.

32. Hans-Eberhard Lohmann, "Die Collectio Wigorniensis (Collectio Londinensis Regia): Ein Beitrag zur Quellengeschichte des kanonischen Rechts im 12. Jahrhundert," *ZRG KanAbt.* 22 (1933), 35–187. For Holtzmann's classification of decretal collections into primitive and systematic categories, see *Studies in the Collections of Twelfth-Century Decretals,* from the papers of Walther Holtzmann, ed. Christopher R. Cheney and Mary G. Cheney, Monumenta Iuris Canonici, Series B: Corpus collectionum, 3 (Città del Vaticano, 1979), pp. xxxi–xxxii. Following the work of Jacoba Hanenburg ("Decretals and Decretal Collections in the Second Half of the Twelfth-Century," *Tijdschrift voor Rechtsgeschiedenis* 34 [1966], 522–99, esp. pp. 591–92) and Peter Landau ("Die Entstehung der systematischen Dekretalensammlungen und die europäische Kanonistik des 12. Jahrhunderts," *ZRG KanAbt.* 65 [1979]), 120–48), however, the "Worcester" group, which Holtzmann called primitive, has been re-classified as systematic, because its members are professional works, devised in books according to subject matter.

Book V. de casibus, in quibus non est deferendum appellationibus (13 chapters).
Book VI. de casibus, in quibus est deferendum appellationibus, etiam si causa sit appellatione remota commissa (4 chapters).
Book VII. ad informandum iudices in diversis casibus quandoque emergentibus (81 chapters).[33]

The Worcester collection was the work of experienced canonists in the circles of the two most famous judges delegate of the period, Bartholomew of Exeter and Roger of Worcester, together with their familiar colleagues Baldwin of Ford, Adam of Evesham,[34] Robert of Kenilworth, and others. Baldwin succeeded Roger at Worcester and archbishop Richard at Canterbury, and these successive stages of his promotion are reflected by the insertion of later decretals to him in these offices, entered by different hands in the manuscript volume. It was from collections of this kind, and especially from the "Worcester" tradition itself, that the later systematic traditions evolved. And, since the decretals dealt with actual cases or answered questions on which bishops and judges required authoritative definitions, they constituted a source of living law, shaped to the pressures and preoccupations of contemporary society. In the execution of their office the papal judges delegate controlled the direction of the evolving law by their handling of the cases, the questions of principle and procedure which they raised, the manner in which they recorded the latest definitions and decisions, and in all such practical and professional ways.

The importance of the new law was quickly recognized in Bologna, where the doctors of the schools sought the latest decretals to supplement their teaching in precisely the same way that professors in law schools today gather and cite the latest laws in their treatment of legislation and judicial decision. But although decretal letters were sent to all parts of the Church, the initiatives taken by English judges delegate in the 1160s and 1170s proved decisive in the formation and consolidation of the new law. The sources from which the Worcester collection (*Wigorniensis*) was compiled were also the seed bed from which the later fully systematic collections were primarily made, first in the *Appendix concilii Lateranensis*[35] assembled in

33. Ibid., pp. 119–23, 123–24, and 125–49.

34. On commissions to Adam of Evesham, and a final report by Adam to the pope, see Katherine Christensen, "'Rescriptum auctoritatis vestre': a judge-delegate's report to pope Alexander III," in *The Two Laws: Studies in Medieval legal history dedicated to Stephan Kuttner*, ed. Laurent Mayali and Stephanie A. J. Tibbetts, Studies in Medieval and Early Modern Canon Law, 1 (Washington DC, 1990), pp. 40–54.

35. So called because the decretals are appended to a copy of the decrees of the Third Lateran Council of 1179 in some early manuscripts.

Oxford or Lincoln from 1184, and then in the closely-related *Bambergensis*,[36] made at Tours, also from 1184. Both compilations were associated with the professional teaching of canon law in the Angevin Empire, respectively in England and Touraine, and mark the reception of the latest decretal law into the academic tradition. From these two sources, the English material was received by the great Bolognese canonist Bernard of Pavia, whose "Leipzig" collection (*post* 1185) formed the basis of his *Compilatio prima* (*post* 1188), which established the form and structure of later collections of decretal law.[37] Bernard's was the first of the "five ancient collections," of which two (Peter of Benevento's *Compilatio tertia* and Tancred's *Compilatio quinta*) were promulgated by popes Innocent III and Honorius III in 1210 and 1226 respectively.[38] From these momentous achievements, it was but a small step to the compilation by Raymund of Peñafort, under papal auspices, of the *Liber Extra* or *Decretales* of Gregory IX in 1234.[39] With characteristic insight, Maitland recognized long ago the essential links in this chain:

> One small step will be taken by Innocent III., another small step by Honorius III., . . . and then Gregory IX. will issue a code of some two thousand sections. The Englishmen who gave Alexander III. the opportunity for issuing a hundred and eighty decretals of permanent importance contributed an ample share to the plentitude of power.[40]

In the state of historical knowledge at that time, Maitland could not know the precise nature of the crucially creative role of the English judges delegate and the canonists in their circles in the genesis of post-Gratian decretal collections, and through them their influence on the later official collections. Indeed, as noted already, the entire professional transmission of the decretals was influenced by the English judges and collectors. In Holtzmann's statistical survey,[41] the total number of decretals in all known collections for the period from 1145 to 1198 was 1055, of which 509 were received in England and 33 in the English king's continental lands; 199 were

36. So called because the manuscript survived in the Staatsbibliothek in Bamberg.

37. Divided into five books, each devoted to a specific topic: *iudex, iudicium, clerus, connubium, crimen*. Indeed, Bernard's earlier collection, *Parisiensis secunda* (the first extant systematic collection, c. 1177–78) had already revealed the influence of the English primitive collections.

38. The "Leipzig" collection and the "five ancient compilations" (*prima, secunda, tertia, quarta,* and *quinta*) are analysed in Friedberg, *Quinque compilationes antiquae*.

39. ed. Friedberg, *Corpus Iuris canonici*, 2.

40. Maitland, *Roman Canon Law*, p. 130.

41. Walther Holtzmann, "Über eine Ausgabe der päpstlichen Dekretalen des 12. Jahrhunderts," *Nachrichten Akad. Göttingen* (1945), 15–36, esp. p. 34 Anh. 1.

received in Italy, including the Norman territories in the south; 133 in the French king's lands; 13 in Germany; and a total of only 7 in Scotland and Ireland.[42] Although these statistics now need minor modifications, they remain valid in their broad implications. The predominance of English decretals in the collections was a consequence not simply of the admittedly large number of decretals received in England, but far more significantly of the creative role of the English judges delegate.

The Judge Delegate's Jurisdiction

The delegate's jurisdiction extended to every level and branch of Western Christian society, from kings, prelates, and magnates, to monastic and religious communities, to simple clerks, and lay men and women. In the course of the great rebellion of 1173–74, for example, King Henry II of England was threatened with interdict if he failed to restore the wife and fiancée respectively of his two eldest sons, Henry and Richard. Margaret and Alice, daughters of Louis VII of France, had been detained by Henry II in retaliation for his sons' involvement in the revolt. Following the complaint of the French king, Alexander III sent the decretal *Non est vobis* to the entire clerical order in the English king's lands, both in England and on the continent, announcing that he had commissioned the archbishop of Tarantaise, the bishop of Clermont, and the prior of Chartreuse (or the prior of Mont Dieu) to admonish the English king to restore Margaret and Alice within forty days of receiving the papal letter.[43] If he failed to do so, divine office should be suspended in the provinces in which they were detained or to which transferred, except for the baptism of infants and penance for the dying, until they were restored. The pope ordered the recipients to induce the king to comply, or to enforce the sentence with-

42. The relatively small number of decretals to French recipients in the collections is *prima facie* surprising, in view of the close relations between the French Church and the Roman curia, notably during the period of Alexander's exile in France from early April 1162 until September 1165, in the course of which he summoned a council at Tours in 1163, and the papal curia functioned at Sens, 1163–65. Indeed, the non-canonical archives in France for the period are rich in records of papal *privilegia*, letters of confirmation of rights, and other letters, many explicitly recording litigation in the presence of papal judges delegate, whose commissions have not survived. In contrast, the almost total absence of decretals to German recipients (only three from Alexander III), in the collections, is easily explained by the emperor's support for a series of anti-popes, following Alexander's election in 1159, until his reconciliation with Frederick I at Venice in 1177, a crucial and formative period in the origin and evolution of decretal collections.

43. *WH* 669, *JL* 12248, 1173 *ex*.

out contradiction or appeal. In the event, Henry II survived the rebellion with his authority enhanced, and it is unlikely that the commissioners—all residents of Henry's continental lands—were able to execute the mandate. The French king's daughters were still in King Henry's company when he returned to England in 1174.[44] Nevertheless, the principle that interdict might be imposed on a whole province for one person's offence was noted in a marginal comment in one English decretal collection—*Ecce quod pro delicto unius tota terra interdicitur*[45]—and a truncated version of the letter was transmitted through the systematic collections from *Bambergensis* to the *Decretales*,[46] no doubt because of the important disciplinary principle involved.

At the lower end of the scale, the "poor clerk" R. took his tearful complaint in person to pope Lucius III at Verona in 1184—*Constitutus in presentia nostra R. pauper clericus lacrimabili conquestione monstravit. . . .* He had obtained the church of Ham[47] in due canonical order, through presentation by the patron and institution by the diocesan bishop, but the clerk H. (or G.), through concealment of the truth, secured papal letters to the bishop of Ely and the abbot of Crowland, who summoned R. to appear before them in a place several days' journey from his church. When his adversary claimed that he had himself been presented to the church first, and the judges unjustly harassed R. with frequent and peremptory citations and many labors and expenses, the latter appealed to the pope. The distinguished canonist bishop Bartholomew of Exeter supported R.'s claims, and assured the pope of their truthfulness, recording that he had himself instituted R. first, and that the latter had been excessively burdened by the earlier judges. The pope therefore ordered the abbot of Ford (Baldwin, later bishop of Worcester and archbishop of Canterbury) and the archdea-

44. For relevant details, cf. Charles Duggan, "English secular magnates in the decretal collections," *Monumenta Iuris Canonici*, Series C, Subsidia, 9 (1992), pp. 595–96.

45. Oxford, Bodleian MS, Tanner 8, p. 696b; cf. Walther Holtzmann, "Die Dekretalensammlungen des 12. Jahrhunderts, I: Die Sammlung Tanner," *Festschrift zur Feier des 200jährigen Bestehens der Akad. der Wissenschaften in Göttingen, phil.-hist. Klasse* (1951), 7.5.20, p. 138.

46. Bamb. 50.34; *X*, 4.1.11. For the full text, derived from a manuscript of St-Victor, in Paris, see André Duchesne, *Historiae Francorum Scriptores* 4 (Paris, 1641) 769, Mansi, 21: 1032, *PL*, 200: 965.

47. *WH* 180, *JL*—, 1184. Pd in Heinrich Singer, "Neue Beiträge über die Dekretalensammlungen vor und nach Bernhard von Pavia," *Sitzungsberichte der Kais. Akad. der Wissenschaften in Wien*, phil.-hist. Kl., 171.1 (1913), 233. Holtzmann considered the place-name of the church in question so corruptly transmitted (ham., ham., n.) that an accurate identification was unlikely, but a very probable location is that of the church of St Pancras in Ham, within the limits of modern Plymouth, almost on the border of Devon and Cornwall, the respective areas of jurisdiction of the archdeacons of Totnes (Devon) and Cornwall in the decretal.

cons of Totnes and Cornwall to restore everything as it was before his adversary's appeal. If they determine that R. was canonically instituted first—as indeed was the case, on the evidence of his own statement and that of the bishop—they are to restrain his adversary from troubling him, impose perpetual silence on the former in respect of the church, and set moderate expenses, to be paid to R. No letters may be effective in prejudice of this decision.

The judges perhaps had little difficulty in executing this mandate, but sometimes the cases presented for their judgment involved very powerful persons and institutions. The stages of a protracted dispute between archbishop Roger of York and the prior and canons of the Augustinian house at Guisborough in Yorkshire are recorded in two decretals of Alexander III and in archival records. The earlier letter, *Dilecti filii nostri,* is of interest for its meticulous instructions to the judges delegate, the bishop of Exeter and the dean of Lincoln. The prior and canons of Guisborough had complained that Roger had suspended the prior after appeal, interdicted their churches, and declared the canons excommunicate if they obeyed the prior. The pope ordered the judges to summon the parties within thirty days when requested to do so. If they found the facts as stated, they must publicly declare that the prior and canons were not bound by the archbishop's sentence, "because if the matter so appeared to us, we would certainly have done the same"—*quia, si nobis constaret, nos hoc idem proculdubio fecissemus.* They must make a full and careful report to the pope, and admonish those who know the truth to tell it and not fail to bear witness through fear or favor of the archbishop or anyone else. The canons had also complained that the archbishop oppressed their vicars and clerics with undue exactions, and granted their churches to his relations. All of this was clearly contrary to the canons and damaging to his reputation. The judges must investigate the truth of the charges. If they find the facts as stated, such grants must be revoked by papal authority, unless the canons maliciously delayed to make appointments; the churches must be restored to the prior and canons, and their vicars and clerics must keep their oaths, unless unjustly extorted by the prior. The judges must order the archbishop to refrain from undue oppressions and exactions, and inform the pope of the truth of all these matters without delay. With unusual emphasis and directness, the pope mandated the judges to ensure that the case was not unduly prolonged by over-refined examination, as many judges did—*sicut a multis fieri solet.* The simple and pure fact itself must be investigated, according to the form of the canons and the institutes of the fathers. If the archbishop were unwilling to appear or obey their judgment, the judges should proceed with the affair, unless he had a canonical excuse.[48]

But in a later commission, *Ex transmissa nobis conquestione*,[49] to bishop John of Chichester and the abbots of Ford and Evesham, the pope replied to a complaint by the prior and canons that, after a papal sentence in their favour concerning the church of Kirklevington, the archbishop had placed the clerk W. de Ridale in their chapel after appeal to the pope and without their knowledge, excommunicated two of the canons, without summons, conviction, or confession, and finally deposed and excommunicated the prior, interdicted divine office for the whole convent unless they showed him obedience and reverence, interdicted their churches, and excommunicated the chaplains who sang in their churches and the parishioners if they paid tithes or oblations to the canons. The pope could not overlook such serious matters. The judges must summon the parties, diligently investigate the matter, *omni gratia et favore postponente*. If the charges brought by the canons are proved, the judges must correct what the archbishop has done after appeal, in respect of deposition, excommunication and interdict, tithes, oblations, and other rights. The judges must forbid the archbishop to harm or oppress the prior and canons in their persons or property.

This case had in fact arisen from Roger of York's attempts to circumvent the grant of Kirklevington and its chapels made to Guisborough Priory by Robert de Brus by appointing his own nominees. The decretals cited here are eloquent witness to his aggressive and intimidating tactics. In the event, an unsatisfactory compromise was worked out in 1180 in the presence of the papal legate Alexius, who had come to Britain to settle, among other things, the even more weighty question of the status of the see of St Andrew's (over which Roger also claimed jurisdiction).[50]

48. *Papal Decretals Relating to the Diocese of Lincoln in the Twelfth Century*, ed. Walther Holtzmann and Eric W. Kemp, Lincoln Record Society 47 (Hereford, 1954), pp. 30–33 at p. 30: ". . . provisuri attentius, ne ita subtiliter, sicut a multis fieri solet, cuiusmodi actio intendatur, inquiratis sed simpliciter et pure factum ipsum et rei veritatem secundum formam canonum et sanctorum patrum instituta investigetis."

49. *Cartularium prioratus de Gyseburne*, ed. W. Brown, Surtees Society 89 (1899), 2: 81 no. 718; cf. *Papsturkunden in England*, 1. ed. Walther Holtzmann, Abhandlungen der Akademie der Wissenschaften zu Göttingen, phil.-hist. Klasse, New Ser. 25 (Berlin, 1930), pp. 443–45 no. 173.

50. I am indebted to Dr. Marie Lovat for advice on the closing stages of this tortuous litigation. The whole process of this and other related cases will be treated in her forthcoming edition of the *York Acta*; meanwhile, cf. *Cartularium de Gyseburne* 2: 46–49 nos 182–84. The archbishop secured a life interest in Kirklevington. See also Raymonde Foreville, *L'Église et la royauté en Angleterre sous Henri II Plantagenet* (Paris, 1943), p. 472. It is a matter of some interest that the compromise was witnessed by Masters Vacarius and Ambrose, both eminent Roman lawyers, among others.

At the other end of the country, another powerful Augustinian house was engaged in a long and acrimonious dispute with the knight Joel of Vautort and his nephew over the *ius patronatus* of the church of Sutton.[51] Two decretals *Ex parte nobilis* and *Cum nuntius canonicorum* record the successive stages in the litigation, and the judges' final settlement is recorded in the Plympton cartulary. According to Joel's report, the parties were brought before the diocesan bishop (Bartholomew of Exeter), but, believing himself oppressed, Joel placed himself and his lands under the protection of St Peter and the pope. Thereupon the bishop allegedly placed all the churches in Joel's lands under interdict, after appeal—which the pope can scarcely believe—with the result that the bodies of parishioners, who had meanwhile died, remained unburied. In *Ex parte nobilis,* the pope ordered archbishop Richard of Canterbury to summon the parties and investigate the matter. If he found that interdict was imposed after appeal, he should publicly declare the sentence void and order the bodies to be buried, unless they were of persons excommunicated or interdicted individually—*nominatim*. Then he should hear the case and reach a judicial verdict, notwithstanding any papal letters impeding truth and justice. If he found that the churches were interdicted before appeal, he should secure sufficient surety from Joel to accept his judgment, then release the churches from the sentence, notwithstanding any contradiction or appeal, and proceed to hear all aspects of the case and bring it to a conclusion, without leave of appeal.

The matter was not immediately resolved, as the commission *Cum nuntius canonicorum* to archbishop Richard of Canterbury and bishop Roger of Worcester makes clear. A messenger from each side appeared in the pope's presence—*in nostra essent presentia constituti*. The canons' messenger produced a copy of a charter (*rescriptum*), which the former bishop of Exeter, William Warelwast, had allegedly granted in their favor against the claims of Reginald, Joel's grandfather. The knight's messenger asserted, in contrast, that he and his predecessors had freely held the right of patronage at that time, that it lawfully belonged to him, and disclaimed all previous knowledge of the document now produced. Since neither side had come prepared to pursue the case, the pope could not fittingly bring it to a conclusion, and therefore he committed it to Richard and Roger, confident in their prudence and honesty. They should summon the parties, and, if authentic letters established that the church was adjudged to the canons, they

51. Now St. Andrew's in Plymouth.

should impose perpetual silence on Joel in respect of it, and confirm the sentence of interdict placed on his lands by bishop Bartholomew because of the loss and injury sustained by the canons. If the knight did not comply with these orders, they should excommunicate him, notwithstanding any letters secured by concealment of the truth. The outcome of the dispute is not recorded in the decretal collections, but the judges' notification of settlement survives among extracts from a lost Plympton cartulary in a seventeenth-century manuscript. The notification rehearses the details of the case, with the additional note that Joel informed the pope that the *ius patronatus* of the church belonged to him and his nephew, whose guardian he was. After the fourth peremptory edict, Joel failed to appear in response to their summons and was judged contumacious. The judges examined authentic letters and seals with the advice of bishop Bartholomew, and by papal authority imposed silence on Joel and those who acted in his name in this matter.[52]

The Guisborough-York and Plympton-Vautort cases exemplify the sophistication and complexity of ecclesiastical cases in the period and the ability of judges delegate to summon very powerful persons before their tribunals. But the delegate's jurisdiction stretched even beyond the confines of the kingdom in which a case was brought. In November–December 1181, pope Lucius III sent letters respectively to John of Oxford, bishop of Norwich, and archbishop Richard of Canterbury, both on behalf of the plaintiff Master Stephen of Blois, concerning sureties which he had given respectively for Master G. de Insula and Master Peter of Blois, the archbishop's chancellor at the time of the Lateran Council (March, 1179),[53] which the bishop of Norwich attended.[54] Stephen complained that he had guaranteed payment of debts incurred by G. de Insula on his departure from Bologna—*in recessu suo a Bononia*—and by Master Stephen. Neither had paid the debt, meanwhile much augmented, and Stephen was harassed by the creditors. The pope mandated the recipient in each case to compel the debtor to release Stephen from the bond if the charges were confirmed; if the debtor denied the debt or interest, he should be compelled to swear

52. For a full discussion of the texts, and the background to the case, see *Decretales ineditae,* pp. 73–77 no 43a; cf. also Cheney, *Roger, Bishop of Worcester,* pp. 95, 143–44, 186, 283–84, 334–35 and 344.

53. R. W. Southern, "Peter of Blois: a Twelfth-Century Humanist?" in Southern, *Medieval Humanism* (New York, 1970), pp. 105–32; cf. Christopher R. Cheney, *English Bishops' Chanceries, 1100–1250* (Manchester, 1950), pp. 33–35.

54. To bishop John of Norwich: *WH* 161, *JL*—, Nov.–Dec. 1181; the letter is known only from the Rochester decretal collection (*Roff.* 121); cf. now *Decretales ineditae,* pp. 113–114 no. 16. To Richard of Canterbury: *WH* 162, *JL* 14963, Nov.–Dec. 1181; transmitted to *X,* 3.22.3.

an oath, notwithstanding custom which is contrary to law—*consuetudine que legi contraria est non obstante, iuramentum calumpnie subire cogatur.* Moreover, since it would be difficult for Stephen to bring his witnesses to England, the respective commissioners (Norwich and Canterbury) should instruct the Bolognese judges to act in their place (*vice tua*), examine and thoroughly question the witnesses, and send back their sealed depositions, indicating what trust should be placed in the witnesses or depositions. If the accused disdain to appear or stand to judgment, they should be deprived of their ecclesiastical benefices, and their incomes assigned to the payment of the debts until the creditors were satisfied. This notable case involving the well-known Peter of Blois reflects the international character of the new law in a striking way. In it the guarantor of debts incurred in Italy seeks relief through an appeal to the pope, which involves collaboration between two judges in England and colleagues in Bologna, who are given the responsibility of establishing the veracity of the plaintiff's allegations. A more revealing example of the supranational character of the new law can scarcely be imagined.

By virtue of his papal commission, the judge delegate's jurisdiction extended to all levels and classes of society. The magnates in their marriages, dynastic interests, and inheritances, their patronage of churches, tithes, and numerous matters were subject to the delegates' rulings in the event of disputes arising.[55] The question of legitimacy in marriage, though essentially a spiritual and religious question, entailed vital political and material interests of property and inheritance. The pontificate of Alexander III was of crucial importance in the development of the Church's doctrine of marriage, and many of Alexander III's commissions dealt with aspects of this question.[56] But the cases themselves reflect the dynastic and political interests which lay behind the doctrinal issues: the dispute between Richard of Anstey and Mabel de Francheville related to the Sackville inheritance; that between Francus de Bohun and Ralph de Arderne recorded one stage in the prolonged Bohun-Arderne dispute which was not finally settled until 1199; and that relating to the marriage of William FitzGodric and Aubrey de Lisours related to the Lacy of Pontefract inheritance.[57] These cases and

55. Cf. Duggan, "English Secular Magnates," pp. 605–10.

56. Charles Donahue, "The Policy of Alexander III's Consent Theory of Marriage," *Proceedings of the Fourth International Congress of Medieval Canon Law, Toronto, 1972,* ed. Stephan Kuttner, Monumenta iuris canonici, Series C: Subsidia 5 (Città del Vaticano, 1976), pp. 251–281.

57. *Letters of John of Salisbury,* 1:227–237 no. 31; P. M. Barnes, "The Anstey Case" in *Medieval Miscellany for Doris Stenton,* Pipe Roll Society, New Series 36 (London, 1962), pp. 1–

numerous others were argued in the delegates' presence on the basis of the canonical and doctrinal principles underlying the Church's law of marriage, but it is evident that great political and material interests in English society were at issue.

Indeed, at the highest level, the crisis of conflicting jurisdictions in England between papal and royal power is most clearly recorded in the dispute between Henry II and Becket, focused in the sixteen clauses framed by Henry II's lawyers at Clarendon in 1164. Among these, the third clause, relating to criminous clerks, attracted most controversy then, and has continued to do so in historical debate. But the eighth clause, concerning appeals, was far more important both in doctrine and in practice, since it sought to establish an invariable procedure whereby appeals should progress from the archdeacon's court to the bishop's, and thence to that of the archbishop; if the latter proves remiss in doing justice, the case should go to the king, to be decided thereafter in the archbishop's court by the king's order in such a way that it should go no further without royal assent.[58] The clause struck at the heart of papal appellate jurisdiction, and therefore also at that of the judges delegate, and would have curtailed the most active and creative function of papal authority in the period had it been implemented. But the post-Becket settlement at Avranches in 1172 with the legates Albert and Theodwin, to the effect that appeals would go freely to the pope except that suspect appellants would swear that no harm to the king or the kingdom would result thereby, ensured that the system would develop without further hindrance.[59]

Eventually the flood of appeals was so great that Gregory VIII, the former chancellor Albert de Morra,[60] sought to curtail them. In failing health, Gregory reigned as pope less than two months (21 October to 17 December 1187), and in the general letter *Vel ex malitia* to all archbishops

24; Charles Duggan, "Equity and Compassion in Papal Marriage Decretals to England," in *Love and Marriage in the Twelfth Century*, ed. Willy Van Hoecke and Andries Welkenhuysen (Leuven, 1981), pp. 68–70; cf. Duggan, "English Secular Magnates," pp. 606–9; *Decretales ineditae*, pp. 123–125 no. 71.

58. *Councils and Synods with Other Documents Relating to the English Church, A.D. 871–1204*, ed. Dorothy Whitelock, Martin Brett and Christopher N. L. Brooke (Oxford, 1981), I/2, p. 880.

59. Ibid., pp. 942–956. For the papal confirmation of the agreement (2 Sept. 1172), see p. 955: "Appellationes autem ad sedem apostolicam factas nec impedies nec impediri permittes, quin libere fiant in ecclesiasticis causis ad Romanam ecclesiam bona fide, absque fraude et malo ingenio, et per Romanum pontificem tractentur et suum consequantur effectum: ita tamen ut si qui tibi suspecti fuerint, securitatem faciant quod malum tuum vel regni non querent"; cf. p. 949 no. 5.

60. See below, at n. 65.

and bishops, he spoke of his own physical frailty—*imbecillitate proprii corporis laborantes,* the malice of litigants, and the failure of the recipient prelates—*ex . . . defectu vestro.*[61] He could not properly attend to all matters arising, nor hear the complaints of those rushing upon him from all sides. Burdened with matters of middling importance, he could not deal with more weighty questions. He therefore set out a series of rulings to limit recourse to the curia to such issues, leaving other questions for settlement in the dioceses in which they arose. For example, cases relating to matters of less than twenty marks value should be resolved in their diocese of origin, cases should not needlessly be appealed to the curia, nor should litigants compel their adversaries to journey to the curia, when the case will be sent back to their area for settlement. Nevertheless, whenever litigants have a just cause for appeal to the pope, the prelates should not neglect to provide them with letters dimissory, containing a full record of the process. The import of the letter was in effect to buttress the traditional hierarchy of jurisdictions in the Church, and to curtail the abuse of the appellate system, while maintaining the pope's authority in appropriate cases.

Conclusion

As suggested at the outset, the development of the judge-delegate system recorded a remarkable development both in papal jurisdiction and the concept of the authority of the law itself, which could not have occurred without the interaction and collaboration of three sets of participants: the litigants who appealed, the popes who responded, and the delegated judges who received and executed their commissions. In this way, the new canon law responded to the changing circumstances of contemporary society and to the demand for clarity, authority, and consistency in the application of norms of behavior throughout the Western Church. It was an expression both of papal authority and of the authority of law itself, but it was also a reflection of a widespread desire to substitute lawful process for arbitrary judgment: to place the authority of the law above that of the person. Appeals to the Roman curia offered a relief from oppression, bias, or illegality,

61. A problem arises in the verbal transmission of this letter: the version of the phrase in the canonical tradition is *ex . . . defectu nostro* (*1 Comp.*, 2.20.47, p. 24), suggesting admission of neglect by the pope himself; the version in the archival tradition (in MSS in Alençon and Paris) is *ex . . . defectu vestro: Papsturkunden in Frankreich,* ed. Johannes Ramackers, new series 2: *Normandie* [Göttingen, 1937], p. 383).

whether real or imagined. The appellate process was itself inevitably open to abuse and exploitation, and both popes and jurists were much concerned with misuse of the system and laid down safeguards to counteract it. But when lawfully and conscientiously applied, the system afforded protection to the weak against the powerful and the reform of long-standing abuses. In the exercise of power in twelfth-century society, the rapid growth of the learned law, both Civil and canon, created new forms and procedures for defending rights and challenging existing power structures. Religious could sue their superiors, clerks could counter the biased or autocratic jurisdiction of their bishops, churches could protect their interests against oppressive lords, and monks and clergy could seek redress of grievance through an objective forum rather than the arbitrary judgment of their prelates. The extraordinary popularity of the appeals procedure is proof of its relevance to the needs of the period. The process was activated from the periphery, not from the center, by litigants not by judges. It was to some extent subversive of established hierarchies. As Alexander III expressed it, "appeals were created for the relief of oppression," and the aggrieved could invoke the process of the law to make the balance of power less uneven.

Simultaneously, these developments brought into existence a new and learned elite, and created a new profession, open to talent and less dependent on birth and privilege. Education, knowledge, and mastery of the processes and procedures of the law opened new paths to influence and status. What distinguished Romano-canonical process from the regional laws of Europe was its universality, its basis in written codes (Gratian's *Decretum* and later the Gregorian *Decretales,* and Justinian's *Corpus iuris civilis*), and its requirement of men skilled in the law for its effectiveness. It is called "the learned law" with good reason. Its practitioners were trained in its procedures and learned in its lore, and litigants were represented in the process by skilled advocates. The demands of the system filled the law schools in Bologna, Oxford, Montpellier, Paris, and elsewhere, produced a new professional elite, and its international character offered career paths across Europe. Gerard Pucelle (later bishop of Coventry) founded a school of canon law in Cologne; Master Ralph of Sarre (in Kent) taught at Reims where he later became dean;[62] the English canonists Gilbert and Alan taught at Bologna and assembled collections of Innocent III's decre-

62. Cf. Ludwig Falkenstein, "Zu Entstehungsort und Redaktor der Collectio Brugensis," *Proceedings of the Eighth International Congress of Medieval Canon Law, San Diego, University of California at La Jolla, 21–27 August 1988,* ed. Stanley Chodorow, Monumenta iuris canonici, Series C: Subsidia 9 (Città del Vaticano, 1992), pp. 117–62 at pp. 140–144, and n. 108.

tals, used by John the Welshman in compiling the *Compilatio Secunda,* the second of the "five ancient collections," from which the Gregorian *Decretales* of 1234 descended.

Appendix: The Judge Delegate Formulary *A. B. C. judices*[63]

The development of the legal learning and professional expertise of judges delegate ran parallel with that of officials in the papal chancery, in the reception of Roman law, and the adoption of Romano-canonical procedures.[64] It was most clearly marked in the Chancery by the evolution of the functions of the chancellor, the notary, the corrector of apostolic letters, and in the development of the *Audientia litterarum contradictarum* under such eminent chancellors as Albert de Morra, legate to the English king in the post-Becket settlement in 1172 and later pope Gregory VIII (1187).[65] The professional learning and its practical application by English canonists and judges are reflected in their construction and use of procedural treatises and *ordines*—notably the Anglo-Norman *Incerti auctoris ordo iudiciorum* (the pseudo-*Ulpianus de edendo*), *c.* 1140, the *Olim edebatur actio* (a post-1177 expansion), the *Ordo iudiciarius* (1182–85), attributed to a canonist in the circle of archbishop John Cumin of Dublin, and William Longchamp's *Practica legum et decretorum* (post-1183).[66] At a practical level, the exercise of the judge delegate's power is continuously recorded in the numerous commissions and their gradual incorporation in canonical collections, but its scope and application are most professionally recorded in judge-delegate formularies. No extant English formularies for the specific guidance of judges

63. For the full Latin text, see F. Donald Logan, "An Early Thirteenth-Century Formulary," *Studia Gratiana* 14 (1967): *Collectanea Stephan Kuttner,* 4: 75–87; cf. n. 67 below.

64. de Zulueta and Stein, *Roman law in England,* p. xix, "This was developed by co-operation between civil lawyers and canonists; at first the civil lawyers took the leading role, but by the end of the century the canonists had largely taken over."

65. Brigitte Meduna, *Studien zum Formular der päpstlichen Justizbriefe von Alexander III. bis Innocenz III. (1159–1216): die* non obstantibus-*Formel,* Österreichischen Akademie der Wissenschaften (Vienna, 1989), pp. 9–13, 23–39, 126–170, *et passim.*

66. de Zulueta and Stein, *Roman law in England,* pp. xl–xliii: Procedural works. For the work of the Anglo-Norman canonists, see Stephan Kuttner and Eleanor Rathbone, "Anglo-Norman Canonists of the Twelfth Century: an Introductory Study," *Traditio* 7 (1949–51), 279–358; Charles Duggan, "The Reception of Canon Law in England in the Later Twelfth Century," *Proceedings of the Second International Congress of Medieval Canon Law, Toronto, 1962,* ed. Stephan Kuttner and J. Joseph Ryan, Monumenta iuris canonici, Series C: Subsidia 1 (Città del Vaticano, 1965), pp. 359–390, esp. pp. 371–377.

delegate pre-date the closing years of the twelfth century, since no predecessor of Innocent III (1198–1216) is named in them, but it is almost certain that earlier versions preceded the first known survivals. Several copies of the group *A. B. C. judices* (briefly analysed below) are found in codices now widely dispersed in manuscript libraries.[67] The provenance of the collection is certainly English, since the custom of the English Church is mentioned in one formula—"tam quia forma rescripti, licet consonet canonibus, tamen consueto cursui et Anglicane ecclesie consuetudini refragatur,"[68] but the extant versions record variants and additions to a common stock—manuscripts in the Vatican and at Montecassino, for instance, include additions of Bolognese material, in evidence of the expansion of an English archetype from Italian sources.

The formulary, briefly summarized below, contains a series of standard letters relating to a range of possible stages in a hypothetical action between two parties, variously identified, concerning title to a certain church, which has been delegated by the pope (identified as "Innocent" in forms 1,14 and 15) to the judges A., B., and C.

1. *Form of the first citation on receipt of the papal mandate.* The judges A. B. C. to the rector T. of a certain church: on receipt of the mandate, the judges set a time and place for the rector of the church in question to appear before them.

2. *Form of the second citation, the first peremptory summons.* The judges to the defendant: on his failure to appear or send a suitable *responsalis,* the judges issue a second citation, the first peremptory.

3. *Form of excuse.* The clerk N. to the judges A. B. C.: he could not appear when summoned, since he was judge in another case, for which he had set the date before citation in the present litigation.

4. *Form of third citation, the second peremptory summons.* The judges to the

67. For the extant manuscripts, now in London (British Library and Lambeth Palace), Cambridge (Gonville and Caius College), Baltimore, the Vatican, Montecassino, and Oxford (Bodley), see Logan, "An Early Thirteenth-Century Formulary," pp. 77–79 and Sayers, *Papal Judges Delegate,* pp. 45–49. The British Library copy is in a volume including the early English primitive decretal collection *Regalis:* cf. Duggan, *Decretal Collections,* p. 82 n. 1.

68. Logan, "An Early Thirteenth-Century Formulary," pp. 77 and 85–86 no. 14. The English origins of the formulary are further supported by incidental references in some of the manuscripts. The Baltimore MS includes Oxford and Northampton references, suggesting "an origin in the nascent university," while the Bodley MS seems clearly based on actual cases, with references to named persons, offices and places, pointing to Cirencester as the likely place of origin (Sayers, *Papal Judges Delegate,* pp. 46–59). A formulary from Canterbury, edited in Jane E. Sayers, "A Judge Delegate Formulary from Canterbury," *Bulletin of the Institute of Historical Research,* 35 (1962), 198–211, is in matter and style of presentation comparable to the *A. B. C. judices* analysed here, but it is a fuller and later work in 30 forms, possibly post 1227 in completion, and influenced by Tancred's *Ordo iudiciarius* (c. 1216: Sayers, "A Judge Delegate Formulary," p. 200).

defendant: the judges issue a third citation, the second peremptory, and warn him that they will proceed with the case, if he fails to appear.

5. *Form of the third peremptory summons, for a person of rank.* The judges to the defendant: in consideration of the defendant's status, the judges can issue a third peremptory summons.

6. *Form of the letter of commission by a judge.* The judge A. to his fellow judges B. and C.: since he is prevented by other commitments from being present in the case between N. and H., he commissions one of his clerks to act in his place, except for the formal presentation of the case and definitive judgment.

7. *Form of a judge's letter of excuse for absence.* The judge C. to his fellow judges A. and B.: he notifies his colleagues that he cannot be present to hear the case committed jointly to them. They are to proceed with their commission, and he is informing the parties.

8. *Form of letter by which the defendant appoints a proctor.* The clerk N. to the judges A. B. C.: since he cannot be present, he commissions a proctor E. (the bearer of his letter) with full powers to act for him, and he is informing the other party.

9. *Form of letter to the judge ordinary ordering execution of an interlocutory sentence.* The judges delegate to the judge ordinary: on N's failure to appear in response to several letters and a peremptory summons, the judges issue an interlocutory judgment against him (after taking counsel), and give possession of the church to his adversary H., pending final judgment, the question of right being reserved—*causa rei servanda.* By the authority of the pope committed to them, they mandate the ordinary not to defer execution of their sentence.

10. *Request to the judges delegate on behalf of a litigant.* To the judges B. and C.: an unidentified source requests the judges to listen earnestly to the plea of H., the bearer the letter.

11. *Form of letter recording a settlement made by the litigants.* General notification by the judges A. B. C. in the case between the clerks N. and H.: the parsonage to remain with H., but N. to have the vicarage, in return for an annual payment.

12. *Form of letter of execution of a definitive sentence.* The judges delegate to the judge ordinary: having fully considered all the evidence presented by N., they adjudge the church to him, and order the judge ordinary to execute the judgment without delay.

13. *Charter containing the judgment* de re iudicata. Formal instrument containing the final sentence.

14. *Form of reference to the pope on a doubtful matter.* The judges A. B. C. to the pope (Innocent III): the judges report their examination carried out by his authority. After examination of witnesses of both sides, their claims and objections, and consultations with legal experts, they decided to refer the matter to the pope, with the form of the rescript and the testimony and allegations of both sides, to secure an equitable judgment from him; and they set a date for both sides to appear in his presence.

15. *Form of letter mandating the judge ordinary to execute the sentence, including the financial penalty imposed on the loser.*

[16. *Form of letter of revocation sent by judges delegate to earlier judges.* Masters C. and D. to bishop A. and abbot B.: on receipt of Pope Innocent's commission, they request bishop A. and abbot B. to withdraw from the hearing and execution of the case between N. and H., which has been transferred to them by papal mandate.][69]

69. Logan, "An Early Thirteenth-Century Formulary," p. 77 n. 4. On all procedural matters, see now Linda Fowler-Magerl, *Ordines iudiciarii and Libelli de Ordine ludiciorum (from the middle of the twelfth to the end of the fifteenth century)*. Typologie des Sources du Moyen Age Occidental (Turnhout, 1994).

Part III

Cultures of Power

John Van Engen

9. Sacred Sanctions for Lordship

Imprisoned in Pavia and frustrated in his episcopal ambitions, Rather of Liège, writing his *Praeloquia* about 935, denounced lordly pretentions among the hereditary nobility. The "patron" or "lord" (*senior*), as he was now customarily flattered,[1] paid no heed to what Augustine, Gregory, and Benedict had set down long ago about human "equality" before God. Distinctions among people arose, Rather pointedly noted, from the human will, not from nature (*non natura sed uoluntate homines a se inuicem distare*). More than three centuries earlier Gregory had described as mysterious the providential ordering of human affairs (*occulta administratio*) by which, though all born equal, some enjoyed less esteem even as others became prelates. He urged humility on the privileged, while ascribing such ranking partly to merit (*variante meritorum ordine*).[2] Rather echoed this passage, then quipped that in his day "people were frequently made lords even over their betters."[3] He addressed lords directly (*tu*): He who proves superior in good works and humbly serves is better than some lord who arrogantly scorns, he who proves faithful in doing what he promises nobler than the lord who mendaciously deceives, and he who keeps the laws of nature by not deserting his place more generous than the lord who violates the great good of "friendship."

1. "Patronus siue—ut usitatiue a multis dici ambitur—senior es?" Ratherius Veronensis, *Praeloquia* 1, 10; ed. Peter L. D. Reid, *CCCM* 46A (1984), pp. 22–27. On Rather, see Jean Flori, *L'idéologie du glaive: préhistoire de la chevalerie* (Geneva 1983), pp. 105–7; and Carlo Guido Mor, "Raterio di fronte al mondo feudale," and Ilarino da Milano, "La spiritualità dei laici nei *Praeloquia* di Raterio di Verona," in *Raterio da Verona*, Studi sulla spiritualità medievale 10 (Todi 1973), pp. 165–86, 35–93.

2. Gregory, *Moralia* 21: 15 (22–24); ed. Marcus Adriaen, 3 vols., *CC* 143 (1979–85), 2: 1082–83. Compare his *Regula pastoralis* 2, 6; (*PL* 77: 34). For interpretation and additional references, see Carole Straw, *Gregory the Great: Perfection in Imperfection* (Berkeley CA, 1988), pp. 81–89, and Robert Markus, "Gregory the Great's Europe," *Transactions of the Royal Historical Society* 31 (1981), 21–36. Compare Georges Duby, *The Three Orders: Feudal Society Imagined*, tr. Arthur Goldhammer (Chicago, 1980), pp. 34ff, who emphasized Gregory's influence.

3. ". . . ut plerumque aliqui dominentur etiam melioribus." Rather, *Praeloquia*, 1, 10; (*CCCM* 46A, 22). This follows on a paraphrase of the text from Gregory's *Moralia* in note 2 above (not seen by the editor).

So familiar had this picture of grasping lords become by the mid-tenth century, Rather contended, that people now imagined the Lord God himself to rule and judge people the same way they did, that is, as jealous of one another's advantage, anxious about power and possessions, swelled up with greed and ambition, convinced that another man's gain was their loss.[4] Rather's social critique, unusual for its perception of a reversed link between the sacred and the social, substituted no radical vision of a society constructed on a divine exemplar. He too presumed a world in which kings ruled supreme and bishops pleaded for recognition, the *miles* represented a warrior rather than a social class, and "laborers" enjoined to "constancy and contentment" in fulfilling their obligations comprised the most numerous group of Christians. Few today, he observed, merited their standing as free men (*libertatem*). It was not lineage but property (*non in genere sed in ipsa consistere possessione*) and possessions (*ea quae circumstant hominibus*), most often, that rendered lords powerful, and this, he insisted, fortune—or rather, the Almighty—could easily alter. He paraphrased Ecclesiastes: I see a servant sitting in the place of the lord.[5] Personal pique as much as social conviction or Christian charity animated his diatribe, an unusual example for the tenth century of direct discourse on Christian society.

Few churchmen—with the singular exception of John of Salisbury in the 1150s (whence the fame and influence of his *Policraticus*)—wrote out general expositions of the sacred and social orders prior to the recovery of Aristotle's *Politics* in the 1260s. They prepared "mirrors for princes" in the ninth century, contended about legitimacy and authority during the Investiture Struggle, and alluded to such matters ever more regularly in scriptural and legal commentaries.[6] But their expositions commonly echoed a restricted number of inherited textual authorities. Jonas of Orleans in the ninth century, like many others, cited Isidore of Seville, another Roman magnate and prelate who had placed more emphasis than Gregory upon order—equality on the spiritual plane but gradations on the social. Though

4. *Praeloquia* 4, 15; (*CCCM* 46A, 119).

5. *Praeloquia* 1, 10; (*CCCM* 46A, 26); see Eccl. 10: 6–7.

6. See now David Luscombe, "Introduction: The Formation of Political Thought in the West" and "The Twelfth-Century Renaissance" in *The Cambridge History of Medieval Political Thought, c.350–c.1450*, ed. J. H. Burns (Cambridge, 1988), pp. 157–73, 306–38; Jürgen Miethke, "Politische Theorien im Mittelalter," in *Politische Theorien von der Antike bis zur Gegenwart*, ed. Hans-Joachim Lieber (Munich, 1991), pp. 47–156; and Hans Hubert Anton, *Fürstenspiegel und Herrscherethos in der Karolingerzeit*, Bonner Historische Studien 32 (Bonn, 1968).

servitude came from sin and that sin was wiped away at baptism, he explained, a "just God (*aequus Deus*) so ordained life for humans that he established some as subjects (*seruos*) and others as lords in order that the license of subjects acting badly could be restrained by the power of lords. For if everyone were without fear, who would there be to stop those doing evil?"[7] The Carolingian bishop Hincmar of Rheims believed that everyone should be "ruled and benefited" (*praeesse ac prodesse:* also a Gregorian phrase) by an "episcopal authority" made manifest in preaching, life, and word, and by a "royal office" (*regia dignitas*) made manifest in ruling and correcting. The impious were to be wiped from the earth (*debet de terra perdere*) by the bishop's "medicinal sword" and the king's "judicial sword."[8] This corrective notion of lordship, rule aimed at upholding or restoring an order threatened by human sinfulness, rested upon the Roman church fathers, especially Augustine.[9] But it was Isidore's formulation that informed most early medieval accounts, including the Council of Tribur in 895 and the two most influential canonistic collections of the eleventh century, by Burchard of Worms and Ivo of Chartres.[10]

Fundamental assumptions about the correlation between sacred and social power lay scattered nonetheless throughout the works of eleventh- and twelfth-century authors. Two authors may be cited as typical, one male and probably of humble origins, the other female and noble. In his scriptural commentaries, the Benedictine monk Rupert of Deutz (d. 1129) allowed for the realities of lordship, of doing what befit lords and fathers (*curare quod dominum uel patrem decet*), providing for the necessities of family and household: licit, he said, but dangerous, for all too easily the

7. Isidore, *Sententiae* 3, 47 (*PL* 83, 717). Compare Jonas, *De institutione laicali* 2, 22 (*PL,* 106, 213–15).

8. Hincmar, *De diuortio, PL,* 125, 772. Compare Anton, *Fürstenspiegel* on the Carolingian texts (here p. 312), and Flori, *L'idéologie du glaive,* pp. 52–57 on Hincmar.

9. Augustine, *De ciuitate Dei,* 19, 15; ed. Bernard Dombart and Alphons Kalb, 2 vols., *CC* 47–48 (1955), 2: 682–83. For interpretation, see Robert Markus, *Saeculum: History and Society in the Theology of St Augustine* (Cambridge, 1970), pp. 89ff, 197–210; Tilman Struve, *Die Entwicklung der organologischen Staatsauffassung im Mittelalter,* Monographien zur Geschichte des Mittelalters 16 (Stuttgart, 1978), pp. 45–67; and Robert Markus, "The Latin Fathers," in Burns, *Medieval Political Thought,* pp. 92–122, esp. 103ff. Ambrose, while teaching that true liberty for Christians arose from their being "in Christ," retained even more forcefully antique notions about an equally just order of domination; see his *Epistola* VII (= 37); ed. Otto Faller, *CSEL* 82/1, pp. 43–66.

10. Burchard, *Decretum,* 15, 43 (*PL* 140: 908), where it was taken over from the Council of Tribur as the concluding canon in a book devoted to lay people. Ivo, *Decretum* 16, 45 (*PL* 161: 915), taken from Burchard for a much larger book "de officiis laicorum et causis eorumdem."

goods could come to dominate you rather than you the goods.[11] He took for granted that people in the world looked out mostly for temporal comforts and earthly well-being (*commodis temporalibus et transitoriae saluti*), indeed more ardently so than did his fellow monks pursuing the things of God, whom he exhorted to rouse themselves with likeminded zeal.[12] As an abbot in charge of a monastic household, Rupert recognized two staffs of authority, one of discipline and pastoral care for the disciples of Christ and another of "domination," as he called it, for the kings of the nations.[13] Churchmen were allowed only the first, the care of souls, not the wielding of sword and judgment. Yet he endowed them—in the midst of the reform struggle—with the riches of cities and castles, the spoils of tyrants subjected to the yoke of Christ,[14] fair exchange in his view for spiritual intercession and a form of rule not equated with "domination." This they were to exercise as imitators of the apostles and Christian kings, not as tyrants or pagan emperors; "domination" suggested coercive force, ideally placed at the service of the church but not exercised by churchmen themselves.[15] Writing before the Investiture Struggle was settled, he noted that the church badly needed (*multum indiget*) the supporting "sword-power of king and emperors," and that when the two fell out nothing proved more ruinous for Christendom's standing (*status*) in this world.[16] In the present era already (or also) Christ and his church should hold sway (*principatum teneret*) in a public religious cult (*publica religione*) by way of a shared celebration of secular power and sacred priesthood.[17]

Hildegard of Bingen, an abbess in the mid-twelfth century, drew from received notions of ordained power a spiritual lesson. She reiterated views that great people were to be feared and revered and that they properly lorded it over others (*magnae personae dominentur*); God caused some people to excel and others to submit precisely to keep people from killing each other. But this order served a higher purpose as well: it was chiefly through submission to outward and secular lordship (*dominationem*), she

11. Rupert of Deutz, *Super Mattheum* vi; ed. Rhabanus Haacke, *CCCM* 29 (1979), 180.

12. *De operibus spiritus sancti* viii.21; ed. Rhabanus Haacke, *CCCM* 24 (1972), 2100.

13. Rupert, *Super Mattheum* viii; ed. Rhabanus Haacke, *CCCM* 29 (1979), 246.

14. *De sancta Trinitate* xvii.15; ed. Rhabanus Haacke, *CCCM* 21 (1971), 984. See John Van Engen, *Rupert of Deutz* (Berkeley, CA, 1983), pp. 265–69, 301–2; Matthäus Bernards, "Die Welt der Laien in der kölnischen Theologie des 12. Jahrhunderts: Beobachtungen zur Ekklesiologie Ruperts von Deutz," in *Die Kirche und ihre Aemter und Stände: Festgabe für Josef Kardinal Frings* (Cologne, 1960), pp. 391–416.

15. *De sancta Trinitate* 19, 17; ed. Rhabanus Haacke, *CCCM* 22, (1972) 1108–09.

16. *De sancta Trinitate* 26, 5 (*CCCM* 22, 920).

17. *De victoria Verbi Dei* 8, 25; ed. Rhabanus Haacke (*MGH* Geistesgeschichte 5), p. 269.

said, through the fear and honor shown humans, that the interior person learned to know the invisible power of almighty God.[18] So deep was her sense of linkage between social and sacral order that the abbess stubbornly and publicly resisted accepting non-noble women into her house. The arrangment of things in society was of God (Rom. 13: 1), and replete with spiritual lessons for the attentive soul. In sum, where Rather thought people were falsely ascribing to God what they had experienced in secular lordship, and Rupert sought a mutually supportive public cult of power and religion, Hildegard expected the display of power in secular lordship to lead people toward a grasp of invisible divine lordship.

Telltale as such representative remarks on sacred and social power may be, few authors dealt explicitly with the concept of "lordship" as it is commonly used by historians today. To uncover the social attitudes that governed such relationships, given the lack of formal political treatises, historians have focused upon the sacred sanctions invested in the notion of "estates" (*ordines* or *status*), what German historians called "Stände-Lehre"[19] and Duby made famous as the *imaginaire* of feudal society. Whichever scheme a medieval writer employed,[20] it presumed the divine ordering of society, with each estate located within the church, each image offering metaphorical testimony to the way things were or ought to be. Such ideas were promulgated primarily through images and rituals, and only secondarily (at least until the later middle ages) through sermons and treatises.

18. *Sciuias* 3, 6, 13–14; ed. Adelgundis Führkotter and Angela Carlevaris, 2 vols., *CCCM* 43 (1978), 1: 441–42. On these passages, see Alfred Haverkamp, "Tenxwind von Andernach und Hildgard von Bingen: Zwei 'Weltanschauungen' in der Mitte des 12. Jahrhunderts," in *Institutionen, Kultur und Gesellschaft im Mittelalter: Festschrift für Josef Fleckenstein zu seinem 65. Geburtstag,* ed. Lutz Fenske, Wesner Rösener, and Thomas Zotz (Sigmaringen, 1984), pp. 515–48, here 535–36.

19. A traditional starting-point was Wilhelm Schwer, *Stand und Ständeordnung im Weltbild des Mittelalters: Die geistes- und gesellschaftsgeschichtlichen Grundlage der berufsständischen Idee,* 2d. ed. (Paderborn, 1952). More recently, Otto Gerhard Oexle has done the most work in this area; see his "Die funktionale Dreiteilung der 'Gesellschaft' bei Adalbero von Laon: Deutungsschemata der sozialen Wirklichkeit im früheren Mittelalter," *Frühmittelalterliche Studien* 12 (1978), 42–44; "*Tria genera hominum:* Zur Geschichte eines Deutungsschemas der sozialen Wirklichkeit in Antike und Mittelalter," in *Institutionen,* pp. 483–500; and "Deutungsschemata der sozialen Wirklichkeit im frühen und hohen Mittelalter: Ein Beitrag zur Geschichte des Wissens," in *Mentalitäten im Mittelalter: Methodische und Inhaltliche Probleme,* ed. Frantisek Graus. Vorträge und Forschungen 35 (Sigmaringen 1987), pp. 65–117 (both with much literature).

20. There were of course many other schemes; for the evidence from letter-writing manuals, see Giles Constable, "The Structure of Medieval Society According to the *Dictatores* of the Twelfth Century," in *Law, Church, and Society: Essays in Honor of Stephan Kuttner,* ed. Kenneth Pennington and Robert Somerville (Philadelphia, 1977), pp. 253–67; for theological authors, see Yves Congar, "Les laïcs et l'ecclésiologie des *ordines* chez les théologiens des XIe et XIIe siècles," in *I laici nella "societas christiana" dei secoli XI e XII* (Milan, 1968), pp. 83–117.

Whether one understands these schemes, images, and rituals as clerical and royal impositions[21] or as collective fictions permeating the entire society (Oexle), they each took for granted a world of lords and subjects.

At issue for this study is the relationship between the language of sacred authority learned authors of the eleventh and twelfth centuries derived from their inherited texts and the language they encountered and presumably used in their social experience, whether indeed the language of experience made its way into that of authoritative exposition. For in the eleventh and twelfth centuries, the sacred and the social, church and politics, churchmen and lords, interacted along a continuum, distinguishable perhaps in texts or principles but conjoined in reality. When bishops acquired vassals and assembled armies, either as dependents of the king or as princes in their own right, they acted as lords comparable in style and authority to counts at least, if not dukes, and were accordingly listed as such in social schemata drawn up by Walafrid Strabo in the ninth century and by Gilbert of Limerick in the early twelfth.[22] Great abbeys and smaller collegiate churches depended upon the exercise of economic lordship to secure for their clerics the leisure to pray; indeed monks may have been more masterful than others in exacting economic claims.[23] Benedictines, seeking to distinguish themselves from their lordly neighbors in the world and stung by the criticism of religious reformers who initially repudiated these forms of lordship, protested otherwise. Peter the Venerable, abbot of Cluny, the most prestigious and grievously attacked house, cited the text from Gregory about the different ranks within this world, implying thereby more than he said about lordly monks and subject peasants, but he went on to contrast the cruel exactions of secular lords evident to all (ascribing to "lordship" thus mostly negative connotations) with the honest and compassionate oversight by monks who treated their subjects as brothers and sisters.[24] In local parish communities, too, when rectors laid claim to

21. The emphasis of Duby, and earlier of Jacques Le Goff, "A Note on Tripartite Society, Monarchical Ideology, and Economic Renewal in Ninth- to Twelfth-Century Christendom," in his *Time, Work and Culture in the Middle Ages,* tr. Arthur Goldhammer (Chicago: 1980), pp. 53–57.

22. Walafrid, *De exordiis* 32; ed. Alfred Boretius and Victor Krause, *Capitularia regum Francorum, MGH, Legum* Sectio II, 2 vols. (Hanover, 1883–97), 2: 515–16; Gilbert, *De statu ecclesie, PL* 159: 997–1004. For the real equivalences in income and consumer households in the later middle ages, see Christopher Dyer, *Standards of Living in the Later Middle Ages* (Cambridge, 1989), p. 20.

23. Georges Duby, *The Early Growth of the European Economy . . .*, tr. H.B. Clarke (Ithaca, NY, 1978), pp. 213ff.

24. *The Letters of Peter the Venerable,* ed. Giles Constable, 2 vols. (Cambridge, MA, 1967) 1: 86–87, 84 (citation of Gregory).

tithes and various legal obligations fulfillable only in their churches, they exercised an authority nearly indistinguishable from that of secular lords. Rectors were commonly addressed as "lords" (*dominus* or *seigneur*) from the eleventh century onwards.

In their writings churchmen certainly recognized these social realities in one way: they often turned forms of social domination into spiritual virtues, depicting peasants as people redeemed by their work and their submission to lordship. Bonizo of Sutri, a reforming canonist who spelled out rules for different groups in society, declared peasants' work "without sin" so long as they learned to keep faith with their lords, avoid stealing, and pay tithes.[25] Churchmen understood fully that the work of peasants was essential to the feeding of the whole church, princes and prelates alike, and that they were therefore to be protected and prayed for.[26] For feeding the people of God and for "living without guile," most of them would be saved, Honorius believed, quite unlike rapacious warriors.[27] Peasants could also be depicted at the other extreme as stupid, grasping, and virtually bestial, especially by secular lords and in courtly literary genres. Churchmen, by contrast, on occasion referred to the poor as "lords of all the churches' things."[28] But calling peasants "lords" drew its ironic force from the stark reality that they were not, and churchmen knew it. Interpreting one of her visions, Hildegard of Bingen noted matter of factly that by the precept of God there are great people who enjoy the strength of secular power (*maiores natu ex fortitudine saeculari potentiae*) and little people who live under the power of lords both secular and ecclesiastical (*minores qui consistunt sub potestate et spiritalium et saecularium personarum*).[29]

Lordship as a category of social analysis, as distinguished from a description of social relations or a form of social address, entered the formal

25. Bonizo, *De uita christiana* 8: 1, ed. Ernst Perels. Texte zur Geschichte des römischen und kanonischen Rechts im Mittelalter 1 (Berlin, 1930), p. 253. See Tilman Struve, "Pedes rei publicae: Die dienenden Stände im Verständnis des Mittelalters," *Historische Zeitschrift* 236 (1983), 1–48.

26. Peter the Chanter said it most fully: "Tertium genus est agricolarum et pauperum atque operariorum, labore et sudore quorum omnes degunt et uiuunt. Isti sane sunt uelut pedes et quasi rectores mundi. . . . Quos tam oratores quam pugnatores tenentur protegere ac defensare atque pro eis intercedere et orare, et non iniquis exactionibus, uiolentis angariis et collectis grauare et expoliare." Richard C. Trexler, *The Christian at Prayer: An Illustrated Prayer Manual Attributed to Peter the Chanter (d. 1197)* (Binghamton, NY, 1987), p. 226.

27. Yves Lefèvre, *L'Elucidarium et les lucidaires* (Paris 1954), p. 429.

28. "Sunt utique pauperes domini ominum rerum ecclesiarum." Trexler, *Christian at Prayer*, p. 225. This referred to their claim on charity; see Michel Mollat, *The Poor in the Middle Ages*, tr. Arthur Goldhammer (New Haven, CT, 1986).

29. *Sciuias* 3, 6, 12 (*CCCM* 43, 441).

writings of churchmen slowly and relatively late. The most common term for the exercise of lordship was "power" (*potestas*). Carolingian authors had commonly distinguished the *potentes* and the *pauperes,* but in the eleventh and twelfth centuries powers of any size, from royal kingdoms to local castellanies, came to be designated as *potestates*.[30] So too in the later twelfth century, when Italian cities established a strong administrative figure, they called him, in the vernacular, the *podestà*. For churchmen, this choice of terminology seemed no accident, whatever vernacular or colloquial usages lay behind and reinforced it. For it echoed the passage in Scripture crucial to Christian notions of a sacral sanction for power, Paul's statement in Rom. 13: 1 that all power was of God and that those powers that exist are ordained of God (*non est enim potestas nisi a Deo; quae autem sunt, a Deo ordinatae sunt*), cited at the outset of nearly all accounts of sacred and political authority, including, for instance, those given by Cardinal Robert Pullen and John of Salisbury.[31] In a treatise on "royal power" written in the midst of the Investiture Struggle, Hugh of Fleury declared it self-evident that the "whole world was separated into ranks and powers" (*totum mundum certis gradibus ac potestatibus*) just like the royal court in heaven, that the two principle powers by which this world is ruled are royal and sacerdotal, and that everyone in power (*in potestate positi sunt*) is to be revered (same word as Hildegard) by those in subjection, if not for their own sakes, then for the order and rank they have received from God (*propter ordinem et gradum quem a Deo acceperunt*).[32] Hugh of St. Victor perceived a universe permeated by ordained power, which he, among the first, described in terms of a Dionysian hierarchy extending from the divine through the angelic to the human.[33] What little he had to say about earthly power (*potestas terrena*) proposed a mutual indebtedness in law and defense between lords and subjects, with all earthly power derived from the king or emperor as head and delegated through local officials, a traditional vision of public order, with its language—*praelati* for lords and *census et tributum* for rents—also inherited.

30. This point made already by Georges Duby, *La société aux XIe et XIIe siècles dans la région mâconnaise* (Paris, 1953), pp. 218ff.

31. Robert Pullen, *Sententiae* 7, 7 (*PL* 186: 919–921); John of Salisbury, *Policraticus* 4, 1; ed. C. C. J. Webb (London, 1909) 1: 236. For the history of scriptural exegesis on this text, see Werner Affeldt, *Die weltliche Gewalt in der Paulus-Exegese: Rom. 13: 1–7 in den Römerbriefkommentaren der lateinischen Kirche bis zum Ende des 13. Jahrhunderts* (Göttingen, 1969).

32. Hugh, *Tractatus de regia potestate et sacerdotali dignitate,* i; ed. Ernst Dümmler et al., *Libelli de lite imperatorum et pontificum,* 3 vols. *MGH* (Berlin, 1891–97) 2: 467, 468, 470. Compare Struve, *Die organologische Staatsauffassung,* pp. 110–15.

33. "Hiis hierarchiis, id est principatibus sacris totus regitur mundus," *PL* 175: 931.

Power experienced in everyday reality and sanctioned by God himself (Rom. 13) was the presumed reality. But churchmen also introduced countervailing themes, such as those in Scripture depicting God and the just as showing "no respect of persons,"[34] which helped blunt the raw force of divine sanctions for ordained power. Some teachings built upon antique traditions that projected the ruler as both just and divine, adapted for Christians in the image of "Saint Constantine." Most highlighted the rulers' responsibilities to the people for justice and mercy, even the place of the people themselves.[35] Seventh-century heirs to Roman tradition, acting as bishops and clerics in the recently converted Germanic kingdoms, began to develop a specifically Christian pattern of teaching about the obligations and expectations of kingship. Isidore of Seville, best remembered for an etymological and moralizing definition of kingship (*reges a recte agendo uocati sunt*), prescribed for "princes" a life of "justice" outwardly and of "mercy" inwardly (*clementia, pietas, patientia*), for they were "bound to the laws." God gave princes rule over people, he insisted with Gregory, to benefit them, not to harm them or lord it over them.[36] At the fourth Council of Toledo (633), plainly inspired if not drafted by Bishop Isidore (d. 636), the king was addressed for the first time as a *minister Dei* and reminded that he was to answer to God for the people entrusted to his care.[37] Yet at that same council bishops mostly spent time assuring the king that his power was God-given, and promising—with implicit conditions—their fidelity. Restraint upon princes hardly exceeded the force of moral exhortation.

The most important contrasting theme developed by churchmen was that of ruling power as service, also captured in a word, *ministerium*. Scripture set it specifically against the "domination" exercised by princes in this world:

> You know that the princes of the gentiles lord it over them [*dominantur eorum*]; and they that are the greater, exercise power [*potestatem*] upon them. It shall not be so among you: but whosoever will be the greater [*maior*] among

34. See John Van Engen, "'God is no Respecter of Persons': Sacred Texts and Social Realities," in *Intellectual Life in the Middle Ages: Studies for Margaret Gibson*, ed. Lesley Smith and Benedicta Ward (London, 1992), pp. 243–64.

35. This aspect receives fuller treatment in the dissertation of Philippe Buc, *Potestas: Prince, pouvoir, et peuple dans les commentaires de la Bible (Paris et France du Nord 1100–1330)* (diss., Paris, 1989). My thanks to Dr. Buc for making his work accessible to me.

36. Isidore, *Sententiae* 3, 48–51 (*PL* 83: 718–24). The basic work remains Eugen Ewig, "Zum christlichen Königsgedanken im Frühmittelalter," now in his *Spätantikes und Fränkisches Gallien* (Munich 1976), pp. 3–71.

37. Toledo 4, 75 (*PL* 84: 385–86).

> you, let him be your minister [*vester minister*]: And he that will be first among you, shall be your servant [*servus*]. (Matt. 20: 25–27)

Gregory the Great accordingly styled himself, as pope, the "servant of the servants of God," even as the emperor Otto III would call himself a "servant of the servants of Christ." Carolingian clergymen seized upon this teaching both to restrain and to rationalize the raw exercise of power. The earliest of all their mirrors for princes, Smaragdus's for King Louis (800/814), described a set of virtues that made up the "royal way," as in another treatise he set out for his fellow monks the virtues appropriate to the "monastic diadem." Power to rule may have come through blood-lines and ritual anointing, his dedicatory letter explained, but a king's share in Christ's eternal kingdom can come only through gracious adoption and its concomitant moral responsibilities.[38] These lordly rulers had to be persuaded that power came ultimately from God, not from family or arms, and that they were therefore answerable to God, not family or arms. From the mid-eighth century, titles such as "by the favor of God" (*a Deo, gratia Dei*) abounded, as did images of the "hand of God" conferring rule—at once admonitory teaching devices and expressions of divine sanction for these kings and their power.[39]

So too these princes were encouraged to think of it as a "ministry," entrusted to them from the Almighty even as they entrusted ministries to various lesser people around them. The notion (*ministerium*), common for clerical duties in worship or servant duties inside a household, appeared in court writers about the time of Charlemagne, and was programatically applied by later ninth-century clerics.[40] Hincmar of Reims, addressing Charles the Bald, dismissed the customary "adulation that pleases lords and princes" (*adulatio principi ac domino terrae placere debet*), addressing instead the "person of the king and his royal ministry" (*de regis persona et regio ministerio*), and he intentionally placed considerations of family and powerful persons after duties owed the church and the commonwealth (*respublica*).[41] Sedulius Scottus opened his dedicatory poem to Charles the Bald with the concept of "ministry." In his dedicatory letter he pressed more forcefully than Hincmar for a notion of rulers (*rectores:* language borrowed

38. *PL* 102, 933.
39. Slightly different emphasis in Ewig, "Königsgedanken," pp. 48–49.
40. Ewig, pp. 59ff.
41. Hincmar, *De regis persona et regio ministerio, PL* 125: 833–34.

from Gregory the Great) understood—and understanding themselves—as "ministers of God" rather than as "lords of the people."[42]

Power, in sum, was presumed; the sanction was to come from "ministry." But such images and teachings contained as yet no clear notion of "office." Just how difficult it was to think of rulers, even wicked rulers, as accountable in terms of human office may be illustrated by the events surrounding the revolt against Louis the Pious in 833. However much churchmen and princes may have orchestrated events extending to a papal excommunication, the imperial dignity was lost in battle on the "field of lies" when his army melted away, that is, by a judgment from God, not a deposition from office. When the bishops gathered subsequently to oversee his public penance, they noted first their own "ministry" in the kingdom of God and then the king's neglect of the "ministry entrusted to him," a neglect which had "displeased" people, "irritated" God, and "scandalized" the church, with the result that the "imperial power had been suddenly withdrawn from him by a divine and just judgement."[43] In Bishop Agobard's memorandum on this affair, he was careful to say that the bishops' role, then and subsequently, was to admonish the king (*ammoneretur . . . et exhortaretur*) and to guide him toward penance.[44] The office itself was granted and taken away by God, whatever human instruments he may have used. In the coronation oath designed for West Frankish rulers a generation later, Bishop Hincmar may have hinted at another possibility, never articulated openly: kings, by so swearing, promised to keep the laws on behalf of the people entrusted to them by God.[45] But Hincmar himself mostly reaffirmed a more commonplace view of sanctions for rule, echoing Isidore: God made good kings, and he permitted evil kings as punishment for the sins of the people.[46]

The Investiture Struggle, with people caught up in frequent attempts

42. "Quid enim sunt christiani populi rectores nisi ministri omnipotentis? Porro idoneus et fidelis quisque est minister, si sincera devotione fecerit quae ei iusserit suus dominus atque magister. Hinc piisimi et gloriosi principes plus se ministros ac servos excelsi quam dominos aut reges hominum nuncupari et esse exultant. . . . Ecce imperator eminentissimus [Constantine] plus gratulabatur se Dei fuisse ministrum quam terrenum habuisse imperium." Siegmund Hellmann, *Sedulius Scottus* (Munich, 1906), pp. 19, 23.

43. *Capitularia* 2: 51, 52–53.

44. *Capitularia* 2: 56.

45. This line of thought developed by Janet Nelson, "Kingship, Law and Liturgy in the Political Thought of Hincmar of Rheims," *EHR* 92 (1977), 241–79.

46. Hincmar, *De regis persona et regio ministerio,* I–II (*PL* 125, 834–835) (the first issue in his treatise!); compare Isidore, *Sententiae* 3, 48, 11 (*PL* 133: 720).

to depose kings, popes, or bishops, considerably sharpened thinking about how a person might be held accountable for "ministry" or a ruling office. Yet from all those pamphlets and letters no clear teaching on office emerged. The arguments were mostly ad hoc, attempting to justify particular actions already taken, and they were perceived as such. Sigebert of Gembloux found it unthinkable that the king appointed as Christ's place-holder, whatever his faults, could be removed by anyone other than God himself.[47] True, Manegold of Lautenbach, in a famous rhetorical gesture, asked whether unworthy swineherders were not removed. Yet Manegold, who advanced most boldly toward a notion of office, put his argument as a question and implied that the pact with the people was broken *first* by the king's own moral unworthiness, loosing them from bonds to a ruler whose function (*officium*) it was to curb evil; in effect the king removed himself ("fell") by violating the essential condition for his position (*pactum pro quo constitutus est*).[48] For thinkers caught in this web of scriptural teaching and social tradition, the difficulty was to hold at one and the same time that all power came from God in various ordered gradations, and that persons could be removed from that entrusted power if they defaulted in their ministry—when, so it seemed and was also taught, people usually "deserved" their rulers and patient forbearance counted as virtue, a small price to pay for keeping order in a wicked world.

From high to low, the world in which people lived was made up of "powers" exhorted by churchmen to act as "ministers of God." But addressed as individuals, those figures were not "powers" or indeed "minis-

47. "Et adhuc sub iudice lis est. Ammoneri quidem possunt, increpari, argui a timoratis et discretis uiris; quia quos Christus in terris rex regum uice sua constituit dampnandos et salvandos suo iudicio reliquit." Sigebert, *Epistola Leodiciensium; Libelli de lite* 2, 459.

48. "*Quod rex non sit nomen nature, sed uocabulum officii* [= function]. Regalis ergo dignitas [= office] et potentia, sicut omnes mundanas excellit potestates, sic ad eam ministrandam non flagitiosissimus quisque uel turpissimus est constituendus, sed qui sicut loco et dignitate, ita nichilominus ceteros sapientia, iusticia superet et pietate. . . . Atqui, cum ille, qui pro coercendis prauis, probis defendendis eligitur, prauitatem in se fouere, bonos conterere, tyrannidem, quam debuit propulsare, in subiectos ceperit ipse crudelissime exercere, nonne clarum est, merito illum a concessa dignitate cadere, populum ab eius dominio et subiectione liberum existere, cum pactum pro quo constitutus est, constet illum prius irrupisse?" Manegold, *Liber ad Gebehardum* 30, *Libelli de lite* 1, 365. The very way of posing the question (most of it in the subjunctive) indicates that a clear declaration of "deposition" was almost impossible to articulate. See I.S. Robinson, *Authority and Resistance in the Investiture Contest* (New York, 1978), pp. 114–31; and Horst Fuhrmann, "'Volkssouveränität' und 'Herrschaftsvertrag' bei Manegold von Lautenbach," in *Festschrift für Hermann Krause* ed. Sten Gagner, Hans Schlosser, and Wolfgang Wiegand (Cologne, 1975), pp. 21–42, who (p. 38) points to the teachings of Isidore: "Recte igitur faciendo regis nomen tenetur, peccando amittitur" (*Etymologiae* 9, 3) and "Reges quando boni sunt, muneris est Dei, quando uero mali, sceleris est populi" (*Sententiae* 3, 48, 11).

ters" but "lords."[49] Assuming, then, the reality of *potestas* and the ideal of *ministerium,* it is time to focus upon notions of "lordship" (*dominium*).[50] For Romans it meant the authority held in a household by a *pater familias,* thence possession or propriety with all ensuing rights; thus it appeared as a palea in Gratian's *Decretum.*[51] In this more precise sense the term was frequently joined with *ius,* meaning possession of and legal right to something. In early medieval usage *dominium* commonly referred in the first instance to proprietary rights over things, especially land, but with overtones of lordship; thus, as Pseudo-Isidore taught in the name of Pope Damasus, offerings made to the church could not remain under the *dominium* of lay people.[52] A Roman synodical ruling from 826, also recorded in Gratian, counterbalanced this crucial principle with a declaration that founders could not be compelled to give up their *dominium* (proprietary rights, but also lordship) over a church—the basis for *ius patronatus* or the right of presentation in the high middle ages.[53] Nearly all other medieval usages rested upon this concrete sense: that which a lord possessed or over which he exercised power. When Rodulfus Glaber in the 1030s referred to Charlemagne and Louis the Pious as subjugating the surrounding peoples to their "lordship" as to a "single household" he was echoing such usages.[54] After the twelfth-century recovery of Roman law teachings, the proprietary meaning was again strengthened, with civilian jurists in the later middle ages attempting to distinguish a strict sense of propriety from a more general sense of power over persons and things. But the larger sense had meanwhile become predominant. Ockham, in his work on politics, reported that in moral philosophy *dominium* was taken to mean the power to

49. Duby, *La société mâconnaise,* pp. 152, 294; Jean Flori, *L'essor de la chevalerie, XIe–XIIe siècles* (Geneva, 1986), p. 227, citing evidence from the region of Chartres.

50. Compare Duby, *La société mâconnaise,* pp. 168–77; Otto Brunner, *Land und Herrschaft,* 4th ed. (Vienna, 1959), pp. 240ff and passim; Peter Moraw, "Herrschaft," in *Geschichtliche Grundbegriffe,* ed. Otto Brunner, Werner Conze, and Reinhart Koselleck (Stuttgart 1982) 3: 5–13 (with literature).

51. "pater autem familias appellatur qui in domo dominium habet," *Digests* 16, 195, 2; *Decretum* C.16 q.3 c.16 = *Codex* 6, 7, 39. For basic orientation, see *Paulys Real-Encyclopädie der classischen Altertumswissenschaft* (Stuttgart, 1903) 101: 302–4.

52. Gratian, *Decretum,* C. 10 q. 1 c. 15; ed. Emil Friedberg (Leipzig, 1879), p. 615.

53. "Monasterium uel oratorium canonice constructum a dominio constructoris eo inuito non auferatur. . . ." Gratian, *Decretum,* C. 16 q. 7 c. 33; ed. Friedberg, pp. 809–10. The meaning may come closer here to a Roman notion of property than a medieval sense of lordship; thus Ulrich Stutz, "Ausgewählte Kapitel aus der Geschichte der Eigenkirche und ihres Rechtes," *Zeitschrift der Savigny-Stiftung für Rechtsgeschichte, Kanonistische Abteilung* 26 (1937), 18ff.

54. *Rodulfi Glabri historiarum libri quinque* 1, 4, ed. John France (Oxford, 1989), p. 10.

do freely whatever one chooses, as in: man is a lord and has lordship over his own acts.[55]

To these basic usages in the social and legal spheres, historians must add a scriptural usage affecting the human images associated with the medieval word *dominium*. When the Lord God cursed Eve for yielding to the Devil's temptation, he decreed (Gen. 3: 16, according to the Douay version of the Vulgate) that "thou shalt be under thy husband's power and he shall have dominion over thee" (Gen. 3: 16 *et sub uiri potestate eris, et ipse dominabitur tui*). The same language of power and dominion authorized by Scripture reinforced notions of lordship at the core of human relationships, of man over woman. Rupert of Deutz, a lifelong monk, observed that of the various curses laid upon Eve such as travail in bearing children, this matter of subjection was the lightest, virtually nothing for chaste and faithful women of good will.[56] Lordship at the domestic level, whatever the naïveté or insensitivity of this monk, was for Rupert a reality so taken for granted that it hardly seemed an imposition and required no defense as divinely sanctioned.

It was in the eleventh century, according to all the available dictionaries and studies, that the term *dominium* acquired a new meaning in society, not lordship but the lands which a lord held directly or in reserve for himself, that is, his demesne, as distinguished from that which he held in fief.[57] This usage presupposed that transformation in the social order by which various public powers, including constraint (*distringere*), had devolved upon local potentates. As a result, *dominium* developed a cluster of new and interrelated meanings, distinguished in modern English as demesne, domain, and lordship.[58] All of them presuppose that lordship takes its meaning less from the proprietary element as such, the lands or peoples possessed, than the person in whom this power or authority inheres, that quality by which one strong man exercises his rule over another,

55. "hoc nomen 'dominium' sepe in philosophia morali accipitur pro potestate qua quis libere potest in actus contrarios, et sic dicunt quod homo est dominus et habet dominium actuum suorum." *Opus nonaginta dierum* i; ed. J. G. Sikes, *Guillelmi de Ockham opera politica* (Manchester, 1940), 1: 307 (where there is a much larger discussion on the various meanings of *dominium*).

56. Rupert, *In Gen.* 3, 21 (*CCCM* 21, 259).

57. *Dictionary of Medieval Latin from British Sources* (London 1986), p. 718 (where a few examples pertaining to royal claims date back to the tenth century); J. F. Niermeyer, *Mediae latinitatis lexicon minus* (Leiden, 1976), p. 353; *Glossarium mediae latinitatis Cataloniae,* in progress (Barcelona, 1960–) 1 (A–D), 1002.

58. Duby, *La société mâconnaise,* pp. 174–76 distinguished a "seigneurie domestique," "seigneurie foncière," and "seigneurie banale." Neither in Latin nor in the various vernacular usages was there, so far as I can determine, any established set of distinctions.

a *senior* over against a *vassus,* a lord over against his peasants. In his study of Picardy Fossier claimed—whatever the danger here of circular argumentation—that one of the few sure ways to identify these potentates with accumulated lands, subject peasantry, and public powers of constraint is to find them addressed as "*dominus*" and their sphere of power identified as a "*dominium.*"[59] On his demesne a *dominus* exercized a form of control over land recognizably different from that over lands held by vassals or rented out to peasants. The sense of that difference generated not only a new and more specific usage of the term *dominium* but also a new word, *dominicatus* or *dominicatura* (especially in Spain), terms which, despite some Carolingian precedents, were essentially eleventh-century constructs.

The notion of territoriality or "domain," of lordship in a region subject to the dominance of some particular lord, developed more slowly. Instances of it remained comparatively rare before the later twelfth century, becoming common only in the thirteenth and fourteenth centuries. When the so-called *Leges Henrici primi* referred to a "witness from another lordship," it probably presumed ties still of a personal rather than a regional sort, but in Champagne by the end of the twelfth century, the entire county was identified as a *dominium* or lordship.[60] In 1232 Frederick II's privilege for the German princes recognized, below the level of princes, noblemen, and ministerials, *domini terre* and people enfeoffed by reason of their *dominium terre.*[61] In time "lordship" came to encompass any region wholly subject to a lord or *senior* (hence *senioritas* and *senioria,* attested from the eleventh century), what would become in the French vernacular a *seigneurie.* In Caxton's English version of Ramon Lull's influential book on chivalry, where all lordship is derived at the outset from God the "lord and souerayne kynge above," his rule over the celestial courts is described as "seygnorye" extending all the way down to the knights who "have power and dominacion over the moyen peple."[62]

The use of "lordship" as an abstract category, taking in a whole range

59. Robert Fossier, *La terre et les hommes en Picardie jusqu'à la fin du XIIIe siècle,* 2 vols. (Paris, 1968) 2: 514ff. Compare Robert Boutruche, *Seigneurie et féodalité,* 2 vols. (Paris, 1959; 1 2nd ed., 1968) 1: 205–6; 2: 286.

60. *Leges Henrici primi,* ed. L. J. Downer (Oxford 1972) c. 48; Michel Bur, *La formation du comté de Champagne, v.950–v.1150* (Nancy, 1977), p. 467.

61. *Constitutio in favorem principum,* c. 7; ed. Ludwig Wieland, *Constitutiones (1198–272), MGH Legum* 4 (Hanover, 1896) 2: 212.

62. "That in lyke wyse owen the kynges prynces and grete lordes to haue puyssaunce and sygnorye upon the knyghtes and the knyghtes by symylytude oughten to have power and dominacion ouer the moyen peple." *The Book of the Ordre of Chyualry, translated and printed by William Caxton,* ed. Alfred T. P. Byles, Early English Text Society, 168 (London, 1926), pp. 1–2.

of social and political relations, developed more slowly still. In all the endless discussions of *regalia* arising from the Investiture Struggle during the early twelfth century, for instance, the word never appeared. Most instances postdate 1200, with the term entering the vocabulary of political theorists in the later thirteenth century. Ptolomy of Lucca, completing Thomas Aquinas's *On the Rule of Princes,* revised the "*potestas*" of Rom. 13: 1 to say matter of factly—and revealingly!—that "all lordship comes from God as the first lord."[63] In the Golden Bull of 1356, lordship ranked among the defining rights and powers inherent in a prince, especially a prince-elector.[64] And in England John Wyclif seized upon the term in his *De civili dominio,* treating lordship in the 1370s as a general political and religious phenomenon extending from God himself down through church and kingdom to a host of lesser lordships. Plainly the differentiation of one meaning of *dominium* from another involved shades of meaning rather than absolute distinctions, with one usage often entailing or assuming another.

Yet the emergence of the word itself, its movement from a form of address to a complex of powers to an abstract political notion after the year 1200, discloses nothing about the sanctions, sacred or otherwise, attached to its usage. For if there was a widespread assumption that all power was of God, there was an equally clear sense that the disordered use of violent force was of the Devil. Here too Augustine stood at the beginning of a long tradition with his oft-quoted quip that without justice kingdoms were little more than "robbers writ large" and his description, in effect, of an illicit lordship in the making.[65] In the tenth century Odo of Cluny offered the image of Gerard of Aurillac, the perfect knight, as anti-type to the gnawing fear (or even certainty) that most *potentes* were "oppressors" and anything but humble and caring.[66] Aggressive lords at all levels in the eleventh century, from local potentates to princes and kings, provoked mostly negative responses. Honorius said about 1100 that warrior lords had little hope of salvation because they lived by plundering.[67]

63. "inde manifeste apparet a Deo omne prouenire dominium sicut a primo dominante." *De regimine principum* 3 1; *Sancti Thomae Aquinatis opera omnia,* 25 vols (Parma, 1845), 17, pp. 250–51. Compare his discussions of "legitimate lordship" in 2: 8–9, pp. 243–45.

64. Thus "principes in principatibus, terris, dominiis et pertinentiis suis" or "libertatibus, iurisdictionibus, iuribus, honoribus seu dominiis principum electorum." *Die Goldene Bulle Kaiser Karls IV. vom Jahre 1356,* ed. Wolfgang D. Fritz, *MGH Fontes iuris germanici antiqui* 11 (Weimar 1972), pp. 64, 69. Benjamin Arnold, *Princes and Territories in Medieval Germany* (Cambridge 1991), pp. 61–73.

65. Augustine, *De civitate Dei* 4, 4; *CC* 47, 101.

66. See Barbara Rosenwein, *Rhinoceros Bound: Cluny in the Tenth Century* (Philadelphia, 1982), pp. 57–83.

67. *L'Elucidarium,* p. 427.

But where then did they fit into the divinely mandated world of lords and subjects, the emerging world of "lordship"? As an evil to be borne, a punishment sent from God? Or an authority to be obeyed? Did allegiance to the Lord Christ implicitly lend authority to all other lords, or only to those few authorities, mostly kings and bishops, who claimed to stand in the place of Christ?

Lordship as unsanctioned and unrestrained violence exercised beyond the divine order, especially against churches and a helpless peasantry: this was the image projected in the eleventh century by those who promoted the Peace of God. The "plundering of warriors and the ruination of the poor" compelled churchmen, as Ademar de Chabannes saw it, to take action themselves,[68] for these "worldly powers" gave the church no peace, invaded sanctuaries, and oppressed poor commoners entrusted to the church. Such violence was anything but sanctioned: by threatening and defrauding churches, they ruined the Sacrifice itself, the ultimate source of sanction.[69] To restore peace and to put down forms of lordship judged destructive, bishops, abbots, and their lay supporters banded together to exercise dominion and wield the material sword themselves. The imperial bishop of Cambrai protested that this was in turn an infraction, a violation of the power vested in public authority.[70] Most churchmen, however, came to see and explain it otherwise: those who broke this peace/truce would incur curses and sanctions (in the negative sense), for on Saturday when the Lord rested, Ivo of Chartres explained to the people of his diocese, they could not be plundering their neighbors and Christ himself in his members; if they observed the written peace to which they had hereby sworn, however, they could expect both material and eternal blessings.[71] The sanctions, both positive and negative, which he and others invoked for peace-keeping and for peace-breaking, were decidedly sacral. They often involved, as here, swearing on relics, and were usually reinforced by an ad hoc assemblage of material force. Two generations into the movement, by roughly the year 1100, public powers began to re-appropriate the pursuit of Peace, in fact or as pretext, to consolidate their authority. In the German

68. Ademar, *Chronicon* 3, 35; ed. Jules Chavanon (Paris, 1897), p. 158; see Harmut Hoffmann, *Gottesfriede und Treuga Dei, MGH,* Schriften 20 (Stuttgart 1964), pp. 26–30 for similar descriptions.

69. Mansi, *Amplissima collectio conciliorum* 19: 509.

70. "Hoc enim non tam impossible quam incongruum uideri respondit, si quod regalis iuris est sibi uendicari presumerent. Hoc etiam modo sanctae aecclesiae statum confundi. . . . Omnes enim communi peccato inuolui, si commento huiusmodi uterentur." *Gesta episcoporum Cameracensium* iii, 27; ed. L. C. Bethmann, *MGH SS* 7 (Hanover, 1844), 474.

71. Ivo, *Epistola* 44; ed. Jean Leclercq, *Correspondance* (Paris, 1949), pp. 182, 184.

Empire, beginning already in 1104 (and in the midst of his struggle against the papacy), the king promulgated the peace and issued sanctions against plunderers, including a penalty clause for those who fled this "judgment" which stipulated that "their lord" (*dominus suus*) should confiscate their benefice or their relatives (*cognati*) their inheritance.[72] Thus peacekeeping eventually enhanced the sanctions attached to the public ruler. Other powers sprung up beyond and within the network of public powers also used the peace to consolidate and in time to sacralize new lordships, both lay and ecclesiastical, claiming for themselves as "peacekeepers" sanctions once reserved for kings and advocates.[73]

The same ironic transition occurred within the Reform movement, it might be noted parenthetically. The earliest and most radical reformers attempted to deny lords any divine sanction over churches or properties not awarded or governed explicitly according to ecclesiastical guidelines. In the end, after successfully separating material and spiritual power in principle and establishing the priority of the spiritual, churchmen, anxious to end a generation of warfare and schism, effectively conceded to rulers who acted according to legal form most of the power they had long possessed, but now with an implicit sanction called the *ius patronatus* or right of patronage. The result at the local level was to confer upon the lord as "founder" or "presenter" the equivalent of a sacred sanction for his continuing domination over the church.

For an image more expressive of lordship as such, historians have turned to that three-part division of the church (later, society) distinguishing among intercessors, warriors, and laborers. The hereditary nobility and ordained churchmen retained a strong interest in distinguishing the obedience and justice owed to *principes* and *praelati* from the shedding of blood done by *milites*, a task that remained suspect within the household of God. For churchmen throughout the eleventh and twelfth centuries, the second figure in this scheme (*pugnatores, agonistae, milites*, etc.) represented a task, not a class of lords. Their whole purpose in ritual blessing or moral admonition was to have swordpower function as a "ministry" supportive of the church or of Christian moral action, most spectacularly in Gregory VII's dream of a "milita of St. Peter" and Urban II's calling out of the First

72. *Constitutiones*, ed. Ludwig Weiland (Hanover 1893) n. 74, p. 125.

73. Hoffmann, *Gottesfriede*, passim; Carl Erdmann, *The Origin of the Idea of Crusade*, tr. Walter Goffart and M. W. Baldwin (Princeton, NJ, 1977); Georges Duby, "Les laïcs et la paix de Dieu," in Duby, *Hommes et structures du moyen âge* (Paris 1973), pp. 227–40; Thomas Bisson, "The Organized Peace in Southern France and Catalonia, ca. 1140–ca. 1233," *AHR* 132 (1977), 290–311.

Crusade. In the 1130s Gerhoch of Reichersberg argued that a *miles* too could follow the Gospel and be saved if he bore the sword rightly as a "minister of God," though the cautions here were plainly more severe than the sanctions.[74] At the end of the century, in a model sermon directed at *milites,* Alan of Lille depicted them as rightly buckling on the sword to restore peace, defend the homeland, and protect the church—but not to pursue gain against their own as plunderers.[75] But whatever qualifications churchmen attached to sanctioning ministry with the sword, their institution of knightly orders, crusader vows, blessings for arms and armies, the cult of chivalry, and so on bespoke more loudly their sanctioning of the task of the *miles*. In the course of the twelfth century notions such as these came ever more frequently to vernacular expression as well.[76]

Deep into the twelfth century, learned discussion about sword power and particularly about the "two swords" was not about two "*potestates*" understood as independent powers, and certainly not about lordship as such, but about two forms of coercion, spiritual and material, two ways of making lordship effective, and above all about when the use of those swords was sanctioned.[77] Churchmen, who could not shed blood or (if they were monks) own property as individuals, could and often did supervise the "proper" use of the material sword. Military coercion became an exercise of lordship sanctioned by the church under certain conditions. Rufinus, in his commentary on Causa 23 of Gratian's *Decretum,* put it very plainly. It is not a sin—note the persistent negative approach to the issue—for laymen to fight for a just cause such as repulsing injury or avenging evil, so long as public powers preside. Clerics, he continued, may not bear arms but under certain conditions can command their use.[78] This influential canonist of the 1150's understood warriors to be "ministering" and not sinning or plundering only when their efforts were sanctioned by public authorities, lay or ecclesiastical. What was sacred and what profane, what

74. "Qui recte gladium exercendo Dei minister est, gladium quasi onus, ordinante Deo, sibi impositium non sine causa portat. Qui autem extra ordinem, non Dei sed suae avariciae minister est, quia in pauperibus uexandis et lucris iniquo mammonae congregandis gladium accipit, nisi legitime poenitendo salvetur, sine dubio flammeo gladio ante paradisam constituto peribit." *De edificio Dei* 43 (*PL* 194: 1301).

75. Alan, *Summa de arte predicatoria* 40 (*PL* 120: 186).

76. Thus Etienne de Fourgères, quoted by Flori, *L'essor de la chevalerie,* p. 317.

77. For this important and complicated field, where much work was done a generation ago, see the summaries (with further literature) in Yves Congar, *L'église de saint Augustin à l'époque moderne* (Paris, 1970), pp. 142–55, 176–97; Friedrich Kempf, *Papsttum und Kaisertum bei Innocenz III* (Rome, 1954); Brian Tierney, "Some Recent Works on the Political Theories of the Medieval Canonists," *Traditio* 10 (1954), 594–625.

78. Rufinus, *Summa decretorum,* ed. Heinrich Singer (Paderborn, 1902), p. 404.

belonged unquestionably to the world of spiritual power and what to the world of earthly power, underwent further refinement in the course of the lengthy twelfth-century dispute between *regnum* and *sacerdotium*. As Stephen Langton put it with remarkable clarity around the year 1200, kings acquired their sword-power from the church in the largest sense, that is, from all the faithful who conferred "rule" upon them, but not from the church in the narrow sense, that is, from hierarchical prelates as such.[79]

The historical complication, as with the inter-related peace and reform movements, was that the function of these warriors (their presumed "ministry") eventually became transformed into the distinguishing mark of a social class: the inherited status of nobleman (*nobilis*) blurred into the task of warrior (*miles*) to become an ever more exclusive caste of "knights." Regional histories have suggested dates varying from the year 1000 (Duby's Mâconnais) to nearly 1200 (the German empire), with the coalescence complete only after the year 1200.[80] What began as an effort to bless and to order a function—the "ministry" of peace-keeping, crusading, and protecting by means of the sword—ended up sanctioning the lordship of a more or less distinct social class. Where Bonizo in the 1090s had regarded warriors as essentially and ideally faithful to lords (*milites dominis suis fidem servare et pro salute eorum et pro republica usque ad mortem decertare*) and Gerhoch in the 1130s had stressed their obligation to obey higher powers (*sui est officii potestatibus sublimioribus subditos esse debere*),[81] Ramon Lull in his book on chivalry made it clear: knights were lords charged with governance of the world.[82] Later medieval authors—without forgetting virtues like fidelity—merged warriors and noblemen into a single lordly group essential to the divine ordering of society.

When after 1200 the notion of lordship emerged with a presumption of divine sanction, it was in large measure because various social powers had appropriated positions once reserved in principle for public officials. They had thereby assumed for themselves the accompanying sanctions, which were often intended originally to accomplish precisely the reverse, to guide and constrain such independent powers. What deserves notice is how haltingly and almost unconsciously that coalescence between material

79. A wonderful passage transcribed by John Baldwin, *Masters, Princes, and Merchants: The Social Views of Peter the Chanter and His Circle*, 2 vols. (Princeton, NJ, 1970), 2: 111.

80. Flori, *L'essor de la chevalerie*, pp. 1–42; see also the essays in *Das Rittertum im Mittelalter*, ed. Arno Borst (Darmstadt, 1976).

81. Bonizo, *Liber de vita christiana*, 2: 43; ed. Perels, p. 56; Gerhoch, *De edificio Dei* 43 (*PL* 194: 1302).

82. *Book of Chyvalrie*, pp. 19–20, 28–30.

force, social class, and sacred sanction proceeded. This shift in attitude toward lordship as a concept in itself and as a part of the divinely sanctioned order is remarkably like that in the gesture for prayer, essential to human intercession of the divine. After 1200 people gradually adopted for prayer to the divine, so most liturgical historians assume, the gestures of submission to the human lord[83]—but with never a word of explanation. Had social lordship sufficiently gained acceptance and an aura of sacred sanction to make such a transference possible?

In their formal writings twelfth-century ecclesiastical authors steadily directed moralizing admonitions at predatory warriors, reserving divine sanctions primarily for recognized or delegated public powers (as the texts above have indicated). The question is whether they ever, beyond moral exhortation, took account of the slippage into private hands of public powers and the claims of those powers to a divine sanction. Did they ever consider lordship in the sense of this broader political fracturing and restructuring? Rarely, it must be said, under the label of "lordship," except in so far as they used this term for demesne or domain. But another term served well for these new lordships: tyranny. This word, too, had a long history going back into antiquity; its associations were nearly all negative, and its basic definitions in Isidore were familiar to most medieval churchmen. Suger of St. Denis, writing in the 1140s, employed it regularly in cases where social historians today might think of "lordship," especially in its more rebellious or autonomous forms. In his life of Louis VI (1108–37) "tyrants" function as various antitypes to the good ruler. Prince Louis first proved his mettle as a young man against the count of Roucy, who preyed upon the churches there (*tirannide fortissimi et tumultuosi baronis*), from whom the prince secured peace (*pacem a prefato tiranno ecclesiis et impetravit et imperavit*).[84] Suger introduced one of Louis's last battles (against Thomas of Marle) with a general statement on the audacity and violence of tyrants, whom kings were pledged by their "duty" (*officium*) to put down with a mighty right arm; his description of tyrannical behavior fit all the more ruthless forms of lordship.[85] Even a cardinal-legate saw fit to move against this tyrant (*eius tyrannidem mucrone beati Petri . . . detruncans*).[86] Such "tyranny" could come in the form of a count (Auvergne), a "wild man" whom the bishop of Clermont asked the royal majesty to restrain

83. Compare the qualifying remarks of G. B. Ladner, "The Gestures of Prayer in Papal Iconography of the Thirteenth and Early Fourteenth Centuries," in Ladner, *Images and Ideas in the Middle Ages* (Rome, 1983), pp. 209–37.

84. Suger, *Vie de Louis VI le Gros*, c. 5; ed. Henri Waquet (Paris, 1929), pp. 24–28.

85. Suger, *Vie*, c. 24, pp. 172–174.

with his sword (*tyrannum effrenatum compescere regiae maiestatis gladio*), the Roman people driving out an elected pope (*a sancta sede eorum tyrannide arceretur*), or all those whom the young king had first to subjugate to defend the weak and the good (*tyrannos potenti uirtute perdomuerat*), for it was the general "mark" of evil rule (*nota tyrannidis et crudelitatis formidine eripit*).[87] By contrast, Suger often used the term "lord" for recognized power, thus the lord pope, or the lord of a castle (*dominus castri se dedere regiae maiestati non differat*),[88] or the king himself on assuming his royal powers and responsibilities.[89]

This portrait of "tyrants" faced down by the king in northern France must be juxtaposed with John of Salisbury's description of "tyrants" a decade later, at the end of his *Policraticus* (VIII cc. 17–23), chapters he probably drafted as a separate tractate, as he did many parts of his "statesman's manual." All attempts to ferret out some cloaked reference to a contemporary ruler have proved unpersuasive.[90] Most scholars now agree that his "doctrine of tyrannicide is purely theoretical, in the sense that John was not proposing it as a plan of action,"[91] one scholar reducing it to the teaching that "tyrants come to a miserable end" and "they are really deserving of it."[92] In other writings John used the term for various evil rulers, greater and lesser, especially the despised German emperor.[93] He also composed a kind of history of tyrants to prove that their end was "misery," concluding with a number of rebellious English lords in Stephen's time, all of whom met unhappy ends and were so remembered to his day.[94] Readers, that is, were led to conceive of "tyrants" primarily as unruly and unsanctioned "lords" like those of the English civil wars[95] and of Louis VI's reign.

The "tyrant," in John's depiction, is a kind of anti-type to the good prince: he oppresses the people by violent lordship (*uiolenta dominatione*), in contrast with the prince who rules according to the laws. The tyrant

86. Suger, *Vie,* cc. 24, 31, pp. 174, 250–56.

87. Suger, *Vie,* cc. 29, 27, 14, 18, pp. 232–34, 200, 84–86, 126.

88. Suger, *Vie,* c. 12, pp. 78, 80.

89. Suger, *Vie,* c. 8, p. 36.

90. A summary of the theories in Cary Nederman, "A Duty to Kill: John of Salisbury's Theory of Tyrannicide," *Review of Politics* 50 (1988), 388, n. 103.

91. Richard H. Rouse and Mary A. Rouse, "John of Salisbury and the Doctrine of Tyrannicide," *Speculum* 42 (1967), 709, despite some dark hints about Henry II (704–9).

92. Jan van Laarhoven, "Thou Shalt NOT Slay a Tyrant! The So-called Theory of John of Salisbury," in *The World of John of Salisbury,* ed. Michael Wilks (Oxford, 1984), pp. 319–41.

93. Van Laarhoven, "So-called Theory," pp. 339–41.

94. *Policraticus* 8, 21; ed. Webb 2: 395.

95. See Hans Liebeschütz, *Mediaeval Humanism in the Life and Writings of John of Salisbury* (London, 1950), pp. 50–55, who came closest to the interpretation I am suggesting.

thinks only how to empty the laws and crush the people in servitude. He is the very image of iniquity, and therefore to be done away with.[96] The will of the tyrant, in casting off the law, becomes itself slave to desire, even as he attempts to impose the yoke of servitude on others. Gideon should be the model for princes: offered the position of lord (*honor dominii*), he refused and instead subjected to the law all those he had liberated from the yoke of servitude.[97] Not only kings (*non soli reges*) but many private individuals as well (*priuatorum plurimi tiranni sunt*), not only lay lords but also ecclesiastical (*siue ecclesiastici siue mundani sint*), under the guise of "duty" turn all their energies toward "tyranny."[98] And who would dare say that such tyrants found in the church should be revered when those in the world deserve their evil ends?[99] John summarized the gospel teaching about not lording it over subjects but rather exercising the "task/duty of ministry" (*sibi uindicet officium ministrandi*). For in human affairs nothing can be more helpful or more harmful than another human being, and among all humans none more helpful than lay or priestly princes and none more harmful than lay or priestly tyrants, with the priestly in each case more harmful or more helpful.[100] What distinguished princes from tyrants was primarily the law (*differentia sola uel maxima*). As the image of divine majesty (*in terris quaedam diuinae maiestatis imago*), evidenced by subjects bending their necks in submission, princes received power from God, and it was not to be resisted. Even when he cruelly raged against subjects, he did so by divine permission and for the subjects' punishment.[101]

All of this—the public and the private, the lay and the churchly, the will to oppression, the repudiation of law—must have read to contemporaries as a perfect cipher for the evolving world of lords and lordship in the early twelfth century; all of it, one would assume, stood well outside divine sanction. Yet these very same tyrants, lay and ecclesiastical, John concedes (*non abnego*) may also act as "ministers of God" through whom evil

96. *Policraticus* 8: 17; ed. Webb 2: 345.

97. "Defertur honor dominii et recusat; legi tamen subicit quos a iugo seruitutis absoluit," *Policraticus* 8, 22; ed. Webb 2: 397.

98. "Nam et in sacerdotio inueniuntur quam plures, id tota agentes ambitione et omnibus artibus eius, ut sub praetextu officii suam possint tirannidem exercere," *Policraticus* 8, 17; ed. Webb 2: 348.

99. "Si enim tirannus secularis iure diuino et humano perimitur, quis tirannum in sacerdotio diligendum censeat aut colendum?" ed. Webb, 2: 357.

100. It is hard to render John's pithy classicizing Latin, which echoes Cicero's *De officiis* 2: 3 at *Policraticus* 8, 23; ed. Webb 2: 401.

101. A more classical statement of what Isidore and the Carolingians also held: "Neque enim potentis est, cum uult [princeps] seuire in subditos, sed diuinae dispensationis pro beneplacito suo punire uel exercere subiectos," ed. Webb, 2: 401.

people are punished and the good tested and corrected.[102] For all power is of God; tyranny refers to the abuse of any power entrusted over subjects, not only that of princes. The power wielded by the tyrant, John says, is therefore in some sense good, even though nothing is worse than tyranny as such.[103] Private tyrants, John goes on, need not be flattered or even killed, because they can readily be restrained by public laws, and the sword cannot be wielded against an ecclesiastical tyrant out of reverence for the sacraments.[104] Remarkably then, and in sum, even "tyrants," though exemplary in their miserable ends, may serve as instruments for the ordained power of God! By that same slippage which allowed conspirators to become sanctioned as peace-keepers, lay investors to become sanctioned as founders and patrons, warriors to become sanctioned as lordly knights, John allowed "tyrants," however reprehensible in themselves and deserving of their unhappy ends, to share in sanctioned power.

In those same years church lawyers were confronted with a teaching from the natural law, equated by Gratian with divine law, which appeared to repudiate that which made lordship possible, namely, property and servitude, for natural law afforded "common possessions to all and a single liberty for all" (*communis omnium possessio et omnium una libertas*).[105] But the realities of lordship were so taken for granted that these lawyers were hardly slowed or forced to reflect critically. Such teachings about community and liberty were declared abrogated by civil law (*nunc enim iure ciuili hic est seruus meus, ille est ager tuus*); they were not binding; they were only inferences, possible goods. Moreover, Rufinus went on to explain, insofar as civil law used force to restrain evil-doers and even reduced some to servitude for relentless rebellion, it merely returned people to the human uprightness of the natural law; so what was lost in sin was now restored in Moses, perfected in the Gospel, and embellished by custom (*in moribus decoratur*).[106] That is, the civil law of servitude bent people back toward the

102. "Ministros Dei tamen tirannos esse non abnego, qui in utroque primatu, scilicet animarum et corporum, iusto suo iudicio esse uoluit per quos punirentur mali et corrigerentur et exercerentur boni. Nam et peccata populi faciunt regnare ypocritam et . . . defectus sacerdotum in populo Dei tirannos induxit." *Policraticus* 8, 18; ed. Webb 2: 358.

103. "Ergo et tiranni potestas bona quidem est, tirannide tamen nichil est peius. Est enim tirannis a Deo concessae homini potestatis abusus. . . . Patet ergo non in solis principibus esse tirannidem, sed omnes esse tirannos qui concessa desuper potestate in subditis abutuntur." ed. Webb 2: 359.

104. Ed. Webb 2: 364.

105. *Decretum* d. 1 c. 7 (= Isidore, *Etymologiae* 5, 4, 1–2).

106. Rufinus, *Summa decretorum*, ed. Singer, pp. 9–10 (though the whole introductory section is relevant). For this topic, the basic work remains Rudolf Weigand, *Die Natur-*

just order of the divinely sanctioned natural law. Other canonists held to a "just servitude" introduced by God himself as punishment for sin, and then worked through the same development from natural law to civil and back to natural. With respect to an original community of property, some canonists, especially from the Parisian school, tried to make sense of it by arguing that God alone had *dominium* over all things, granting human beings only "usage" and making them "*quasi-domini.*"[107] The first man who made exactions from subjects and exercised lordship (identified from Scripture as Nimrod) committed sin against the natural law, but through long usage, Rufinus argued, these proprietary rights had become customary law and were now, as law, above reproach.[108] That is to say, as argued more generally and less legalistically above, custom and usage were understood over time to have conferred sanction.

Theological masters were more uncertain how to deal conceptually with the realities of worldly power, and found no fixed place for it in their systems. Master Peter Lombard's *Four Books of Teachings* (*Sententiae*), compiled at roughly the same time as John's *Policraticus* and Rufinus's commentary, attained paradigmatic status as the standard textbook. He inserted brief remarks on worldly power at the end of a long section on sin (*Sententiae* II.44). He began with a traditional conundrum, whether the power to sin came from God or the Devil; he was inclined to ascribe it, like all other power in the universe, to God. "Another question arises," he continued, "which is not to be passed over in silence." Since all power is of God and he who resists power resists the ordination of God (Rom. 13: 2), it would seem that the Devil's power to effect evil must also be ordained of God and therefore is not to be resisted. To escape this unacceptable conclusion Master Peter introduced a distinction: People are not to resist that in secular power (*de seculari potestate, scilicet rege et principe et huiusmodi*) which has been ordained by God, but they are to resist a prince or the Devil or some other human person insofar as he orders something contrary to God. As his authorities for this traditional view of ordained power he drew upon exegetical materials assembled around Romans 13, and in this backhand way created an opening for future generations of medieval theologians.

Thomas Aquinas's commentary on this passage, expanded upon in

rechtslehre der Legisten und Dekretisten von Irnerius bis Accursius und von Gratian bis Johannes Teutonicus, Münchener Theologische Studien 26 (Munich, 1967), pp. 259–82 on "liberty."

107. The *Summa Monacensis,* a development of the *Summa Parisiensis,* as quoted by Weigand, *Die Naturrechtslehre,* p. 324.

108. Rufinus, *Summa decretorum,* p. 21.

his *Summa* (I 1. 96 aa. 3–4), conceded the existence of numerous unjust lordships, and was careful to ascribe *dominium* to God only insofar as it was good. While the domination of one person over another in coercive lordship and submissive servitude sprang from sin, forms of lordship by which one person directed another were inherent in the human condition, he argued, because humans are naturally social creatures (Aristotle) and one is gifted with greater learning and justice than another. Ranked ordering had obtained in Paradise, as in the choirs of angels. A society without some form of lordship had become, quite literally, unimaginable. In fact by the mid-thirteenth century thinkers used both the word and the concept freely, even in theological arguments. Where Anselm and Bernard in the early twelfth had rarely employed the word outside a legal or political setting, Thomas and later medieval schoolmen deployed it on occasion in their discussion of God's power, even of relations within the Trinity.

Bonaventure, the Franciscan schoolman, master general, and preacher, offered a commentary remarkable for its social detail and assumption of lordship as a notion central to the sacred sanctioning of the social order. He summarized the question Peter Lombard had posed as whether "all lordship is of God" (*utrum omnis potestas dominandi a Deo sit*). And for Bonaventure it was, both in itself and with respect to the person ruled,[109] even as it is God who conferred the quality or strength (*virtus*) of dominating. When someone ruled others justly, his lordship was quite simply of God;[110] when he ruled by violence or trickery, it was of the Devil with respect to the lord's acts and intentions, though not with respect to the person ruled who might be undergoing some test (*bonorum probationem*) or punishment (*malorum punitionem*). There is, in sum, no power of lordship which may be said not to have come from God (*ideo de nulla potentia praesidendi dici potest quod non procedat a Deo*). Even when things seem disordered, the foolish ruling the wise, for instance, one must assume some hidden purpose or just order.

Bonaventure then proceeded to the second question, and explicitly took on Augustine and Gregory's texts about a natural equality, the same ones Rather knew and nearly all medieval thinkers were forced to contend with. Was this lordship therefore instituted in humans by nature or as punishment for sin? To answer, Bonaventure distinguished three forms. The

109. "Concedendum est igitur quod omnis potestas praesidendi secundum id quod est et etiam respectu eius super quem est iusta est et a Deo est. . . ." *In Sent.* II d.44 a.2 q.1: ed. *S. Bonaventurae opera omnia,* ed. 10 vols. (Quarrachi, 1885), 2: 1006.

110. "Quando autem praeest aliquis aliis per iustitiam, tunc illa potestas dominandi, simpliciter loquendo, a Deo est. . . ." *In Sent.* II d.44 a.2. q.2: ed. Quaracchi, 2: 1005.

first and broadest was that by which a person could rule at will, thus as lord of his own possessions, something common to every state of human nature, the primordial, the fallen, and the glorified.[111] A second form of lordship consisted in that superiority of power by which someone has command over another rational human being. This too existed in both the primordial and the fallen states, as in a man ruling a woman or a father his son, though it will not persist into the glorified state. The third, lordship in the *strict* sense, Bonaventure explains, to which servitude corresponds, is the power of coercing subjects and restricting their liberty; this was in fact the result of punishment, and therefore peculiar to the fallen human nature.[112] Bonaventure then countered several objections which would have projected this form of lordship back into the primordial state. With respect to the male-female relationship, he noted that though man was called the "head" (1 Cor. 11: 3, Eph. 5: 23) of the woman, he was not called her "lord"—thus making the form of address a crucial component of his argument. She was made originally to be his companion (*socia*), not his maid or his mistress (*ancilla, domina*). With respect to that lordship inherent in social or political office (*quod dominium est proprietas dignitatis*), Bonaventure declared that while this might seem honorable or empowering to the person ruling (*proprietas dignitatis in eo qui praesidet*), it was dishonoring to the person ruled (*indignitatem tamen dicit in eo qui subest*). In the relationship of one rational being to another it represented something unnatural, a penalty for sin (*quodammodo praeternaturaliter, uidelicet in punitionem peccati*). With respect to lordship and servitude as necessary to preserve a certain natural order, Bonaventure repeated points held as well by the lawyers: in the primordial state all was held in common, in the fallen state private property was introduced to quell strife; in the primordial state humans were equal, in the fallen state one person was subjected or made servant to another so that the wicked could be restrained and the good defended. For if there were no lordships to constrain the evil (*huiusmodi dominia coercentia malos*), one person would oppress another and people could not live together. Throughout the same ambiguity persisted: lordship in the broad

111. "Largissime dominandi potestas dicitur respectu omnis rei qua homo potest ad libitum et uotum suum uti, et hoc modo dicitur homo esse dominus possessionum suarum siue mobilium siue immobilium. . . . Primo modo potestas dominandi communis est omni statui. . . . *In Sent.* II d.44 a.2 q.2: ed. Quarrachi, 2: 1008.

112. "Tertio modo potestas dominandi dicitur potestas coercendi subditos, et haec potestas dicit quondam arctationem libertatis, et *talis potestas dominandi proprie dicitur dominium* [my emphasis], cui respondet seruitus. . . . Inest enim ei secundum culpae punitionem, non secundum naturae institutionem, et hoc quia seruitus sibi correspondens . . . est poena peccati," ed. Quarrachi, 2: 1008.

sense as inherent in the nature of things; lordship in the "strict" sense as a result of sin but essential to preserving order and restraining evil. Bonaventure's entire discussion, though rooted in Romans 13, was not of *potestas* but of *dominium* and the *potestas dominandi*. Lordship had become the common social coin, even for learned theologians.

The message was simple enough that most people must have understood it, even if they construed it more as some mysterious fate or bad fortune than as the providential ordering of the biblical God. Yet the broad and abstract notion rested ultimately upon the specific power exercised by individual *domini*, within their households, on their lands, over their men, and in government. Stated most simply, lordship extended to anything over which a lord could exert his will, from land and rights to serfs and women, or still more concretely, to any relationship requiring that a person be addressed as "lord," from the lord pope in Rome to the lord of the manor, from the lord priest of the village to the lord of a household. Through most of the eleventh and twelfth centuries, the world of lordship as such suggested too much of blood and greed, tyrannical power rather than princely law. At some point after the year 1200—when village lords had become "patrons" of the parish and peacekeepers coopted as public officials, when warriors and noblemen had merged to become "knights," when the autonomous status of earthly kingdoms had gained grudging recognition from churchmen, when schoolmen had begun to think about the political order anew, when lordship had become a common reality for everyone including theologians—the language and even the gestures of lordship imperceptibly crept into the language of theology, of prayer, and of political reflection. It was understood, in a wicked world, as both regrettably necessary and divinely sanctioned. There was no revolutionary cultural moment, no great new visionary or intellectual representation of medieval society. But the social order of lordship was fit no less remarkably into the general perception of divine lordship.

John W. Williams

10. León: The Iconography of the Capital

In Legionensi civitate unde regnum ducitur[1]

Among the earliest of Romanesque tympana is one over the door opening into the southern aisle of the church of San Isidoro in León. At first glance the choice of the ancient theme of the Agnus Dei seems to reflect the pioneering state in the early twelfth century of the tradition of figured tympana. The pairing on the central axis of the Lamb and the Offering of Isaac apparently establishes a eucharistic iconography of a type which was to remain marginal for such public settings. However, when the relief is read across its horizontal axis a theme of far different import emerges. Abraham is the key figure in an iconography that is decidedly nonsacramental. Sarah is seated at the right near her son Isaac, who rides off to Moriah. She balances in the tympanum and in the scales of divine economy Hagar and her son Ishmael, the warrior mounted at her right. Abraham's offering sealed God's final election of the Chosen and elicited the Almighty's pledge that "your descendants shall possess the gates of their enemies" (Gen. 22: 17), a promise recalled yearly in the Vigil of Easter in the liturgy in which the Leonese rulers had been raised.[2] The election set in motion a salvational scheme cast in terms of genealogy. Hagar and Ishmael belonged, in fact, to that genealogy, but in an outlaw branch doomed to defeat. In his submission Isaac assumes the role, in prefiguration, of the sacrificial Lamb. In sharp contrast, his half brother Ishmael aggressively aims an arrow at the Lamb. Through his action and by his act of shooting while riding *a la jinete* Ishmael personifies the pagan conquerors of Andalusia whom the chronicles of Astur-León habitually referred to as Agarenes and Ishmaelites, in accordance with the ancient belief that these outcasts were the

1. This is the phrase used in the *Chronica Adefonsi Imperatoris* when Alfonso Raimúndez arrived in the capital to assume the throne vacated by his mother Urraca's death in 1126, ed. Luis Sánchez Belda (Madrid, 1950), 1:1, p. 5.

2. *Liber Commicus*, ed. Justo Pérez de Urbel and A. González y Ruíz-Zorrilla (Madrid, 1950), 2, pp. 371–72.

progenitors of the Arab race.[3] While it is true that the Lamb is based on the New Testament, the pivotal figure, both in terms of composition and theme, is the patriarch Abraham. In depending on the Old Testament, the Leonese tympanum was one of the least canonical by the iconographic standards that came to prevail. However, unorthodox as it was in comparison with the development of tympanum iconography, our relief could scarcely be more apt for the principal entrance of the palatine church of the capital of the kingdom of León, for through the intersection of Hispanic traditions, claims to a special authority and responsibility within the Peninsula came to be identified with León and hence with the genealogy of a particular family and place. From this fact emerged the concept of the capital as a self-conscious emblem of that authority, and an artistic program to make this concept obvious.

If the medieval idea of the capital is less easy to circumscribe than the modern one,[4] the capital in the sense of fixed, urban, sites that served as the actual, principal, seats of power is not debatable. Credentials of various sorts such as metropolitan status may be evoked for exclusionary purposes; ephemerality may have been the fate of all but a few, but capitals were not planned with that in mind. Monumentalization, the erection of buildings and the fashioning of objects that communicate through conventional iconographies but also serve as visible signs of wealth and the command of craft, is a mode of projecting authority of considerable power, yet often unrecognized in discussions of the capital.[5] León, the capital of Astur-León, registered its identity as seat of authority by accumulating under Fernando

3. "Sarraceni perberse se putant esse ex Sarra; uerius Agareni ab Agar et Smaelite ab Smael filio Abraam et Agar," *Chronica Albeldensia,* 16, in *Crónicas asturianas,* ed. J. Gil Fernández, J. L. Moralejo, and J. I. Ruíz de la Peña (Oviedo, 1985), p. 181. For the iconography of this tympanum see John Williams, "Generationes Abrahae: Reconquest Iconography in León," *Gesta* 16, 2 (1977), 3–14.

4. Among recent studies are Eugen Ewig, "Résidence et capitale pendant le haut moyen age," *RH* 87 (1963), 25–72. More restrictive is Carlrichard Brühl, "Remarques sur les notions de 'Capitale' et de 'Résidence' pendant le haut moyen âge," *Journal des savants* (1967), 193–215; Brühl, "Zum Hauptstadtproblem im frühen Mittelalter," *Festschrift für Harald Keller* (Darmstadt, 1963), pp. 45–70. For Spain, see José María Lacarra, "Panorama de la historia urbana en la península ibérica desde el siglo V al X," in *La città nell'alto medioevo,* Settimane di studio del Centro italiano di Studi sull'alto Medioevo, 6, 1958 (Spoleto, 1959), pp. 319–55; Claudio Sánchez Albornoz, "Sede regia y solio real en el reino asturleonés," *Asturiensia medievalia* 3 (1979), 75–86; Lauro Olmos Enciso, "Los conjuntos palatinos en el contexto de la topografía urbana altomedieval de la península ibérica,' in *Arqueología medieval española,* II Congreso, Madrid, 19–24 January 1987 (Madrid, 1987), 2: 346–352.

5. For Speyer as this type of "capital" in the eleventh century see Stefan Weinfurter, "Herrschaftslegitimation und Königsautorität im Wandel: Die Salier und ihr Dom zu Speyer," in *Die Salier und das Reich I: Salier, Adel und Reichsverfassung,* ed. Stefan Weinfurter and Jelmuth Kluger (Sigmaringen, 1991), pp. 55–96. I thank Benjamin Arnold for leading me to this article.

I (†1065) and his successors a panoply of attributes that distinguished the city effectively from mere royal residence. Those attributes that were significant were a royal palace, a specially favored palatine church that served a special cult, a dynastic cemetery, and a significant production of luxuriously crafted objects sponsored by the ruler, even if not all objects ended up in a treasury on the palatine site. Through their identification of the ruler as a patron of royal munificence, these objects served as *Herrschaftszeichen*.[6] A fundamental step in the process of establishing León as a capital had been taken when Ordoño II (914–24) transferred the capital of the Asturias to León from Oviedo and installed a bishop on the site where the cathedral still stands. But with the criteria I have proposed, the city of León became a capital only under Fernando I, ruler of the kingdom of Astur-León from 1038 to 1065.

Fernando was crowned and anointed, in the Visigothic manner, king of León on 22 June 1038 in the capital's cathedral. Since 1029 he had been count, then briefly the first king, of Castile. His Leonese ascendancy was the result of his marriage in 1032 to Sancha, the Leonese *infanta,* and the death of her brother Vermudo in battle with Fernando on 4 September 1037. Fernando moved into a palace on the north side of the city. We do not know much about it; there are no material remains and its very location can only be deduced. In the tenth century the palace had been moved from its initial installation in the remains of the Roman baths next to the east wall to a site against the south wall.[7] Probably as the result of the devastations visited on the city by Muslim attacks in the late tenth and early eleventh centuries, the palatine complex was then shifted into the northern sector when Alfonso V restored the city early in the eleventh century. This new palace would have been integral with the present church of San Isidoro, for it was served by the church of St. John the Baptist. No remains of this church have been discovered, but charters and chronicles put them close together. Under Fernando the role of palace church would be taken over by a new church on, it would seem, the same site. Although we have only a presumption of it, part of the palace as it expanded under Fernando's successors is available for inspection, as we shall see.

With Fernando's new church we may be more specific. Its dedication,

6. See generally Percy Ernst Schramm, *Herrschaftszeichen und Staatssymbolik,* 3 vols. (Stuttgart, 1954–1956); and Schramm, *Denkmale der deutschen Könige und Kaiser* (with Florentine Mütherich) (Munich, 1962). For France, see Danielle Gaborit-Chopin, *Regalia: les instruments du sacre des rois de France* (Paris, 1987); Gaborit-Chopin et al., eds., *Le trésor de Saint-Denis,* Musée du Louvre, Paris, 12 March–17 June, 1991 (Paris, 1991).

7. *Sampiro: su crónica y la monarquía leonesa en el siglo X,* ed. Justo Pérez de Urbel (Madrid, 1952), p. 311.

an occasion attended by seven bishops of the realm and abbots of the important Galician and Castilian monasteries, took place on 21 December 1063.[8] Some of its fabric survives as parts of the north and west walls of the actual basilica of San Isidoro in León. These portions plus the foundations lying beneath the floor permit a reliable reconstruction of Fernando's new palatine church.[9] We are, moreover, extraordinarily well informed about the circumstances surrounding the new palatine complex, for a detailed account appears in an early twelfth-century chronicle termed the *Historia Silense,* a work announcing itself as a biography of Alfonso VI but which actually focuses on his father, Fernando. The assignment of the *Silense* to an author from Sahagún, the great Leonese monastery so favored by Fernando and his son Alfonso VI, is far preferable, as José M. Canal has shown, to the traditional one of Santo Domingo de Silos.[10] With the *Silense* we are close to the Leonese court. Although the dedication of the new church coincided with the creation of a major new cult around the figure of St. Isidore of Seville, the initiative for its construction stemmed not from the arrival of his body but from a different decision, that to create a dynastic cemetery. The *Silense* is explicit on this point and on Sancha's role in it:

> Seeking an audience with the lord King, Queen Sancha persuaded him to make a church in the cemetery of the kings in León, where their bodies ought to be interred in state. For King Fernando had originally decreed his burial would be in Oña, a place he always loved, or in the church of San Pedro de Arlanza. But since her father, Alfonso of blessed memory, rested in Christ in the royal cemetery of León as did the most serene king Vermudo, her brother, Queen Sancha labored hard that she and her husband might be buried with them after death. Acceding to the petition of his faithful wife, the king ordered builders assiduously to work on such a worthy task.[11]

San Isidoro is today possessed of a splendid narthex of six vaulted bays called since the eighteenth century the "Pantheon"[12] (see Figure 1).

8. Those who presided also witnessed the charter of gift with which he endowed the new church on the same day. See *Colección diplomática de Fernando I (1037–1065),* ed. Pilar Blanco Lozano (León, 1987), pp. 169–72. Peter of Le Puy also was present, probably on his way to or from Santiago de Compostela.

9. John Williams, "San Isidoro in León: Evidence for a New History," *Art Bulletin* 55 (1973), 171–84, esp. 171–72. For the history of the site see Walter Muir Whitehill, *Spanish Romanesque Architecture of the Eleventh Century* (Oxford 1939; reprint 1968), pp. 143–54.

10. José M. Canal Sánchez-Pagín, "Crónica Silense or Crónica Domnis Sanctis?" *Cuadernos de Historia de España,* 63–64 (1980), 94–103. For the text see *Historia Silense,* ed. Justo Pérez de Urbel and A. González Ruíz-Zorrilla (Madrid, 1959). Future references to the *Silense* will be to this edition.

11. *Silense,* pp. 197–98.

12. The designation "Pantheon" was introduced in Spain with the royal mausoleum of the Escorial. The León example was called originally the capilla de Santa Catalina or the Capilla Real.

Figure 1. San Isidoro de León. Section of Pantheon of the Kings, with tower and part of palace above. Property of the author.

Some of the dozens of tombs of members of the Leonese royal families of the eleventh and twelfth centuries which filled it are still found there. Although for years this vaulted narthex was seen as the very funerary chapel built by Fernando to honor Sancha's request, modern scholarship tends to reject such a precocious date.[13] We do not know by what formal means Fernando's and Sancha's royal cemetery was accommodated. Perhaps it occupied part of the space eventually covered by the actual Pantheon and was only updated, with a French vocabulary, as we shall see, by his son and daughter. At any rate, it is difficult to imagine that a dynastic cemetery was not part of Fernando's complex. Indeed, it is central to it in the *Silense* account.

The day following the dedication Fernando and Sancha gave to the church property and church furnishings of a scope that made clear the extraordinary nature of the palatine center. The list of gifts was headed by an altar frontal of pure gold encrusted with emeralds and sapphires, followed by three silver frontals, three golden votive crowns, two others of the regalia type, including that being worn at the moment of the gift, a crown presumably resembling that worn by Fernando in the frontispiece of the Diurnal given in 1055 (see Figure 2 below),[14] a chalice and paten of gold and gems, two censers of the same precious metal and a gold Cross studded with jewels and enamels. The list continues with numerous luxury items, including a number of textiles of Muslim manufacture.[15]

Of all these items, only the "ivory cross with the effigy of the crucified Lord" with the names of Fernando and Sancha is certainly identifiable today.[16] Other objects, such as the gold and ivory casket of Saints John the Baptist and Pelagius,[17] an ivory casket with an unusual iconography of the Beatitudes,[18] and an ivory plaque in the Louvre with a Majesty and SS.

13. See John Williams, "San Isidoro in León."

14. Pedro de Palol and Max Hirmer, *Early Medieval Art in Spain* (London, 1967), pl. 19.

15. Archivo de la Real Colegiata de San Isidoro. See *Colección diplomática de Fernando I*, pp. 166–72. This charter of donation is considered by the editor as a faithful copy dating from only a short time after the event. It was witnessed by those who had participated in the dedication of the new church.

16. For items of the treasury of San Isidoro see now John W. Williams, "León and the Beginnings of Spanish Romanesque," in *Art of Medieval Spain, A.D. 500–1200* (New York, 1993), pp. 167–73, cat. nos. 109–113, 118, 120, 143.

17. W. W. S. Cook and José Gudiol Ricart, *Ars Hispaniae* (Madrid, 1950), 6: figs. 269, 270. This had been given earlier, in 1059, as we know from an inscription removed during the Napoleonic occupation of San Isidoro. See M. Gómez Moreno, *Catálogo monumental de España: Provincia de León* (Madrid, 1925), p. 193.

18. Julie Harris, "The Beatitudes Casket in Madrid's Museo Arqueológico: Its Iconography and Content," *Zeitschrift für Kunstgeschichte* 53 (1990), 134–39.

Peter and Paul[19] cannot be easily identified among the objects of the translation gift, but were, at any rate, the result of the largesse of Fernando and Sancha, which had begun at least by 1047 when they gave a lavish copy of the Commentary on the Apocalypse by Beatus of Liébana.[20] All these ivories are so homogeneous stylistically that a Leonese ivory workshop of royal sponsorship must be assumed. To be sure, Córdoba had ceased to be such only a half century earlier, but this is an unusual phenomenon for Christian kingdoms anywhere. It indicates a peculiar concentration of patronage of the kind we associate with such imperial centers as Aachen and, in the tenth and eleventh century, with the Ottonians. An Ottonian origin for the Leonese ivory style has, in fact, been proposed,[21] but it is difficult to conclude from comparisons with such Ottonian exemplars as the Echternach Master's that German workers were involved. A North French source has been advanced for the inhabited vinescroll of the cross.[22] In any event, these works seem to be based on transpyrenean models.

When we turn to the casket which received the remains of Isidore, the Ottonian connection is not debatable. This arca[23] is a gilt silver casket now displaying Genesis reliefs of the Formation of Adam, the Fall of Adam and Eve, the Admonishment of Adam and Eve, and the dressing of Adam and Eve, having lost the Naming of the Animals and the Formation of Eve, whose inscriptions survive. The ruler, bareheaded and seemingly in a non-regal, penitential guise, completes the ensemble.[24] The epigraphy

19. See Cook and Gudiol Ricart, *Ars hispaniae* 6: fig. 273. From its size and proportions we may suppose it was carved as part of the cover of the great Bible of 960 at San Isidoro (Cod. 2), which Fernando had probably taken from the Castilian monastery of Valeranica.

20. Biblioteca Nacional, Vitr. 14–2; John W. Williams, *The Illustrated Beatus: A Corpus of Illustrations of the Commentary on the Apocalypse*, 5 vols. (London, 1994–), 3 no. 11 [in press].

21. Robb, "Capitals," 172–73.

22. Marlene Park, "The Crucifix of Fernando and Sancha in its Relationship to North French Manuscripts," *Journal of the Warburg and Courtauld Institutes* 36 (1973), 77–91.

23. Palol and Hirmer, *Early Medieval Art*, pls. 71–73. See María Jesus Astorga Redondo, *El Arca de San Isidoro: historia de un relicario* (León, 1990); Manuel Gómez Moreno, "El Arca de las reliquias de San Isidoro," *Archivo español de arte y arqueología* 8 (1932), 205–12; John Williams, "Tours and the Early Medieval Art of Spain," in *Florilegium in honorem Carl Nordenfalk octogenarium contextum*, (Stockholm, 1987), pp. 197–208, esp. 203–4. Ambrosio de Morales, *Viage por orden del rey d. Phelipe III a los reynos de León y Galicia y principado de Asturias* [1572] (Madrid, 1765 [Oviedo, 1977]), pp. 46–47, described a much larger gold reliquary of San Isidoro formerly on the high altar and attributed it to Fernando. It was c. 5.5 ft. wide and c. 1.5 ft. tall, with figures of Christ in Majesty and the Apostles, with enamel medallions with figures. See also Risco, *Historia de la ciudad y corte de León y sus reyes* (Madrid, 1792), 2: pp. 145–46.

24. See Karl Werckmeister, "The First Romanesque Beatus Manuscripts and the Liturgy of Death," in *Actas del simposio para el estudio de los codices del "Comentario al Apocalipsis" de Beato de Liebana*, 1** (Madrid, 1980), pp. 167–92, for the penitential nature of this figure. The lid has the effigies of a crowned king with four attendants. Gómez-Moreno (Manuel Gómez-

of the inscriptions is outside of the Leonese traditions,[25] and both style and iconography point to an Ottonian source. I have speculated elsewhere that Hugh of Cluny was the agent linking Ottonian artistic resources and Leonese consumption.[26]

With the treasury of Fernando and Sancha it is possible to speak of a "first Romanesque style" in northern Spain, related to currents north of the Pyrenees.[27] Their church, however, employed a distinctly Spanish style. When the first Leonese palatine church, San Salvador, was built by Ramiro II near the south wall of León c. 982, the "Mozarabic" style with its references to the vocabulary of Islamic architecture had been employed as a matter of course.[28] However, the best parallel for Fernando's church is the vaulted church of San Salvador de Valdediós built by Alfonso III more than a century and a half earlier, in 893, near the Cantabrican coast.[29] In its shape and fabric, therefore, the building proclaimed a kinship with royal building as it had been practiced by the Asturian kings. Moreover, the idea of a royal cemetery, a "Pantheon," could be traced back most certainly and in similar urban, palatine, capitaline, terms to Alfonso II (†842), who had erected a funerary chapel dedicated to Mary next to the Cathedral of San Salvador in his new capital at the end of the eighth century.[30] Royal burial took place in a room in the western end of the nave. At the heart of a dynastic cemetery is a genealogy. Fernando chose to attach himself to a dynastic tree with traditions that were crucial, as we shall see, to the establishment of his capital. In effect, the appeal by Sancha resulted in Fernando's discarding the Castilian identity imposed on him by his father when Sancho

---

Moreno and Vázquez de Parga, "En torno al crucifijo de los reyes Fernando y Sancha," in *España en la crisis del arte europeo* [Madrid, 1968], pp. 79–83) identified this scene as Sancho Mayor with his four sons, and the crownless effigy on the side as Sancho's father, García of Navarre. This conclusion cannot be dismissed out of hand, but see the next note.

25. Vicente García Lobo, "Las inscripciones medievales de San Isidoro de León," in *Santo Martino de León*. Ponencias del I Congreso internacional sobre Santo Martino en el VIII centenario de su obra literaria, 1185–1985 (León, 1987), pp. 373–98, esp. 377, 382, 393, characterized the epigraphy as "carolina" and "Catalan o ultrapyrenaica" and dated it to c.1063.

26. John Williams, "Cluny and Spain," *Gesta* 27 (1988), 93–101, esp. 203–5.

27. The label "premier art roman" traditionally belongs, of course, to the architecture of the eleventh century in Italy, Gaul, and Catalonia.

28. See Manuel Gómez-Moreno, *Iglesias mozárabes* (Madrid, 1919), pp. 253–59.

29. Williams, "San Isidoro," 173.

30. Pedro de Madrazo, "La primitiva basílica de Sta. María del Rey Casto y su real panteón," *Boletín de la Real Academia de la Historia,* 16 (1890), 177–81. According to later claims King Silo (774–83) planned a "pantheon" for the narthex of the church of his residence at Pravia, but it seems doubtful. For this church after excavations see José Menéndez Pidal in *Actas del Simposio para el estudio de los códices del "Comentario al Apocalipsis" de Beato de Liébana,* 1**, pp. 281–97.

gave Fernando the eastern part of his realm, and assumed a Leonese one.[31] This is marked by his rejection of burial in one of the great isolated Castilian monasteries, Oña, where he had interred his own father in 1035, or San Pedro de Arlanza. The existence of these options, in particular interment of Sancha at Oña in western Castile, the first of this Navarrese family to lie there, testifies to the absence of any concept of Pantheon on the part of Fernando's patrilineal side.

In attaching himself to the Asturian line, Fernando engaged a tradition reflected in the use of imperial titles in charters of Astur-León beginning in the tenth century. This usage gave rise to a substantial modern literature.[32] Although Leonese imperialism has virtually disappeared from recent histories, even being explicitly denounced as an invention of the "nationalism" of the "historical-romantic school,"[33] the appearance of imperial terminology in allusions to Leonese royalty, and virtually exclusively to them, is a fact even if the precise meaning of the concept reflected by this language is elusive. Most discussions of Leonese "imperialism" have invoked two other concepts which are equally hard to render precise. One is Neo-Gothicism, the quest for a restoration of a unified Christian Spain as it had existed before the invasion of the Muslims. This ideology was invoked as early as 881 when the *Chronica albeldense* described the capital of Oviedo as it was founded by Alfonso II: "omnemque gotorum ordinem, sicuti Toleto fuerat, tam in eclesia quam palatio in Ouetao cuncta statuit."[34] The other is the Reconquest, the effective corollary of the Neo-Gothic ideal of a restored Christian Spain. There are reasons for thinking Fernando was conscious of both of these aspects of the "imperial" phenomenon. Under him, beginning in 1056, military campaigns were successfully directed against Muslim strongholds at all points of the compass: Viseo to the west, Valencia to the east, Zaragoza to the north, and Sevilla to the south. To be sure, these conquests were part of a policy of collecting tribute rather than of reoccupation, and rulers other than the Leonese also

31. See Charles Julian Bishko, "Fernando I and the Origins of the Leonese-Castilian Alliance with Cluny," *Studies in Medieval Spanish Frontier History* (London, 1980), Study II, p. 69, for the part played in this reorientation by Fernando's defeat of his elder, Navarrese brother, García at Atapuerca in September 1054.

32. See, for example, Ramón Menéndez Pidal, *El imperio hispánico y los cinco reinos* (Madrid, 1950); José Antonio Maravall, *El concepto de España en la edad media* (Madrid, 1954), pp. 427–86; Hermann J. Hüffer, "Die mittelalterliche spanische Kaiseridee," in *Etudios dedicados a Menéndez Pidal,* 7 vols. (Madrid, 1950–1962), 5: 361–95.

33. Antonio Ubieto et al., *Introducción a la historia de España,* 14th ed. (Barcelona, 1983), p. 122.

34. *Chronica Albeldensia,* pp. 174, 249.

attempted to wrest territory from Muslims. However, it is a striking fact that Fernando's aggressive campaigns fell in the last decade of his life, the one that saw the establishment of the "imperial" capital. That decade began in 1055 at Coyanza (Valencia de Don Juan), where both Fernando and Sancha convened a council, "cum episcopis et abbatibus et totius nostri regni optimatibus," "ad restaurationem nostre Christianitatis."[35] The council, with the Navarrese bishops of Pamplona and Nájera as well as those from León and Castile, represented a renewal of conciliar activity of a national kind, inspired by a desire to "restore the traditional discipline of the Spanish church."[36] At the same time, in its acknowledgment of the Benedictine as well as the Isidoran monastic customs and other concerns, the Council was not exclusively conservative.[37] The transpyrenean dimension of Fernando's new ambitions is registered artistically too in this same year, 1055, when Sancha commissioned a luxurious prayer book (Santiago de Compostela, Bibl. Universitaria Res. 1; see Figure 2) whose illumination introduces the Romanesque style to northern Spain. The nature of the change within the royal scriptorium is measurable because it contained an elaborate Alpha page based on that of a Beatus Commentary carried out for the royal couple eight years earlier.[38] This was two years after Fernando's first contacts with Cluny, and the beginning of an association that implicitly acknowledged the spiritual headship of the great Burgundian abbey, while leaving intact the notion of Leonese imperialism, a tradition jeopardized by papal claims to hegemony in the peninsula.[39] Probably in the very year the new palatine church was dedicated and endowed, enormous sums of Leonese gold began to be channeled to the Burgundian abbey. In acknowledgment, Cluny's liturgical commemoration of the Leonese royal family would match that accorded the Holy Roman Emperors.[40]

---

35. Alfonso García Gallo, "El Concilio de Coyanza; contribución al estudio del derecho canónico español en la alta edad media," *Anuario de Historia del Derecho Español* 20 (1950), 275–633, esp. 353, 364.

36. In the interpretation of García Gallo, "El Concilio," 630.

37. See Bishko, "Fernando I and Cluny," 26–27.

38. Manuel Gómez-Moreno, *El arte románico español: esquema de un libro* (Madrid, 1934), pl. I (Beatus of 1047, f. 6), pl. II (Diurnal, f. 1); Perrier, "Spanische Kleinkunst," figs. 46, 45.

39. See Bishko, "Fernando I and Cluny," passim, esp. 80.

40. Charles Julian Bishko, "Liturgical Intercession at Cluny for the King-Emperors of León," *Studia monástica* 3 (1961), 53–76, in Bishko, *Spanish and Portuguese Monastic History, 600–1300* (London, 1984). While this instance of imperial "rivalry" is well documented, another, in which Henry III protested Fernando's use of the imperial title at a council in Florence or Tours in 1050 or 1055 depends solely, it seems, on Juan de Mariana's late-sixteenth-century *Historia de España* (Toledo, 1601, Latin version 1592), which in turn seems to have drawn on literary inventions; see Ramón Menéndez-Pidal, *La España del Cid*, 5th ed., 2 vols.

Figure 2. Prayer Book of Fernando and Sancha of León: the King and Queen with the book's scribe (Petrus) or painter (Fructuosus). Santiago de Compostela, Biblioteca Universitaria Ms. Res. 1, fol. 3v. Copyright © 1993 by the Metropolitan Museum of Art. Reproduced by permission of the Metropolitan Museum of Art.

Although his campaigns never freed the ancient Visigothic capital itself, Fernando put an emphatic Neo-Gothic stamp on his capital by moving the body of St. Isidore from Seville to León and inaugurating around it a prominent, and to a real extent new, cult. This possibility came as a result of Fernando's successful campaign of the summer of 1063, the outcome of which is recorded in some detail in the *Silense*. Al-Mutadid of Seville agreed to yield up not only gold, but the body of a Sevillian saint as well. Fernando consulted with the *curia ordinaria* while still encamped at Mérida, and asked for the body of Santa Justa,[41] one of two sisters martyred in Seville around 300. An important embassy consisting of Alvitus and Ordoño, bishops of León and Astorga respectively, and count Muñoz was sent to recover it and bear it to León. In the passion apparently composed not long after their deaths at the end of the third century, Justa and her sister were buried in the cemetery outside Seville.[42] Then, after three days of prayer by Bishop Alvitus, Isidore appeared, identified himself, exposed his own tomb by cracking open the floor with his staff, and offered his body as a fitting substitute for Justa's.

On the surface, it would appear that the visit to Seville resurrected the name of its most powerful prelate. It is possible that Isidore's body had been lost, for it is likely his tomb was displaced when the first principal mosque was erected in Seville in the ninth century. There is no reliable reference to the location of Isidore's tomb. A poetic epitaph recorded in a (northern?) Spanish manuscript written c. 800 indicates that Isidore had been buried with his siblings, Leander and Florentina.[43] In the brief but contemporary biography of Isidore by Redemptus, the final days and the death of Isidore are recounted in some detail. Since the setting is the church of St. Vincent where Isidore had a cell, and no removal to another site is referred to, burial within St. Vincent's is implied.[44] Unresolved, as well, is the identification of the cathedral of Seville. In 830 St. Vincent's became the

---

(Madrid, 1956) 2: 670–71. Nevertheless, the episode is included in Mansi (19: 839–840) and Hefele-Leclercq (C. J. Hefele and H. Leclercq, *Histoire des conciles,* 20 vols. [Paris, 1907–38], 4^2, 1117).

41. *Silense,* 198. We learn that the consultation and decision was made before returning to León from the diploma in which Fernando rewarded Bishop Ordoño of Astorga for his services in recovering the body, *Colección diplomática de Fernando I,* no. 67, pp. 173–75.

42. Angel Fábrega Grau, *Pasionario hispánico,* 1 (Madrid, 1953): 131–36; 2 (1955): 296–97.

43. BN, Ms. lat. 8093. Item 5. I am grateful to Ann Boylan for describing this manuscript for me. For the epitaph see J. B. de Rossi, *Inscriptiones christianae Urbis Romae,* 2 vols. (Rome, 1867–88), 2: 296–97; José Vives, *Inscripciones cristianas de la España romana y visigoda,* (Barcelona, 1969), no. 272, pp. 80–81.

44. *PL* 81, 30–31.

site of the first principal mosque of Seville, a fact that suggests, by analogy with the pattern of Córdoba and Toledo, that it was indeed the cathedral.[45] Bishop Isidore's burial there would seem logical, as would Leander's. With the building of the mosque in 830 the original tomb would have been disturbed. Perhaps the tradition whereby Leander and Florentina were buried in the church of SS. Justa and Rufina, accepted in the *Bibliotheca Sanctorum,*[46] records the outcome of their dislocation.[47] If Isidore's body had also been moved there, the coincidence of location would lend a certain level of plausibility to the narrative in the *Silense.*

Still, the *Silense*'s translation scenario with its tale of frustration seems patently an attempt to cover the shift from Justa to Isidore by connecting St. Isidore himself with the decision. The need for such a contrivance, if Isidore's body was truly the target, would seem to lie in the overwhelming superiority of Justa as a cult figure. She was a martyr whose cult, helped by Isidore, had spread in Spain from an early date.[48] Fernando's request matched the pattern established by Alfonso III when he made the bodies of the Cordobese martyrs Eulogius and Lucrecia part of his peace negotiations with Córdoba in 883.[49] Although he appeared under 4 April in the martyrology composed by Usuard after his Spanish trip,[50] in Spanish calendars Isidore, Confessor, was not ubiquitous before the translation of 21 December 1063.[51]

Even the prayer book of 1055 given to the Cathedral of Santiago de

45. L. Torres-Balbás, "La primitiva mezquita mayor de Sevilla," *Al-Andalus* 11 (1946), 425–39. See Pedro de Madrazo, *España: sus monumentos y artes—su naturaleza e historia; Sevilla y Cádiz* (Barcelona, 1884), p. 455 for the identification of St. Vincent with the cathedral. This conclusion is still debated, however. In the *Bibliotheca Sanctorum,* 12 vols. (Rome, 1961–67), 5: col. 849, the cathedral is the church of SS. Justa and Rufina, but that seems to have been a suburban church. The councils of Seville were held in the church of Holy Jerusalem, but councils need not take place in the cathedral. See the discussion in Carmen García Rodríguez, *El culto de los Santos en la España romana y visigoda* (Madrid, 1966), pp. 234, 360; Rafael Puertas Tricas, *Iglesias hispanicas (siglos IV al VIII): testimonios literarias* (Madrid, 1975), pp. 56, 301–2. In the note of gift in the Biblia Hispalense, given to the Cathedral of Seville in 988, the cathedral has a new identity as St. Mary's, Martín de la Torre, and Pedro Longás, *Catálogo de códices latinos, I: Bíblicos* (Madrid, 1935), p. 11.

46. *Bibliotheca Sanctorum,* 5: col. 849; 7: col. 1158–59.

47. See García Rodríguez, *El culto,* p. 234, app. no. 86 for reference to a Muslim historian's statement that a church of Santa Rufina outside the city was eventually used as a Muslim residence.

48. For Justa and Rufina see *ES,* 9: 276–81; Zacarías García Villada, *Historia eclesiástica de España,* 5 vols. (Madrid, 1929–36), i, pt. 1, 268–271; García Rodríguez, *El culto,* pp. 231–34.

49. Armando Cotarelo y Valledor, *Alfonso III el Magno* (Madrid, 1933), pp. 289–91.

50. *Le Martyrologe d'Usuard,* ed. Jacques Dubois. Subsidia Hagiographica 40 (Brussels, 1965): Société des Bollandistes p. 206.

51. Of the nine Mozarabic calendars collected by Marius Férotin (*Liber mozarabicus sacramentorum,* [Paris, 1912], pp. 43ff.), only five include Isidore.

Compostela by Fernando and Sancha omits Isidore! This manuscript is paradigmatic in still another sense, for its calendar is followed by a poem, *Florus Isidoro Abbati*, honoring Isidore.[52] As *doctor egregius*, the title accorded him at Toledo VIII,[53] he had never been forgotten. In the ninth and tenth centuries the kingdom of Astur-León had been singularly rich in manuscripts of Isidore's works, usually from monastic centers, but with one of them, the *Etymologiae* in the Escorial (MS. P.I.7) carrying the ex-libris of Alfonso III. In a Spanish church filled before the conquest with such illustrious names as Braulio, Julian, and Ildefonsus, Isidore stood in a class apart.[54] With the translation came a cult. He would flourish now as thaumaturge, and the author of the *Silense* claimed it would take a number of volumes to record all the miracles that rewarded those who approached him as healer and miracle worker.[55] As the thirteenth century opened he could be seen as a hero of the Reconquest in the manner of Santiago Matamoros, with a claim that he aided of Alfonso VII at the Battle of Baeza.[56] Although in the *Silense* Fernando's conquest of Coïmbra involved a prediction of its fall by St. James, and Santiago de Compostela is singled out as a devotional site favored, along with Oviedo, by the ruler, Fernando's efforts to reinforce Leonese authority did not involve the Apostolic shrine in an appreciable way. It was only in the reign of his son, Alfonso VI, and under bishop Diego Gelmírez that the shrine took on extraordinary importance as a pilgrimage goal and was housed within a building of monumental scale richly decorated in the new Romanesque manner. If the two cults, Isidore's and Santiago's, cannot fairly be termed rivals, at least Fernando's translation of Isidore gave León, whose history as an ancient Christian center scarcely registered, a distinguished link with the ancient peninsular church. In the charter rewarding Ordoño of Astorga for his role in the translation, the learned saint was referred to as *Totius Hispaniae Doctor*,[57] a title which shows how Isidore could serve the imperialist cause.

52. Marius Férotin, "Deux manuscrits wisigothiques de la Bibliothèque de Ferdinand Ier," *BEC* 62 (1901), 374–87, esp. 377–79.

53. José Vives, *Concilios visigóticos e hispano-romanos* (Madrid, 1963), p. 276.

54. For Isidore's importance in Spain see M. C. Díaz y Díaz, "Isidoro en la edad media," in *Isidoriana*, ed. M. C. Díaz y Díaz (León, 1961), pp. 345–87 (= *De Isidoro al siglo XI* [Barcelona, 1976], pp. 143–201, esp. 175–82).

55. A book was so filled by Lucas of Tuy at the end of the twelfth century. See note 90.

56. Lucas of Tuy, *Chronicon Mundi* in *Hispaniae illustratae*, ed. Andreas Schott (Frankfort, 1608), 4: 104; Julio Puyol, *Crónica de España por Lucas, obispo de Tuy* (Madrid, 1926), p. 394. In the *Primera crónica general*, ed. Ramón Menéndez Pidal, 2 vols. (Madrid, 1955), 1: cap. 478, 266, excerpted by Colin Smith, *Christians and Moors in Spain*, (Warminster, 1988), 1: 5, Isidore almost thwarted the Conquest when his agents just missed seizing Muhammad when he came to Córdoba to preach his evil doctrines.

57. *Colección diplomática de Fernando I*, no. 67.

Indeed in looking for the proper context for the translation, Bishko chose to see it as a "Leonese and imperialist phenomenon, exclusively explicable in the context of the Gothicist tradition of the Leonese church."[58] One document not appealed to roundly confirms the "Gothicist" framework of the arrival of Isidore's remains in León. It is the so-called "Acts of Translation," an account of the mission to bring Justa's body back to León and her substitution by Isidore.[59] The narrative is closely related to that in the *Silense,* and, for most who have considered the issue, an account written not long after the event and subsequently drawn on by the *Silense*'s author.[60] In the "Acts" a preamble providing a resumé of events that is spread over chapters in the *Silense* provides the context for Fernando's establishment of a cult of Isidore in León. It begins with the devastation visited on the Christian peninsula by the Muslims. Churches and monasteries were destroyed, books burned, treasuries pillaged, "omnes incolas ferro, flammas, fame cosumptos." Then king Pelayo, sprung from the royal line, took on the Saracens at Covadonga, and with the help of God subjected them to the sword. Slowly and almost imperceptibly "*the kingdom of the Gothic peoples* grew like the shoots from a reviving root, sees were restored, basilicas founded, treasuries enriched with gold and gems, and books provided."[61] It is immediately after this statement that Fernando and his request to Benabet (Al-Mutatid) for the body of Justa are introduced and the story continues almost exactly as in the *Silense.* In this compressed format, then, not just the translation but Fernando's embellishment of his capital appears as a neatly enframed Neo-Gothic program.[62]

58. Charles Julian Bishko, "Fernando I and the Origins of the Leonese-Castilian Alliance with Cluny," in Bishko, *Studies in Medieval Spanish Frontier History* (London, 1980), Study II, p. 51.

59. *ES* 9, 370–75.

60. Manuel Gómez Moreno, *Introducción a la Historia Silense* (Madrid, 1921), p. xvii (as by same author); *Historia Silense,* pp. 45–49; Viñayo González, "Cuestiones histórico-críticas en torno a la traslación del cuerpo de San Isidoro," in *Isidoriana,* ed. M. C. Díaz y Díaz (León, 1961), pp. 285–97; Geoffrey West, "La 'Traslación del cuerpo de San Isidoro' como fuente de la Historia llamada Silense," *Hispania Sacra* 27 (1974), 365–71.

61. "Illo ex tempore rursum gloria & regnum Gothicae Gentis sensim atque paulatim coepit veluti virgultum ex rediviva radice pullulare, & industria Regum qui regali stemmate progeniti apicem regni nobiliter gubernabant singulis momentis succrescere. Fuere namque armis & viribus famosi, consilio clari, misericordia atque justitia praecipui, religione dediti, quique antiqua Episcopia innovarunt, Basilicas fundarunt, & thesauris ditarunt, auro et gemmis, librisque ornarunt, ac pro viribus Christiani nominis gloriam dilatarunt. Ex quorum illustri prosapia emersit vir clarissimus Fredinandus Sancii Regis filius" (*ES* 9, 371).

62. If Bernard Reilly ("Sources of the Fourth Book of Lucas of Tuy's *Chronico Mundi,*" *Classical Folia* 30 [1976], 127–37, esp. 132–33) is right, there was a twelfth-century chronicle drawn on by the onetime Leonese canon, Lucas of Tuy, in which the Neo-Gothic interpretation of events was reinforced by speaking of the rulers of the Reconquest after Pelayo as "Goths." In its introduction of Alfonso VI, Fernando's son and successor, the *Silense* states he is *ex illustri Gotorum prosapia ortus* (p. 119).

Only with Alfonso VI's successful campaign of 1085 would the former Visigothic capital itself become a city within the boundaries of León. In its actual state it can have provided Fernando with little in the way of guidance toward realizing his capital-making ideal. It would have been the first Leonese capital, Oviedo, that provided him with the effective model in his ambition. Oviedo was subsequently so overshadowed by the Apostolic shrine at Santiago de Compostela, the invention of the same Alfonso II (791–842) who founded Oviedo, that we forget Oviedo's significance in Fernando's and Sancha's era. In its summary of Fernando's character, the *Silense,* whose author is obviously familiar with Oviedo and its history, makes Fernando's recognition of its special character as a cult center explicit: "He honored over the cults of many sacred and venerable sites, the church of the Savior in Oviedo."[63]

The chronicles agree in giving to Alfonso II the responsibility of establishing Oviedo, a site with no previous history as a city, as the capital of Asturias,[64] and with endowing it with a cathedral dedicated to the Savior, a properly imperial advocation, with relics of all of the Apostles(!), a royal Pantheon in the church of St. Mary's next to the cathedral, a special sanctuary, the *Cámara Santa,* for the extraordinary collection of relics we identify with the *Arca Santa,* palaces, baths, as well as the great gold cross we call the "Cross of the Angels" after the account of its miraculous manufacture by an angelic team.[65] The gift to the cathedral of church furnishings in precious metals, made by Alfonso in 812 provided a model for the magnificent gift of Fernando and Sancha in 1063.[66] Enough remains today of Alfonso's elaborate endowment of his capital to enable us to appreciate how spectacular and exceptional it was. It is only necessary to refer to murals of the suburban (palace?) church of Santullano with their echo of ancient schemes of fictive architectonic decoration to measure the truth

63. *Silense,* p. 205.

64. *Estudios sobre la monarquía asturiana* (Oviedo, 1949; reprint 1971); Juan Ignacio Ruiz de la Peña Solar, "La cultura in la corte ovetense del siglo IX," in *Crónicas asturianas,* p. 13. For the monuments see Joaquín Yarza, *Arte y arquitectura en España, 500–1250* (Madrid, 1979), pp. 43–53. Still useful is the overview by José María Quadrado, *España, sus monumentos y artes—su naturaleza e historia: Asturias y León* (Barcelona, 1885), pp. 69–101.

65. Helmut Schlunk, "The Crosses of Oviedo," *Art Bulletin,* 32 (1950), 91–114, esp. 110–11.

66. The charter in the Cathedral of Oviedo dated 16-XI-812 is sometimes rejected in whole or in part but has been defended in recent times by such authors as Antonio C. Floriano, *Diplomática española del periodo astur (718–919)* 1 (Oviedo: Universidad Dorielo, 1949), no. 24, pp. 118–19; Claudio Sánchez Albornoz, *Desoblación y repoblación en el valle del Duero* (Buenos Aires, 1966), pp. 38ff.; M. Díaz y Díaz, "La historiografía hispana hasta el año 1000," in *De Isidoro al siglo XI* (Barcelona, 1976), pp. 205–34, esp. 214, n.24.

of this.[67] In the ninth-century chronicle known as the *Albeldense* Alfonso's enterprise is placed under the rubric of a reconstitution of Toledo: "omnemque gotorum ordinem, sicuti Toleto fuerat, tam in eclesia quam palatio in Ouetao cuncta statuit."[68] This would not mean that the Asturian versions of what was proper to a capital resembled their Toledan counterparts.[69] Rather, behind the elaboration of the new city stood the notion that it would function as the capital in the way the ancient Christian capital of Toledo had, even as Toledo would have modeled itself ideally on Constantinople.[70] The prominent place of the cross in the Visigothic liturgy of royal victory[71] must have contributed to the focus on the cross in Asturian iconography and inspired the inscription of the Cross of the Angels ("Beneath this sign the enemy is defeated"), yet the artistic language of the Cross of the Angels is post-Visigothic. His new church aside, Fernando's capitalizing in turn involved forms that actually rejected Spanish traditions while employing recognizable peninsular modes. Thus the cross donated by the royal couple in 1063, in ivory with a carved corpus and numerous other figures, stands in marked contrast to the golden Cross of the Angels of Alfonso II and to the "Cross of Victory" of Alfonso III,[72] itself a formal "updating" of the Cross of the Angels.

Whether Bishko is right to conclude that the translation deserves to be seen "exclusively" in Neo-Gothic terms is debatable. Thanks to Isidore's literary output, no other Spanish saint's name so resonated internationally as his.[73] For this reason, the selection of Isidore rather than the martyr Justa may be compared to the new transpyrenean character of Fernando's imagery and his Cluniac alliance. The choice may have seemed especially apt at a time which witnessed such openings to the north as association with Cluny and with the revolutionary artistic language, imported from the north, employed in the treasury of the palatine church. Even the idea of the capital may have fed on such northern models as Aachen, though

67. Helmut Schlunk and M. Berenguer, *La pintura mural asturiana de los siglos IX y X* (Madrid, 1957).

68. *Crónicas asturianas,* pp. 174, 249.

69. See Jerrilyn Dodds, *Architecture and Ideology in Early Medieval Spain* (University Park, PA and London, 1990), pp. 27ff. for the problems involving the meaning of the *Albeldense*'s statement, and an argument that it reflects the ideology of its own era more than that of Alfonso II's. That is debatable.

70. Ewig, "Résidence et capitale," 31ff.; Brühl, "Remarques," 206, 215.

71. Michael McCormick, *Eternal Victory: Triumphal Rulership in Late Antiquity, Byzantium, and the Early Medieval West* (Cambridge, 1986), pp. 308ff.

72. Palol and Hirmer, *Early Medieval Art,* pl. 8, p. 39; Schlunk, "Crosses," pp. 101ff.

73. For a review of Isidore's influence outside the peninsula see Jocelyn Hillgarth, "The Position of Isidorian Studies," *Studi medievali* 24, ser. 3 (1983), 817–905, esp. 883–93.

only an imprecisely known ideal Aachen, the actual one having lost by this time its importance as a royal seat. It is legitimate to raise the issue of the extent, if any, to which the reliance on Germanic models for the reliquary for St. Isidore and the introduction of an ivory corpus to the cross reflects a conscious attempt to employ a language known for its association with the Holy Roman Emperors.[74]

The dedication of the church of San Isidoro was followed by more military campaigns, but the last one, directed against Valencia, had to be broken off because of Fernando's failing health. Back home, his death followed swiftly, on 27 December 1065. Far from trailing off with Fernando's death and Sancha's two years later, the effort directed toward enhancing the palatine site actually gathered momentum. With the decisive assumption of power by Alfonso VI in 1072 and his successes in the campaigns against Andalusia, the means were at hand. Beyond financial resources, however, it is not clear to what extent Alfonso himself was directly involved in the enterprise. From his itinerary[75] we know he spent relatively little time in the capital city, much preferring the great monastery at Sahagún, two days journey southeast. He and his wives would be buried there. However, it is apparent that Alfonso's older sister, Urraca, the firstborn of Fernando and Sancha, took extraordinary interest in her father's foundation.[76] The *Silense* goes out of its way to acknowledge her role as donor: "All of her life she [Urraca] followed her desire to adorn sacred altars and the vestments of the clergy with gold, silver, and precious stones."[77] Unfortunately, we have lost a spectacular example of this largess, a crucifix with an ivory corpus on a cross of gold and silver studded with gems (Manzano claims it was 7 feet tall). It included an effigy of Urraca at the foot, in gold repoussée, identified by inscription.[78] We gain some idea of the sumptuousness of conception,

74. See Joaquín Yarza Luaces, "Peregrinación a Santiago y la pintura y miniatura románicas," *Compostellanum* 30 (1985), 369–93, esp. 373 for the purple color of the Diurnal of 1055 in Santiago de Compostela and details of initials as "imperial" details.

75. Bernard F. Reilly, *The Kingdom of León-Castilla Under King Alfonso VI, 1065–1109* (Princeton, NJ: 1988).

76. For Urraca's interest in the artistic embellishment of San Isidoro consult Susan Havens Caldwell, "Urraca of Zamora and San Isidoro in León: Fulfillment of a Legacy," *Woman's Art Journal* 7, 1 (Spring–Summer 1986), 19–25. The chronology proposed there differs substantially from the one assumed here.

77. *Silense,* p. 123.

78. See Manzano, *Vida y milagros,* p. 383, Risco, *Historia de León,* 2: 146–47 and *ES* 35: 357. According to Manzano the stem was 2½ *varas* tall and the cross bar 1½. In *Romanesque Sculpture of the Pilgrimage Roads,* 1: 40–41 Porter proposed that the ivory corpus purportedly from the Cistercian convent founded in the mid-twelfth century at Carrizo de la Ribera (Astorga) and now in the Museo Arqueological Provincial in León (Palol and Hirmer, *Early Medieval Art,* pl. 78) was from this cross. Its relatively small size of 33 cm in height would rule

however, from the surviving chalice carrying her name (see Figure 3). It ingeniously and uniquely incorporates two antique onyx cups so that one can function as the bowl and the other, inverted, as the foot. These are encased in gold filigranes uniting gems and pearls and small plaques of enamel.[79] The Germanic background of the techniques employed are as apparent as they were in the case of the Isidore casket. Like the lost crucifix, this offering to San Isidoro is identified by inscription as the gift solely of Urraca, daughter of Fernando and Sancha. The *Silense*'s praise of her generosity seems to have been more than puffery.

It was only after Fernando's death that the Pantheon assumed its actual form. Although, as we have seen, Fernando's commissions broke in decisive ways with Hispanic traditions and employed extra-pyrenean ones, they did so in the realm of the minor arts, manuscripts, and reliquaries. His church, as we saw, took shape according to an Asturian model. Now, however, the compound piers of the Pantheon displayed an architectural plasticity unprecedented in the peninsula (Catalonia excepted), but present c.1030 at a Gallic site, the crypt of Saint-Etienne d'Auxerre.[80] Moreover, the engaged half-columns in the Pantheon were crowned by historiated capitals. Although Leyre in Navarre had employed figured capitals as early as mid-century,[81] they belonged to a pre-Romanesque phase, as did those of San Pedro de Teverga, close to León, in the 1060s.[82] Although relatively primitive, the Pantheon's formal language represents the new Romanesque art being shaped north of Spain. Gallicization of this sort is understandable within a Leonese royal cultural orientation in which its ruler would be married from 1074 to 1078 to Agnes (Inés), daughter of the Duke of Aquitaine, and from 1079 to 1093 to Constance, daughter of the Duke of Burgundy and niece of Hugh of Cluny and Robert, King of France. The Pantheon would have arisen in this period when one must imagine Gallic cultural standards prevailed. Within the 1080s is the most likely term, for there are traces of the inventions taking place in the capitals at Saint-Sernin de Toulouse. Thus two of the themes particularly associated with

---

this out if Manzano's description is to be trusted, as does the bejeweled golden skirt described by Manzano. Urraca also gave a large gold and gemmed cross with an ivory corpus to the Cathedral of León at the foundation of a new building by Bishop Pelayo in 1073. It is lost but see Risco, *ES* 36 (1787), app. 28, p. lix.

79. See Gómez-Moreno, *Provincia de León,* pp. 205–6.

80. Kenneth John Conant, *Carolingian and Romanesque Architecture, 800–1200* (Baltimore, 1959), pl. 47.

81. Palol and Hirmer, *Early Medieval Art,* pls. 60, 61.

82. Helmut Schlunk and J. Manzanares, "La iglesia de San Pedro de Teverga y los comienzos del arte románico en el reino de Asturias y León," *Archivo español de Arte* 24 (1951), 277–305.

Figure 3. Chalice of Urraca of León. León, Colegiata of San Isidoro. Copyright © 1993 by the Metropolitan Museum of Art. Reproduced by permission of the Metropolitan Museum of Art.

the Portes des Comtes there, the punishment of lust through the figure of a woman with serpents at her breasts and the punishment of some unspecified sin by means of a dragon biting the head of a man,[83] are present in the Pantheon. On the other hand, influences from the other major development in the 1090s on the Pilgrimage Road nearby at Sahagún and Frómista are not detectable.[84] This provides a bracket of post-1080 and pre-1090s.

Urraca's epitaph indicates that there is good reason to assign her a preponderant role in the expansion of the palatine complex. It states that she "amplified" the church and enriched it with gifts.[85] Although it used to be customary to see this "amplification" as a reference to the actual basilica, I identified the claim instead with the Pantheon just described.[86] Perhaps, however, she should still be given credit for getting a new, much expanded, basilica under way. The only document related to the building of the church is a charter of 12 October 1110, eight years following her death, when Didacus Alvitiz, maiorino of the king and queen, that is, of Urraca and Alfonso the Battler, sold a house in the city of León and gave the proceeds, 100 solidos, *in illo labore Sancti Isidori ad illos magistros in presentia de illas infantas.*[87] This, of course, confirms nothing about the state of building. Foundations continuing the line of the aisle walls but running through the transept reveal an earlier, transeptless, plan. From the sutures made necessary by the new apsidiols attendant on the introduction of the transept, we know that the east end of this first church was far advanced. In fact, the columns that stand in front of the easternmost aisle windows, additions made necessary by the decision to vault the aisles, indicate it had reached the first bay of the nave.[88] From the fact that the Pantheon was designed to front a facade no wider than Fernando's church and retained its original door, the new church had not been conceived at that time. It is possible, however, that before she died Urraca had realized that a new, Romanesque, church would be required.

The church of 1063 had been erected just before the Romanesque era introduced more monumental building schemes, and had been conceived

83. Gómez-Moreno, *Arte románico,* pls. LXIII, LXIV. For the comparable examples at Toulouse see Marcel Durliat, *L'Haut-Languedoc roman* (Zodiaque, 1978), pls. 17, 18.

84. For Sahagún and Frómista see Serafín Moralejo, "Tomb of Alfonso Ansúrez (†1093): Its Place and the Role of Sahagún in the Beginnings of Spanish Romanesque Sculpture," in *Santiago, Saint-Denis and Saint Peter: The Reception of the Roman Liturgy in León-Castile in 1080,* ed. Bernard Reilly (New York, 1985), pp. 63–100.

85. "Hic resquiescit Domna Urraca regina de Zamora filia regis magni fernandi. Hec ampliauit ecclesiam istam multis muneribusque ditauit . . ."

86. J. Williams, "San Isidoro in León."

87. *Cartulario del monasterio de Vega,* ed. Luciano Serrano (Madrid, 1927), p. 37.

88. Gómez-Moreno, *Arte románico,* pl. CXXIII.

as a palatine chapel. This role was confirmed in the next generation by the intimate association of palace and church allowed by the design of the large vaulted tribune which was carried by the Pantheon.[89] This area eventually became a chapel, but it was originally designed to function as a part of the palace and communicated with the city wall and the tower. By means of a large window looking down into the nave of the church, royal devotions could take place in view of the altar. This original function of the tribune as part of the palace is reflected in one of the Isidoran miracles appearing in the collection written by Lucas of Tuy, sometime canon of San Isidoro. One miracle involved the appearance of St. Isidore to Sancha, the sister of Alfonso VII († 1157), as she knelt in prayer before the window of the tribune. He reproved her, a lay person, for living in such close proximity to the religious. In response she quit the tribune and built a palace adjacent to its southern side, incorporating a window which allowed a view into the church. This story probably reflects the replacement in 1148 of the nuns of San Pelayo/San Isidoro with the canons of Sta. María de Carbajal.[90]

Although until recently it was customary to assign the frescoes of New Testament subjects on the Pantheon vaults toward the latter part of the twelfth century, that is, a century after the Pantheon's erection, Urraca's initiative is, if problematic, not precluded.[91] The identity of the saints painted on the vaults of the Pantheon is as Frankish as the style of the architecture on which they lie. Martin of Tours is present and Martial of Limoges,[92] and a remarkably early version of St. Eligius of Noyon as goldsmith. But there is no Isidore. The customary tardy date followed from an identification of the FREDENANDO REX kneeling at the foot of the Crucifix as Fernando II. Surely, however, this is not Fernando II, whose initiative led Master Matthew in 1168 to undertake at Santiago de Compostela the splendid west facade known as the "Portico de la Gloria" and who was buried in that great pilgrimage church. This would be an effigy of the founder of

89. Williams, "San Isidoro," figs. 2b, 16.

90. For the appearance of St. Isidore see Lucas of Tuy, *De miraculis S. Isidori* (Bibl. de la R.C. de San Isidoro, MS. 61, fols. 46rv (also as translated in Juan de Robles, *Libro de milagros de Sant Isidro, arçobispo de Sevilla* [Salamanca, 1525], cap. 35, and Joseph Manzano, *Vida y portentos milagros de el glorioso San Isidoro, arzobispo de Sevilla* [Salamanca, 1732], pp. 152–53. Modern edition by J. Pérez Llamazares [León, 1947]). For the exchange with Carbajal see García M. Colombás, *San Pelayo de León y Santa María de Carbajal* (León, 1982).

91. For reproductions of the frescoes of the Pantheon see Antonio Viñayo González, *Pintura románica: Panteón real de San Isidoro, León* (León, 1971).

92. "Marcialis Pincerna and the Provincial in Spanish Medieval Art," in *Hortus Imaginum: Essays in Western Art,* ed. Robert Enggass and Marilyn Stokstad (Lawrence, KN, 1974), pp. 29–36.

the church, Fernando I, and it would be retrospective.[93] The formula followed here, with the king accompanied by his *armiger,* is closely matched by the depiction of Alfonso II in the *Liber Testamentorum* of the cathedral of Oviedo, from c.1120.[94] The series employs other iconographic peculiarities matched again by a work in Oviedo. Unusually, Anna is present in the frescoes in both the Annunciation and the Flight into Egypt, just as she is on the *Arca Santa* of the Cathedral of Oviedo.[95] The *Arca* is traditionally seen as the immediate outcome of the opening of the fabulous collection of relics in the Cámara Santa of Oviedo by Alfonso VI and Urraca in 1075. However, when he restored the Arca Gómez-Moreno invented the date 1075,[96] and the diploma in the Cathedral archive which documents the event has been shown by Bernard Reilly to be a forgery.[97] These facts do not in themselves prove that the *Arca* was not produced in 1075, but the style of its reliefs would not seem to point to so early a date. It is possible, even, to imagine the Arca as an aspect of Bishop Pelayo's promotion of his see after his elevation in 1099. At any rate, the Arca would date no later than the early part of the twelfth century, and provides, through the iconographic parallels alluded to, still another indication that we should place the frescoes of the Pantheon closer to the erection of the Pantheon. It is true that the frescoes present a remarkably developed Romanesque style, one not too distant from that employed for the standing saints in the crypt of Notre-Dame-le-Grand in Poitiers, usually dated around 1100.[98] If the style of the Spanish frescoes is more plastically conceived, it is even less so than the Leonese ivory plaque of the Noli Me Tangere and its companion plaques dated by Goldschmidt to this same time.[99] If it is not possible on this evidence finally to conclude that the frescoes were part of the program carried out under Urraca, they would have been part of a scheme belonging to the early part of the twelfth century rather than toward its end.

This would place the virtually continuous campaign of building and

93. Williams, "San Isidoro in León," 181. For the Crucifixion see Viñayo, *Pintura,* pl. 27.

94. Palol and Hirmer, *Early Medieval Art,* pl. 22.

95. Palol and Hirmer, pl. 75.

96. Manuel Gómez-Moreno, "El Arca Santa documentada," *Archivo español de Arte y Arqueología* 18 (1945), 125–36.

97. Reilly, *Alfonso VI,* p. 84.

98. Otto Demus, *Romanesque Mural Painting* (London, 1970), p. 420, pl. 124, as end of eleventh century; Paul Deschamps and Marc Thibout, *La peinture murale en France* (Paris, 1951), pp. 64–67, pl. 21, as mid-eleventh century.

99. Adolph Goldschmidt, *Die Elfenbeinskulpturen* . . . , 4 vols. (Berlin, 1914–26), 4, p. 32, no. 108; Palol and Hirmer, *Early Medieval Art,* pl. 79. In fact, the peculiar knots found in the drapery of the plaques have counterparts in the angel of the Annunciation to the Shepherds and the symbols of Evangelists in the Pantheon frescoes.

embellishment which we have reviewed within the lifetimes of only two generations. The familial nature of the enterprise and its commemorative character surfaces clearly in the frescoes. We have identified the kneeling ruler in the Crucifixion of the Pantheon as Fernando I. The woman opposite is not labeled, but is most likely Sancha, for there is an allusion to the couple in the vault over their effigies, where there are three separate scenes based on the first chapter of Revelation. In the first scene the angel who stands to the right receives the book, in a scene accompanied by an inscription that is not Biblical: UBI ANGELUS A DNO. In the next scene, at the western end of the vault where St. John bows before the angel, the viewer is told that the scene is UBI PRIMITUS IOHANES CUM ANGELO LOCUTUS EST, again a non-Biblical text. The final scene shows John falling at the feet of Christ: UBI IOANNES CECIDIT AD PEDES DNI. These inscriptions identify the sources of the composition of the vault: all accompany the depictions of these same subjects in the copy of the Commentary on the Apocalypse commissioned by Fernando and Sancha in 1047[100] and there can be no doubt that it was followed by the mural painter. Indeed, the choice of this particular Apocalyptic subject, the Commissioning of the Book of Revelation, would have been inspired by the desire to honor the commissioners of the sumptuous copy of 1047, Fernando and Sancha.

In the restoration of the murals several years ago it was discovered that a cavity plastered over in the tympanum over the original doorway leading from the Pantheon to Fernando's church exactly matched in size an ancient commemorative plaque installed early in this century in the north transept of the basilica.[101] The text of this plaque epitomizes the history of the site:

> This church which you see, formerly that of St. John the Baptist, made of brick, was built of stone by the most excellent king Fernando and queen Sancha. They brought here from Seville the body of archbishop Isidore. It was dedicated 21 December, 1063. Then on 26 April 1065 they brought here from Avila the body of St. Vincent, brother of Sabina and Christeta. In that same year the king, returning here from the enemy forces before Valencia, died on 27 December 1065. Queen Sancha then dedicated herself to God.[102]

100. See note 19.

101. The plastered cavity may be seen in Viñayo, *Pintura románica,* pl. 33. For the inscription, Viñayo, *L'Ancien royaume de León roman* (Zodiaque, 1972), pl. 51.

102. The failure to include Sancha's death date (1067) may indicate, but does not require, that it was carved between 1065 and 1067.

The exact manner in which the hands of the angels hold the plaque leaves little doubt that this inscription was carried by them from the conception of the frescoes. But the plaque they offer is, to judge by its epigraphy, the very one installed by the founders of the site over the door to their church some decades earlier.[103]

The Agnus Dei of these frescoes offers a reprise of the Agnus Dei of the south doorway, where we began. There it presided over an Old Testament narrative promising victory over the descendants of Ishmael, the very forces contesting with the kings of León the possession of the peninsula. While this iconography is apt, as we have seen, for the capital of the Reconquest, it is apt too in having at its heart a genealogy, for that is a theme implicit in the enterprise from the decision to elect the site for a dynastic cemetery to an explicit honoring in the frescoes of the founders, Fernando and Sancha. It is fitting, too, that females, Sarah and Hagar, have prominent places in the carved tympanum, for as we have seen the site was substantially indebted to spouses and daughters, from Sancha's initial request to Fernando for a pantheon to Urraca's crucial initiatives.[104] With her sister Elvira, Urraca had been given dominion over the monasteries of the realm at Fernando's death, the portion of the patrimony within the *infantazgo,* on condition that marriage did not take place.[105] In the *Silense* the two daughters seem to have enjoyed as conscientious an education as the sons: "Fernando undertook the education of his sons and daughters so that they were first instructed in the liberal disciplines to which he too had been educated. Then, at the proper age, the sons were put to running horses in the Spanish way and in arms exercises and hunting, but the daughters, so that they would avoid idleness, were instructed in all feminine virtue."[106] This passage is difficult to take at face value, however, for, as Pérez de Urbel noted, it is substantially indebted to Einhard's *Vita*

103. The tympanum would belong to the renovation accompanying the construction of the Pantheon, but Fernando and Sancha installed a similar inscription in the wall above the door of San Miguel de Escalada. See V. García Lobo, *Las inscripciones de San Miguel de Escalada* (Barcelona, 1982), no. 11, pp. 68–69.

104. By the thirteenth century in the *Primera crónica general* 2: 492, cap. 812, Sancha's initiative is even behind the Reconquest in the claim that she purchased arms for Fernando's forces with the "gold, silver, precious stones, and textiles" from her treasury.

105. See Luisa García Calles, *Doña Sancha, hermana del emperador* (León-Barcelona, 1972), pp. 113–16.

106. "Rex vero Fernandus filios suos et filias ita censuit instruere, vt primo liberalibus disciplinis, quibus et ipse studium dederat, erudirentur; dein, vbi etas patiebatur, more Ispanorum equos cursare, armis et venationibus filios exercere fecit, sed et filias, ne per otium torperent, ad omnem muliebrem honestatem erudiri iusit," *Silense,* p. 184.

Karoli Magni.[107] Elvira would have played a minimal role at San Isidoro, for she took up residence in Oviedo.[108] San Isidoro would have fallen to Urraca's responsibility as part of the *infantazgo*. Moreover, because it was a palace chapel, an extension of the royal household, queens and infantas may have felt an extraordinary proprietary interest, and the income from the *infantazgo* may have aided its embellishment.

In the more turbulent reign that followed, Urraca the daughter and successor of Alfonso VI[109] acquired a reputation as a despoiler of the site, deserved or not. According to the unsympathetic *Historia Compostelana*, in 1122 she "stripped the churches throughout her kingdom of their gold and silver and their treasures,"[110] and the *Chronicon Mundi* of Lucas of Tuy puts Urraca and her husband Alfonso the Battler at the center of an aborted wholesale appropriation of the "crosses and chalices, images and reliquaries," from the treasury of San Isidoro, including a clear reference to the chalice of Urraca.[111] It is, nonetheless, during Urraca's reign that the only known donation *ad laborem* takes place, and work must have proceeded.[112] It is even likely that the basilica in its final state advanced significantly during her reign, for it is probable, to judge by the style of the sculpture of transept portal and the masons' marks employed, that the transept was added by shops brought from Santiago de Compostela in the second decade of the twelfth century. When she was succeeded in 1126 by her son Alfonso VII (†1157), the situation returned to its previous state, that of a reigning brother, continuously campaigning, with little time in

107. "Liberos suos ita censuit instituendos, ut tam filii quam filiae primo liberalibus studiis, quibus et ipse operam dabat, erudirentur, tum filios cum primum aetas patiebatur, more francorum equitare, armis ac venationibus exerceri fecit. Filias vero . . . ne per otium torperent, operam impendere, atque ad omnem honestatem erudiri iussit," *Vita* 19, *Silense*, p. 184, n. 193. See Gómez-Moreno, *Introducción*, pp. xxx–xxxi. In María Isabel Pérez de Tudela y Velasco, "El Papel de las hermanas de Alfonso VI en la vida política y en las actividades de la corte," in *Estudios sobre Alfonso VI y la reconquista de Toledo*. Actas del II Congreso internacional de Estudios mozarabes, Toledo, 20–26 Mayo 1985. (Toledo. 1988), 2: 163–80 the account is taken at face value.

108. According to a document of 1074 cited by R. Escalona, *Historia del real monasterio de Sahagún* (Madrid, 1782), p. 90.

109. Bernard Reilly, *The Kingdom of León-Castilla Under Queen Urraca 1109–1126* (Princeton, NJ, 1982).

110. *Historia Compostelana*, ed. Emma Falque Rey. CCCM, 70 (Turnhout: Brepols, 1988), 2: 53.7, p. 322.

111. *Crónica de España por Lucas, Obispo de Túy*, ed. Julio Puyol (Madrid, 1926), pp. 384–85. In his edition of the "Chronica Adefonsi Imperatoris" Prudencio Sandoval (*Chronica del inclito emperador de España Don Alonso VII* [Madrid, 1600], p. 40) recorded still another legend of Urraca's rapacity in which she was said to die upon entering the treasury of San Isidoro to despoil it.

112. See above, note 89.

León, business taking him far more often to Burgos and Toledo, while an older sister supervised the palatine complex in León. This sister, Sancha, played a far greater role in the life of the site than did Alfonso's queen, Berenguela.[113]

An epitaph on a tomb that used to stand in the south aisle of the basilica and is now in an annex of the Pantheon states that Petrus Deustamben "overbuilt" (*superedificavit*) the church at the command of Alfonso VII (1126–1157) and his sister Sancha, in what is taken to be a reference to its vaulting.[114] The vaulting is indeed remarkable, for it includes two great polylobed arches at the crossing, a motif originating in Islamic architecture but frequently used later both north and south of the Pyrenees in church building.[115] It is possible that these are included not merely because they were considered beautiful but because in some sense they were trophies, representing Islam in the way Ishmael did on the tympanum of the basilica. At Palermo a short time later in the palatine church of the Normans, forms and iconographies were drawn from the Constantinopolitan, Roman, and Islamic worlds in the service of an ideal that may be termed "imperial."[116] Although we have no guarantee they were not present merely as part of some neutral pan-Iberian storehouse of beautiful forms, San Isidoro's polylobed arches may too have played such a programmatic role.

The only formal consecration of the church of San Isidoro we know of after that of 1063 took place in 1149, long after its assumed completion. It must have been essentially ceremonial, taking advantage of the presence of eleven bishops and secular magnates in León for conciliar duties.[117] From the chronicle of the reign of Alfonso VII we learn that a decade after his original enthronement he staged an elaborate coronation ceremonial that has left us with a portrait of the powerful appeal exercised by the Leonese imperial tradition:

113. For Sancha see García Calles, *Doña Sancha.*

114. Whitehill, *Spanish Romanesque Architecture,* p. 153. For the tomb see Gómez-Moreno, *Provincia de León,* p. 189. He credits him only with the vaulting of the final western bays, but that does not seem a task worthy enough to receive such a dignified memorial.

115. Etelvina Fernández González, "El arco: tradición e influencias islámicas y orientales en el románico del reino de León," *Awraq* (Revista editada por el Instituto hispano-arabe de Cultura), 5–6 (1982–83), 221–42; Eliane Vergnolle, "Les arcs polyobes dans la Centre-Ouest de la France: Limousin, Angoumois, Saintonge," *Information d'Histoire de l'Art,* 14 (1969), 217–23.

116. See Slobodan Ćurčić, "Some Palatine Aspects of the Capella Palatina in Palermo," *Dumbarton Oaks Papers* 41 (1987), 125–44, esp. 141–42 for the Byzantine imperial model behind the inclusion of Islamic elements at Palermo.

117. Williams, "San Isidoro," 184.

> After these events, in 1135, the king summoned a meeting of a council to be held in the royal city of León, on the second of June, the feast of the Pentecost, with archbishops and bishops, abbots, counts, princes, and leaders who were gathered in the kingdom. On that day the king arrived with his Queen, Berenguela, and his sister, the Princess Sancha, and with them García [Ramírez], King of Navarra, and as the king decreed, all gathered in León. Then a great assemblage of monks and clerics, as well as a great number of people, gathered to see, to hear, and to speak the divine word. On the first day of the council great and small gathered in the Church of St. Mary with the king and concerned themselves with that which the clemency of the Lord provided and those things that involved the salvation of the souls of the faithful. On the second day, when the descent of the Holy Spirit on the Apostles is celebrated, the archbishops, and bishops, abbots, and all the higher and lesser nobles as well as all the people gathered again in the Church of the Blessed Mary, and with King García and the sister of the king, accepted divine council that they call the king emperor, since King García and Zafadola, king of the Saracens and Raymond, Count of Barcelona and Alfonso, Count of Toulouse, and many counts and leaders from Gascony and France were obedient to him in all things. After the king was dressed in a magnificent mantle, they placed on his head a crown of pure gold and precious stones and placed a scepter in his hands. With King García taking his right arm and Arrianus, Bishop of León, his left, they led him to the bishops and abbots before the altar of St. Mary, singing the *Te Deum* to its end and reciting "Long live Emperor Alfonso!" After the Benediction a High Mass was celebrated.[118]

It is true that this is an imperialism far different in mode from the amorphous tradition that preceded it, but it confirms the ideal's reality.[119] At the same time it marks the swansong of León's ascendency, for after Alfonso's death Burgos would outweigh León, but do so without a comparable palatine complex to articulate its position.

118. Henrique Flórez, *ES*, 21: 345–347; Robert Folz, *The Concept of Empire in Western Europe*, tr. Sheila Ann Ogilvie (London, 1969), Doc. XIII, p. 191.

119. Hermann J. Hüffer, "Die mittelalterliche spanische Kaiseridee," cited note 32, 361–95, esp. 375ff.

Laura Kendrick

11. Jongleur as Propagandist: The Ecclesiastical Politics of Marcabru's Poetry

> He was very well known and listened to throughout the world and feared because of his tongue, for he was so slanderous that the castellans of Aquitaine, of whom he had said much evil, finally did away with him.[1]

So ends a biography (or *vida*) prefacing a group of poems attributed to the vernacular poet and performer Marcabru in a thirteenth-century manuscript collection of lyrics.[2] What is the historical value of such a statement? Literary scholars have shown that many of these *vidas* are based solely on interpretations of the poetry that follows in a particular manuscript collection, poetry mostly composed, in the case of Marcabru, over a century before it was written in surviving manuscripts. Furthermore, lyrics ascribed to Marcabru in one manuscript may be ascribed to other poets in other manuscript collections.[3] There must have been an individual who composed lyrics and internally "signed" some of them by including a verse in which he said explicitly, "Marcabru made the words and the song," as in the second line of a widely disseminated crusade exhortation begin-

1. *Biographies des troubadours,* ed. Jean Boutière and A. H. Schutz (Paris, 1973), p. 12, the version of the A songbook (Vatican 5232, f. 27): "E fo mout cridatz et ausitz pel mon, e doptatz per sa lenga; car el fo tant maldizens que, a la fin, lo desfeiron li castellan de Guian[a], de cui avia dich mout gran mal." All English translations in this essay are my own unless otherwise noted.

2. The only modern edition of all the lyrics ascribed to Marcabru (until the appearance of a new edition by Simon Gaunt and Ruth Harvey) remains that of J. M. L. Dejeanne, *Poésies complètes du troubadour Marcabru* (Toulouse, 1909), which assigns each lyric a Roman numeral. When more recent critical editions of individual lyrics exist, I have used these in my text and cited them in footnotes; in the absence of any such note, the Dejeanne edition is the printed source of the lyric, identified by its Roman numeral.

3. For example, "Courteously I want to begin" ("Cortesamen vuoill comensar," XV), which is directed by a final strophe to Jaufre Rudel and the French "beyond the sea," is ascribed in a majority of manuscripts to Marcabru, but in others is either left anonymous or ascribed to Uc de la Bacalaria, Bertran de Saissac, or Bertran de Pessars.

ning "Pax in nomine domini." Many of the poems ascribed to Marcabru in thirteenth- and fourteenth-century collections bear no such signatures, but are supposed to be his because they show thematic and stylistic similarities to "signed" poems or because they quote him by name, "Marcabru says." If qualifying quotation marks did not grow so tiresome, we might well make a rule of surrounding the name Marcabru with them to remind readers that we are not necessarily talking about an individual man, but a critical tradition represented by over forty surviving lyrics in variant manuscript versions. Marcabru was the name used by an individual poet-performer who may have begun composing as early as 1115–1120,[4] but also the name to which other poet-performers attached and by which they authorized their lyric imitations or adaptations of Marcabru's verse,[5] and it was also the name to which later compilers assigned hitherto "anonymous" lyrics that displayed a set of critical themes and a slanderous style dangerous enough, or so thought the later composer of the *vida,* to get a poet killed by angry castellans.

Nowhere in the group of poems ascribed to Marcabru does the first-person speaker specifically predict his own murder, although in one lyric he complains that, in going about chastizing others' folly, he seeks his own harm, and in other lyrics, he claims that he dares to say no more or that fear holds him back.[6] Unless the composer of the *vida* is relying on oral tradition, his account of Marcabru's punishment must be an inference based on his interpretation of the verse attributed to Marcabru and of what sort of harm might come from it to its composer/performer. Although there is no historical evidence that a jongleur who called himself Marcabru really did get murdered for his evil tongue, the thirteenth-century *vida* still offers a fascinating glimpse into a society in which vernacular poetry was believed to matter, in which criticism couched in poetry, performed publicly as song, was believed to have sufficient persuasive force or propaganda value to pose a serious threat to men in power.

4. See Appendix A.

5. The generalizing, figurative, euphemistic style of Marcabru's verse not only makes it very difficult to place or date, but very easy to reuse and adapt to new situations. Specific historical references tend to come in final strophes that could be replaced as occasion demanded. Surviving lyrics attributed to Marcabru are probably more often than not adaptations of earlier lyrics that have been specified or generalized to fit a new situation either by Marcabru himself, by other poet-performers, or they may be imitation Marcabru (of his "school"), authorizing themselves and proclaiming their partisan sympathies by repeating his rhymes, his diction, and his themes.

6. For these claims see, for example, numbers IX (strophe 2, "I don't dare say what I want"), XXXII (strophe 4, "I will not clarify my meaning . . . because of the sons who do vile things; I fear bad treatment too much to wait for worse"), XLI (strophe 5, "And if I try to go about chastizing their folly, I am seeking my own harm").

Indeed, during the thirteenth century in southern France and northern Italy (where the *vidas* were written), one of the instruments of resistance used by local secular lords against the French monarchy and the clergy was the vernacular lyric genre of the *sirventes*—a song with bellicose intentions that dished up political advice to rulers with shaming, slanderous criticism of them.[7] Most famously, the castellan Bertran de Born wielded the words of his *sirventes* to taunt late-twelfth-century rulers (Alphonse of Aragon, Richard I, the young Henry and Henry II of England, and Philip Augustus of France) for their avoidance of battle and their stingy, mercantile behavior.[8] At the very head of this critical vernacular poetic tradition stands the verse ascribed to Marcabru, the themes of which suggest that it was initially sponsored by the church in an effort to exert the pressure of negative public opinion upon unruly nobles. The purpose of Marcabru's lyric blame was to change the behavior of secular lords by threatening them with the loss of esteem and willing support of their dependents—to erode their legitimacy—if they did not live up to their own ancestors' ideal behavior as defined anachronistically in the song, with newer, ecclesiastical ideals of lordly behavior posing as ancient secular ones.

In order to demonstrate how the verse ascribed to Marcabru threatens the legitimacy of secular lords, we need to consider it in more detail, beginning with the poem in which the first-person speaker says that his criticism may lead to his own harm. After an evocation of the awakening of nature in springtime, the speaker says that he is worried about various natural and unnatural things he has heard noised about among the people ("lo poble"). The poet thus sets himself up as a spokesman for popular opinion, which is scandalized, as he tells us in the second strophe, by rampant cuckoldry:

> Because cuckoldry spreads / and one cuckold flatters the other, / let them come and go. / Who cares who is the winner at this? / For I wouldn't give two cents / to figure out their tangles.[9]

7. On later uses of the *sirventes,* see Martin Aurell, *La vielle et l'épée: troubadours et politique en Provence au XIIIe siècle* (Paris, 1989); on the rise of this genre, see Dietmar Rieger, *Gattungen und Gattungsbezeichnungen der Trobador Lyric: Untersuchungen zum altprovenzalischen Sirventes* (Tübingen, 1976).

8. For more detailed discussion, see the chapter devoted to Bertran de Born in my unpublished doctoral dissertation "Criticism of the Ruler, 1100–1400, in Provençal, Old French, and Middle English Verse" (Columbia University, 1978).

9. Dejeanne, XLI, strophe 2:

> Pus la cogossia s'espan / E l'us cogos l'autre non blan, / Laissem los anar e venir. / Cuy cal quals que chaps an primiers? / Qu'ieu non daria dos deniers / Per lor mesclanhas devezir.

While claiming not to be interested in knowing who is the winner of this game (although popular rumor presumably *is* interested), Marcabru nevertheless publicizes the scandal and, in the next strophe, accuses its "burning" players, whom he calls "boastful seculars," of diminishing "pretz" (noble worth) and setting folly loose by "redoubling" their "crimes" in ways that the speaker (to protect himself or, rather, to elicit curiosity?) says are "worse than I dare to uncover."[10] Marcabru further dishonors the objects of his criticism, both noblewomen and noblemen, by attributing their games of cuckoldry to a mercantile avarice:

> The female traffickers, trafficking, / bending (their bodies), trembling (with eagerness) for traffic, / who cause Worth and Youth to be destroyed, / traffic with the traffickers.

At least some of these offenders who destroy Worth and Youth ("pretz" and "jovens," virtues which are supposed to distinguish the nobility from the merchant and laboring classes) have to be nobles themselves; the cuckoldry of ordinary folk among themselves would have no effect on noble virtues.

The language Marcabru uses to bring these nobles down is not pretty; it sullies and shames with the exaggerated vulgarity of its low vocabulary and the harsh sounds of plosive and sibilant consonants, as in the lines just translated above:

> Las baratairitz baratan, / Frienz del barat corbaran / Que fan Pretz e Joven delir, / Baraton ab los baratiers.

Yet the speaker takes the moral high ground in the next strophe by using a Christian metaphor (of preaching as sowing seed, based on Matthew 13) to describe his relationship to those he criticizes:

10. XLI, strophe 3:

> Qu'aissi.s vai lo pretz menuzan / E.l folhatges hieis de garan, / Non puesc, sols, lo fuec escantir / Dels seglejadors ufaniers, / Qui fan los criminals dobliers, / Pejors que no.us aus descobrir.

The boastful secular men who "redouble" their crimes may well recollect Duke William IX of Aquitaine's poem, "I want many to know" ("Ben vueill que sapchon li pluzor"), wherein he boasts of his sexual prowess and of how he successfully rose to the challenge of a woman's inviting him to "redouble" ("doblier") his efforts. Marcabru's pointed denigration of William IX's boasts will be discussed later in this essay.

I go sowing my chastizements / over natural rocks / that I see neither sprout nor flower.[11]

This suggests that the criticism is intended for the nobles' own good, to change their behavior for the better, and not just to debase and dishonor them in the eyes of the people. Is the jongleur who performs these verses not, rather, performing a service of counsel for the nobles, whose names he never divulges, by informing them of how rumors of their cuckoldry debase their virtue in the people's opinion?

The threat implicit in these verses is veiled in several ways, not least by the written form in which we perceive them today. Let us try to imagine a performance context with another lyric attributed to Marcabru. In "The other day at the end of April" ("L'autrier, a l'issida d'abriu"), the speaker gives us an example of how the lives of ordinary folk are disrupted by the behavior of the great. In a pasture in the springtime, the speaker overhears a shepherd trying to persuade a servant girl to couple with him, only to be refused by the girl, who is preoccupied by the rumors she hears that "Prowess" and "Youth" and "Joy" have declined to the extent that no one can trust in another. She goes on to describe the source of the problem: powerful men create the conditions for the debasement of their own lineages by shutting their wives in houses so that no stranger may touch them and keeping at their hearths good-for-nothings whom they command to guard their wives:

And according to what Solomon says, / these could not welcome worse robbers / than such companions / who bastardize the new generation; / and they [husbands] caress the little good-for-nothings, / and believe they are sympathizing with their own sons.[12]

Through the mouth of this servant girl, in vernacular terms, the poem's speaker accuses powerful lords of allowing the corruption of their lineages, the adulteration and decline of the noble virtues of "Pretz e Jovens e Jois."

11. XLI, strophe 5:

Semenan vau mos castiers / De sobre.ls naturals rochiers / Que no vey granar ni florir.

12. Dejeanne, XXIX, strophe 5:

E segon que ditz Salamos, / Non podon cill pejors lairos / Acuillir d'aquels compaignos / Qui fant la noirim cogular, / Et aplanon los guirbaudos / E cujon lor fills piadar.

The new, adulterated generation of nobles is a mixture in which, according to this girl the people are saying, one can have no confidence.

Although no lords' names are given in this lyric, that does not necessarily make it less threatening. The place of such a poem's performance could serve to turn the general into the specific in the minds of listeners; lords in general could be understood as *our* lord. The withholding of specific names, much like the extremely vulgar *senhals* or nicknames (such as Lady Good-Fuck and Lord Costs-So-Much) that Marcabru uses to designate noble ladies and lords in other lyrics, may arouse curiosity and make the poem relevant in many places rather than in just one. Even the voicing of the poem's criticism through the humble servant girl makes it, in some respects, *more* rather than less threatening; her complaint suggests that knowledge of the noble husbands' shame has spread so far down the social ladder that it has undermined popular confidence in their lineage's purity and virtue (hence in the justice of their right to rule over ordinary folk). This little *pastourelle,* general as it is, could have brought considerable critical pressure to bear by shaming and questioning the legitimacy of specific nobles in specific performance contexts. Nevertheless, with its clever indirection, for the speaker claims to be repeating a servant girl's repetition of popular views, such a lyric hardly seems the sort of thing that could get its composer killed (even if only in the imagination of a later medieval *vida* writer).

In other lyrics, prototypical *sirventes,* the speaker assumes a more bellicose role to castigate for their base qualities, especially avarice and sloth, and accuse or taint with insinuations of illegitimacy (of not truly being their fathers' sons) lords who are stingy with wages, feasts, or rewards for their "soudadiers" or their "maisnada" (soldiers in their pay or their households). In such poems, the speaker is a disgruntled "soudadier" who claims to be responding to the rumors he hears among others like himself, men who feel that they have not had their fair share of the wealth because of the avarice and laziness of the great.[13] In one lyric, which he initially signs with

13. In *The Troubadour Marcabru and Love* (London: Westfield College, 1989), pp. 13–14, Ruth Harvey has suggested that Marcabru identified himself with the *soudadiers* in some poems (for example, III and XIX) because he actually was one: "If he were one of the sons of a family of the lesser nobility, he may have been obliged to seek his fortune as a *soudadier,* whether by means of his *trobar* talents or by the sword or both. Such a hypothesis would help to account for . . . his complaints about the avarice of the seigneurial classes damaging the prospects of the young men." Whatever Marcabru the man's social origins, there are compelling rhetorical and propagandistic reasons why the first-person speaker of several lyrics attributed to him should identify himself with the *soudadiers.*

praise of his own verse-making, "Listen to the song, how it advances and improves" ("Aujatz de chan, com enans'e meillura"), Marcabru summons himself to "war" against the "meanness" ("malvestat," the exact opposite of noble worth) that "many people warn is on the increase and worsening." Signs of this are that "youth offers no comfort . . . since the lords have commenced extracting and pass giving through the holes of a sieve." Avarice is responsible for the reversal of the "just and reasonable" order of things, so that wealth alone turns a base-born servant into an emperor, and the worst are rewarded instead of the best. The speaker goes on to charge,

> Whoever through avarice loses shame and moderation / and throws honor and valor to oblivion / seems by manner to be of the brotherhood of the hedgehog and the lapdog and the robber.[14]

In short, the lord whose love of wealth gets the better of his concern for honor and valor delegitimizes himself by proving that his blood is not truly noble: his true brothers must be cowardly beasts and robbers.

Marcabru's verse does more than insinuate the debasement and illegitimacy of the nobility by accusing *Joven* (the younger generation of nobles) of seeming good but being undermined or hollowed out by *Malvestat* (baseness).[15] In another lyric, the movement of the criticism is, as is often the case, from insinuations of illegitimacy to outright accusations of it, although always generalized. The speaker begins, "At the very beginning of winter" ("Al prim comens de l'ivernaill"), announcing that prowess should not be a seasonal matter, as it is among lowborn men ("avols hom") who do things according to the weather. Having described the behavior of non-noble men in pejorative terms (he also calls them "acropitz" or "squatters"), the speaker turns to "good-looking noble youth" ("Joves

14. Aurelio Roncaglia, "Marcabruno: Aujatz de chan," *Cultura neolatina* 17 (1957), 20–48, strophe 6 (Dejeanne, IX):

> Qui per aver pert vergonh'e mezura / e giet'honor e valor a non cura / segon faisson es del semblan confraire / a l'erisson e al gos e al laire.

15. The term *Joven* (or *Jovens*) in Marcabru's verse can designate young heirs (who should head adventurous groups of "companions"), these groups of unmarried companion-followers, and the youthful bravado and eagerness to prove themselves that constitute the behavioral ideal appropriate to young noble heirs and their bands. The effect of this semantic overlap is that any criticism of the leader's corruption threatens the reputation of the followers.

homes de bel semblan"), whom he accuses of being "corrupted by baseness" ("per Malvestat deceubutz"), so that their boasts of military action remain empty:

> For they go about boasting, / "During this year we'll make a thousand assaults, / in the springtime." / But there remain the boasts and the vaunts.[16]

After two strophes on the behavior of "avols hom" and two on that of "Joves homes" who are no more willing to take action than the lowborn, the speaker turns to the married and established noblemen ("moillerat") and accuses them of debasing *Joven* through their cuckoldry:

> Husbands, you would be the best in the world, / but each of you makes himself a lover, / which confounds you, / and the cunts are sent to market, / because of which Youth is debased, / and people call you cuckolds.
>
> The "noble reputation" to be got from damage and trickery, / from wherever it may come, / husbands have, / and I willingly grant it them, / and that "Joy" is celebrated among them / and that "Giving" is maintained somewhat.[17]

This last strophe is dripping with irony as the speaker affirms the sort of "pretz" or noble reputation to be got from the boasting about sexual con-

16. The best edition of this lyric is by Simon Gaunt and Ruth Harvey, "Text and Context in a Poem by Marcabru: 'Al prim comens de l'invernaill,'" in *The Troubadours and the Epic: Essays in Memory of W. Mary Hackett,* ed. Linda M. Paterson and Simon B. Gaunt (Coventry, 1987), pp. 59–101 (Dejeanne, IV):

> Joves homes de bel semblan / vei per malvestat deceubutz; / que van gaban: / 'de so mil essais encogan / farem qan lo temps er floritz'. / Mas lai reman lo gabs e.l brutz. (A ms. version, strophe 4)

17. A ms. version, strophes 6 & 7:

> Moillerat, li meillor del mon / foratz, mas chascus vos faitz drutz, / que vos confon! / E son acaminat li con, / per q'es jovens *fora*ba*n*ditz [ms., astrobauditz] / e vos en apell' om cornutz.
>
> Lo pretz del dan e del barat, / de calqe part sia vengutz / ant moillerat, / e ieu ai lo lor autreiat; / e jois es entr'els esbauditz, / e donars alqes mantengutz.

The modern emendation of "astrobauditz" to "forabanditz" ("abandoned") seems highly conjectural. What "astrobauditz" might mean is not clear, although it must be an expression of debasement. The I manuscript reading, "acropauditz" ("turned into squatters"), echoes Marcabru's imprecations against squatters elsewhere. On the possible ironies of the expression "pretz del dan e del barat," see Gaunt's textual notes, p. 77.

quests by noble husbands (such as, most famously, Duke William IX of Aquitaine). What noble husbands are really doing, the speaker charges, is encouraging the adulteration of their own blood; it is they who are responsible for *Joven*'s (the younger generation's) lack of prowess, its base behavior.

This is the major theme of the verse attributed to Marcabru, whether the debasement of the young nobles' blood is announced outright in criticism of cuckoldry or whether it is insinuated through analogies with animals or plants (as when their behavior is compared to that of a lapdog or when they are said to be disappointingly barren plants, fruit trees that turn out to be willows and elders, implicitly due to the grafting of worthless trees onto the parent fruit trees' stocks [III]). These natural metaphors and analogies are not merely ways of attacking powerful noblemen indirectly; they add great force to the criticism. If the nobility *naturalizes* its power in order to justify it, attributes to itself superior natural virtues passed down through blood and preserved in a pure state by restrictive breeding (or marriage) policies, then, according to this same argument, any "pollution" of the breed would lessen its natural virtue and right to rule. Thus, in another lyric, "I will tell you in my own language" ("Dirai vos en mon lati"), Marcabru repeats folk wisdom about the breeding of plants and animals to set up his criticism of noble husbands for allowing the adulteration of their lineages. This lyric begins with the speaker repeating what he "sees and hears," but with a prophetic twist, for he announces that the world may soon end because "the son fails the father / and the father the son," just as Scripture says will happen. These failures, as Marcabru goes on to explain, are due to the debasement of noble blood and virtue, the corruption of the breed. He gradually gets to specifics, as usual, through a series of generalizations and insinuating analogies. In the second strophe he announces the decline and "deviation from its path" of "Jovens," as well as the stealthy flight of "Donars" (Giving), who used to be the "brother" of *Joven*. The perversion of noble virtues is summarized in the punning nickname of the treacherous lord Costs-So-Much ("dons Costans l'enganaire"), whom the speaker accuses of never having welcomed Joy or Youth.

How such lords got to be stingy, how noble virtues were perverted, is the subject of the next stanzas. First Marcabru repeats the proverbial wisdom that a rich man who takes into his house and feeds a "bad neighbor . . . of bad lineage" ("mal vezi . . . de mal aire") is sure to have trouble in the morning. What kind of trouble is insinuated in the next strophe through proverbs about breeding:

> The miller judges at his mill: / whoever ties well also unties well. / And the peasant says behind the plow: / good fruit comes from a good garden, / and a base son from a base mother / and from a worthless horse a nag.[18]

This folk wisdom is followed by a prophetic-sounding strophe announcing the birth of two beautiful, frisky, blonde-maned colts that immediately begin to turn colors, from white to a changeable grey, and finally come to resemble asses. Appearances are deceptive. Joy and Youth "cheat" now, the speaker says, and Baseness issues from them. Figurative, enigmatic speech arouses curiosity and speculation, and encourages rumor. Having whetted the audience's appetite, the speaker criticizes more directly, albeit still in generalizing pluralities:

> Husbands with the mentality of goats / prepare the cushions / with which the cunts become robbers; / for such (a husband) says, "My son is smiling at me," / who had nothing at all to do in his making.[19]

The final strophe justifies Marcabru's criticism by asserting its corrective intention:

> It does me no good if I chastize them, / for they return immediately [to their former behavior], / and not a one do I see / extract himself from this game of cunt.[20]

Avowedly, Marcabru is interested only in the welfare of those he criticizes (at his own risk).

Such criticism of the stinginess of lords might be dismissed as the

18. Dejeanne, XVII, strophe 4:

Lo mouniers jutg'al moli: / Qui ben lia ben desli; / E.l vilans ditz tras l'araire: / Bons fruitz eis de bon jardi, / Et avols fills d'avol maire / E d'avol caval rossi.

19. XVII, strophe 6:

Moillerat, ab sen cabri, / Atal paratz lo coissi / Don lo cons esdeven laire; / Que tals ditz: "Mos fills me ri" / Que anc ren no.i ac a faire. . . .

20. XVII, strophe 7:

Re.no.m val s'ieu los chasti, / C'ades retornan aqui, / E puois un non vei estraire / Moillerat del joc coni. . . .

self-serving effort of a jongleur to squeeze out a reward with the threat of bad publicity, but Marcabru consistently presents himself as speaking for others, especially for those who are being harmed by noble avarice and unwillingness to act, the lord's dependents or "soudadiers." In another lyric, after describing the intercourse of a married noblewoman and a lowborn servant as that of a greyhound with a lapdog, the speaker turns to plant metaphors to accuse the servant of having the "first fruits," that is, debasing the blood of the first-born, the heirs, who are consequently stingy:

> For between them is neither key nor partition / to keep them from having what is deepest, / and of the fruits both the first and the second; / these make baseness flourish, / when they cause us to be given "no" instead of "yes."[21]

The metaphoric insinuation that even the first-born have been debased is a serious threat to the legitimacy of a nobility that increasingly restricted inheritance to first-born males (or first-born females for lack of any males). Such a restriction on inheritance, as well as concentrating possessions and power, would seem to protect lineal purity in the sense that the legitimate paternity of first-born children might more easily be assured by newlywed ardor and by strict surveillance of the bride, especially when the noblewoman was given very young in marriage. Marcabru undermines this assurance by insinuating that the useless and corrupting men ("guasta-pa," bread-wasters / destroyers of "bread") whom the noble husbands cherish for guarding their wives cuckold them in the secrecy of the household, with the result that the debased first-born, the heirs, lack the noble virtue of generosity and are stingy to "us" (Marcabru and all the lords' dependents). Over and over, the verse attributed to Marcabru demonstrates how the act of guarding "li don" (ladies) leads to the adulteration of noble lineages and thus to the withholding from deserving men of gifts ("don" in another sense).

Although Marcabru justifies his public criticism of noble cuckolds and corrupted Youth as a corrective intended for their own good and not just to shame and undermine them, to call a nobleman a son-of-a-bitch is a ter-

In the last line, I have continued to follow the A manuscript reading, which Dejeanne uses as his base, although he switches here to a later copy's transposition of line order.

21. Peter T. Ricketts, "A l'alena del vent doussa" de Marcabrun," *Revue des langues romanes* 78 (1968), 109–15, strophe 7 (Dejeanne, II):

> Qu'entr'els non a clau ni meja / qu'els non aion del plus preon / e del frug lo prim e.l segon; / cist fan la malvestat rebon / quan no.s fan donar non per oc.

rible insult in the twelfth century; he bastardizes and "disinherits" nobles with his images of noble wives (and mothers) as bitches in heat mating with lapdogs. Such vilifying criticism might speak to the interests of other men who could not justify their own claims to power or possessions by the nobility of their ancestry, the "generosity" of their blood: bastard sons of noblemen, soldiers and "soudadiers" recently risen from the peasantry, merchants and artisans in the cities, and even peasants resentful of lordly exactions. By calling into question the true paternity of the "first fruits," by accusing young heirs of avarice and cowardly laziness, Marcabru turns an ideology whereby nobles might explain and justify their power against them, and challenges them to live up to it. If noble virtues are inherent in blood, then any heir who does not display generosity and energy must have debased blood—must be no more worthy to inherit than bastard sons, less so than younger sons, less "pure" in his breeding (therefore less worthy to inherit), even, than many of his vassals and dependents.

Public insinuations, accusations, and, in the case of the church, official proclamations of the illegitimacy, for breeding purposes, of particular marital unions among the nobility are in this period a potent form of interested propaganda aimed at eroding the support of vassals and dependents and thus forcing concessions from particular noblemen. With increasing frequency from the mid-eleventh through the twelfth centuries, popes and bishops excommunicated nobles and placed their lands under interdict for partisan motives in order to protect church property and advance church interests. Such strong acts of verbal censure were performed for the explicit purpose of correcting the ruler's sins, which often took the form of a stubborn refusal to break off a sexual union considered by the church to be illegitimate and polluting, usually incest (as the church defined it) or bigamy.[22] To the extent that nobles adopted the clerically elaborated justification of their own power as being grounded, not in sheer force, but in the purity of their blood and inherent virtues, they had to pay some attention to public charges of the pollution of incest, which was a danger they ran in carrying their purity- (and power-) ensuring endogamy too far.

It was ecclesiastical policy during the Gregorian reform movement, when expedient, to taint and dishonor, to stir up and wield the force

22. On innovations in and implications of excommunication, see Elisabeth Vodola, *Excommunication in the Middle Ages* (Berkeley, CA, 1986), especially pp. 1–26. Georges Duby, *Le chevalier, la femme, et le prêtre: la mariage dans la France férdale* (Paris, 1981), provides examples of the political use of excommunication, especially for persistence in an "incestuous" union, to force rulers into obeying the church.

of public opprobrium to force secular lords into behaving as the clergy wanted. Public shame in the form of excommunication, a verbal act of sullying the offender, of dramatizing the pollution he had supposedly brought upon himself (and his lineage) by his illegitimate union, was the church's strongest weapon against those who would not follow its orders, not the least because excommunication rendered them, by their "uncleanness," dangerous to the spiritual health of others who had social contact with them. Excommunication could be "contagious" (like heresy), automatically contracted—hence the necessity for vassals and dependents to break off contact with the offending lord whose contamination had been officially proclaimed.

Marcabru's invective was the vernacular poetic equivalent of excommunication; it sullied reputations, contaminated lineages, and thereby threatened to cast nobles out of their inherited positions. Within the general territory and time when lyrics attributed to Marcabru were being performed, there is an interesting historical case of vassals justifying their revolt against their lord by accusations that his sons are not his own.[23] Although it would not at first appear that the church had anything to do with such accusations, closer inspection suggests that it probably did. In 1130 the vassals of Isembert de Châtelaillon successfully rose against their lord, proclaiming that they would not obey the "adulterous sons" of Isembert, who had long tolerated the notorious conduct of his wife Aeline, that "daughter of Belial."[24] Although there is never any explicit reference by name to Isembert in verse ascribed to Marcabru, his themes would certainly have made excellent propaganda in support of such a revolt, and in particular one poem, "The winter departs and the weather grows mild" ("L'iverns vai e.l temps s'aizina"), which contains references in its final strophes to "Lady Aiglina" and "Lord Eblo." Allowing for the vagaries of medieval spelling, one wonders whether the name of Isembert's infamous wife, Aeline, may be suggested in the name "Aiglina" (from the phrase "trut dullurut n'Aiglina," the ditties of or about Lady Aiglina) in the pen-

23. The themes of Marcabru's poetry also seem to fit an incident that occurred in 1125, although in the north of France: Hugh, Count of Champagne, supposedly in a fit of jealousy at seeing his young wife caress her infant son (whom Hugh believed was not his own), repudiated wife and son, gave his inheritance to his nephew Thibaut IV of Blois, entered the order of the Templars, and left for Jerusalem. This incident is recounted by Reto Bezzola, *Les origines et la formation de la littérature courtoise en Occident, 500–1200*, 3 vols. (Paris, 1960–66), Part 2, ii. *Les grandes maisons féodales après la chute des Carolingiens et leur influence sur les lettres jusqu'au XIIe siècle*, p. 368.

24. Alfred Richard, *Histoire des comtes de Poitou, 778–1204*, 2 vols. (Paris, 1903) 2:16.

ultimate strophe of this lyric, which castigates, in the most vulgar images, the lady who cuckolds her husband by copulating with a household servant and giving birth to greedy "nobles":

> The lady knows nothing of pure love / who loves a household servant. / Her desire "mastifs" her / like the female greyhound does it with the lapdog. / Aye! / From such are born the rich wretches / who give neither hospitality nor pay, / Yes!, / just as Marcabru declares.
>
> This one enters into the kitchen / to watch over the fire in the ashes / and drink the steam from the basin / of his lady, Lady Good-Fuck. / Aye! / I know how they linger and lie / and separate the grain from the straw. / Yes! / He cuckolds his lord.
>
> Whoever has good love nearby / and lives from its provisions, / Honor and Valor incline to him / and Worth without dispute. / Aye! / He keeps such faith with truthful speech, / that he need not be worried, / Yes!, / about the ditties of Lady Aiglina.[25]

The phrase "trut dullurut n'Aiglina" may evoke vulgar songs of seduction to taunt and shame the cuckolded lordly husband.[26] In this last strophe, the description of good love seems to be influenced by the church, as is even more clearly the case in an earlier strophe where Marcabru contrasts adulterous love, which leads to "perdition," with a love that "carries medicine / to cure its companion." Not only was proper marriage, in the eyes of the church, a sort of good love because it was a "medicine" for and curative of sexual passion, but ecclesiastical censure was also described as a medicine

25. Dejeanne, XXXI, strophes 6–8:

> Dompna non sap d'amor fina / C'ama girbaut de maiso; / Sa voluntatz la mastina / Cum fai lebrieir' ab gosso; / Ai! / D'aqui naisso.ill ric savai / Que no fant conduit ni pai; / Hoc, / Si cum Marcabrus declina.
>
> Aquest intr' en la cozina / Coitar lo fuoc el tizo / E beu lo fum de la tina / De si donz na Bonafo; / Ai! / Ieu sai cum sojorn' e jai / E part lo gran e.l balai, / Hoc, Son seignor engirbaudina.
>
> Qui bon' Amor a vezina / E viu de sa liurazo, / Honors e Valors l'aclina / E Pretz sens nuill' ochaio; / Ai! / Tant la fai ab dig verai / Que no.il cal aver esmai / Hoc, / Del trut dullurut n'Aiglina.

26. Ruth Harvey, *The Troubadour Marcabru*, pp. 59–60, suggests that Aigline may be a name—like Marion, Marote and Aelis—given to the female character of popular songs of love or seduction, songs that sometimes have alliterative nonsense refrains similar to "trut dullurut."

for sin, a cure motivated by brotherly love and concern for the sick soul.[27] The speaker of this poem suggests that his criticism is motivated by this kind of good, because curative, love.

Nevertheless, one has to wonder how such slanderous criticism could possibly be motivated by anything but a partisan desire to shame and delegitimate, and thereby to further the interests of the speaker's side. Is Marcabru not using a conventional tactic of ecclesiastical censure in order to shield himself from counterattack? Ecclesiastical censure and "discipline" were often means of destroying the opponent's support and turning his people or vassals against him (or giving them a justification to desert or rebel against him). So was the slander attributed to Marcabru. That is why, as we have seen, Marcabru addresses or claims to be speaking for the people or the "soudadiers" in denouncing the cuckoldry of lords and the corruption of *Joven*. If there is reason to doubt the sincerity of Marcabru's concern for the welfare of the lords he criticized, there is also reason to question the sincerity of his identification with the concerns of the "soudadiers" or the people. He seems to be giving public expression to and stirring up their discontent in an effort to threaten and pressure lords, but to be doing this in the interest of the church, even if that interest is not overtly expressed.

Investigation into the background of the Châtelaillon affair of 1130 suggests that, here too, the church may have had something to gain from shaming the lord and his wife. Local monasteries had long complained of the lord of Châtelaillon's depredations, and Eble de Châtelaillon had twice been excommunicated for these. Indeed, Pope Urban II threatened Duke William IX of Aquitaine with the interdiction of all his lands in 1096 if he did not force his vassal, Eble, to restore the Island of Oléron to the monastery of the Trinity of Vendôme (which was then headed by the highly political Abbot Geoffrey).[28] The more generalized criticism of noble cuckoldry in Marcabaru's "L'iverns vai e.l temps s'aizina" may be pointed

27. The fundamental text for the view that marriage serves to curb sexual passion is St. Paul's "It is better to marry than to burn" (1 Cor. 7: 9). See also Duby, *Le Chevalier,* p. 36, for Jonas of Orleans's medicinal concept of marriage. Matthew 18: 17, on the Christian duty of fraternal correction, was used to justify social ostracism as a therapeutic discipline. On this see Vodola, *Excommunication,* pp. 5–6.

28. Richard, *Comtes de Poitou,* 1: 403–4, 410–11, 413–14. Gerald Bond, in an appendix to his edition, *The Poetry of William VII, Count of Poitiers, IX Duke of Aquitaine* (New York, 1982), pp. 102–7, provides the Latin text and English translation of a charter of William IX dated 10 December 1096, wherein William narrates his side of the story: soon after his father died and while William IX was still a boy, his vassal Eble had forced him with threats of desertion to give him lands the monks of Vendôme had held for over forty years, but a certain portion of which Eble claimed had been "granted to his ancestors a long time ago."

toward Isembert of Châtelaillon by the final strophe (which appears only in some versions) denouncing the "troba n'Eblo":

> Never will I engage myself on the side / of the inventions of lord Eble, / who maintains a foolish judgment / against reason. / Aye! / And I say and said and will say / that love and burning love ("am-ars") cry out, / and whoever blames love slings dung.[29]

Although literary scholars have taken this strophe as a criticism of a style of adulterous love poetry associated with the court of Eble of *Ventadorn*—indeed this strophe has provided some of the most "solid" evidence that such verse was promoted by Eble of Ventadorn[30]—a politically partisan reading of this criticism of the "troba n'Eblo" and of Marcabru's contrast of "amors" with "amars" seems appropriate. Isembert of Châtelaillon's ancestral territorial claim is being delegitimized, presented as a mere "invention of lord Eble" maintained against right reason and therefore not the sort of claim that a vassal or "soudadier" should engage himself to defend. Not only does the speaker offer himself as an example for his audience to follow when he announces that he will never support lord Eble's foolish inventions, but he also announces his partisanship in the propaganda war between "amors" and "amars": between seculars, who are characterized by passionate or sensual ardor, and religious, who are characterized by pure love, or, more specifically, between the lord or lineage of Châtelaillon and monks. Marcabru repeats what has been, is, and will be his position in the verbal battle: whoever blames the religious is wrong, is just slinging dung.

One begins to suspect, however, that the real dung-slinger in this dispute is Marcabru in his partisan support of the monks. As is so often the case in monastic chronicles, which paint an offending lord's wife as the bad influence urging him on in his depredations and disobedience, so with Isembert's wife Aeline, who was considered by chroniclers to have her

29. XXXI, strophe 9:

> Ja non farai mai plevina / Ieu per la troba n'Eblo, / Que sentenssa follatina / Manten encontra razo; / Ai! / Qu'ieu dis e dic e dirai / Quez amors et amars brai, / Hoc, / E qui blasm' Amor buzina.

30. See, for example, M. Dumitrescu, "Eble II de Ventadorn et Guillaume IX d'Aquitaine," *Cahiers de Civilisation Médiévale* 11 (1968), 379–412, and the discussion of Eble II of Ventadorn's supposed "school" in Ulrich Mölk, *Trobar clus, trobar leu* (Munich, 1968), pp. 19–39.

weak-willed husband in her whorish powers.[31] Marcabru's slander of ladies who satisfy their lusts with household servants sounds very like a clerical invention aimed not just to explain a lord's behavior, but to delegitimize his lineage in the eyes of others, especially his vassals and "soudadiers," to foment and justify their rebellion. If the ousting of Isembert profited the monks, it could do so only if Duke William X of Aquitaine, in repossessing the lands of his vassal, respected the monks' rights, which they might reasonably expect he would do. As opposed to his father William IX, who was excommunicated twice for defying the church, William X collaborated more cooperatively with the clergy and monks of his domain (although he too was excommunicated, but for being too obedient—to Pope Anaclete, the eventual loser of the papal schism of the 1130's, and to local bishops and abbots who supported Anaclete).

The religious partisanship driving Marcabru's poetic blame of secular lords is further elucidated by two poems addressed to Emperor Alphonse VII of Castile and León and probably composed, at least in initial versions, in 1138 and 1139.[32] Because of Alphonse's crusades against the Moslem Almoravides in southern Spain, Marcabru praises his "proeza" in the first lyric, "Emperaire, per mi mezeis" ("Emperor, I myself"), which is an exhortation to mount a new crusade, but in the second, "Emperaire, per vostre prez" ("Emperor, for your worth"), he criticizes Alphonse for not rewarding him sufficiently and threatens to bring down Alphonse's reputation by stigmatizing him as base and cowardly. Marcabru concludes with an insinuation of his ignoble mercantilism: no emperor or king will ever get such a "bargain" out of him as Alphonse has had. Indeed, no living ruler does receive such high praise from Marcabru in surviving lyrics attributed to him. Marcabru's vocation is not to praise secular rulers, but to blame them, to threaten to destroy their reputations and their legitimacy if they do not do what the church wants.

In addressing Alphonse, Marcabru assumes the role and authority of divine messenger; after an initial strophe describing the noble virtues that

31. Richard, *Comtes de Poitou,* 2: 16.

32. For this dating argument, see Paul Boissonnade, "Les personnages et les événements de l'histoire d'Allemagne, de France et d'Espagne dans l'oeuvre de Marcabru (1129–1150)," *Romania* 48 (1922), 207–42, here 235–37. Critical editions of "Emperaire, per mi mezeis" and "Emperaire, per vostre prez" have been published by Aurelio Roncaglia, "I due sirventensi di Marcabru ad Alfonso VII," *Cultura neolatina,* 10 (1950), 157–83, who proposes a date of 1143 (instead of 1138) for "Emperaire, per mi mezeis." The latest discussion of these arguments may be found in Ruth Harvey, "Marcabru and the Spanish *Lavador,*" *Forum for Modern Language Studies* 22 (1986): 125–26.

have merited his own visit, Marcabru rapidly proceeds to put Alphonse in his "place":

> Because the Son of God summons you / to avenge him on the lineage of Pharaoh, / you ought to rejoice.[33]

Alphonse is Christ's vassal, bound to serve him for his fief, and Marcabru is there to remind him of his obligations—and not only him, but all Christian lords.

The third strophe of this crusade lyric begins Marcabru's castigation of rulers on the other side of the Pyrenees: they spend their time (like a bunch of women) "weaving a cloth of envy and wrong"; wealthy lords prefer lounging and comfortable sleeping ("mol jazer e soau dormir") to conquering "honor and wealth and merit"; shameless they covet one another's possessions and think they will save themselves through riches; Youth fails due to greed. Marcabru rounds off these accusations with a challenge to the legitimacy of the young French king Louis VII who, by his marriage in 1137 to Eleanor, William X's eldest daughter and heiress, became Count of Poitou (and Duke of Aquitaine):

> Since France, Poitou, and Berry / bow to a single lord, / let him come here and do service for his fief!
>
> For I don't know why the prince exists / if he does not do service to God for his fief.[34]

Here Marcabru tries to shame Louis VII into crusading in Spain by defining kingship as a feudal contract with God, which would justify royal dominion only so long as the king fulfills his defensive obligations to protect God's kingdom (the Christian church, here being equated with Christians under attack in Moslem Spain). Any king who does not live up to his

33. Roncaglia, p. 160, strophe 2 (Dejeanne, XXII):

Pois lo Fills de Dieu vos somo / que.l vengetz del ling Farao, / ben vos en devetz esbaudir.

34. Roncaglia, p. 162, first and second *tornadas:*

Mas Franssa, Peitau e Beiriu / aclin'a un sol seignoriu, / veign'a Dieu sai son fieu servir!

Qu'ieu non sai per que princes viu / s'a Dieu no vai son fieu servir.

obligations to his overlord God, Marcabru implies, is worthless and does not deserve to be kept alive.

In the general territorial and political interests of the church, and perhaps of particular monasteries that profited from the outright gifts and pawning of lands by crusaders, Marcabru sought the support of Alphonse VII and provided him with poetic propaganda that, by shaming other lords into joining military expeditions against the Almoravides under Alphonse's "imperial" leadership, promoted his territorial interests and ambitions for greater prestige. Yet Alphonse was by no means immune from criticism. In Marcabru's verse the only truly good secular lord is a dead one, for the dead lord's virtues can be deliberately idealized in ways that challenge his descendants' imitation or diminish them by comparison.

In his most famous crusade lyric, "Pax in nomine domini," Marcabru's religious partisanship is clearly announced in the first line by the Latin proclamation of peace (the peace at home that is supposed to accompany crusading abroad). Like the fulminating of anathema, his invective works to pollute the noncrusading noble and cast him out of the ranks of the nobility. Those who behave ignobly show their true origins; to refuse to honor God by crusading is to risk being confounded with the descendants of Cain (as the Muslims were said to be):

> Near here, there are so many / of the lineage of Cain, / the first felon, / that not a one does honor to God . . .
>
> And the sensualist criers-after-wine, / dinner-gobblers, blowers-on-the-coals, / squatters-in-the-path, / will remain in their squalor.[35]

Marcabru's invective epithets are deliberately vulgar and ugly, bristling with harsh combinations of sound ("corna-vi," "coita-disnar," "bufa-tizo," "crup-en-cami"). The most powerful leaders ("plus rics captaus") are "broken, flawed, tired of prowess" ("fraitz, faillitz, de proeza las"). The French are "denatured"—they demonstrate that their natural condition of

35. Ricketts and Hathaway, p. 2, strophe 5 & 6 (Dejeanne, XXXV):

> Probet del linatge Cai, / del premiran home fello, / a tans aissi / c'us a Dieu non porta honor . . .
>
> E.l luxurios corna-vi, / coita-disnar, bufa-tizo, / crup-en-cami / remanran inz el folpidor . . .

being "franc" or noble has been corrupted—if they refuse God's business ("Desnaturat son li Frances, / si de l'afar Dieu dizon no").

Even though the explicit concern of much of Marcabru's verse is the decline of noble virtues, and especially the debasement of lineages through illegitimate sexual unions, this concern is, as we have seen, an excuse for delegitimizing and often quite slanderous criticism aimed at stirring up discontent and putting pressure on lords from below. Instead of spending words threatening nobles with hellfire and damnation to keep them in line (although he occasionally does that too),[36] he threatens them with being the debasers of their own blood, the destroyers of their natural virtues and of the justification for their own rule. He threatens lineages with loss of honor and power in this world rather than the next. In this respect, Marcabru's slanderous lyrics supplement other verbal means the church used at this time—in a prolonged struggle for power we call the "peace" and Gregorian reform movements—to pressure secular lords into obedience. To the extent that people accepted the clerically elaborated ideology that justified noble power and possession by grounding it upon notions of the "purity" of noble blood, nobles were vulnerable to criticism for improper breeding practices. The church pressured noble lords by excommunicating them, or threatening to, for their contumacious persistence in bigamy or incest (and the dissolution of loyalties and feudal vows that could result from a lord's excommunication put teeth into these threats); similarly, Marcabru's vernacular lyrics pressured them with the publication of their adulteries (which threatened to undermine the legitimacy of their lineages).

Some rulers, such as Duke William IX of Aquitaine, fought back against ecclesiastical attempts to dishonor and control them. Because of the church's refusal to recognize his father's second marriage (to a daughter of the Duke of Burgundy), William was born illegitimate in 1071, and his younger brother Hugh remained so all his life. Although at the age of five William was legitimized by the pope to insure a peaceful succession, the marriage of his mother to his father was never recognized, his parents were shamed by their "incestuous" union (which they apparently did not break off), and William's mother's name did not appear on any official charters until after her husband's death.[37] Whether or not William IX's opposition to church interference in noble marriages was grounded in this childhood experience, resist he did. In 1100 he forcibly tried to break up the council of Poitiers before the members could renew an excommunication of

36. See Appendix B.

37. Richard, *Comtes de Poitou,* 1: 310–22, 380–81.

his overlord, King Philip I of France, for remaining in a marriage considered illegitimate by the church (because Bertrade de Montfort had left her husband, Fulk le Rechin, Count of Anjou, to marry Philip, who had left his wife for her).[38] When William IX was himself excommunicated on two occasions around 1115, by the bishops of Poitiers and Angoulême, for refusing to separate from the wife of his vassal, the viscount of Châtellerault, each time he reacted by threatening to kill, taunting, or exiling the excommunicating bishop.[39] The lyrics ascribed to the count of Poitou are of a piece with this sort of resistance. In effect, by performing or having these performed in his lands, William IX thumbed his nose at the church. Nor did his reputation for facetious, lascivious song go unreproved by monastic chroniclers[40] or, albeit more implicitly, through their own lyric ripostes by Marcabru and his continuators.

Only eleven lyrics ascribed in the manuscripts to the "Count of Poitou" have come down to us, often in unique copies, only two sufficiently specific about the lordship involved to be fairly certainly by William IX.[41] What several of these poems share is their theme: jocular boasting about sexual dominance and accounts or hints of sexual exploits with the wives of the boaster's vassals. In "Companions, I will make a suitable lyric" ("Companho, farai un vers covinen"), the speaker gradually reveals that the two fine saddle horses about whom he has been speaking with a number of sexual innuendos are two women, Ladies Agnes and Arsen, whom he has given in marriage to two of his vassals (probably with the castles and lands the ladies inherited, "Gimel" and "Niol" [Nieuil]) but with the jocular stipulation that his vassals' proprietorship is merely temporary, that he will retain possession of the women (as well as of the fiefs). In another lyric, "In Auvergne, near the Limousin" ("En Alvernhe, part Lemozi"), which he begins in some versions by castigating ladies who love monks or clerics

38. Richard, *Comtes de Poitou,* 428–30.

39. See Richard, *Comtes de Poitou,* 468–69 & 472–73; Bond, *Poetry of William VII,* pp. 128–33, for Latin texts and English translations of William of Malmesbury's account of William IX's violent resistance to these two excommunications and for Hildebert of Lavardin's poem praising Bishop Peter of Poitiers as a saintly martyr for applying the "knife" of excommunication (Peter died soon after William IX exiled him), and accusing William of polluting his lands with his illicit union: "He had chased the bride from the wedding bed, the wife from the throne, / Harming temple, bed, and country with violence, whoredom and ruin."

40. See Bond, *Poetry of William VII,* 118–21, for selections and translations from Orderic Vitalis and William of Malmesbury.

41. The critical edition is by Nicolo Pasero, *Guglielmo IX d'Aquitania* (Modena, 1973). "Pos de chantar m'es pres talenz," William's lyric *congé* taking leave of this world, is the only one in which the speaker identifies himself as the lord of Poitou. From his boasts of overlordship of "Gimel" and "Niol" in "Companho, farai un vers covinen," we might deduce the speaker's identity.

rather than knights, William describes how he tricked Ladies Agnes and Ermessen, the wives of "En Guari" and "En Bernart": by pretending to be deaf and dumb, he assured the wives that they might use him for their sexual pleasure with impunity. In the secrecy of their chamber, after a good meal at their hearth and a painful proof of his muteness, he claims to have obliged them 188 times. "I want many to know" ("Ben vueill que sapchon li pluzor") is another boasting lyric in which the speaker narrates a sexual exploit, this time via dicing metaphors, and claims such mastery that women always want him again, for "I well know how to earn my bread / in all markets" ("que be.n sai gazanhar mon pa / entotz mercatz"). William IX castigates husbands for "guarding cunt" (especially from the likes of himself) in two poems addressed by their initial word to his "companions," presumably his vassals or soldierly retinue. In the first of these, "Companions, I can't help being shocked" ("Compaigno, non puosc mudar qu'eo no m'effrei"), the speaker, assuming a lordly judicial role, announces that he has just received a lady's complaint that her jealous husband, against law and right, keeps her shut up by three vulgar, unrefined guardians. Then, directly addressing the "gardador" (the jealous husbands), he warns them that they are sure to be cuckolded by these low guardians: "for if you keep good company away from her, / she'll accommodate herself to what she finds around her" ("Si.l tenez a cartat lo bon conrei, / adoba.s d'aquel que troba viron sei"). William's moral is that it is better to be cuckolded by "good company" than bad. Indeed, the sexual intercourse of a vassal's wife (or of other females of his family) with good company such as himself, as William implies in "Companions, I have had such a poor reception" ("Companho tant ai agutz d'avols conres"), is downright profitable to the vassal. The speaker warns those who have not shown him the expected hospitality that they break the natural "law of cunt," which increases, rather than diminishes, with use, just as several trees grow in a woods in place of one chopped down. (Indeed, for William to take his "cut" of a vassal's woods [women] would be to improve the stock.) By means of such analogies to nature, William IX suggests that any progeny he might sire on a vassal's wife or other women in his protection would be all to the good.

Marcabru mines William IX's lyric boasts of his sexual dominance for their dishonoring implications. For example, through his hearthside feeding metaphors for sexual intercourse between ladies and baseborn household servants,[42] Marcabru recollects a situation William had boasted of in

42. See, for example, Dejeanne XXXI, strophe 7; XXXVIII, strophes 4 and 5.

"En Alvernhe, part Lemozi," but with an important difference: whereas a duke incognito presents no serious threat to the nobility of the blood of the cuckolded husband's lineage, Marcabru's churlish servants do. He takes William's point—that noblemen's wives, when left unsupervised by their husbands, will be perfectly happy to have sexual intercourse with a deaf-mute stranger in the secrecy of their kitchens—and turns it against noble husbands, like William himself, who spend their time trying to cuckold other husbands. While William was holed up with Ladies Agnes and Ermessen, what was his own wife doing?

If guarding wives and keeping "good company" away from them will result in the jealous husband's cuckolding by base guardians, as William warns in another lyric ("Compaigno, non puosc mudar qu'eo no m'effrei"), Marcabru announces that that is just what is happening, whether the wives are guarded or not. Ladies Agnes and Ermessen are not very reassuring; they serve to prove Marcabru's repeated accusation (which smacks of clerical misogyny) that all women are basically prostitutes ("putas"). This is what the speaker charges, for example, in the single surviving version of "I am glad when the waves grow bright" ("Bel m'es can s'esclarzis l'onda"):

> With difficulty nowadays will the prostitute / feel shame over rude testicles, / but she welcomes violation by the crude baboon / because he plumbs her / often, no matter who complains,
>
> Because he has the second key, / whereby the lord, I assure you, / wears a cap of cunt horns; / for only by means of a graft does his lady / grow round, so says Marcabru.[43]

Here the "second key" is both a sexual metaphor and a reference to the office of the cuckolder, a guardian entrusted with surveillance of the lady, a trusted, baseborn household servant.[44]

43. Dejeanne, XII bis:

> A! greu aura ia vergonda / Putia de gros bosin, / Mas nafrot baldit baboin / Ja acueilh, car li aprionda / Soven, qi qe s'en graus.
>
> Car el n'a la clau segonda / Per qe.l segner, so.us afin, / Porta capel cornut conin, / C'ab sol un empeu[t] redonda / Si donz, lo ditz Marcabrus.

44. The blatantly phallic second-key imagery in Marcabru's verse (where the lowborn servants are the possessers of the "second keys") may mock William IX's call for a "counterkey" to someone's casket with the last word of his enigmatic poem of "strictly nothing." See Harvey, *The Troubadour Marcabru,* pp. 77–78.

In "On a song gone astray, cantor" ("Al son desviat chantaire"), Marcabru's attack is pointed by allusions to William IX's lyrics. Those Marcabru explicitly blames for reviling Prowess in one strophe of this poem are "dukes and kings and emperors," but he targets William IX's riddling lyric beginning, "I will make a poem about strictly nothing" ("Farai un vers de dreit nien") when he declares himself to be the "sermonizer of folly" and the "chastizer of nothing" ("nien"). In the two strophes wherein Marcabru denigrates husbands for their games of cuckoldry, there is an allusion to Saint Hilary that may also point to William IX:

> Husbands, by Saint Hilary, / are brothers ("confraire" or, punning, "cunt-brothers") in a / single folly, / for among them war is waged / so that the horned husband makes a horned wife, / and the cuckold blamed makes the cuckoldress blamed; / then even the tail starts shouting.[45]

Saint-Hilaire was an important monastery of Poitiers of which the Count had, for generations, been the official Abbot.[46] That the "*con*-fraternity" of cuckolded and cuckolding husbands should be assembled under the patronage of Saint Hilary seems to point to the pernicious influence of Abbot William IX.

William IX's sexual boast of his ability to "earn his bread in any market" Marcabru also turns against him with his many debasing descriptions of these cuckolding contests as mercantile and deliberately deceptive trade (or "barat"). For example, in "I like to hear the frog sing" ("Bel m'es quan la rana chanta"), a lyric variously attributed to Marcabru or Alegret (a jongleur whose verse shares Marcabru's themes and style),[47] the speaker says that noble cuckolders will be cuckolded by their own wives and will have no right to complain about this, because this is the law of trade:

> The husband who scratches another man's cunt / may be sure that his own goes fishing / and shows men how to engage it, / so that he is beaten with his own stick; / and he will be wrong to complain, / because law and reason

45. Dejeanne, V, strophe 4:

> Moillerat, per saint Ylaire, / Son d'una foldat confraire, / Qu'entr'els es guerra moguda / Tals que cornutz fa cornuda, / E cogotz copatz copada, / Puois eis la coa de braire.

46. Since 942, Richard, *Comtes de Poitou*, 1: 82. Stopping such lay retention of ecclesiastical benefices was one of goals of the Gregorian reform movement.

47. For Alegret's verse, see *Jongleurs et troubadours gascons des XIIe et XIIIe siècles*, ed. Alfred Jeanroy (Paris, 1923), pp. 4–11.

demonstrate / that whoever buys dearly sells dearly / now, according to the law of Pisa.[48]

In the strophe leading up to this, the speaker accuses dukes and kings of being the first to close Prowess's mouth by making "a big noise about a little deed / because giving makes them ashamed" ("Qu'ill fan de pauc fag gran nauza / Quar Donars lur fai vergonha"). Whether the little deed dukes and kings have boasted about is to be understood as a deed of cuckoldry (one thinks of the wife-stealing of William IX and Philip I of France) is uncertain.

In the strophe after the one accusing the cuckolders of ignoble mercantilism, the speaker is careful to point out the deleterious effects of their greed on their lineage, and consequently on their followers; the white-shirted, flattering upstart whom the lord sets guard over his wife cuckolds him at his own pleasure:

From this one is born that low-down merchandise, / the wealthy lord—may death and God strike him down— / who never gives feasts or holds dances. / May he not be stuffed with praise / who famishes his followers; / this one puts on a white robe / and makes his lord indulgent / and "keeps" his lady at his own pleasure.[49]

The natural metaphors William IX used to argue that lesser men should not guard their wives (at least not from him), Marcabru counters with less reassuring natural metaphors. Whereas William assured his companions that three trees would quickly grow in place of the one chopped down in their woods, Marcabru complains of the grafting of worthless trees—willows and elders—onto the noble stocks of old fruit trees, the degeneration of noble lineages.[50]

48. Dejeanne, XI, strophe 7:

Maritz qui l'autrui con grata / Ben pot saber que.l sieus pescha / E mostra com hom li mescha, / Qu'ab eis le sieu fust lo bata, / Et aura.n tort si s'en clama, / Car drech e racos deviza / Que qui car compra car ven, / Ar, segon la lei de Piza.

49. XI, strophe 8:

D'aqui nais l'avols barata, / Ric cui mortz e Dieus descresca! / Qu'us non fai condug ni tresca; / Non sia lauzenja plata / Cell qui sa maisnad' afama; / Cest vest la blancha camiza / E fai son seinhor sufren / E ten si dons a sa guiza.

50. Aurelio Roncaglia, "Marcabruno: 'Al departir del brau tempier,'" *Cultura Neolatina* 13 (1953), 7 (Dejeanne, III): "fuelhs e flors, paron de pomier, / son al fruchar sautz e saucs" (the

"As long as good Youth was father / of the world and loyal Love mother, / Worth was maintained in secret and in the open, / but now they have debased it, / dukes and kings and emperors."[51] The past that Marcabru idealizes in strophes such as this—when lords were generous to their households and dependents (not avaricious), when they were content to hold their own (and did not spend their time envying and fighting against one another to accumulate wealth), when they fought the infidels to protect the church in fulfillment of their duty as God's vassals (and did not luxuriate at home scheming against one another), when they maintained the purity of their blood by maintaining the strictures of marriage (and did not try to keep their own wives and enjoy other men's too)—this past is surely a fiction, but not a naive one. Marcabru deliberately challenges the lord who buys into glorification of his ancestry to live up to an ecclesiastical ideal of secular lordship (in which fiscal exactions, the judgment and punishment of wrongdoers, and military prowess exercised against other Christians are notably absent), an ideal sanctioned by its attribution to noble forebears, even though it is really a recent invention, a project for bringing present lords under control, and propaganda of the "peace" movement.

Appendix A

Nineteenth-century Occitan scholars such as Friedrich Diez and Hermann Suchier believed that Marcabru was a contemporary of Richard-the-Lionhearted. Paul Meyer first argued that Marcabru's verse was composed during the reign of William X, Duke of Aquitaine, from approximately

---

fruit and flowers appear to be those of apple trees, / but at fruition they prove to be willows and elders).

51. Dejeanne, V, strophe 7:

> Tant cant bos Jovens fon paire / Del segle e fin' Amors maire, / Fon Proeza mantenguda / A celat et a saubuda, / Mas er l'ant avilanada / Duc e rei et emperaire."

The imagery of the final strophe of this lyric seems, once again, intended to critically revise that in a lyric attributed to William IX. Whereas, in "Ab la dolchor del temps novel," William celebrates the poignant fragility of an illicit love with the natural metaphor of a budding branch in a treetop that trembles in the freezing night rain before leafing out under the warm sun of the following day, Marcabru preaches a legitimized love that "is born in a noble place / and the spot where it grows / is enclosed by branching boughs and [protected] from heat and cold / so that no stranger can reach it" ("L'amors don ieu sui mostraire / Nasquet en un gentil aire, / E.l luoc ou ill es creguda / Es claus de rama branchuda / E de chaut e de gelada, / Qu'estrains no l'en puosca traire").

1135–1150.[52] Paul Boissonnade pushed the beginning of Marcabru's career back to 1129 and judged, "Because he nowhere mentions Guillaume VII the troubadour [IX as Duke], it is certain that the prince who was his principal and constant protector, at whose side he undoubtedly acquired his poetic reputation, is solely Guillaume VIII."[53] Subsequent scholarly dating arguments have remained within the parameters set by Boissonnade. I believe that Marcabru (that is, the man at the beginning of the tradition), whose true patron was the church and not any particular secular lord, probably began composing earlier in the 1120s in the general context of the "peace" movement and in critical response to Duke William IX's and his imitators' lyric resistance to ecclesiastical pressures for behavioral reform of the nobility. Although there is general scholarly consensus that the verse ascribed to Marcabru shows many signs of a clerical education, and Richard Goddard, in a 1985 Oxford dissertation, has suggested that Marcabru was a court cleric as well as a jongleur,[54] we will probably never know precisely how the man at the head of this tradition (whose given name was almost certainly not Marcabru) was linked to the church. One might well view the variety of rulers addressed in different areas of southern France and northern Spain in verse ascribed to Marcabru, not as signs of the precarious livelihood of a lay jongleur in constant search of the patronage of secular lords, as we have tended to do, but rather as signs of a successfully prosecuted, church-supported, propaganda campaign by an itinerant poet-preacher who communicated, in part, through vernacular lyrics. In a recent essay that draws on Goddard's study, Simon Gaunt notes, "Marcabru's poetry can be read almost as a form of church propaganda which carefully foregrounds issues like cuckoldry and illegitimate children that will strike a chord with a lay audience. It may well be no accident that the only troubadour consistently to concern himself with sexual morality, and particularly with the condemnation of adultery, should have been active at a time when the Church was attempting to reform the marital practices of lay society."[55]

52. Paul Meyer, "Marcabrun," *Romania* 6 (1877), 119–29.

53. Boissonnade, "Les personnages," p. 210.

54. Richard Goddard, "The Early Troubadours and the Latin Tradition," diss., Oxford, 1985, pp. 72–75.

55. Simon Gaunt, "Marginal Men, Marcabru and Orthodoxy: The Early Troubadours and Adultery," *Medium Aevum* 59 (1990), 67.

Appendix B

In a lyric ascribed in two of five manuscript versions to Bernart de Ventadorn and in three to Marcabru, "Pus mos coratges s'es clarzitz" ("Since my mood is lightened,") (XL), the speaker preaches the value of "good love" and threatens with hell's punishments a list of sinners that occupies three whole strophes. Among many other types of sinners such as homicides, traitors, simoniacs, and magicians, the speaker includes some that typify Marcabru's concerns elsewhere: false married people, cuckolds, and "burning prostitutes / who consent to others' husbands" ("putas ardens / Qui son d'autrui maritz cossens"). The two manuscripts (C and E) that ascribe this lyric to Bernart de Ventadorn apparently regard the expression "Marcabru ditz," not as an internal signature, but a reference to Marcabru's prior verse criticism. The strophe in question, which appears in all manuscript versions, particularly singles out for the punishments of hell, on Marcabru's authority, "drunkards and cuckold / false priests and abbots / false male and female recluses" ("Ebriaic et escogossat, / Fals preveire e fals abat, / Falsas recluzas, fals reclus, / Lai penaran, ditz Marcabrus"). This linking of Marcabru with criticism of false priests, abbots, and recluses may suggest his opposition to one of the games Duke William IX (hereditary Abbot of Saint-Hilaire of Poitiers) is reported to have played: "at a certain castle called Niort he built some little houses, almost like monastic huts, and wildly proclaimed that he would found an Abbey of Whores. And he sang that he would establish this girl or that one, whom he named, all from famous brothels, as his abbess, his prioress, and his other officials."[56]

56. See Bond, *Poetry of William VII,* pp. 120–21, for the Latin text and English translation of this passage from William of Malmesbury's *Gesta regum.*

C. Stephen Jaeger

12. Courtliness and Social Change

ich schilt die âventiure niht, / swie uns ze liegen geschiht / von der âventiure rât, / wan si bezeichenunge hât / der zuht unde der wârheit.

(What the romances tell us may be a pack of lies, but I do not criticize them, for they contain symbols of courtesy and truth)
—Thomasin von Zirclaere, *Der welsche Gast*, 1121–25

This study suggests ways of assessing the part played by courtly literature and courtly ideals in the social changes of the twelfth century. It is not easy to assess the role of literature and ideas in any climate of social crisis and change.[1] For twelfth-century court society, where imaginative literature forms a large part of the documentation, the problems are great, and that makes methodology a fundamental concern. Courtly literature is fantastic and artificial;[2] the society in which it arose was rough, rude, and violent.[3] The society produced social codes that seem to mediate between literature and reality, or at least to occupy an intermediary position,[4] but there is no

1. Gabrielle Spiegel, "History, Historicism, and the Social Logic of the Text in the Middle Ages," *Speculum* 65 (1990), 59–86; and Spiegel, "Social Change and Literary Language: The Textualization of the Past in Thirteenth-Century Old French Historiography," *Journal of Medieval and Renaissance Studies* 17 (1987), 129–48. See the extensive survey of research by Otto H. Baumhauer, "Kulturwandel: Zur Entwicklung des Paradigmas von der Kultur als Kommunikationssystem: Forschungsbericht," *Deutsche Vierteljahrsschrift* 56 (1982), Sonderheft, 1–167.

2. See Erich Auerbach's reading, in *Mimesis: The Representation of Reality in Western Literature*, tr. Willard R. Trask (New York, 1957), pp. 107–24 ("The Knight Sets Forth").

3. See Joachim Bumke, *Höfische Kultur: Literatur und Gesellschaft im hohen Mittelalter*, 2 vols. (Munich, 1986), 1: esp. 9–14, 430–32; tr. Thomas Dunlap, *Courtly Culture: Literature and Society in the High Middle Ages*, (Berkeley, CA, 1991); Arno Borst, "Das Rittertum im Hochmittelalter: Ideal und Wirklichkeit," *Saeculum* 10 (1959), 213–31, rpt. in *Das Rittertum im Mittelalter*, ed. Arno Borst, Wege der Forschung 349 (Darmstadt, 1976), pp. 212–46; Georges Duby, "Youth in Aristocratic Society," in his *The Chivalrous Society*, tr. Cynthia Postan (London, 1977), pp. 112–22.

4. For instance, on chivalric honor, see Jean Flori, *L'idéologie du glaive: préhistoire de la chevalerie* (Geneva, 1983); Flori, *L'essor de la chevalerie, XIe–XIIe siècles* (Geneva, 1986). On courtly manners, see C. Stephen Jaeger, *The Origins of Courtliness: Civilizing Trends and the Formation of Courtly Ideals, 939–1210* (Philadelphia: University of Pennsylvania Press, 1985); and courtly love, Bumke, *Höfische Kultur* pp. 503–82, and Rüdiger Schnell in a series of works,

agreement on the ability of such codes to set standards of social behavior.[5] And yet one of the hard and accepted facts of the history of chivalry is that the ideal of the chivalric courtly knight in literature created a social ideal;[6] shortly after the emergence of courtly literature, "knighthood" has risen from humble beginnings as mounted soldiers to a noble order comprising the entire nobility.[7] And dukes, counts and kings are proud to have themselves and their ancestors represented in family chronicles as modest, debonair gentlemen, who overlook insult and abuse and never seek revenge.[8]

Society changed; it sought the trappings of chivalric romance;[9] it staged festivals that were themselves the stuff of romance.[10] But did warriors become "verhöflicht," and if they did, what part did courtly literature have in their reformation? [11] There is a large gap that separates the sublime idealism of romance from the realities of court society. What, if anything, does that gap say about the engagedness of courtly literature in the process of civilizing the knighthood?

Romantic and Victorian scholarship tended to make courtly literature into documentation of social realities.[12] For the past few decades the major

---

most recently, "Die 'höfische Liebe' als 'höfischer Diskurs' über die Liebe," in *Curialitas: Studien zu Grundfragen der höfisch-ritterlichen Kultur* ed. Josef Fleckenstein (Göttingen 1990), pp. 231–301. Also his *Causa amoris: Liebeskonzeption und Liebesdarstellung in der mittelalterlichen Literatur* (Bern-Francke, 1985).

5. See Bumke, *Höfische Kultur,* pp. 439ff. The non-existence of "courtly love" as a social practice is virtually an accepted tenet of current literature. Cf. Schnell in *Curialitas,* p. 300, referring to the current scholarly consensus: "der höfische Frauendienst war keine gesellschaftliche Realität; die 'höfische Liebe' existierte lediglich als 'a mode of thought' bzw. nur in der Literatur."

6. The result of Joachim Bumke's *Studien zum Ritterbegriff im 12. und 13. Jahrhundert,* 2nd ed. (Heidelberg, 1977).

7. Bumke, *Studien* esp. pp. 130ff.; also Bumke, *Höfische Kultur* (with extensive bibliography); Georges Duby, "The Origins of Knighthood," in *The Chivalrous Society* (note 3 above), pp. 158–70; Maurice Keen, *Chivalry* (New Haven, CT, 1984); Flori, *L'idéologie* and *L'essor* (note 4 above).

8. Jaeger, *Origins,* pp. 195–210.

9. See Bumke, *Höfische Kultur,* pp. 137–275 ("Sachkultur und Gesellschaftsstil").

10. See Bumke, *Höfische Kultur,* pp. 276–318; also the studies in *Höfische Repräsentation: Das Zeremoniell und die Zeichen,* ed. Hedda Ragotzky and Horst Wenzel (Tübingen, 1990); *Das Fest,* ed. Walter Haug and Rainer Warning (Munich, 1989); *Feste und Feiern im Mittelalter,* ed. Detlef Altenburg, Jörg Jarnut, and Hans-Hugo Steinhoff (Sigmaringen, 1991). The study by John Baldwin, "Jean Renart et le tournoi de Saint-Trond: Une conjonction de l'histoire et de la littérature," *Annales ESC* 45 (1990), 565–88, is valuable for showing the literary representation of court practice.

11. "Verhöflichung der Krieger" is Norbert Elias's term: *Über den Prozess der Zivilisation: Soziogenetische und Psychogenetische Untersuchungen,* 2d ed., 2 vols. (Bern, 1969), 2: 351–69. See Sabine Krüger, "'Verhöflichter Krieger' und miles illitteratus," in *Curialitas,* pp. 326–49.

12. For instance, Alwyn Schultz, *Das höfische Leben zur Zeit der Minnesinger,* 2 vols., 2d ed. (1889; rpt. Osnabrück, 1965); Hans Naumann continues this tradition and represents the

work in the area has reacted against that trend. It was an important corrective to the nineteenth-century view of the middle ages. But it has its limits. It tends to relegate courtly literature and the social values it conveys to the realm of "the ideal" and privileges non-fictional documents as spokesmen of "reality." This view has prominent adherents: Johan Huizinga,[13] Erich Auerbach, and Erich Köhler. Joachim Bumke recently published a study of major importance that draws in part on this paradigm for its conceptual framework.[14] E. R. Curtius deserves mention in this connection for tending to isolate literature in a realm by itself. Curtius helped us look on literature as a composite of received forms, isolated in literary traditions—as texts generated by earlier texts—and discouraged us from looking on it as texts charged with ideas and social issues alive and influential in the period which produced them.[15]

The opposition of the ideal and the real accommodates post-

---

moral values of courtly literature as actual social values in *Deutsche Kultur im Zeitalter des Rittertums* (Potsdam, 1938). See Bumke, who comes to terms with this entire trend in *Höfische Kultur* pp. 14–17. It is easy to do an injustice to much of the earlier literature in a kind of wholesale dismissal of its premises. Still instructive for the moral force of courtly literature, without succumbing to the fallacies Bumke warns against, is Kenelm Digby's *The Broad Stone of Honor or, The True Sense and Practice of Chivalry*, 4 vols. (London 1877). See the fascinating survey by Mark Girouard, *The Return to Camelot: Chivalry and the English Gentleman* (New Haven, CT, 1985).

13. Huizinga represents the strengths and weaknesses of the Ideal vs. Real paradigm. His judgment of chivalry as a historiographical idea: "The confused image of contemporaneous history being much too complicated for their comprehension, they simplified it, as it were, by the fiction of chivalry as a moving force. . . . A very fantastic and rather shallow point of view, no doubt. How much vaster is ours. . . . Still, this vision of a world ruled by chivalry, however superficial and mistaken it might be, was the best they had. . . . It served them as a formula to understand, in their poor way, the appalling complexity of the world's way" (*The Waning of the Middle Ages: A Study of the Forms of Life, Thought, and Art in France and the Netherlands in the XIVth and XVth Centuries*, tr. F. Hopman [London, 1924], p. 68). The voice of the patriarch chastising his silly, ungovernable subjects sounds wherever Huizinga talks of chivalry. Its ideals are symptomatic of "the spirit of a primitive age, susceptible of gross delusions and little accessible to the correction of experience" (p. 129). They are comforting lies: "In order to forget the painful imperfection of reality, the nobles turn to the continual illusion of a high and heroic life. They wear the mask of Lancelot and Tristram. It is an amazing self-deception. The crying falsehood of it can only be borne by treating it with some amount of raillery" (p. 80).

14. Bumke, *Höfische Kultur*, esp. pp. 9–14, 430–50; also Auerbach, *Mimesis;* Erich Köhler, *Ideal und Wirklichkeit in der höfischen Epik* (Tübingen Niermeyer, 1970); Johanna Maria van Winter, *Rittertum: Ideal und Wirklichkeit* (Munich, 1969); Klaus Schreiner, "Hof (*curia*) und höfische Lebensführung (*vita curialis*) als Herausforderung an die christliche Theologie und Frömmigkeit," in *Höfische Literatur, Hofgesellschaft, Höfische Lebensformen um 1200: Kolloquium am Zentrum für Interdisziplinäre Forschung der Universität Bielefeld*, ed. Gert Kaiser and Jan-Dirk Müller (Düsseldorf, 1986), pp. 67–138.

15. Ernst R. Curtius, *European Literature and the Latin Middle Ages*, tr. Willard R. Trask (New York, 1963). See Peter Godman, "The Ideas of Ernst Robert Curtius and the Genesis of *European Literature and the Latin Middle Ages*," Epilogue to *ELLMA* (rpt. Princeton, NJ, 1990), with extensive bibliography on recent studies of Curtius.

structuralist thinking without being beholden to it. It creates a category into which literature can be banished to a detached aesthetic existence with no ties to the other category, "the real." That is the direction in which post-structuralist theory tends to push literature.[16] Chivalry and courtly love, the norms governing behavior in courtly literature, are placed in a kind of limbo, and to ask about them as social realities is to repeat the mistake of Don Quixote.

* * *

In the present state of the question, a central methodological problem is how to judge the historical value of texts that bear on knighthood in the twelfth century when a large body of documentation gives sharply conflicting views.[17] The following reflections deal with the process by which determinants of social behavior are established through a conflict of ideas and interests.

Sociologists and cultural anthropologists have wrestled with the inherent impossibility of documenting the "realities" of social behavior reliably, and have tended to focus discussion on the "patterns of and models for behavior, received and transmitted by symbols,"[18] or on "the conceptual structures individuals use to construe experience."[19] The "cultural patterns" that organize experience and the "conceptual structures" that explain

16. See the methodological reflections of Gabrielle Spiegel, "History, Historicism, and the Social Logic," who summarizes a large body of theoretical literature and suggests possibilities for historical criticism in a post-structuralist theoretical climate. On the problem of non-referentiality and post-structuralist conceptions of the text, Rodolphe Gasché, *The Tain of the Mirror: Derrida and the Philosophy of Reflection* (Cambridge, 1986), esp. pp. 109–76, rescuing Derrida from an over-simplified view that sees him as abolishing referentiality ("There is nothing outside of the text"—Gasché, *The Tain,* pp. 278–93). Whatever its precise views on referentiality, post-structuralism moves away from questions like literature's role in social change and towards the questions raised by problematized discourse and hermeneutic. A general criticism of post-structuralism, Manfred Frank, *Was ist Neostrukturalismus?* (Frankfurt, 1984); trans. *What Is Neostructuralism?,* tr. Sabine Walke and Richard Gray (Minneapolis, 1989).

17. A problem analyzed evenhandedly by Yuri Bessmertny in his study "The Peasant as Seen by the Knight (Based on French Data of the 11th–13th Centuries)," in Bessmertny, *Social and Political Structures of the Middle Ages* (Moscow, 1990), pp. 45–61. Cf. p. 49: "The gap [between the ideal and the real] did not preclude the ideal from performing its ideological functions, nor did it preclude the ideal from making an impact on social realities."

18. A. L. Kroeber and Clyde Kluckhohn, "Culture: A Critical Review of Concepts and Definitions," *Harvard University Peabody Museum of American Archeology and Ethnology Papers* 47 (1952), 189. For more recent literature see the survey of research by Baumhauer, "Kulturwandel."

19. Clifford Geertz, "The Politics of Meaning," in Geertz, *The Interpretation of Cultures: Selected Essays* (New York, 1973), p. 313.

it are the object of ethnology, and not some comprehensive inventory of the actual observable forms of behavior. Cultural anthropology aims at formulating "the norms for and standards of behavior . . . the ideologies that legitimize certain select patterns of behavior or give them a rational explanation."[20] The discussion of courtly literature and courtly society would profit by moving to this more abstract level, at which symbolic models compete for dominance in a conflict of ideas aimed at establishing norms, instructing, informing, explaining, and representing behavior.

A letter of Peter of Blois will get us into the issues.[21] Letter 94 is addressed to a certain Archdeacon John. It criticizes the behavior of his two nephews, who are knights, and develops a general criticism of knighthood. He makes the following accusations. Knights slander and malign clerics; their speech is scurrilous; their behavior is inordinate; they esteem most him whose speech is filthiest and whose curses are foulest, who fears God and the church least; they claim the license to rob and slander; hardly girded with the sword, they turn to plundering the church, persecuting the poor and suffering mercilessly; they let their exorbitant lusts and desires run wild; they are slothful and drunken; corrupted by *otium,* they neglect the practice of arms; they go to battle as if to a banquet, their pack animals laden with wine, cheese, sausage, and roasting forks instead of weapons; they carry gilt and jewel-encrusted shields, which of course they are concerned to protect from sword blows; they have scenes of combat painted on their saddles and shields, "so that they may take pleasure in a kind of fantasy vision of battles [*quadam imaginaria visione*], which in reality they would not have the courage so much as to look upon, let alone take part in."[22]

Listing the accusations in this bald way strips the letter of its rhetorical structure and of the social values which move it. Now we should try to restore the syntax of thought and of argument in which these criticisms are imbedded.

The occasion for writing is the slandering of clerics. Knights have an obligation to defer to clerics, which they are neglecting shockingly. The

20. Kroeber and Kluckholn, "Culture," 189.

21. *PL,* 207, 293–97. Bumke called attention to the letter. He quotes it at length opposing its realism to the idealism of the courtly knight of romance (*Höfische Kultur,* 2: 430ff.). Some brief comments on the letter in Flori, *L'essor,* pp. 332–33. Informative on Peter of Blois's letters, though not for our context, Ethel Cardwell Higonnet, "Spiritual Ideas in the Letters of Peter of Blois," *Speculum* l 50 (1975), 218–44. Also R. W. Southern, "Peter of Blois: A Twelfth Century Humanist?" in Southern, *Medieval Humanism and Other Studies* (Oxford, 1984), pp. 105–32.

22. *PL,* 207: 296A: "Bella tamen et conflictus equestres depingi faciunt in sellis et clypeis, ut se quadam imaginaria visione delectent in pugnis, quas actualiter ingredi, aut videre non audent."

tensions between knights and clerics are a reality of social life in the period. The many testimonies to them[23] include the debate poems on the question of the comparative virtues of knights and clerics as lovers. Peter of Blois is speaking in the interests of his own social group. He has not fabricated the social tensions in which the letter originates, nor is he standing back from a disengaged distance.

The language of his accusations is conventional and easily recognized. The concerns of the peace movement since the late tenth century register in some of the complaints: the knights' obligation to protect clerics, the church, the poor, widows, and the suffering; the attack on the ungovernable and contentious character of knights and lay nobles.[24] But alongside this discourse is another: an attack on sloth, corruption, debauchery, drunkenness, and the resultant slackening of the warrior spirit. This is the language of polemics against the corruption of knights through life at the court, polemics that surfaced in the mid-eleventh century and continued into the thirteenth.[25] In Peter of Blois's letter both directions of the polemics are represented: the knights are violent outdoors; they are slothful, debauched, and corrupt at court.

Along with Peter of Blois's polemical language there is a language of chivalric ideals. He posits an "order" of knighthood, high in dignity and excellence, and a code governing its behavior.[26] Each of the knightly abuses is presented as a betrayal of the knightly code. In the conceptual syntax of his argument, ideal and abuse are set in a relationship of mutual interdependency. The knights' maligning of clerics comes from the conviction of "the eminence of knighthood"[27]; they ignore the "code of knights" in abusing clerics and in not tempering their scurrilous speech with "a kind of maidenly modesty"[28]; their corruption is all the worse because as youths they learned from their uncle "modesty and good conduct" (*modestia et hones-*

23. See Josef Fleckenstein, "Miles und clericus am Königs– und Fürstenhof: Bemerkungen zu den Voraussetzungen, zur Entstehung und zur Trägerschaft der höfisch-ritterlichen Kultur," in *Curialitas,* pp. 302–25.

24. See, among many other works, Hans-Werner Goetz, "Kirchenschutz, Rechtswahrung und Reform: Zu den Zielen und zum Wesen der frühen Gottesfriedensbewegung in Frankreich," *Francia* 11 (1983), 193–239.

25. See Henri Platelle, "Le problème du scandale: les nouvelles modes masculines aux XIe et XIIe siècles," *Revue Belge de Philologie et d'Histoire* 53 (1975), 1071–96; Jaeger, *Origins of Courtliness,* pp. 176–94.

26. On the gradual development of a knightly code of honor in the eleventh and twelfth centuries, see Flori, *L'essor,* pp. 265–67.

27. 293C: ". . . vitae militaris eminentiam jactitantes clericorum sortem multiplici detractione depravant."

28. 293D–294A: ". . . si essent milites, aut quae militum professio esset, cognoscerent, deferrent clericis; et se a scurrilitate verborum quadam puellari modestia temperarent."

tas)[29]; they receive their swords from the altar, only to turn them against the church[30]; they dishonor both the reputation and the ethics of knighthood[31]; they have received the "solemn honors" or "solemn distinction" of knighthood (= were knighted).[32]

This pattern shows us the dominant structure of the letter, the perversion of an ideal order: "their honor is dishonor; their modesty is immodesty; their weapons are sausages." Of course the agenda of this polarized discourse requires it to position knights squarely at the negative pole. But that pole plays its part as the negation of an ideal, not as an unopposed perspective onto the real world of knights. Knighthood true to its "order" is "eminent" and "excellent." It behaves with "girlish modesty," it follows the law of *honestas*. "Ordinate" knights protect widows and orphans and fight boldly for a good cause. Membership is acquired through solemn, sanctifying rituals.[33]

An important element of this idealizing is the projection into the Roman past of the ideal of knighthood. It has its exemplary embodiment in Aeneas, Scipio Africanus, Trajan, Pompey, and Caesar[34]. The military discipline, boldness, and self-sacrifice of the ancient Roman heroes are conjured to show how far the nephews of Archdeacon John have declined.

The letter gives us abundant material to convict medieval knights of bad habits. But it also sets tensions in place between an ideal and a corrupted knighthood. So, shall we credit the abuses, or the ideal, with a higher degree of "reality"?

Peter of Blois's writing gives us a second perspective on his character as polemicist. It is a help in judging the value of his polemics as testimony to real conditions. He wrote a letter against the clerics of Henry II's court which became a classic work of court criticism. His accusations were as vehement and extreme as those against the knights, but in this case he received an answer. The chaplains wrote a reply, unfortunately lost, which brought their accuser up short. He then wrote a chastened apology (Let-

29. 294A: ". . . illi a pueritiae cunabulis solam in vobis modestiam noverint, solam a vobis didicerint honestatem."

30. 294B: ". . . et hodie tirones enses suos recipiunt de altari, ut profiteantur se filios Ecclesiae . . . Porro res in contrarium versa est . . ."

31. 294C: ". . . vitam . . . degenerem in immunditiis transigentes nomen et officium militiae dehonestant."

32. 297A: ". . . nepos vester S. . . . solemnes militiae titulos acquisivit"

33. For a balanced view of ideals set against abuses, see Flori, *L'essor,* pp. 271–84. It is clear from Flori's discussion of critics of knighthood (particularly Orderic Vitalis) that blame sits in the larger context of praise.

34. *PL* 207: 295 A–C.

ter 150) with fervent praise of court clerics, their good offices, and their "laudable and glorious service." He commends them for virtues which are the reverse of the vices his first letter attacked.[35]

So much for the polemicist as spokesman for "reality." If he was deflating what Huizinga called "an amazing illusion" or tearing off the "mask of Lancelot or Tristram,"[36] then he certainly could not be relied on to stick to his guns. As soon as he was challenged he retreated. His swift retraction shows that he was back-pedaling on his own exaggerations. The principle of gross, barely defensible exaggeration probably applied to his attack on knighthood as well, as it does to much of medieval polemics especially in and after the investiture controversy.[37]

Peter's two letters show us what social pressures were exerted on courtiers and knights, not what an entire class "was really"—something we can never learn. A social class is not like a chemical element with a single discernible internal code which governs its behavior. The two letters mark off a field of social forces within which the court clerics and the knights live and work, and the two extremes are the parameters within which—in the reality of late twelfth century knighthood—an unlimited variety of individual behavior could take place. The polemicist pressures them towards compliance with the values of a code. In the case of the clerics of Henry II's court, we see the courtier's code emerge as a real functioning ethic, because the polemicist backs into it and away from his criticism (though of course the courtiers' vigorous defense says nothing about the degree of compliance, only that a code exists to which they can appeal against charges of abuse). Peter of Blois's polemic against knights likewise confirms ex negativo the existence of chivalric ideals as social values.

Reading polemics against knighthood along with the idealizing litera-

35. Epist. 14, *PL* 207: 42–51. On court criticism, see Bumke, *Höfische Kultur,* pp. 583–94. On Peter's Epist. 14, Claus Uhlig, *Hofkritik im England des Mittelalters und der Renaissance: Studien zu einem Gemeinplatz der europäischen Moralistik* (Berlin and New York, 1973), pp. 99–105; Rolf Köhn "'Militia curialis': Die Kritik am geistlichen Hofdienst bei Peter von Blois und in der lateinischen Literatur des 9.–12. Jahrhunderts," in *Miscellanea Mediaevalia 12: Soziale Ordnungen im Selbstverständnis des Mittelalters,* ed. A. Zimmermann (Berlin and New York, 1979), pp. 227–257. For letter 150, *PL* 207: 439–42.

36. Note 13 above.

37. An illustrative exchange is the letter of Abbot William of Hirsau accusing the Saxon clergy of simony and corruption (ca. 1082–1085) and the answer from the accused. The former is a model of extreme polemics, the latter a model of measured, reserved correction of the abbot's hyperbole. *Briefsammlungen der Zeit Heinrichs IV.*, ed. Carl Erdmann and Norbert Fickermann, *MGH,* Briefe der deutschen Kaiserzeit 5 (Weimar, 1950), pp. 41–46 (Hildesheimer Briefe, Epist. 18 & 19).

ture would seem to leave us either with the category ideal-real, or stymied in indeterminism. I want to suggest a way around this difficulty.

The two sides of Peter of Blois's polemics work together. Medieval social criticism in general operates within a two-pronged discourse: one prong skewers the objects of attack on their gross abuses, the other fixes them into codes and norms. The first finds or invents inflated wrongs, the second fashions sublime ideals.[38] In the polemics of Peter of Blois the dichotomy of good knight-bad knight, restraint and violence, is a unified discourse aimed at urging civilized behavior on the warrior class.

A hindrance to integrating both aspects of the discourse in reading medieval polemics is a mode of interpreting that I will call the mimetic fallacy. This is the assumption that a text like Peter of Blois's letter 94 operates in the mode of empirical, mimetic observations, that it wants to reproduce reality. It is a fallacy because it accepts the illusion of objectivity as a fact of the text's discursive mode. Certainly any medieval writing that brings disapproval to bear on a social group or practice is speaking a polemical language of extreme distortion. The statement, "knights are slothful brutes" has the historical value of the statement, "police are violent racists." Both comments conceal an agenda of social change beneath the appearance of an objective observation. They say silently, "disapprove of brutality." They mask the imperative or optative mode in the indicative.

This mask only exercises deception and creates a misread modality once the issues it faces die, fade, or disappear. No one living in a crisis of competing social values would fail to recognize the engagedness of statements that take positions on the issues at stake. "Police brutality" will certainly now find a lot of agreement, but also a lot of opposition. But a hundred years from now a historian will face that statement with a methodological problem. Once the issues die, the statements remain, and the appearance of objective observation establishes itself as the "true" mode of the statements. The undertow of their agenda for change no longer exercises its pull. That is precisely the condition in which Peter of Blois's polemics or Wolfram's *Parzival* confront the modern historian. The issues on which they took a strong position are no longer present in the mind of

38. This helps us deal with the difficult case of Guibert of Nogent, regarded as at once the most scurrilous and the most "objective" and "critical" historian of the Middle Ages. See the survey of views on Guibert in John Benton, *Self and Society in Medieval France: The Memoirs of Abbot Guibert of Nogent* (New York, 1970), pp. 7–11.

the reader, and the texts take on the appearance of "art" or some kind of objective imitation of reality.

Readings of panegyric literature are especially susceptible to the mimetic fallacy. We can imagine a poem in praise of a king, describing him as chaste, generous, wise, and clement. In the spell of mimesis, we think him admirable. Then we read other sources, and these persuade us that in reality he was lascivious, stingy, foolish, and vengeful. Still in the spell of mimesis, we now see the poem as lying flattery because we are measuring its "genuineness" by its loyal rendering of reality. Since it appears to have betrayed that principle, we brand it a lie. The panegyrist's extravagant praise may well be intended to oppose the vices of a notoriously vicious king by fulsome praise of what he lacked. He was prodding and stinging the king by false praise, pushing him to change, and if the rest of the court heard it, so much greater the power of its irony to push him toward reform.[39] But that motive and that immediate effect are lost to the view of the modern reader, since the agenda of reform has vanished, and a mimetic thrust the text never contained is the only one we credit. The exemplary thrust of panegyric in general—that is, not only in ironic praise—removes it from the mimetic mode, and tries to impose its idealizing on reader and subject alike. A modern reader's urge to find the man "as he really was" behind panegyric is ordinarily naïve, not because it is lying flattery, but because it aims at recreating the subject and others in the image of its ideals. It does not represent anything objectively.

Another anti-mimetic element in representation is policy, its documentation, legitimation, and monumentalizing. Any portrait of a ruler aims at more than representing the man "as he was," an aspect necessarily subordinated to the monumentalizing intent. If an art historian writing centuries later read the portrait for its physiognomic information, he would be in the spell of the mimetic fallacy.

The same process by which the illusion of mimesis replaces the reality of advocacy is at work in Peter of Blois's letters. With his polemics he wanted to change reality; he did not care particularly about describing it in some sense we would call "objective." Advocacy is the modality of texts engaged in an economy of competing social issues exercising power and exerting pressure through the written or spoken word. That is why the dis-

39. An example of this didactic impulse in ironic praise is a letter from a student of the Mainz cathedral school to the students of the school at Worms (1033), *Die ältere Wormser Briefsammlung,* ed. Walther Bulst, *MGH,* Briefe der deutschen Kaiserzeit 3 (Weimar, 1949; rpt. 1981), pp. 47–48.

course of polemics is polarized. Its negative pole is insult and ridicule: the abuses opposed have to cry out to heaven, and if they do not, the polemicist will invent them. His voice is shrill to muster disapproval.[40]

Its positive pole does the opposite. It speaks a language of ideals that allure and promise social rewards (esteem, prestige, honor), and that have the exemplary force of a charismatic human being, the power to draw others into its orbit. One pole works through extravagant glorifying, the other through extravagant vilifying. The knighthood placed between these two poles is meant to be repelled by the negative and attracted by the positive, and extreme exaggeration at both ends turns up the pressure.

Peter of Blois's response to the alleged violence and sloth of knights was a push to turn them into members of that *ordo militiae,* modest as maidens, serving the needy, the clergy, and the *res publica,* hard, wise, and disciplined as that elite order of ancient knights. This aligns them with many clerics engaged in an important contest of social ideals from the second half of the eleventh century on, among them the authors of courtly romance, who opposed the violence of the lay nobles with ideals of restraint, moderation, and courtesy. We will look at examples of this conflict first in social history, then in literature.

In late 1073 or early 1074 Abbot Walo of St. Arnulf (Metz) wrote two letters to his Archbishop, Manasses I of Rheims (1070–1080), explaining his resignation from the abbacy of St. Remi of Rheims after a brief, unhappy period as abbot.[41] These letters and the other documents that touch on the clash of Walo and Manasses are a lucid illustration of the issues. The abbacy of St. Remi had been vacant since 1071, and this caused concern in Rome.[42] By the end of 1073 Manasses had appointed Walo, who resigned the position within a short time of accepting it. In the letters the freed abbot wrote to Manasses, he heaps vituperation on the archbishop. The latter appears in the letters as an abusive monster who has insulted, threatened, and cursed Walo. "I must have been a fool," he complains, "to

40. See Laura Kendrick's paper on Marcabru in this volume. It is instructive to read the ugly polemics against Henry IV in Bruno of Merseburg, *Brunos Buch vom Sachsenkrieg,* ed. Hans-Eberhard Lohmann, *MGH,* Deutsches Mittelalter: Kritische Studientexte des Reichsinstituts für ältere deutsche Geschichtskunde 2 (Leipzig, 1937), cc. 5–15, pp. 16–22, along with the critical commentary by Karl Hampe, *Herrschergestalten des deutschen Mittelalters,* 6th ed. (Heidelberg, 1955; rpt. Darmstadt, 1978), pp. 134–46.

41. On Manasses I, see John R. Williams, "Archbishop Manasses I of Rheims and Pope Gregory VII," *AHR* 54 (1949), 804–24. Also Max Manitius, *Geschichte der lateinischen Literatur des Mittelalters,* 3 vols. (Munich, 1923; rpt. 1976), 2: 724ff.

42. See William, "Manasses I," p. 808–9. Manasses received a letter from Gregory VII urging him to fill the vacancy post haste and to mind his manners, *Das Register Gregors VII.,* ed. Erich Caspar, 2 vols. (Berlin, 1920–23), 2: 1 Epistle 13 (June 30, 1073).

come to a beast so ungentle, so fierce, so violent, so horrendous!"[43] Part of Walo's inducement to accept the position in the first place was the opportunity to convert a man so fierce and truculent from his harsh ways.[44] And indeed he claims in one letter to Manasses that he repeatedly tried to "mitigate his raging" by citing holy scripture, singing it to him, as it were, to drive out the demon in his soul, like another David before Saul.[45] But Manasses holds to his warrior-like ways. It becomes evident that he is not clinging to inborn and habitual savagery, but to an ideal of behavior. He is wrathful and violent as a privilege of his class, and he has the nerve, moreover—says Walo—to suggest that the abbot, being a peaceful, humble, and quiet man, constantly given to reading, is not comfortable with the "manners of the French" and of Manasses.[46] This perversion of values sets off a tirade:

> O monster whom no single virtue redeems from vice! Is it not true that you regard a life tempered by peace, modesty, and sobriety as lower in virtue than one given to harsh and bold combat in wars, since [as you claim] peace is wont to weaken strong minds, while battle strengthens the weak and idle? That distinguished orator has argued justly, ingeniously, and persuasively that weapons take second place to the toga, since those who can live continently

43. Walo's letter, *Briefsammlungen der Zeit Heinrichs IV*, p. 184 "nisi enim ego follis fuissem, ad te tam inmitem tam trucem tam violentam tam inmanem bestiam non venissem."; also in *PL*, 150: 879–80, together with other letters of Walo. Also on Manasses's rude ways, *Vita Theoderici Abb. Andaginensis*, c. 20 *MGH SS* 12: 49 (ca. 1090): "in disciplina liberalium artium apprime eruditus, vir saeculi dignitatem nobiliter natus, ad omnia sagax et strenuus, episcopatu quidem dignus, sed natura et moribus plus quam oporteret ferus . . ." Abbot Theoderich's influence on Manasses: "Multum ergo feritatis ab eo admonitus deposuit . . . et cum pluribus esset frequenter immitis et truculentus, huic uni pro gloria et admiratione virtutum eius semper fuit mitis et placidus." The biographer identifies this archbishop wrongly as Gervasius, Manasses's predecessor. On the error, see Williams, "Manasses I," p. 806, note 7.

44. *PL* 150: 879–80, referring to "illius ferae pessimae monstrique horribilis saevitia," he believed the promises of Manasses and accepted, "non levis meriti minimaeve remunerationis arbitrans fore, si per me posset illius truculentia temperari." Hanover collect. Epist. 108, *Briefsammlung*, p. 183: [he desired the archbishop's release from "canine manners"] "ut, si fieri posset, mentis sevitia morumque bestialitate deposita tu quoque mecum de suavissima caritate et carissima suavitate gauderes." See also note 43 above, Abbot Theoderich's influence on Manasses.

45. *Briefsammlung*, Epist 109, p. 183: "O quotiens adhibui tibi medicamina scripturarum! quotiens celestibus verbis quasi quibusdam carminibus tuum temptavi mitigare furorem! Quotiens non Treicia sed Davitica cythara conatus sum illud vel expellere vel sedare demonium, quo vexaris!"

46. Epist 109, p. 183: "Asserebas enim in illis litteris tuis me hominem esse pacificum, humilem et quietum, lectioni semper intentum, ac per hoc non me Francigenarum tuisque moribus convenire."

> in peace are rarer than those who can suffer the toils and dangers of warfare patiently.[47]

This passage has the flavor of a continued debate between the two men, and it is not improbable to imagine this kind of debate crystallizing around Walo's efforts to tame the wildness of Manasses.

But the clash is also a debate between two classes defending their social mores at a critical moment in the history of those mores, when they were in a serious struggle for dominance the one over the other. Manasses is the spokesman of archaic warrior ways (a posture known in high clergy, though all the more flagrant and inordinate for that reason in the eyes of the pacifiers), Walo the advocate of peace. The abbot places the archbishop's values in the context of warfare and armed combat. His complaint is that the archbishop has brought warrior ways to bear also on domestic and ecclesiastic affairs. This debate is in the air in the eleventh and twelfth centuries.

Walo's letters show us Manasses spitted on the two-pronged discourse of ideal and abuse. The other documents that bear on Manasses's period of office show the champion of warrior ways losing to the party of peace and restraint. He was excommunicated and never restored to his office.[48]

It was not a foregone conclusion that the Christian-courtly agenda of civilizing would win the day against militant nobles generally. An archbishop was more vulnerable than a count or baron. The move to civilize the warrior class operated in a larger field of forces, where it was opposed by assertions of the right to violence and warlike ways as the "customs of our ancient ancestors." For many nobles, lay and cleric alike, "maidenly mod-

47. P. 485:

> O monstrum nulla virtute redemptum a vitiis, putasne inferioris esse virtutis in pace temperanter, modeste et sobrie conversari quam in bello acriter et fortiter preliari, cum pax soleat fortes etiam animos enervare, pugna vero inbelles et desides roborare? Unde non immerito ille insignis orator arma toge cedere persuadet subtiliter, nimirum considerans pauciores esse, qui possint in pace vivere continenter, quam qui pati bellorum labores et pericula patienter.

The "insignis orator" is Cicero. Cf. *De officiis* 1, 22, 77 (ref. from Erdmann ed., p. 185, n. 2).

48. There were other things at stake, but fierceness versus charity, friendship, and "suavitas" recurs in virtually all the documentation (cf. notes 42–47 above). Also Guibert de Nogent, *Autobiographie,* 1.11 ed. Edmond René Labande (Paris, 1981), pp. 62–64. Whatever the issues of policy at stake, the discourse of peace vs. violence structured the rhetoric.

esty" meant womanish cowardice, a sense of shame was an excuse not to fight, and politeness was a form of lying. Warrior ways were their traditions, and restraint meant effeminization and sapping the strength of their manly customs.

The resistance to courtesy is badly recorded.[49] It probably expressed itself ordinarily in acts of violence. But the conflict of violence and restraint also played itself out on the field of literary representations—in fact far more abundantly and dramatically than in non-literary ones.[50] The literary medium of this opposition to restraint, mercy, and moderation was the heroic epic and chanson de geste, though it registers in numerous clerical complaints about the slackening of the warrior spirit. Both kind of sources appeal to "the customs of our ancient ancestors," though the ancestors are not Julius Caesar and Trajan but Dietrich of Bern, Roland, and Raoul de Cambrai. An arch-conservative like Saxo Grammaticus, resisting precisely the civilizing trends of courtly society and lumping together civility and corruption, could even advocate a fierce warrior ethic of revenge.[51] The poet of the *Nibelungenlied,* if he did not represent revenge as glorious, did show it as heroic and awe-inspiring as opposed to the prissy niceties of courtliness. This conservative trend sought to restore an archaic ideal of warrior honor that was in a crisis, and it could do so often by pitting it directly against courtly-Christian values. In the chanson de geste *Raoul de Cambrai,* Bernier tricks his enemy into stepping naked into a fountain, then refuses to kill the helpless man. This chivalric act of restraint makes him an object of scorn for the rest of his life.[52] Siegfried defers to King Gunther in *Nibelungenlied* just before getting speared in the back, and the poet comments: "That was the reward for his courtesies."[53]

The literary advocate of restraint was the courtly romance. This new

49. A brief comment by Hugh of Flavigny gives us a rare look at the ideology of noble fierceness. He says that Richard of Saint-Vanne's efforts to institute the *treuga Dei* in France met with resistance from "certain perverse and indomitable spirits," who regarded "peace by divine revelation" as a "violation of ancestral institutions through the adoption of new and unheard of ideas" (*Chronicon,* 2.30 [*anno* 1041], ed. G. H. Pertz, *MGH SS* 8: 403). The passage shows how resistance to the issues reverses the positive and negative poles: peace is "unheard-of novelty"; unobstructed warfare is "ancient custom." See the commentary of Hartmut Hoffmann, *Gottesfriede und Treuga Dei* (Stuttgart: Hiersemann, 1964), pp. 87–88.

50. See Jaeger, *Origins of Courtliness,* pp. 176–94.

51. *Origins of Courtliness,* pp. 185–90.

52. Cited in Sidney Painter, *French Chivalry: Chivalric Ideas and Practices in Medieval France* (Ithaca, NY, 1967), p. 33.

53. *Das Nibelungenlied,* ed. Karl Bartsch and Helmut de Boor, 12th ed. (Leipzig, 1949), Stanza 980, 1: "Do engalt er sîner zühte."

narrative form from the mid-twelfth century appropriates clerical norms of courtesy and uses them to represent the behavior and speech, the combat and lovemaking, of knights. Its hero combines warfare and courtly-Christian restraint. The romance creates a model in which ideals of courtly restraint are integrated into an exalted lay aristocratic style of life. In some romances both poles of the discourse we observed in Peter of Blois's letter are present.

The Parzival romance of Wolfram von Eschenbach is the best example. Written within a decade of Peter of Blois's letter, it dramatizes the poles of ideal and abuse by showing a knight's progress away from the bad and toward the good. Its hero starts out as a blunt rustic with a good heart, and ends as Grail king, highly honored in both the Arthurian and the quasi-religious Grail court. He spans this broad ethical gap by a progress away from unfeeling egotism. He is held responsible for the death of his mother and the disgrace of a young woman whom he all but rapes; in his blind eagerness to become a knight he attacks and kills another man and strips the armor off his corpse; his victim turns out to be his own uncle; he is responsible for prolonging the sufferings of the old Grail king and his community. Lack of compassion is generally seen as the fundamental flaw that permits the commission of this string of atrocities.[54] Ill-digested lessons from three teachers of uneven quality harm him as much as they help. In the end, suffering, loyalty to his wife, and insistence on the value and dignity of his identity bring him to the virtues of a true knight, husband, and Grail king: gentleness, modesty, loyalty, compassion, and a sense of shame.

This progress covers the same span as the polemics of Peter of Blois. Parzival's misdeeds and the moral flaws from which they derive are comparable to those of Archdeacon John's nephews. In part Parzival's educators Gurnemanz and Trevrizent speak the same ethical language as Peter of Blois.[55] Peter of Blois and Wolfram were clearly addressing some of the same social issues. They share a program of social change, and employ both prongs of a polemical discourse, the negative more strongly emphasized in the one, the positive in the other. The common issue is the move of the warrior class from violence to restraint, from irresponsibility to social en-

54. See the summary of the problem in Joachim Bumke, *Wolfram von Eschenbach*, 6th ed. (Stuttgart, 1991), pp. 128ff. (with recent literature).

55. *Wolfram von Eschenbach*, ed. Albert Leitzmann, 6th ed. (Berlin, 1926), 170, 25: "iuch sol erbarmen nôtec her: / gein des kumber sît ze wer / mit milte und mit güete. / vlîzet iuch diemüete"; 171, 13: "gebet rehter mâze ir orden"; 171, 25: "lât die erberme bî der vrevel sîn."

gagement, a move that the clergy had advocated in varying contexts and ideologies since the tenth century.[56]

Wolfram von Eschenbach and Saxo Grammaticus were evidently engaged in the same conflict of social ideas, and they took up positions near opposite ends of the spectrum. Their works testify to that conflict and its acuteness, no less than do the letters of Walo of St. Arnulf and Peter of Blois.

* * *

Works that engage in the project of shaping and changing social and political consciousness do so by entering into the competition of ideas clustered around issues. Competition that occurs when the norms, values, mores, and laws of a society are in flux or crisis generates friction among contending groups, and this friction places a heavy charge on language and concepts that address the issues at stake. The competition of ideas for dominance gradually focuses power and shapes consensus. The stakes are always high in conflicts for the shaping of social consciousness. If they were not, there would be no friction and no competition of ideas.

But in fact every generation experiences the convulsiveness of such competitions. A systematic ordering of society through widely accepted mores and values is troubled when new values emerge and challenge the old. Then a once systematic ordering of forces turns chaotic. Ideas, sentiments, and convictions—old, new, and intermediate—are tumbled about in this chaos. The combatants carry them like shields and hurl them like weapons. The ideas, sentiments, and convictions are generated by a spectrum of interests that break from the issues at stake. While social practices dominate society unchallenged, they create vested interests, and a challenge to them produces conservative resistance and an ideology that supports it. Along the line formed by the two outer parameters, challenge and resistance to it, a variety of intermediate positions and their defending ideologies form, and all of these vie for consensus and victory. The analysis of such an unstable system is complex and could be aided by a kind of "chaos theory" of social change. The analysis of historical conflicts is especially fraught with the danger of over-simplifying, since the unstable system has normally come to equilibrium when anyone besides journalists begins

56. For recent literature on the peace movement, see note 24 above; also *The Peace of God: Social Violence and Religious Response in France around the Year 1000*, ed. Thomas Head and Richard Landes (Ithaca, NY, 1992).

to analyse it. By the time the historian gets to it its issues and positions have rigidified, amalgamated, or disappeared altogether. Some ideas which fought bravely succumb and fade; others which stood on the sidelines and watched emerge strong, and the historian is confronted with the appearance of a unified system, because all possible outcomes of a once complex and chaotic melee ossify into a single constellation; an unstable and complex mix of issues comes to equilibrium. The point is not to describe the ossified constellation but rather, so to speak, to restore it to chaos in order to see once again the issues in their various interactions.

In the case of the present issue—violence vs. restraint—a dynamic is at work that stands above particular social circumstances, and could be formulated abstractly as a general theory of social change and used to analyse a variety of similar historical and social trends.[57]

The ideas engaged in conflicts of social ideology are borne by any available medium: fiction, lyric, polemics, epistle, broadsheet, legislation. The primary medium is the human beings who are engaged in the conflict. The clash of Walo and Manasses shows the embodiment of ideas that later will confront each other in the writings of Saxo Grammaticus and Wolfram von Eschenbach. This means for the historian that narrowing the body of documentation on a social issue is bad methodology. Considerations of genre inject one-sidedness into selection of texts, and while studies like "the investiture controversy in late eleventh century lyric" are valuable as building blocks and contributions to the narrower discipline, the greater picture of social and institutional change must be drawn from the broadest possible base of documentation.

The same applies to the transition from warrior society to courtly society. Ideas in conflict do not select a particular medium as their bearer, though they may favor one over another. A saint's life may bear on the point of friction as much as church legislation, panegyric as much as slander. The spectrum of competing attitudes unfolds in a variety of statements, acts, legislations, and written documents. The issues generate what we might call their own culture, and a broadly comparative reading of that culture is the basis of good methodology.

An essential characteristic of the conflict of social ideologies is that opposite generates opposite. Offensive attitudes, acts, or statements call

57. Norbert Elias, *Prozess der Zivilisation,* formulated this dynamic for European lay aristocratic society. But the context in that case was the life of the court, and his theory cannot account for the role of spiritual sanctions and popular opinion in the first phase of resistance to warrior ways.

forth opposing attitudes; these provoke and strengthen opposition, which claims as sanctioned behavior what appears to be abuse. Rape, mistreatment of women, and anti-feminism call forth a cult of the revered woman and an ethical obligation to respect and speak well of ladies.[58] Facing this opposition, anti-feminism articulates itself all the more vehemently and self-righteously, looking to any writings for ammunition, but finding it especially in scripture and antiquity. Andreas Capellanus's *De amore* is a self-enclosed friction zone, where the tendencies to idealize and to vilify women face each other in an oddly static confrontation.[59] It both instructs in courtly love mores and opposes them by a fierce anti-feminism. Feuds, private wars, and despoiling of church goods call forth opposition in the peace movement with its rich culture. The recalcitrant nobility responds by appeal to ancestral customs.

In these two cases it would be justified to say that if women were not being raped and mistreated, there would be no cult of woman in courtly literature, and if there were no private wars and church ransacking, there would be no ideal Christian knight. The abuse gives offense, causes suffering, and calls forth the corrective, or at least creates a discursive net to throw over the offenders. The corrective exercises whatever force on the abuse it can muster, using extreme idealizing models, extreme slander, and maligning. Those who are slandered, maligned, and provoked are sensitized to the issue and respond, perhaps capitulate, perhaps retaliate. Then the opposition culture arises. It is highly unlikely that the courtly love lyric arose as a response to a widely-shared adulation of woman, but it is quite likely that it responded to their wretched treatment.

Now let us consider three propositions about conflicting social ideologies.

First. the conflict of ideologies can only exist when norms are in crisis and flux. If the prevailing norms are strong, they may still generate opposition, but opposing ideas have no strength. They are suppressed, voted

58. In reading through the documents on the peace movement for this and another study, it became evident that the protection of women emerges gradually as a social concern. Early documents include women among the threats to peace, later ones among the threatened. It is a rewarding research topic. Cf. the study by Werner Rösener, "Die höfische Frau im Hochmittelalter," in *Curialitas*, pp. 171–230 (with rich bibliography).

59. The two dominant voices recently on the reading of this dissonant work, Rüdiger Schnell, *Andreas Capellanus: Zur Rezeption des römischen und kanonischen Rechts in De Amore* (Munich, 1982); and Alfred Karnein, *De amore in volkssprachlicher Literatur: Untersuchungen zur Andreas Capellanus-Rezeption in Mittelalter und Renaissance* (Heidelberg, 1985).

down, or shouted down as soon as they surface. The norms dominate either in public opinion or in the mechanisms of enforcement or both. There were democratic sentiments in Iraq before the Gulf War, but there was no effective voice advocating them; there was opposition to anti-semitism in Nazi Germany, but it was silent.

Second. no statements addressing the issues in competition can be made that do not engage in the conflict. Where social values are being re-forged and asserting themselves against conservative opposition, everything touching on the conflict is polemical, and the intentions of the author cannot change that.[60] Talking about peace or clemency when these values are asserting themselves against an ethic of revenge is asking for conflict, no matter in what mode or tone of expression the talk is couched. If the vital interests of a social group depend on or are perceived as depending on enforcement through revenge, then the advocate of peace is asking for a fight. The American scientist (a white man) who claimed experimental results arguing the genetic inferiority of blacks experienced the working of this principle. His "research" addressed a fiercely fought social issue, and his appeal to alleged scientific objectivity, far from pacifying the contestants, gave offense and inflamed the issues. His position was comparable to that of a man who enters a battle zone armed with a rifle and wearing the uniform of one side. He can claim neutrality, but he will be shot at anyway.

This proposition also applies in whatever medium or genre the issues in conflict are propagated. It is a principle well known to any office of censorship serving a tyrannical government. A children's fairy tale suffused with ideology can be as inflammatory as a propaganda leaflet and far more effective indoctrination. Imaginative literature can have a much more powerful effect on the imagination than polemical prose.

Third. ideas engaged in competition for dominance in a society have the power to influence behavior. This includes the ideas on the offensive and those on the defensive. This proposition is axiomatic because such competitions aim at establishing dominant social values, and social values determine behavior. Any group of Americans can at present be polarized, troubled, outraged, or sensitized by a charge of anti-feminism or racism.

60. A vital point for weighing the engagedness of courtly romance in social change. It suggests that the idiom of courtliness was engaged in the competition of ideas no matter which author speaks it. The frivolous voice of courtly entertainment narrative is a provocation to the opposing front no less than the high ethical tone of Wolfram's *Parzival*. Authorial intention plays no role.

These charges throw a discursive net over anyone they are directed at, a net that holds them captive in a certain field of conflict. The reaction would be strong whether or not the charge is true. The same result would not be achieved by calling any group of contemporary Americans a pack of Cathars, Anabaptists, or Unitarians. These are curiosities with no power to offend, fossils from dead friction zones, though all were once issues over which blood was spilled and reputations ruined. An accusation of racism now exerts power and influence over the person it is directed at, true or not. It makes that person a combatant in a social issue. It puts him either on the offensive or the defensive. It sets off an internal alarm system which makes him guard his words and those of other people against traces of racism. That is, it creates sensibility, and that means it has successfully influenced behavior in favor of its agenda.

* * *

Was courtly romance a factor in the spread of courtly values? Was the outward enthusiasm with which this genre was accepted by lay society answered by an internal realignment of ethical values? The framework developed in this article says yes. Both Peter of Blois's Letter 94 and Wolfram's *Parzival* addressed social issues engaged in an important contest. The literary work broke through the aesthetic encapsulation within which literary historians have tended to view courtly literature. If the three propositions developed above are valid, then *Parzival* was probably more effectively engaged than Peter of Blois's polemical letter.

But in order not to subject historical analysis to the power of the syllogism, I close with two questions that offer the criterion of falsification or verification of a thesis that courtly literature favored the social acceptance of courtly values.

First. did courtly romance compel identification with its hero and his values? The hero of narrative embodies the crisis playing itself out in the society or social group generally. He or she dramatizes the contradiction at the root of the crisis. He repeats in the phylogeny of his personal development the ontogeny of social change and its stages: normal conditions, anomaly, polarization, and so on. He is charged with the whole field of forces pressing for and against social change. Through identification and immersion, the reader/listener can live in the friction zone, and feel the advantages of the author's agenda and the disadvantages of the opposite. The narrative exemplum charged with authority is one of the most important didactic instruments, certainly in the Middle Ages,[61] perhaps in human society generally. Hence there is no reason to rule out the effectiveness of the courtly-chivalric knight as "Bildungsgedanke."[62] But this is not an argument, only a methodological suggestion.

There is a passage of Peter of Blois's Letter 94 that bears directly on the problem, and it is worthwhile interpreting it in the context of the first question. He says that the corrupted knights want battle scenes painted on their saddles and shields "so that they may take pleasure in a kind of fantasy vision of battles, which in reality they would not have the courage even to look upon, let alone take part in."[63] Here a contemporary observer points to a predilection of knights themselves for the "ideal" in preference to a "reality" they would rather not face. Hartmann von Aue expressed a similar attitude at the beginning of his adaptation of Chretien's *Yvain.* He says that in King Arthur's day men loved bold deeds and actions. But while men of the present day are no longer bold, they have the stories of those men of action. If he, Hartmann, had to choose, he would prefer the present life with the pleasures of these stories to the past with its story-less life of action.[64] In both cases avoidance of action finds compensation in the artifice of chivalric representation.

Did the courtly romance have the effect of alienating its readers from a life of action? Did it pamper the sloth of a slackened warrior class, hand them over to a decadent aesthetic existence, and render them yet more useless for the active life? Extravagant fantasy does seem to work a kind of enchantment. It did on Don Quixote. Samuel Johnson was "immoderately fond of reading romances of chivalry" throughout his life, and he attributed "to these extravagant fictions that unsettled turn of mind that prevented his ever fixing in any profession."[65]

But this should not encourage us to imagine a warrior class stunned

61. See the exhaustive study by Peter von Moos, *Geschichte als Topik: Das rhetorische Exemplum von der Antike zur Neuzeit und die historiae im 'Policraticus' Johanns von Salisbury* (Hildesheim, Zürich, New York, 1988), passim, esp. pp. 13–21.

62. Bumke, *Studien zum Ritterbegriff,* p. 147: "Das adlige Rittertum, von dem die höfische Dichtung erzählt . . . ist ein Erziehungs– und Bildungsgedanke von weitreichender Bedeutung und ein Phänomen der Geistesgeschichte viel mehr als der Sozialgeschichte." On the Arthurian literature and the model of Arthur as an instrument of education of nobles, see Peter Johanek, "König Artus und die Plantagenets: Über den Zusammenhang von Historiographie und höfischer Epik in mittelalterlicher Propaganda," *Frühmittelalterliche Studien* 21 (1987), esp. pp. 358–60.

63. See note 22 above.

64. Hartmann von Aue, *Iwein,* 7th ed., ed. G. F. Benecke, K. Lachmann, and L. Wolff (Berlin, 1968), vv. 54–58: "ichn wolde dô niht sîn gewesen, / daz ich nû niht enwaere, / dâ uns noch mit ir maere / sô rehte wol wesen sol: / dâ tâten in diu werc vil wol."

65. *Boswell's Life of Johnson,* ed. G. B. Hill and L. F. Powell, 3 vols. (Oxford, 1934), 1: 49.

to inaction by the recitation of romances or by "imaginary visions" of a Camelot world and of chivalric combat. That charge is part of Peter of Blois's polemics, and like medieval polemicists generally, he represents the extreme as the norm. Far more likely is an interpretation that sees in this passage testimony to the power of chivalric representation to compel identification. There is much more evidence for that argument, the Arthurian imitations of Ulrich von Lichtenstein being among the earliest and best known.[66] The Arthurian–chivalric cast of courtly representation in many courts of the late Middle Ages and Renaissance represents the dramatic success of courtly enculturation through romances. The madness of Don Quixote and the instability of Samuel Johnson—the possibility that derangement lurks at the dark fringes of courtly enculturation—does not deny the romance's power over behavior, but rather confirms it.

The second question: did courtesy and courtly love become factors in the economy of honor and prestige at court? Did behavior like Gawain's raise a man's standing and did behavior like Kei's lower it? Did it do a woman honor and raise her reputation to receive homage from a knight in the form of a love declaration? Parzival behaved like a boor, and the result was disgrace and exclusion. Did boorishness actually spell exclusion from aristocratic society?[67] The answer tells us whether the lay nobles internalized the ethical values of the courtly knight or merely appropriated from romance the trappings of court festivals and rituals. If courtesy became integrated into the economy of honor at court, then it was not only a real social force, but an indispensable instrument of worldly esteem, and that is the prime moving force of aristocratic society. Those who sought to live in court society without it might well find reason to regret their neglect of the lessons of chivalric romance.

But that is a conjecture that further research would have to test. My purpose here has been to provide a framework within which courtly ideals can be studied as real forces shaping behavior, not just a fanciful overlay

66. David Tinsley, "Die Kunst der Selbstdarstellung in Ulrich von Lichtensteins 'Frauendienst,'" *Germanisch-Romanische Monatsschrift* 40 (1990), 129–40; Jan-Dirk Müller, "Lachen–Spiel–Fiktion: Zum Verhältnis von literarischem Diskurs und historischer Realität im Frauendienst Ulrichs von Lichtenstein," *Deutsche Vierteljahrsschrift* 58 (1984), 38–73; Ursula Peters, *Frauendienst: Untersuchungen zu Ulrich von Lichtenstein und zum Wirklichkeitsgehalt der Minnedichtung* (Göppingen, 1971).

67. These values were thoroughly integrated into the society of Theresa of Avila. She complained about religious houses turned into "courts and schools of good breeding." Her fears of giving offence to people "who think these observances essential to their honor" competed with her religious observances. Santa Teresa de Jesús, *Libro de la Vida* (chapter 37), ed. Otger Steggink (Madrid, 1986), p. 506.

of disengaged discourse beneath which reality could go its dreary way. I believe that the answers to these questions, based on historical data, will reveal the close connections between the ideals of courtly romance and the realities of contemporary social life. The unreality of courtly narrative, its enchantments, wizards, dragons, noble combats, and sublime love affairs are not masks over society's imperfections. If they mask anything, it is an agenda of social change.

Philippe Buc

13. *Principes gentium dominantur eorum:* Princely Power Between Legitimacy and Illegitimacy in Twelfth-Century Exegesis

You know that barbarian princes dominate (*dominantur*) their people, and the great wield power (*potestatem*) over them. It shall not be thus among you.

—Matt. 20: 24–26

Who does not know that kings and princes derive their origin from men ignorant of God who aspired to lord over (*dominari*) their fellow men (*pares*) by pride, plunder, treachery, murder, and lastly by every kind of crime, at the instigation of the Devil, the prince of this world?

—Gregory VII to Hermann of Metz

Potestas and *dominatio:* even when denoting traditional rulers of royal rank, power and lordship were highly sulfurous concepts within clerical *Herrschaftstheologie*.[1] I have quoted from one of Gregory VII's famous letters to Hermann, bishop of Metz; I could as well have called on Augustine's earlier condemnation of Roman lust for domination, *libido dominandi*.[2]

1. The following pages draw on the conclusions of my 1989 (École des Hautes Études en Sciences Sociales, Paris) dissertation, *Potestas: prince, pouvoir, et peuple dans les commentaires de la Bible (Paris et France du Nord, 1100–1330)* (5 vols)—henceforth Buc, *Potestas*. It has now been reworked as *L'ambiguïté du livre: prince, pouvoir, et peuple dans les commentaires de la Bible*, Théologie Historique 95 (Paris, 1994)—henceforth Buc, *L'ambiguïté*, where fuller bibliographic references can be found. I must acknowledge here my debts to Gerard Caspary's and Guy Lobrichon's guidance, friendship, and *grundlegende Werke*, to Amy Remensnyder's comments and help, and to Igor Gorevitch's comforting support.

2. Register, 4, 2 and 8, 22, ed. Erich Caspar, *Das Register Gregors VII., MGH, Epistolae selectae*, 2, 2 vols. (Berlin, 1955), 1: 293–97 and 2: 544–63; tr. Ephraim Emerton, *The Correspondence of Pope Gregory VII* (New York, 1932), pp. 102–5 and 166–75, the above quotation is from 8.22 (Caspar, 2, 552: 13–7; Augustine, *De civitate dei*, e.g., 1, preface, 2, 30; 15, 4–5. See also the contrast between *spiritalis prelatio* and *secularis dominatio* in Gregory the Great, *In primo libro Regum*, ed. Pierre Verbraken, *CCCM* 144 (Turnhout: 1963), 297: 62ff., with R. A. Markus's recent "Gregory the Great on Kings: Rulers and Preachers in the *Commentary on Kings*," in D. Wood, *The Church and Sovereignty, c. 590–1918: Essays in Honour of Michael Wilks*, ed. Diana Wood (Oxford, 1991), pp. 7–21. Intensified, the contrast between carnal and spiritual governance could easily serve as a template for a radicalized opposition between secular

What became of this negative face of power and domination in the century following Gregory VII? John Van Engen has argued for the progressive clerical acceptance, over the course of the twelfth and thirteenth centuries, of domination exercised by non-royal or princely lords.[3] The process he describes is one of delayed but unavoidable legitimization: the institutional phenomena of the turn of the millenium, that is, the devolution of power and the establishment (or revelation) of new forms of lordship, were slowly seized by medieval churchmen and integrated into the social imaginary. Yet any social imaginary is only intelligible as one among many contending models. Alternatives reveal the meaning of the construct finally dominant. As Van Engen himself admits, reforming churchmen initially resisted the legitimization of lordship. I would like to look in more detail at a specific twelfth-century reformist milieu, that of the exegetes educated in northern France, and at its reaction to the process of political modernization begun around the turn of the millenium. I hope to demonstrate that if there was an acceptance of the new order, it was only after a revealingly contentious and politicized debate, in which influential commentators of the Bible reactivated the negative face of *potestas* and *dominatio*. Thus, the legitimization of the new forms of political power did not go without a fight, and, I would argue, was never complete and irreversible—just as Carolingian and Ottonian *Herrschaftstheologie* had never eliminated the theme of a ruler "anointed to kill."[4]

* * *

Why look at the exegetes? The commonplace that the Bible contains the principles of medieval government is not without truth.[5] But it ignores

and sacred, lay and ecclesiastical; cf. Gerard Caspary, *Politics and Exegesis: Origen and the Two Swords* (Berkeley, CA, 1979), pp. 32, 189–91.

3. In this volume, Chapter 9.

4. The expression is Wazo bishop of Liège's, or rather his biographer Anselm's, *Gesta episcoporum leodiensium* 66, ed. Rudolf Koepke, *MGH, SS,* 7, 230: 4–7 (here identical to the oftentimes shriller version, ed. Georg Waitz, *MGH, SS,* 14, 118: 35–38), twisting into a polemical statement a pairing known to Alcuin and Hrabanus Maurus—cf. Karl F. Morrison, *The Two Kingdoms: Ecclesiology in Carolingian Political Thought* (Princeton, NJ, 1964), p. 120. Morrison's classic work suggests that the negative conception of power could be found even among figures considered as Carolingian propagandists (such as Alcuin). This duality was a constant, see now Wolfgang Stürner, *Peccatum und Potestas. Der Sündenfall und die Entstehung der herrscherlichen Gewalt im mittelaterlichen Staatsdenken* (Sigmaringen, 1987).

5. Walter Ullmann, "The Bible and Principles of Government in the Middle Ages," in *La Bibbia nell' alto medioevo,* Settimane del Centro italiano di studi sull'alto medioevo 10 (1962) (Spoleto, 1963), pp. 181–227, with Beryl Smalley's remarks p. 334.

the role of exegetical tradition in fashioning and refashioning the Scriptures' meaning. Biblical commentaries and glosses were simultaneously dictionaries of, and agents in the elaboration of the vocabulary of power. Even more than that, they were a full-fledged source of political thought.[6] Yet historians—with such notable exceptions as Beryl Smalley, Gerard Caspary, and Guy Lobrichon—have hardly tapped this rich documentary vein.[7]

This relative neglect would call for a systematic analysis of the sociopolitical models transmitted in, and elaborated by medieval exegesis. The schools of northern France in the twelfth, thirteenth and early fourteenth centuries, which produced numerous and influential commentaries used as textbooks for higher education, form the natural focus for such a study, in this case limited to an era which has its own unity, ca. 1100–ca. 1240, with occasional forays into earlier and later periods.[8]

The commentators' own agendas and debates have directed my analysis to three questions. First, what is the nature of political power at two key moments: at sacred history's beginning in the Garden of Eden and at its imprecise end when the Heavenly Jerusalem shall descend to earth? Second, what are the theoretical and metaphorical foundations of lay and clerical power? Third, what are the material relationships between the ruler and his people? Although I cannot detail here the language and logic exegetes employed in debating such issues, their lexicon and methods have informed my reading of their texts.[9] I shall only mention here how exegetes took a stance in their commentaries on a given scriptural passage: that is, by reproducing, omitting, or adding to traditional exegetical interpretations,

6. Caspary, *Politics,* is the fundamental work on the grammar of exegesis and its relationships with political theory.

7. Caspary, *Politics*; Beryl Smalley, *The Becket Conflict and the Schools: A Study of Intellectuals in Politics* (Totowa, NJ, 1973); Guy Lobrichon, *L'Apocalypse des théologiens au XIIe siècle,* Ph.D. dissertation, Paris X, 1979 (soon to be published); Lobrichon, "L'ordre de ce temps et les désordres de la fin," in *The Use and Abuse of Eschatology in the Middle Ages,* ed. Werner Verbeke, Daniel Verhelst, and Andries Welkenhuysen (Louvain, 1988), pp. 221–41. One should also mention Werner Affeldt, *Die weltliche Gewalt in der Paulus-Exegese Röm.* 13, 1–7 (Göttingen, 1969), and Ian S. Robinson, "'Political Allegory' in the Biblical Exegesis of Bruno of Segni," *Recherches de Théologie Ancienne et Médiévale* 50 (1983), 69ff.

8. The first "glosses" on the Bible date to the turn of the eleventh century, cf. Guy Lobrichon, "Une nouveauté, les gloses de la Bible", in Pierre Riché and Guy Lobrichon, *Le Moyen Age et la Bible,* Bible de tous les temps 4 (Paris, 1984), pp. 95–114. In the 1230s, the mendicants establish themselves in Paris for educative purposes, a move reflected in the production of an influential commentary, the Dominican *Postilla super totam Bibliam* (see below, n. 13).

9. See Buc, *L'ambiguïté,* pp. 40–49, and Buc, "Pouvoir royal et commentaires de la Bible," *Annales E.S.C.* 40, 3 (1989), 691–713, here 691–95. Cf. also John J. Contreni, "Carolingian Biblical Studies," in *Carolingian Essays,* ed. Uta-Renate Blumenthal (Washington, DC: 1983), 71f.

or by referring to other Biblical verses or glosses. Such touches may seem light to us, or obscure in their significance; to those within the exegetical tradition, they were transparent and powerful in meaning.

It was thus, touch by touch, that twelfth-century commentators revised, inflected, and fought over their patristic inheritance relating to the existence of a form of domination at the beginning and at the end of time. Was there a form or even a foreshadowing of political power in the Garden of Eden? Isidore of Seville (d. 636), followed by the ninth-century compiler Hrabanus Maurus, had answered this question through allegories. Man, to whom God had said, "dominate the fish of the sea, the beasts of the earth, and the fowls of the air," signified the prelate, the spiritual man supremely endowed with reason. Three categories of animals (*reptilia, bestiae, iumenta*) created on the fifth day signified the three orders: clerics, the great (*potentes*), and the simple laity (*simplices*). The division between the sexes was similarly hierarchical in meaning: the true male dominated the obedient feminine populace. Allegorically, hierarchical power, just like the Church, belonged to the order of nature, that is, to God's original plan.[10]

Composed in the early twelfth century, the first version of the so-called *Ordinary Gloss on Genesis* omitted the Isidorian allegories. Judging from the hand and illuminations of one of its early manuscripts, we owe this non-hierarchical reading of the Creation to the influential school of Laon. But toward the middle of the century, anonymous masters, possibly in Paris, reworked the Laon *Gloss*. They reinserted Isidore's hierarchies both into the Garden of Eden and the sacred page's choicest spot, that is between its lines.[11] This layout and text would remain almost unchanged throughout

10. On the three orders, see Georges Duby, *Les trois ordres ou l'imaginaire du féodalisme* (Paris, 1978), tr. Arthur Goldhammer, *The Three Orders: Feudal Society Imagined* (Chicago, 1978), and now Dominique Iogna-Prat, "Le baptême du schéma des trois ordres fonctionnels . . .," *Annales E.S.C.* 41, 1 (1986), 101–26, and Otto-Gerhardt Oexle, "Deutungsschemata der sozialen Wirklichkeit im frühen und hohen Mittelalter," in *Mentalitäten im Mittelalter* ed. Frantisek Graus, Vorträge und Forschungen 35 (Sigmaringen, 1987), pp. 65–117 (with references to latest scholarship). Could not this exegetical tradition have provided the simplest vehicle for the tripartite model between Isidore and the school of Auxerre? Analogies between the exact nature (royal? constitutional? despotic?) of the relationship between man and woman within the family and, on the one hand, the human being's psychic/somatic structure, as well as, on the other, the political order, were as old as Aristotle, *Politics* 1, 5, 1254a: 30–1254b: 25; 1, 12, 1259a: 35–1259b: 15; English translation Benjamin Jowett (New York, 1947), pp. 58–60, 62–63.

11. *In Gen.* 1: 24–25: "*Reptilia* § scrutantes terrena per que intelligant celestia"; "*bestias* § ferocitate superbientes"; "*iumenta* § simplices" (Paris, BN MS Latin 63, fol. 7rv; lacking in Paris BN Latin 14398, fol. 11r). See the Isidorian original (*PL,* 83, 211c) mediated by Hrabanus Maurus (*PL,* 107, 468b); Buc, *L'ambiguïté,* pp. 87–96. I owe to Patricia Stirnemann the origins of Paris, BN Latin 14398. Throughout the notes I shall respect the medieval convention,

the history of the *Gloss*. Hierarchy thus seemed to be enshrined definitely in the very first of the sacred pages.

But other Parisian masters immediately reacted. Both Andrew of Saint-Victor (d. 1175) and Peter Abelard (d. 1142)[12] recalled that man should dominate animals, not other men—a quotation of Gregory the Great truncated with pro-egalitarian scissors. Peter the Chanter (d. 1197), the most influential master of the last quarter of the century, tempered the lesson of the *Gloss* by denying the constant animality of man after the Fall. Calling on other Biblical verses and their patristic interpretation, he concluded that power could be exercised when and only when there was transgression: as long as they did not sin, human beings were essentially not subjects.[13] He and his followers—among them Stephen Langton (d. 1228)—effectively rejected the constant action of rulership. This pro-egalitarian parry became authoritative. In the thirteenth century the exponents of domination in the Garden of Eden shifted their focus to the pair male-female. They emphasized sharp inequality between the genders, whereas twelfth-century Parisian exegesis had tended to argue for a more balanced relationship—an egalitarian *societas* tempered with a moderate degree of hierarchy. This trend had its parallel in sacred iconography: the twelfth-century Triumph of the Virgin gave way in the following era to the Coronation of the Virgin. In the former, the New Eve, bride and queen, sat on a par with her royal husband, Christ, the New Adam. In the latter, she now bent her head to accept submissively the crown proferred by the bridegroom.[14]

---

to underline the biblical text commented upon. Passages borrowed from the *Gloss* appear in bold.

12. Andrew, *Super Heptateuchum,* ed. Charles Lohr and Rainer Berndt, *Andreae de Sancto Victore opera, CCCM* 73 (Turnhout, 1986), 22: 575–78; Peter Abelard, *In Hexaemeron, PL* 178: 761d–2a.

13. Peter the Chanter, *in Gen.* 1: 28, Paris, Arsenal MS. 44, p. 7a; corrected on the Pseudo-Hugh of Saint-Cher, *Postilla in Genesim,* 7 vols. (Venice, 1621) 1: 3va, quoted in Buc, *L'ambiguïté,* p. 98 n. 71. See now Agneta Sylwan, ed., *Petrus Cantor, Glossae super Genesim 1–3* (Göteborg: Studia Graeca et Latina Gothoburgensia 55, 1992), 40: 12–16. On Peter and Stephen, cf. John W. Baldwin, *Masters, Princes, and Merchants. The Social Views of Peter the Chanter and his Circle,* 2 vols. (Princeton, NJ, 1970). As shown by Robert E. Lerner, "Poverty, Preaching, and Eschatology in the Revelation Commentaries of 'Hugh of Saint-Cher,'" in *The Bible in the Medieval World: Essays in Memory of Beryl Smalley,* ed. Katherine Walsh and Diana Wood (Oxford, 1985), pp. 157–89, the Dominican *Postilla* cannot be attributed to a single author—hence not to its nominal compiler, Hugh. Cf. the Jewish exegesis of *Gen.* 1: 28 in Jeremy Cohen, *Be Fertile and Increase, Fill the Earth and Master it* (Ithaca, NY, 1989).

14. Buc, *L'ambiguïté,* ch. 1. Langton balanced the somewhat hierarchical *in Gen.* 3: 15, Paris Mazarine MS 177, fol. 6v, v(a), with the more egalitarian *in Gen.* 2: 22, BN MS lat. 14414, fol. 145va, deriving from Hugh of Saint-Victor and Peter Lombard. This compensation is lacking in Nicolas of Gorran, cf. *in Gen.* 3: 16, BN lat. 15560, fol. 26vb = Mazarine 169,

Scholastic debates were not divorced from the language of political society. A speech of Obert archbishop of Milan reported (or composed) by Rahewin, Frederick Barbarossa's biographer, portrayed the emperor as a second Adam, using the language of the exegetes of *Genesis* 1. Echoing the Ambrosian *felix culpa*, the author of the speech, whether Obert or Rahewin, presented the occasion—the 1158 Diet of Roncaglia—as a day of grace (*dies gratie*) for now *felix Italia*. Former rulers had perverted the right order by ruling over good rational men and sparing sinners; Frederick, arresting and reversing the country's process of political degeneration, exercised his dominion not over the virtuous but over sinners:

> Truly, it is you, O most illustrious prince . . . who have called back again into use the long-lapsed freedom (*licentiam*) vouchsafed the first man in the [Biblical] dictum which said: *Be fruitful and multiply, and dominate the fish of the sea and the fowl of the air* . . . [you who have] returned this sentence to its true meaning. For our sins, man lords over man, but by divine ordinance man rules over the fish of the sea and the fowl of the air.[15] O Italy, how many kings—nay, tyrants—have you endured who have taken this command in an opposite sense! Turning it about, they dominate men, nay, they oppress all the good and the wise who, as rational beings, desire to use their reason. But they favor the fish of the sea, that is to say, smooth rascals, grasping and given over to filthy pleasures, and those who have wisdom only in loftily empty matters . . . O most august emperor, thou shall dominate the fish of the sea and the fowl of the air . . .[16]

That *The Deeds of Frederick Barbarossa* does not present us with a carbon copy of Parisian ideology is all the more interesting. The schools provided a language, but not necessarily a dogma for political discourse. The schoolmen's formulas gave the prince a subordinate position at best in the Garden of Eden. If he was present there, it was as one of the irrational beastly *potentes* dominated by the true man. In fashioning Frederick as just this true

---

fol. 21ra–b. Texts quoted in Buc, *L'ambiguïté*, pp. 106–7, nn. 94–95, 97. On iconography see Penny S. Gold, *The Lady and the Virgin* (Chicago, 1985), pp. 51–65.

15. Closest exegetical text, Andrew of Saint-Victor (as above, n. 12).

16. *Ottonis episcopi Frisingensis et Rahewini Gesta Frederici seu rectius Cronica: Textum imperatori transmissum IV*, 5, ed. F.-J. Schmale (Berlin, 1965), pp. 516: 17–518: 32; tr. Charles C. Mierow (New York, 1953), pp. 235–37. I have modified Mierow's translation. Rahewin was notary to Otto I of Freising, the latter educated in the French schools and notably in Saint-Victor of Paris (see next note). Schmale believes Obert's speech to have been "freely rendered" by Rahewin. Notably, the speech begins with a mention of shared nature and fraternity: "Felix tandem Italia . . . que modo principem invenire meruisti, qui nos homines, immo proximos ac fratres recognoscat"—see below, at note 43.

man, the Roncaglia speech shows how exegetical models could be adjusted to praise the prince.

When we turn to the political models of the end of time, we meet similar debates. In his study of the several stages of the *Gloss on Revelation,* Guy Lobrichon has shown how, at the turn of the eleventh century, the influential masters teaching at the school of Laon proclaimed that the three orders would last only as long as did profane history.[17] I have found that the Laon masters did not stop there. Their early *Gloss on the Pauline Epistles* incorporated a startling denial of the permanence beyond the end of history of any form of hierarchical authority. On *1 Corinthians* 15: 24, "When He will abolish every principality, every power and every virtue," the masters commented:

> As long as the world lasts, angels govern angels, demons govern demons, and human beings, humans beings, to serve or deceive the living. But when all shall have been gathered, then all power (*prelatio*) shall cease, for it will no longer be necessary.[18]

This text remained authoritative until the end of the twelfth century. Before the middle of the century, Peter Lombard (d. 1160) further underlined the egalitarianism of this final order and thus implicitly the inferiority of the this-worldly hierarchical dispensation. To the gloss "as long as the world lasts" he added a text borrowed from the late Carolingian commentator Haymo of Auxerre: "fear shall cease, charity shall reign, there will not be any dissension between rulers and subjects"—a promise, as it were, of the abolition of socio-political strife and of the ultimate victory of egalitarian *caritas* over hierarchical *timor.* Furthermore, the Lombard quoted "As long as the world lasts" twice in his extremely influential *Sentences* (1155–57). Peter Comestor alluded to it in his *Historia Scholastica* (1169–73), the textbook for first year studies in theology, and in his *Gloss on the Gloss on Mark.*[19]

17. Lobrichon, *L'Apocalypse,* pp. 157–60; Lobrichon, "L'ordre de ce temps."

18. *Parva glosatura* (also known as "*Pro altercatione*") *in 1 Cor.* 15: 24, Paris BN Latin 14409 (Saint-Victor, 2nd quarter of 12th century), fol. 52va = Paris BN Latin 2579, fol. 70rb, Latin text in Buc, *L'ambiguïté,* p. 130 n. 18, distant echo of Augustine, *De civitate Dei* 19.16, *PL* 41: 644; *CCSL* 48: 683: 10–13.

19. Peter Lombard, *Collectanea, in 1 Cor.* 15: 24, *PL,* 191, 1679, cf. *PL* 117: 597; *Libri quatuor sententiarum,* IId, 6, c, 4 and IVd, 5, 47, c. 5, ed. Patres collegii sancti Bonaventure, 2 vols., 2nd ed. (Florence, 1916), 1: 331; 2: 1021; Petrus Comestor, *Historia scholastica in Evangelium,* c. 90, *PL* 198, 1583–4; Comestor, *in Glosa in Marc.,* 10: 42, Paris BN Latin 620, fol. 122vb: "Scitis quia hii qui videntur dominari [*sic.,* principari] gentium dominantur eis, etc, id est inter homines bene apparet qui sint domini et principes, scilicet illi quibus alii subditi ministrant, sed non est ita, id est non ita debet esse inter vos; non enim ille cui ministratur maior est, sed qui ministrat. Fieri maior. Glosa: '**In celo,**' sed quia in celo secundum apostolum post iudicium nulla erit prelatio, expone, maior, id est gloriosior."

Peter the Chanter and Stephen Langton inserted this same theme in their discussions of the Jubilee or peace at the end of time in *Exodus* 25–27.[20] By nature all human beings are equal, but the Fall put one above another; at the end of time, all power shall cease. The influence of this reading spread beyond the schools—after the turn of the century, it was adopted by Eike von Repgow in his *Mirror of the Saxons*.[21]

Yet, at the very moment when the idea of power's ultimate abolition diffused itself beyond its exegetical cradle, a new generation of exegetes turned against it. The reaction was in full, triumphant bloom toward the middle of the thirteenth century, but debates had been raging since shortly after 1200. Stephen Langton, unlike his predecessor Peter the Chanter, had had to defend "As long as the world lasts" against interpretations which sought to neutralize its implicit egalitarianism. Langton may have come in contact with the scholastic *questio* we first find before 1217 in Gerald of Wales's *De principis instructione*. The end of time would witness the abolition of domineering and forceful power, but not the elimination of the hierarchical order of inferior and superior dignities. This subtle nuance allowed mainstream Dominican and Franciscan exegetes to outflank the authoritative Gloss and rediscover inferiors and superiors in the world to come. Eschatological hierarchy now legitimized the this-worldly hierarchical order just as eschatological equality had, in the twelfth century, delegitimized it.[22]

20. Langton (full commentary) *in Lev.* 25: 39–40, Paris BN Latin 384, fol. 75ra–b (cf. BN lat. 14415, fol. 203rb): "[Si paupertate compulsus] vendiderit se tibi [frater tuus] subdendo se consilio tuo et doctrinis non eum opprimes servitute famulorum quia non est habendus subditus bonus ut servus. Servitute iam non dicam vos servos, servus tamen a servitute esse potest, ut Paulus servus Iehsu Christi, et papa servus servorum dei. Sed quasi mercenarius et colonus erit, sic terram corporis bene excolens, spinas et tribulos removens, et in labore penitentie se exercens. Egredietur. Ieremias: In die illa non docebit frater proximum suum [cf. *Ier.* 34: 5], et Paulus: 'Cum evacuaverit omnem principatum et potestatem' [cf. *1 Cor.* 15: 24] et *Iob* [3: 19], ibi erit 'parvus et magnus' 'et servus liber a domino suo.' Cum liberis suis 'Iusto non est lex posita' [*1 Tim.* 1: 9], etc. Item, Ubi non delinquimus pares sumus. Vel, Cum liberis, bonis operibus ut videas filios filiorum et opera illorum sequuntur illos. Item, Usque ad annum iubileum. Id est, plenam remissionem iniquitatis. Operabitur. Ier[onimus]: Semper aliquid boni operis fac. Exibit homo ad opus suum, etc. Postea in vespera vite nullus recipit denarium nisi in hora vespertina laboraverit. Ne affligas eum per potentiam. Simile in *Ecclesiastico* [32: 1]: 'Rectorem te posuerunt? Noli extolli,' sed 'esto in illis quasi unus ex illis.' Item Petrus in canonica epistola: 'Non ut dominantes in clero, sed forma gregis facti ex animo' [*1 Petr.* 5: 3]. Item in *Ezechiele* [34: 5], 'Quod perierat non quesivisti, sed cum austeritate imperabatis ei et cum potentia.' (. . .)'. On the full commentary, the *Expositio moralis,* and the *Expositio litteralis,* see Gilbert Lacombe and Beryl Smalley, "Studies on the Commentaries of Cardinal Stephen Langton," *Archives d'Histoire Doctrinale et Littéraire du Moyen Age* 5 (1931), 1–220, at 81–86 and 156–60, with Buc, *L'ambiguïté,* p. 144 at n. 49.

21. *Sachsenspiegel* Landrecht 3: 42, ed. Karl A. Eckhardt, *MGH Fontes iuris germanici antiqui Nova series* 1: 1–2 (Göttingen, 1955–56) 1: 223; cf. Buc, *L'ambiguïté,* pp. 139–42.

22. *De principis instructione,* i.1, ed. G. F. Warner, *Giraldi Cambrensis opera* 8 (London, 1881), 8–9; Buc, *L'ambiguïté,* ch. 2: 3, pp. 147–61.

In the first half of the thirteenth century, *1 Corinthians* 15 also became embroiled in the struggles between *regnum* and *sacerdotium*. Some exegetes distinguished between *prelatio* and *prelatio* in arguing that lay power would indeed be abolished at the end of time, but that sacerdotal power would last into eternity. The princes' partisans countered this not so subtle denigration of secular rulership. The disciples of Amaury of Bene—men secretly backed by Philip Augustus's son Louis and trained in the schools on the same benches as the hierocrats—pretended that at the end of time all orders would be abolished, including the hierarchy of the Church, but that the king of France and his son would receive *potestas* as well as the science of the Scriptures and would never die.[23]

This episode of 1210 not only reveals the monarchist version of the debate on the end of time, it also highlights how the lay princes' propagandists or panegyrists proposed exegetical science to their patrons as a foundation for their authority. In a symmetrical fashion, prelates had long since adopted violent symbols (such as the metaphorical eating of their subjects) to suggest terror and hierarchy.

The lay rulers' relationship to exegetical reason was complex. As a corporate group, clerics excluded the prince from knowledge, that is, from the virtue most essentially theirs. Their interests incited them to deny to secular rulers wisdom in general, and in particular the comprehension of the scriptures' true meanings, all the while simultaneously proclaiming that this understanding was crucial for good governance, be it lay or ecclesiastical. Did not the Bible contain the true law? Exegetes elaborated theoretical models of power which proclaimed both this exclusion and this necessity. They also embodied this lesson in their reading of *Isaias* 11: 4, "The lion, tantamount to an ox, shall eat straw." The lion, that is the king, just like the ox, the peasant, should content himself with the literal, surface sense of the Scriptures and refrain from seeking to understand its hidden marrow, the preserve of the clergy. In matters of knowledge, princes were simple laymen, *simplices*. They depended for their instruction on the doctors of the faith, and could not judge the preaching of even the least worthy of clerics. In terms of the Isidorian scheme in *Genesis* 1, because they shared in the

23. See the Pseudo-Hugh of Saint-Cher, in *1 Petr.* 2: 9 (7: 328rb), adopted by Peter of Tarentaise, O.P., with minor variations, BN Latin 15265, fol. 199va; BN lat. 15597, fol. 125ra. Cf. Buc, *L'ambiguïté,* ch. 2: 4, pp. 161–66. On the Capetians and Amalric's disciples, see Robert E. Lerner, "The Uses of Heterodoxy: The French Monarchy and Unbelief in the 13th Century," *French Historical Studies* 4, 2 (1965), 188–202.

same irrationality, the *potentes* were on a par with the *simplices*. This was a message intended for princes; the *Bible moralisée* conveyed it to Louis IX.[24]

Yet this corporate exclusiveness often faded in the face of individual agendas. Some clerics, driven by ambition, sought patronage and the service of lay princes. Others simply had faith in their lay ruler. The individual cleric could thus attribute a quasi-science of the scriptures to magnates such as Baldwin II, count of Guines, or Henry the Liberal of Champagne, and kings such as Louis IX. The Investiture Contest may have spelled the death of the model of the priest-king—whatever that was. But already in the twelfth century, individual princes could endow themselves or be endowed with a virtue, "Clergie," which made them tantamount to priests. Indeed, because of the schools, the definition of priesthood now increasingly centered on knowledge and reason.[25]

The clerics' position vis-à-vis symbols of violence mirrored almost exactly that of the princes vis-à-vis reason. Strictly speaking, violence did not belong to the essence of the priesthood. To the contrary, clerics were forbidden to exercise it. Yet exegetes recognized that any political organization must be able to coerce. Even the strongly egalitarian Peter the Chanter understood the corollary of this necessity: power must express and symbolize the violence it potentially exercises.[26] Thus *regnum* and *sacerdotium* competed for the possession of, or strove to exclude each other from, the most strikingly violent symbolism. Clerics tried to render diabolic the hunt, a practice from which they were themselves excluded and which demonstrated power's violent potential. No wonder princes claimed the authorship of hunting treatises, as did Frederick II (d. 1250) with his most celebrated *Art of Falconry*.[27] Such authorship was proof both of expertise

24. Clearest in Langton, *Glose super Glosas Ysaie, in Is.* 11: 7, BN lat. 14417, fol. 188rb, Latin text quoted in Buc, *L'ambiguïté,* ch. 2: 1, p. 189, n. 45: "Leo quasi bos comedet paleas, id est quilibet **principes** vel nobiles sicut et plebeius gaudebunt **superficie hystorie,** etc. Proponetur ei in ecclesia cum aliis, audiet attente, quia eque **simplices** sunt reges et principes ut plebeii. Glosa: '**principes enim,**' etc"; *Bible moralisée, in Is.* 11: 7 (BN lat. 11560, 109v); ed. André de Laborde, *Bible moralisée,* 5 vols. (Paris, 1912–27), 2: pl. 333. I owe this important text to Amy G. Remensnyder.

25. Buc, *L'ambiguïté,* 173–205; see Buc, "Pouvoir royal," 699–704. Fundamental are Herbert Grundmann, "*Sacerdotium—Regnum—Studium,*" *Archiv für Kulturgeschichte,* 34 (1951), pp. 5–21; Grundmann, "Litteratus—illiteratus. Der Wandel einer Bildungsnorm vom Altertum zum Mittelalter," ibid., 40 (1958), pp. 1–60; and Alexander Murray, *Reason and Society in the Middle Ages* (Oxford, 1978), esp. pp. 211–310.

26. E.g., Peter on Nemrod (*Gen.* 9: 10), quoted in Buc, "Pouvoir royal," 698–99.

27. Cf. Charles H. Haskins, "The *De Arte Venandi cum Avibus* of the Emperor Frederick II," *EHR,* 36 (1921), pp. 334–355; Haskins, "Some Early Treatises on Falconry," *Romanic Review* 13 (1922), 18–27.

in matters of symbolic violence[28] and of the possession of the reason which characterized the prelate.

The Church's own claim to violence took the potent form of the metaphorical eating of the subject. The prelate eats his subjects and assimilates them into the political body of which he is the head. Taking pleasure in descriptions of this process, exegetes lingered on its rawest aspects: the good prelate immolated his subjects and shed the blood of sin, then ate the thus-purified individuals, thereby incorporating them into the Church. This was figurative violence, since theoretically clerics could not shed blood. The Eucharist provided the equally bloody reciprocal process: Christ the King immolated himself and distributed himself to his subjects in order to aggregate them into himself. The Church's incoporation entailed devouring the secular kingdoms. According to Peter the Chanter and Innocent III, it was by "immolating and eating" that the Church constructed itself. This mystical body would in the end consume all secular kingdoms.[29]

Exegesis also elaborated on the lay prince's eating of his subjects, but only as the negative mirror image of good clerical incorporation. The polity's construction was made diabolic. The lay ruler did not incorporate his people; tantamount to a cannibal, he devoured it raw. He ate "bloody flesh", that is (as exegetical chains centered on *Genesis* 9: 4 explained) he annihilated his people through exactions, a murderous coercive power, and a grasping justice employing stool-pigeons and aiming at despoiling its hapless victims.[30]

This metaphor of manducation allows us to observe again the interpenetration of exegesis and other forms of political discourse. Two legends centered on royal dreams provide negative and positive versions of princely eating. The first was reported by three twelfth-century authors, Benedict

28. Cf. Buc, "Pouvoir royal," at 697–99, and *L'ambiguïté,* ch. 1: 4, 112–22. Pierre Toubert has drawn my attention to a related phenomenon: princely menageries—see Karl Hauck, "Tiergarten im Pfalzbereich," *Deutsche Königspfalzen,* 3 vols. (Göttingen, 1963–75) 1: 30–74. I am indebted to Dr. Igor Gorevitch for further information on medieval animal lore and for pointing out Wilhelm Schouwink, *Der wilde Eber in Gottes Weinberg: Zur Darstellung des Schweins in Literatur und Kunst des Mittelalters* (Sigmaringen-J., 1985).

29. Buc, *L'ambiguïté,* ch. 4: 1, pp. 206–17.

30. Buc, *L'ambiguïté,* ch. 4: 2, pp. 217–27; e.g., Langton, *Expositio moralis in Lev.* 7: 26, BN lat. 385, fol. 12va–b = BN lat. 355, fol. 114rv: "Sanguinem quoque omnis animalis non sumetis in cibo. Hoc tripliciter exponitur. Primo de raptoribus, secundo de invidis, tercio de detractoribus. Primo sic. Per sanguinem labor et sudor intelliguntur pauperum, quem divites et tyranni huius mundi bibunt. Hii sunt sub quorum alis est sanguis pauperum et innocentum, qui conterunt ossa pauperum in lebete et comminuunt et dirimunt pellem desuper ossibus eorum [cf. *Mich.* 3: 3]. Hii sunt qui de sudore pauperum ornant equos faleris et se veste varia."

of Sainte-Maure, Walter Map, and Gerald of Wales.[31] On the eve of his last, fatal hunt, King William Rufus dreams that he devours a man raw. For Gerald, the ravenously intensive governance of Henry II and his Plantagenet sons was exactly that: royal cannibalism. A different dream was attributed to Louis VII: his son Philip ministered a cup of blood—whose?—to France's principal barons. According to the same Gerald of Wales, this vision signified the reintegration of France's political body. It provides us with a monarchical version of the eating metaphor.[32]

* * *

Commentators did not limit themselves to discussions of transcendental legitimacy and virtues (or symbols) legitimizing princely power. Using the logic of exegetical language, they also dealt with an issue which belongs more clearly to the ambit of modern political science, the relationship between king and people. Central to this issue were two questions, royal taxation (if I may use a half-anachronistic concept) and the constitutional position of the *populus*. Both questions were inextricably tied to a third, the Biblical origins of secular power.

Beginning with the twelfth century, a whole web of interconnected scriptural passages dealt with—here I quote the *Ordinary Gloss*—"what the king should exact from the people" and "what the people must give him."[33] This textual network centered on *1 Kings* 8, the historical origins of the Jewish monarchy. The Jews rejected God's immediate governance and asked Samuel—the last Judge of Israel—to provide them with their first king.[34] The Lord told Samuel to accede to their petition but in a final attempt to dissuade Israel from abandoning divine rule, commanded him to spell out to the people the *ius regis*, the king's law or privileges:

31. Cf. André Queffelec, "Représentation de la chasse chez les chroniqueurs anglo-normands du douzième siècle," *in La chasse au Moyen-Age: actes du Colloque de Nice, 22–24 juin 1979* (Paris, 1980), pp. 423ff.

32. Giraldus Cambrensis, *De principis instructione* 1, 20, 3, 1, ed. Warner, pp. 135, 227–28, deriving from an interpolation to Rigord, *Gesta Philippi Augusti*, c. 1, ed. Henri-François Delaborde, *Oeuvres de Rigord et de Guillaume le Breton*, 2 vols. (Paris, 1882–85), 1: 8–9]. Cf. Buc, *Potestas*, ch. 4: 2. On eating metaphors, see Caroline W. Bynum, *Holy Feast and Holy Fast: The Religious Significance of Food to Medieval Women* (Berkeley, CA, 1987). On Gerald and William Rufus, see Robert Bartlett, *Girald of Wales 1146–1223* (Oxford, 1982), p. 93.

33. *Gloss in 1 Reg*. 10: 25, BN Latin 17204 (c. 1210), fol. 7ra: "[legem regni] Scilicet quid rex a populo exigere et quid populus regi dare deberet."

34. On this episode, see Joseph Funkenstein, "Samuel und Saul in der Staatslehre des Mittelalters," *Archiv für Rechts- und Sozialphilosophie* 40 (1952–53), 129–40, and, for early mod-

> This shall be the *ius* of the king who shall command you: he shall seize (*tollet*) your sons and put them in his chariots and make them his horsemen and the forerunners of his quadrigae, and he shall establish for himself tribunes, and centurions, and tillers for his fields and reapers of his crops and armorers for his weapons and chariots. Further, he shall turn your daughters into his ointment-makers, his cooks, and his bread-makers. He shall seize (*tollet*) your fields, your vineyards, and your best olive-groves, and give them to his servants. As for your crops and the produce of your vineyards, he shall tithe them to give to his eunuchs and members of his *familia*. And he shall take your servants, male and female, your best young men and your donkeys to make them work in his fields. He shall also levy a tithe on your flocks, and you shall be his serfs. And on that day you shall clamor and shrink away from the face of that king whom you have elected, but God shall not hear you, since you asked for a king.[35]

The people refused to bow under this threat and received their first king, Saul.

Compelling evidence exists that some thinkers saw in this text the Biblical justification of royal demands on the people. But for the majority of twelfth-century exegetes the *ius regis* did not describe the absolute prerogatives of a fully legitimate authority, but rather the excesses in taxation and lordship (*exactionem et dominationem*) to which a kingship created against God's will was naturally prone.[36] Through references to other passages of the Bible, these commentators argued for the existence of another law of the kingdom (*lex regni*). Enshrined in the tabernacle next to the Holy Books themselves, it limited the authority and especially the material demands of the kings of Israel and Judah.[37] These masters also underlined the original illegitimacy of royal power. It originated in a rebellion against God whose constitutional consequence the Lord had only reluctantly accepted. God could thus say through the prophet Hosea (13: 11): "I gave them a king in my anger." The canonical distinction between a permission and a precept served to express the exact status of Israelite kingship. God had never prescribed kingship, he had merely allowed it—as a lesser evil,

---

ern Europe, Annette Weber-Möckl, *Das Recht des Königs, der über euch herrschen soll.* Studien zu 1 Sam 8, 11ff. in der Literatur der frühen Neuzeit (Berlin, 1986).

35. *1 Kings* 8: 11–18.

36. *Gloss in 1 Reg.* 8: 7, BN Latin 17204, fol. 5v; see Buc, *Potestas,* ch. 5: 1, pp. 248–51.

37. See the *Epithoma in Libros Regum* (last quarter of the twelfth century), *in 1 Reg.* 10: 25, BN lat. 15074, fol. 86v = BN Latin 2674, fol. 6v: "Descripsit Samuel legem regni, **quid** videlicet **deberet [rex] exigere a populo** et **quid** illi **dare**, et ipsam scripturam coram Domino, id est in loco sancto reposuit, ut ibi iugiter conservanda maneret, ut si quando amplius re quireret [rex] a subiectis, per hanc scripturam condemnaretur, quam ille sanctus propheta Domino dictante conscripserat."

just as Moses had permitted the Jews to divorce.[38] To hammer home the frail status of royal authority, our exegetes drew a series of parallels: first, between the end of the regime of the Judges of Israel and the coup d'état which had abolished the Roman Republic—a crime made into law, according to the words of the poet Lucan[39]; second, between Israel's refusal of God's immediate governance and the Jews' shout at Christ's judgment, "We have no other king but Caesar";[40] third, between this act of rebellion and all prior refusals to obey God—implicitly all the way back to the Fall. Born from the sin of rebellion against God, could royal power sinlessly increase its domination over the people and tax it without limits? The twelfth-century answer was almost unanimously negative.[41]

Exegetes tried another bridle with which to check the growth of Angevin and Capetian lordship. They emphasized the essential proximity of the king's status and that of the *populus*—a group which encompassed the *plebs* or *multitudo* for which they also tried to secure constitutional rights.

This leveling enterprise used the language of moral theology and Christology. Peter the Chanter, in commenting on the anointing of David, figure of Christ the King, emphasized the Lord's humanity rather than his divinity. Royal accession was a wedding uniting king and people. The hierarchical components were faint, for the polity's head and body, thus united, participated in a same community of nature.[42] The Parisian master's political Christology sought to convey a message: rulers (lay as well as ecclesiastical) shared too much with their people to pretend to be of

38. Cf. *Gloss in Deut.* 17: 14, Paris BN Latin 186 (ca. 1150), fol. 47r: "[Constitues eum] Permittit, non commitit."

39. Langton, *in 1 Reg.* 8: 11, Carpentras Bibliothèque Municipale 12, fol. 24r: "Et predic eis ius regis qui regnaturus est super eos id est potestatem regis. Simile: iusque datum sceleri canimus populumque potentem. Ius ergo vocat **exactiones** et **dominationes** regis"—Cf. Lucan, *Civil War* 1: 2 ed. A. Bourgery, 2 vols. (Paris, 1926), 1: 1.

40. *Gloss in 1 Reg.* 10, BN lat. 17204, fol. 6vb: "Seniores Israel, reprobato Samuele, regem sibi petierunt, et Scribe cum Phariseis, repulso Christo vero sacerdote clamaverunt, 'Non habemus regem nisi Cesarem'."

41. Cf. Langton, *in Deut.* 17: 14, BN Latin 14415, fol. 265rb; corrected on Cambridge Trinity College 86, fol. 394rb: "Cum ingressus fueris terram. Hic agitur de rege faciendo, sed non est preceptum de rege quod hic dicitur, sed permissio, quia **non precepit** hic quod facerent, sed si facturi essent, quod saltem de tribu sua esset. Domino itaque non placuit quod regem facerent, immo **displicuit,** unde Osee [cf. *Os.* 13: 11], 'Dedi eis regem in ira mea.' Item Samuel improperans eis quod regem desideraverant retulit exactiones tirannicas regis futuras, non quia licitas, sed in penam eorum **permis**sas"; cf. Buc, *L'ambiguïté,* ch. 5: 1–2, pp. 246–70. I examine thirteenth-century exegetes' progressively greater approval of royal demands, as well as the issue of clerical immunities, in ch. 5: 3–4.

42. Buc, *L'ambiguïté,* ch. 6: 1a, pp. 322–27. The reverse, pro-hierarchical reasoning could be derived from Christology; cf. E. H. Kantorowicz, *The King's Two Bodies: A Study in Medieval Political Theology* (Princeton, NJ, 1957), pp. 42–78, esp. 74.

another nature and above the laws. Ideally, humanity, humility, mercy, and fraternity derived from this community of nature. These virtues balanced the hierarchical preeminence vested in the ruler by his office.[43]

In thirteenth-century iconography, Heaven would become a celestial court structured as a pyramid. But Peter, the *Dominican Postil on the Psalms,* and other commentators represented community with the image of the circle: in the model order of the Heavenly Jerusalem, Christ the King is in the center, *in medio,* and all are equally distant from him. The Roncaglia panegyric used this language: Frederick Barbarossa was "*in medio populi . . . mitissimus.*"[44]

The favorite political formula of Peter the Chanter's school "*Ubi non delinquimus pares sumus,*" "when we do not sin we are equals," conveyed the same ideology: whenever there is no transgression, the king (or the prelate) and his subjects are peers; the ruler has no authority over the people. The formula was far from innocent in a twelfth-century context. It implied a refusal of the nascent administrative power and its propensity to intervene in the life of the people.[45] The Chanter hammered upon this point with special eloquence in commenting on *Matthew* 20: 25—"Barbarian princes dominate their people," a lesson he earmarked for both Christian kings and ecclesiastical prelates:

> Indeed, when we do not sin we are equals, and the Lord said, *Dominate the beasts of the earth* [Gen. 1: 28], that is, those who live bestially . . . . To dominate . . . unless coerced by necessity, that is when there is bestiality, is tyranny and cupidity . . . . The rule is therefore that power should never be wielded except where iniquity [itself] dominates.[46]

The revolutionary consequences of twelfth-century masters' reactionary agenda are evident elsewhere. Exegetes endowed the people with con-

43. E.g., Peter the Chanter, *in Eccli.* 32: 1, Mazarine 176, fol. 140vb: "Rectorem te posuerunt, etc. **Qui dignitate preest non [debet] superbi[r]e.** Unde: **"Qui maior est vestrum, fiat sicut minor"** [*Matt.* 23: 11]. Non venit Christus ministrari sed ministrare, et Apostolus se servum dicit hominum et dominus papa, quia ubi non delinquimus pares sumus. Esto in illis quasi unum ex illis, id est, in privato natura, in publico dignitas; or Langton, on Salomon's designation by David, *in 1 Par.* 28: 2, ed. Avrom Saltman, *Commentary on the Book of Chronicles* (Ramat-Gan, 1978), pp. 139–40: "Et stetisset. Ecce qualiter et quomodo rex debet loqui ad populum et quibus verbis: Audite me fratres mei per naturam populus meus per regiminis curam."

44. The expression *in medio* is used twice—*Gesta,* 516: 20, 23–24. The speech is thus a striking (but quite common in political Christology) conflation of egalitarian and hierarchical themes. It begins with the fraternal emperor in the center, but ends with Justinian's "What pleases the prince has the force of law . . . ." Law-making unifies it: the emperor is in the center "to lay down the laws of peace." Cf. Buc, *L'ambiguïté,* ch. 6: 1b, pp. 333–38.

45. Buc, *Potestas,* ch. 6: 1c, pp. 338–50.

46. Latin text in appendix.

stitutional rights and advocated popular duties with far-reaching—at least in theory—political consequences. Toward the end of the century, Peter the Chanter, Stephen Langton, and Radulphus Niger (d. ca 1200) found a place for the *populus* in royal accessions and made it a participant in the coronation oath. Both Peter and Stephen pleaded for the common people's participation in important royal decisions—for a popular *consilium*.[47]

More boldly still, many authors between 1175 and 1215 endowed the people with a duty to reprimand (*correctio*) its delinquent rulers. The prime Biblical authorities for this idea were the Lord's precept, "Should your brother fault against you, reprimand him" (*Matthew* 18: 15–17), and the *Gloss on Romans,* 1: 32, "To remain silent although one could reprimand is to consent to sin." These commentators even envisaged favorably a popular right of resistance against princes or prelates when they committed evil, a theory anchored in the *Glosses* on *2 Kings* 24 and *Psalm* 81. The first text maintained that the Jewish *populus* had been struck by a plague because it had not opposed (*non restitit*) king David's adultery with Bathsheba and his murder of Uriah.[48] According to the other, the inferiors (*minores*) should have opposed Christ's arrest, unjust trial, and crucifixion. Given their numbers, they could have exerted a threatening pressure on their rulers (*maiores*) and forced them to release the Lord.[49] Thirteenth-century exegesis, led by mainstream mendicant commentators, would attempt to roll back egalitarian interpretations, including the duties of popular reprimand and resistance. But the conciliar movement, the Hussite crisis, and sixteenth-century constitutionalism attest to their survival. They had by then become part of the stock concepts available to medieval political theory.[50]

47. Buc, *L'ambiguïté,* pp. 313–14, 366, n. 154; see also Baldwin, *Masters* 1: 172–73.

48. *Gloss in 2 Reg.* 23: 39, Paris BN Latin 17204, fol. 33ra, quoted in Buc, *L'ambiguïté,* p. 357, n. 128.

49. I cite the earliest known version of the Gloss on the Psalms, the *Parva glosatura,* produced at the beginning of the twelfth century in Laon, *in Ps.* 81: 4, Paris BN lat. 442, fol. 101va; Latin 17213, fol. 120va: "Eripite. [Augustinus:] Ostendit nec illos immunes qui permiserunt principibus Christum, cum pro multitudine timerentur et possent illos a facto et se a consensu liberare; [Cassiodorus:] qui desinit obviare cum possit consensit." Cf. Augustine and Cassiodorus *in Ps.* 81: 4 *CCSL* 39: 1138 and *PL,* 70: 594.

49. Buc, *L'ambiguïté,* ch. 6: 3, pp. 378ff.

50. C. Warren Hollister and John W. Baldwin, "The Rise of Administrative Kingship: Henry I and Philip Augustus," *AHR* 83 (1978), 867–905, have emphasized twelfth-century transformations in government, French historians since at least Georges Duby the intensification of lordship in general, anarchically in the eleventh, with a striving for organization in the twelfth century. See his "Recherches sur l'évolution des institutions judiciaires pendant le Xe et le XIe siècle dans le Sud de la Bourgogne," *Moyen Age* 52 (1946), 149–94; 53 (1947), 15–38; reprinted in Duby, *The Chivalrous Society,* tr. Cynthia Postan (Berkeley, CA, 1977), pp. 15–58, and most recently Dominique Barthélemy, *L'ordre seigneurial* (Paris, 1990), ch. 3. See also Robert I. Moore, *The Formation of a Persecuting Society: Power and Deviance in Western*

"Barbarian princes dominate their people, and the great wield power over them; it shall not be thus among you"—Christ's warning to the apostles found a special echo in the twelfth century. This was an age of princely consolidation, an age in which the forceful tactics of lordly domination were rationalized and applied with intensified method, finally an age during which judicial authority no longer simply reacted to complaints, but also acted on their own cognizance of crimes and invented in the inquisitive prosecution of transgression a rationale for increases in its own power.[51] This phenomenon was of course paralleled (and in many cases anticipated) by the growing institutionalization of papal power and the hardening of local churches' control over their subjects.[52] It was thus no accident that lordship, *dominatio,* and the cognate verb, to dominate (*dominari*), became important topics of discussion for the masters of the northern French schools. In the face of a perceived increase in government's claims over society, these schoolmen—a novel class of specialists in educa-

---

Europe 950–1250 (Oxford, 1987), pp. 100–140. It should be clear from this essay that while I am in agreement with the general picture Moore presents, I believe he underestimates clerical resistance to the new order. *Literati,* who as such stood to profit the most from the "triumph of reason," could oppose increases in the very repressive apparatus which provided their class with careers. Far from seeking pretexts for persecution, Peter the Chanter—and other *magistri*—showed favor to the Waldensians, see my "*Vox clamantis in deserto?* Pierre le Chantre et la prédication laïque," *Revue Mabillon* 4 (1993), 5–47.

51. Something Peter the Chanter well perceived. For him church authority was primarily to be directed against oppressive princes, not against the people or the lower clergy. Cf. infra, appendix, and *in Ex.* 7: 1–2, Paris, Arsenal MS. 44, fol. 65a–b: "Constitui te deum Pharaonis, id est potentem super Pharaonem et in terra eius, ut quod volueris precipias ei, et facias in terra eius in signis et [65b] prodigiis sicut deus imperat creature sue ut vult. Gregorius: Deus quandoque dicitur nuncupative, ut hic, quandoque essentialiter vel natura[liter], quandoque adoptive, 'Ego dixi, dii estis.' Vel Augustinus: Ego dedi te deum Pharaoni. Licet ad populum mitteretur, non ei dictum est, dedi te deum populo, quia nisi si delinquimus pares sumus. Nil ergo imperet maior prelatus minori nisi de contingentibus omittenti, quia [non] datus est illi deus, sed Pharaoni et complicibus eius, precipue principibus secularibus. (. . .)." It was a perversion when Church officials deprived parish priests and other smaller clergy of jurisdiction, cf. *in Lev.* 13: 2–3 [170b–1a]: "Adducetur [reus]. A quibus? ab alii fidelibus, a iusticie amatoribus, quos cognita hominis perversitate negligere non oportet, si zelus domus domini comedit eos qui non habentes iudicandi potestatem, sacerdoti tamen suo hominem illum debent offerre, et de eo quid cognoverint insinuare. [Ad Aaron sacerdotem vel] ad unum quemlibet [filiorum eius]; ergo minores sacerdotes possunt cognoscere de criminalibus sicut et pontifices. Hii tamen de supercilio Phariseorum reservaverunt sibi quorundam peccatorum cognitionem, ut publicorum incendiariorum et huiusmodi. Ad arbitrium eius [separabitur]. Contradic ecclesie [171a] et Apostolus ait, 'Cum spiritu meo et vestro' [cf. *1 Cor.* 5: 4–5]. Verum auctoritas solius eius requiratur ad ligandum vel solvendum populi consensu, sed maiores modo non sinunt ut minores sacerdotes immundos mundent et concordes red[d]ant sine eorum consciencia [consensu?] quia lucrari volunt, sicut patet de filio divitis cuiusdam qui filium pauperis sagittando interfecit, quorum patres minor sacerdos pacificasset et potestas regia, nisi obstitisset avaritia archidiaconi vel episcopi inmisericorditer pretium et penam sanguinis exigere volentis." Remark the role of the people in the judicial process.

tion to whom students flocked from all over Europe—attempted to assess domination's position between the poles of legitimacy and illegitimacy.

Appendix: Peter the Chanter, *in Matt.* 20: 25 and *Luc.* 22: 25–26

Scitis quia principes—Lucas: reges, etc—ac si diceret, vos more similarium per prelationem venire vultis ad regni possessionem.[1] Non est ita. Potestatem exercent : quod malum. Ubi enim non delinquimus pares sumus, et dominus ait, "Dominamini bestiis terre" [Cf *Gen.* 1: 26–28], id est bestialiter viventibus. Alias autem dominari nisi ubi cogit necessitas, scilicet ubi fuerit bestialitas, tyrannis est vel cupiditas. Unde et preceptio mulacia[2] mala est; bonum tamen est ei[3] obedire, sed malum precipere.[4] Est ergo regula quia nusquam exercenda potestas nisi ubi dominatur iniquitas. Lucas [22: 25] melius: Qui potestatem habent super eos, benefici [vocantur], non malefici, non raptores, non usque ad modicum munus exactores ·/[5] ut modo. Olim enim principum largitio in omnes diffundebatur, adeo ut dignum dono [P, 140rb] nulli denegarent quod peteret,[6] etiam de tributis et censu remittebant. Nunc autem nostri stipendiis non sunt contenti,[7] sed tallias, et decimarum et aliorum iniustas exactiones in subditos faciunt.[8] Prelati etiam ecclesiastici dominantes in clero [cf. *1 Petr.* 5: 3] laicos in dominatione excedunt, precipientes suffraganeis ut nepotibus et clericis suis dent prebendas. Cum maior princeps seculari non precipiat minori ut sic vel sic distribuat feuda sua, sed hec omnia in potestate sua relinquit, multo magis et ecclesiasticus superior hoc deberet concedere minori prelato, nisi dilapidaret et male distribueret res ecclesiasticas.

Principes gentium. Videtur dominus velle principes et reges christianorum debere sectari illam humilitatem quam et illi sectabantur quorum

Paris BN Latin 15585, fol. 140ra–va (P); Paris Mazarine 298, fol. 8ra–b (M)

1. Thus corrected in M,P: passionem.
2. Meaning, calling for absolute, automatic, and asinine obedience to an order, whatever its content. Cf. Buc, *Potestas*, ch. 1: 3 n. 73.
3. P: tibi.
4. P: precipere est.
5. M, ***in margine***: ·/ exhaustores loculorum pauperum.
6. P: petent.
7. M: n. s. non contenti.
8. P: faciunt dominantes in subditos.

erat cor unum et anima una. Cur enim[9] diceret principes gentium nisi hoc vellet non licere principibus christianorum, scilicet ut alii aliis dominentur? Sed obicis quod[10] oportet ut dominentur ne alii in alios degrassentur. Licet quoque[11] in tales sed non in humiles et iustos. Sic etiam omnem ornatum vestium videtur velle principibus nostris prohibere, similiter reginis, ita et apostoli %.[12] Hoc verum est.[13] Sed obicitur quia his utendum est ne cadat dignitas et fastus palatii, et item, utere delitiis non pro te [M, 8rb] sed regina [*sic.*, regno?], et utinam pro his causis vel alia honesta hec fierent.

Non ita erit inter vos, . . . cum econtra ad summam virtutum non imperando, non dominando perveniatur sed ministrando. : Sed in quibus hodie[14] tenet huius dominice preceptionis verbum immutabile et apostolistice humilitatis et servitutis exemplum?[15] Et cum dominus sine mutatione hoc preceperit teneri ut esset vestigium huiusmodi humilitatis in aliquibus, non videtur hodie posse teneri. Prelati enim qui regalia habent et predia et villas, sic et abbates, tenentur movere castra, sequi exercitum, intonare et imperare aliis ut hec fiant. Et quod peius est fundere sanguinem. Habent enim monomachias suas. Sic igitur videtur standum sermonem cuiusdam prelati inepti qui ait pro quodam servo quem nolebat sequi uxorem suam, hoc preceptum quidem tunc habebat locum quando piscatores et pauperes prelati erant in ecclesia, hodie autem non tenet cum divites facti sunt et ecclesia lac[tavit] ma[milla] regum. Caderet enim dignitas ecclesie eo observato. Dictum [P, 140va] est ergo apostolis, reges gentium dominantur eorum, vos autem non sic. Nos vero plus multo quam sic in dominio et oppressione subditorum, et non ita erit inter vos, immo multo magis erit inter nos ut amplius, scilicet eis, dominemur in subditis. Marcus [10, 42] ait, non ita est inter vos, Matheus cautius non ita erit quia tunc[16] adhuc fuit ita inter eos quia appetebant primatum terrenum. Maior in merito et premio sit vel erit vester minister in terra, non primatum ambiendo sed humiliter devitando respuendo : ut nec oblatum recipere /.[17] consentiat.

9. M: autem.
10. P: quia.
11. P: quidem.
12. M: *in margine:* Petri et Pauli. *Read:* a. p. et p. prohibent? See note 17.
13. M, P: Hoc videntur.
14. P: prelatis hodie.
15. P: exemplum, Nescio.
16. P: certe.
17. M, *in margine:* nisi necessitas cogat. Signs such as % or /. in the main text of a manuscript refer the medieval reader to a *notula extravagans* in the margins (cf. notes 5 and 12 above), considered as part of the text.

Thomas N. Bisson

Conclusion

People feared the great in the twelfth century, and wondered who was great. Men with power, worried when they lacked status or recognition, struggled to secure customary—that is, legal—assurance of rank. It is a characteristic oddity that ***ministeriales*** tainted with servitude often rose higher in their societies than the untainted *famuli,* mayors, and provosts of western France. But it is clear that service created power. By the later eleventh century one no longer needed to seek out kings to rise and gain; dukes or counts would do, and not a few of these could envy the engaging courtliness of greater castellan lords and barons. Domination not office, lordship rather than kingship, was preponderant in this aristocratic world. That domination was masculine no one could doubt. But women could partake of such masculinity when circumstances required (or permitted), and they shared more fully in the conceptualizing of dynastic power than historians of government have allowed.

Nobility and lordship, the latter especially, loom larger than ever in our understanding, whether by virtue of a more searching inquiry into the old problematic of aristocratic societies, or by virtue of newly directed studies of sacrality, theology, and biblical exegesis. Law may seem less central than is habitually supposed, not for lack of good examples of "lawful societies" but because (perhaps even in Flanders) it could be used or evaded so easily as to invite us to substitute societal or ideological norms for its characteristic function. And perhaps also because we are enabled to see more clearly that judicial process sometimes lay closer to strategic action, to power than to law. Likewise strategic or instrumental was the diverse resort to ritual and commemoration in the royal courts of England, France, and León. On the other hand, canon law assumed prescriptive force in the mechanisms of spiritual courts delegate in the later twelfth century. And as judges virtually made "new law" in the twelfth century, many could see how official action differed attractively from the affectively proprietary ways of lordship.

Was this to insinuate a specifically clerical model of power? Perhaps so, but it would be mistaken to conclude in terms of secular and religious cultures of power. Ideas of office, of functional qualification, may be known to us as ecclesiastical ideas in the twelfth century, but they were easily referred to lay lordship both in its expression and its perversion. Bishops like kings and castellans were vulnerable to charges of (lordly) violence and excess. Nevertheless, our studies of lordship, courts, esoteric expression, and exegesis touch on a subsistent preoccupation with peace as an imperative of moral order that may be recognized as a characteristically clerical theme. It has often been suggested that the religious peace was secularized in the twelfth century, yet it may prove instructive to think of pacification as a persistently clerical—and cultural—influence on the remodelling of justice in the twelfth century.

Here as on other salient points we merely look out on beckoning fields. Prospectors, we envisage no new synthesis. We can see more clearly what topics here omitted or merely touched on—violence, politics, office, and literacy, for example—would contribute to a better understanding of the seed-time of European government. What happened in the twelfth century was that ways of interacting and of thinking about power were juxtaposed or run together more easily than in societies with well developed and specialized institutions and discourses. An example from yet another pertinent topic, accountability, will illustrate this point.

Toward 1118 the monk Lambert of Saint-Omer was at work on his illuminated *liber floridus* when he ran out of parchment while copying Saint Anselm's *Cur Deus homo*. It looks as if he drew on a (discarded?) fiscal account for the local domains of the Count of Flanders in order to carry on, scraping the parchment bare to make way for his theological text. Luckily for us, a few inked strokes of the account escaped erasure where to this day in the manuscript's binding they attest to the confluence of the sublime and the ephemeral. Lambert was filled with lofty imaginings about God's power manifest not only in inspired texts but also in the genealogies of kings and counts and the histories of peoples and of natural things. Did he also understand, even practice, the incipient culture of fiscal control? Or was that work for harder-headed brothers whom he had to raid or cajole? We do not know, and our ignorance is the deeper for the misfortune that the palimpsest Flemish account of ca. 1110 (?) is too incompletely preserved for us to be sure that it was a *ratio* of the new type of dynamic fiscal balance rather than one of the old form of prescriptive inventory.[1] What is

1. *Lamberti S. Audomari canonici Liber floridus*, ed. Albert Derolez (Ghent, 1968), fol. 147v; R. C. Van Caenegem, "The Sources of Flemish History in the Liber Floridus," in *Liber*

clear enough is that power in this burgeoning Flanders evoked by Raoul Van Caenegem was finding expression in practical and inspired forms of literacy, cultural streams that flowed together in the clerical communities of Saint-Omer.

The history of medieval power is to be sought in its microcosms, its locales. It is a cultural history to be recreated from evidence that is comparatively abundant (as in all societies) but also diverse, often incongruent, problematic, and baffling to the inexpert that most of us are beyond our familiar domains. Once we have the collaborative field well in sight it would be worth asking again how Europeans came to govern themselves.

Floridus colloquium, ed. Albert Derolez (Ghent, 1973), p. 71. My own study of this matter will appear elsewhere.

Contributors

BENJAMIN ARNOLD, Reader in Medieval History at Reading University, England, is the author of *German Knighthood 1050–1300* (1985); *Princes and Territories in Medieval Germany* (1991); and *Count and Bishop in Medieval Germany* (1991).

DOMINIQUE BARTHÉLEMY is Professor of Medieval History at the University of Paris XII–Val de Marne. His works include *Les deux âges de la seigneurie banale; Coucy (XIe–XIIIe siècle)* (1984); *La société dans le comté de Vendôme, de l'an mil au XIVe siècle* (1993); and other books and articles about French "feudal" society. He plans new research on knighthood, serfdom, and justice.

THOMAS N. BISSON is Henry Charles Lea Professor of Medieval History at Harvard University. Among his books are *Assemblies and Representation in Languedoc in the Thirteenth Century* (1964); *Fiscal Accounts of Catalonia Under the Early Count Kings (1151–1213)*, 2 vols. (1984); and *The Medieval Crown of Aragon: A Short History* (1986). He is presently working on power in the twelfth century.

PHILIPPE BUC is Assistant Professor of History at Stanford University. He is the author of *L'ambiguïté du livre: prince, pouvoir, et peuple dans les commentaires de la Bible* (1994) as well as of several articles on exegesis and politics. He is now working on a study of medieval theories of political rituals.

CHARLES DUGGAN is Reader Emeritus in History, University of London, and Fellow of King's College London. His works include *Twelfth-Century Decretal Collections* (1963); "From the Conquest to the Death of John," *The English Church and the Papacy in the Middle Ages*, ed. C. H. Lawrence (1965); *Canon Law in Medieval England: The Becket Dispute and Decretal Collections* (Variorum Reprints, 1982); *Decretales ineditae saeculi XII* (1982), with Stanley Chodorow; and numerous articles on decretals, decretal collections and jurisdictional conflicts (including the Becket Dispute).

GEORGES DUBY, Member of the Académie Française, is Emeritus Professor of the History of Medieval Societies in the Collège de France. He is the author or editor of many books, including *La société dans la région mâconnaise aux XIe et XIIe siècles* (1953) and *The Early Growth of the European Economy: Warriors and Peasants from the Seventh to the Twelfth Century*, tr. H. B. Clarke (1974).

THEODORE EVERGATES is Professor of History at Western Maryland College. His works include *Feudal Society in the Bailliage of Troyes Under the Counts of Champagne, 1152–1284* (1975); *The Cartulary and Charters of Notre-Dame of Homblières* (1990); and *Feudal Society in Medieval France: Documents from the County of Champagne* (University of Pennsylvania Press, 1993).

C. STEPHEN JAEGER is Professor of German and Comparative Literature at the University of Washington. He is the author of *Medieval Humanism in Gottfried von Strassburg's Tristan und Isolde* (1977); *The Origins of Courtliness* (University of Pennsylvania Press, 1985), and *The Envy of Angels: Cathedral Schools and European Social Ideals* (University of Pennsylvania Press, 1994).

LAURA KENDRICK, Professor of English at Rutgers University, is the author of an unpublished dissertation on poetry and politics in the Middle Ages, books and articles on the troubadours, Chaucer, and Deschamps, and a forthcoming interdisciplinary study *Animating the Letter: Writing and Illumination in the Middle Ages*.

GEOFFREY KOZIOL is Associate Professor of History at the University of California at Berkeley, and author of *Begging Pardon and Favor: Ritual and Political Order in Early Medieval France* (1992). He is currently studying the interaction of tenth-century monastic reforms and political discourse.

R. C. VAN CAENEGEM is Emeritus Professor of Medieval History and of Legal History in the University of Ghent. Among his publications are *The Birth of the English Common Law* (2nd ed., 1988); and *Royal Writs in England from the Conquest to Glanvill* (1959).

JOHN VAN ENGEN is Professor of Medieval History and Director of the Medieval Institute at the University of Notre Dame. He is the author of *Rupert of Deutz* (1983) and *Devotio Moderna: Basic Writings* (1988) and editor of *The Past and Future of Medieval Studies* (1994).

STEPHEN D. WHITE is Asa G. Candler Professor of Medieval History at Emory University. He is author of *Custom, Kinship, and Gifts to Saints: The Laudatio Parentum in Western France, 1050–1150* (1988) and of various articles on related topics.

John W. Williams is Distinguished Service Professor of History of Art and Architecture at the University of Pittsburgh. He has published on the history of peninsular art and architecture, most recently in *Art of Medieval Spain, 500–1200* (1993) and *The Illustrated Beatus: A Corpus of Illustrations of the Commentary on the Apocalypse,* 5 vols. (1994–).

Index

The following abbreviations are employed: abss. = abbess; abt. = abbot; abp. = archbishop; bp. = bishop; ct. = count; ctss. = countess; cty. = county; d. = duke; e. = emperor; k. = king; q. = queen.

University of Pennsylvania Press
MIDDLE AGES SERIES
Edward Peters, General Editor

F. R. P. Akehurst, trans. *The* Coutumes de Beauvaisis *of Philippe de Beaumanoir.* 1992

Peter L. Allen. *The Art of Love: Amatory Fiction from Ovid to the* Romance of the Rose. 1992

David Anderson. *Before the Knight's Tale: Imitation of Classical Epic in Boccaccio's* Teseida. 1988

Benjamin Arnold. *Count and Bishop in Medieval Germany: A Study of Regional Power, 1100–1350.* 1991

Mark C. Bartusis. *The Late Byzantine Army: Arms and Society, 1204–1453.* 1992

Thomas N. Bisson, ed. *Cultures of Power: Lordship, Status, and Process in Twelfth-Century Europe.* 1995

Uta-Renate Blumenthal. *The Investiture Controversy: Church and Monarchy from the Ninth to the Twelfth Century.* 1988

Daniel Bornstein, trans. *Dino Compagni's* Chronicle *of Florence.* 1986

Maureen Boulton. *The Song in the Story: Lyric Insertions in French Narrative Fiction, 1200–1400.* 1993

Betsy Bowden. *Chaucer Aloud: The Varieties of Textual Interpretation.* 1987

Charles R. Bowlus. *Franks, Moravians, and Magyars: The Struggle for the Middle Danube, 788–907.* 1995

James William Brodman. *Ransoming Captives in Crusader Spain: The Order of Merced on the Christian-Islamic Frontier.* 1986

Kevin Brownlee and Sylvia Huot, eds. *Rethinking the* Romance of the Rose*: Text, Image, Reception.* 1992

Matilda Tomaryn Bruckner. *Shaping Romance: Interpretation, Truth, and Closure in Twelfth-Century French Fictions.* 1993

Otto Brunner (Howard Kaminsky and James Van Horn Melton, eds. and trans.). Land *and Lordship: Structures of Governance in Medieval Austria.* 1992

Robert I. Burns, S.J., ed. *Emperor of Culture: Alfonso X the Learned of Castile and His Thirteenth-Century Renaissance.* 1990

David Burr. *Olivi and Franciscan Poverty: The Origins of the* Usus Pauper *Controversy.* 1989

David Burr. *Olivi's Peaceable Kingdom: A Reading of the Apocalypse Commentary.* 1993

Thomas Cable. *The English Alliterative Tradition.* 1991

Anthony K. Cassell and Victoria Kirkham, eds. and trans. *Diana's Hunt/Caccia di Diana: Boccaccio's First Fiction.* 1991

John C. Cavadini. *The Last Christology of the West: Adoptionism in Spain and Gaul, 785–820*. 1993

Brigitte Cazelles. *The Lady as Saint: A Collection of French Hagiographic Romances of the Thirteenth Century*. 1991

Karen Cherewatuk and Ulrike Wiethaus, eds. *Dear Sister: Medieval Women and the Epistolary Genre*. 1993

Anne L. Clark. *Elisabeth of Schönau: A Twelfth-Century Visionary*. 1992

Willene B. Clark and Meradith T. McMunn, eds. *Beasts and Birds of the Middle Ages: The Bestiary and Its Legacy*. 1989

Richard C. Dales. *The Scientific Achievement of the Middle Ages*. 1973

Charles T. Davis. *Dante's Italy and Other Essays*. 1984

William J. Dohar. *The Black Death and Pastoral Leadership: The Diocese of Hereford in the Fourteenth Century*. 1994

Katherine Fischer Drew, trans. *The Burgundian Code*. 1972

Katherine Fischer Drew, trans. *The Laws of the Salian Franks*. 1991

Katherine Fischer Drew, trans. *The Lombard Laws*. 1973

Nancy Edwards. *The Archaeology of Early Medieval Ireland*. 1990

Richard K. Emmerson and Ronald B. Herzman. *The Apocalyptic Imagination in Medieval Literature*. 1992

Theodore Evergates. *Feudal Society in Medieval France: Documents from the County of Champagne*. 1993

Felipe Fernández-Armesto. *Before Columbus: Exploration and Colonization from the Mediterranean to the Atlantic, 1229–1492*. 1987

Jerold C. Frakes. *Brides and Doom: Gender, Property, and Power in Medieval Women's Epic*. 1994

R. D. Fulk. *A History of Old English Meter*. 1992

Patrick J. Geary. *Aristocracy in Provence: The Rhône Basin at the Dawn of the Carolingian Age*. 1985

Peter Heath. *Allegory and Philosophy in Avicenna (Ibn Sînâ), with a Translation of the Book of the Prophet Muḥammad's Ascent to Heaven*. 1992

J. N. Hillgarth, ed. *Christianity and Paganism, 350–750: The Conversion of Western Europe*. 1986

Richard C. Hoffmann. *Land, Liberties, and Lordship in a Late Medieval Countryside: Agrarian Structures and Change in the Duchy of Wrocław*. 1990

Robert Hollander. *Boccaccio's Last Fiction:* Il Corbaccio. 1988

John Y. B. Hood. *Aquinas and the Jews*. 1995

Edward B. Irving, Jr. *Rereading* Beowulf. 1989

Richard A. Jackson, ed. Ordines Coronationis Franciae: *Texts and Ordines for the Coronation of Frankish and French Kings and Queens in the Middle Ages, Vol. I*. 1995

C. Stephen Jaeger. *The Envy of Angels: Cathedral Schools and Social Ideals in Medieval Europe, 950–1200*. 1994

C. Stephen Jaeger. *The Origins of Courtliness: Civilizing Trends and the Formation of Courtly Ideals, 939–1210*. 1985

Donald J. Kagay, trans. *The Usatges of Barcelona: The Fundamental Law of Catalonia.* 1994

Richard Kay. *Dante's Christian Astrology.* 1994

Ellen E. Kittell. *From* Ad Hoc *to Routine: A Case Study in Medieval Bureaucracy.* 1991

Alan C. Kors and Edward Peters, eds. *Witchcraft in Europe, 1100–1700: A Documentary History.* 1972

Barbara M. Kreutz. *Before the Normans: Southern Italy in the Ninth and Tenth Centuries.* 1992

Michael P. Kuczynski. *Prophetic Song: The Psalms as Moral Discourse in Late Medieval England.* 1995

E. Ann Matter. *The Voice of My Beloved: The Song of Songs in Western Medieval Christianity.* 1990

A. J. Minnis. *Medieval Theory of Authorship.* 1988

Lawrence Nees. *A Tainted Mantle: Hercules and the Classical Tradition at the Carolingian Court.* 1991

Lynn H. Nelson, trans. *The Chronicle of San Juan de la Peña: A Fourteenth-Century Official History of the Crown of Aragon.* 1991

Barbara Newman. *From Virile Woman to WomanChrist: Studies in Medieval Religion and Literature.* 1995

Joseph F. O'Callaghan. *The Cortes of Castile-León, 1188–1350.* 1989

Joseph F. O'Callaghan. *The Learned King: The Reign of Alfonso X of Castile.* 1993

Odo of Tournai (Irven M. Resnick, trans.). *Two Theological Treatises:* On Original Sin *and* A Disputation with the Jew, Leo, Concerning the Advent of Christ, the Son of God. 1994

David M. Olster. *Roman Defeat, Christian Response, and the Literary Construction of the Jew.* 1994

William D. Paden, ed. *The Voice of the Trobairitz: Perspectives on the Women Troubadours.* 1989

Edward Peters. *The Magician, the Witch, and the Law.* 1982

Edward Peters, ed. *Christian Society and the Crusades, 1198–1229: Sources in Translation, including* The Capture of Damietta *by Oliver of Paderborn.* 1971

Edward Peters, ed. *The First Crusade: The* Chronicle of Fulcher of Chartres *and Other Source Materials.* 1971

Edward Peters, ed. *Heresy and Authority in Medieval Europe.* 1980

James M. Powell. *Albertanus of Brescia: The Pursuit of Happiness in the Early Thirteenth Century.* 1992

James M. Powell. *Anatomy of a Crusade, 1213–1221.* 1986

Susan A. Rabe. *Faith, Art, and Politics at Saint-Riquier: The Symbolic Vision of Angilbert.* 1995

Jean Renart (Patricia Terry and Nancy Vine Durling, trans.). *The Romance of the Rose or Guillaume de Dole.* 1993

Michael Resler, trans. Erec *by Hartmann von Aue.* 1987

Pierre Riché (Michael Idomir Allen, trans.). *The Carolingians: A Family Who Forged Europe.* 1993

Pierre Riché (Jo Ann McNamara, trans.). *Daily Life in the World of Charlemagne.* 1978

Jonathan Riley-Smith. *The First Crusade and the Idea of Crusading.* 1986

Joel T. Rosenthal. *Patriarchy and Families of Privilege in Fifteenth-Century England.* 1991

Teofilo F. Ruiz. *Crisis and Continuity: Land and Town in Late Medieval Castile.* 1994

James A. Rushing, Jr. *Images of Adventure: Ywain in the Visual Arts.* 1995

Steven D. Sargent, ed. and trans. *On the Threshold of Exact Science: Selected Writings of Anneliese Maier on Late Medieval Natural Philosophy.* 1982

James A. Schultz. *The Knowledge of Childhood in the German Middle Ages, 1100–1350.* 1995

Pamela Sheingorn, ed. and trans. *The Book of Sainte Foy.* 1995

Robin Chapman Stacey. *The Road to Judgment: From Custom to Court in Medieval Ireland and Wales.* 1994

Sarah Stanbury. *Seeing the* Gawain*-Poet: Description and the Act of Perception.* 1992

Robert D. Stevick. *The Earliest Irish and English Bookarts: Visual and Poetic Forms Before A.D. 1000.* 1994

Thomas C. Stillinger. *The Song of Troilus: Lyric Authority in the Medieval Book.* 1992

Susan Mosher Stuard. *A State of Deference: Ragusa/Dubrovnik in the Medieval Centuries.* 1992

Susan Mosher Stuard, ed. *Women in Medieval History and Historiography.* 1987

Susan Mosher Stuard, ed. *Women in Medieval Society.* 1976

Jonathan Sumption. *The Hundred Years War: Trial by Battle.* 1992

Ronald E. Surtz. *The Guitar of God: Gender, Power, and Authority in the Visionary World of Mother Juana de la Cruz (1481–1534).* 1990

Ronald E. Surtz. *Writing Women in Late Medieval and Early Modern Spain: The Mothers of Saint Teresa of Avila.* 1995

Del Sweeney, ed. *Agriculture in the Middle Ages.* 1995

William H. TeBrake. *A Plague of Insurrection: Popular Politics and Peasant Revolt in Flanders, 1323–1328.* 1993

Patricia Terry, trans. *Poems of the Elder Edda.* 1990

Hugh M. Thomas. *Vassals, Heiresses, Crusaders, and Thugs: The Gentry of Angevin Yorkshire, 1154–1216.* 1993

Ralph V. Turner. *Men Raised from the Dust: Administrative Service and Upward Mobility in Angevin England.* 1988

Mary F. Wack. *Lovesickness in the Middle Ages: The* Viaticum *and Its Commentaries.* 1990

Benedicta Ward. *Miracles and the Medieval Mind: Theory, Record, and Event, 1000–1215.* 1982

Suzanne Fonay Wemple. *Women in Frankish Society: Marriage and the Cloister, 500–900.* 1981

Kenneth Baxter Wolf. *Making History: The Normans and Their Historians in Eleventh-Century Italy.* 1995

Jan M. Ziolkowski. *Talking Animals: Medieval Latin Beast Poetry 750–1150.* 1993

This book has been set in Linotron Galliard. Galliard was designed for Mergenthaler in 1978 by Matthew Carter. Galliard retains many of the features of a sixteenth-century typeface cut by Robert Granjon but has some modifications that give it a more contemporary look.

Printed on acid-free paper.

CPSIA information can be obtained at www.ICGtesting.com
Printed in the USA
LVOW062031220312

274298LV00002B/17/A